Lecture Notes of the Institute for Computer Sciences, Social Informatics and Telecommunications Engineering 111

Jun Zheng   Nathalie Mitton
Jun Li   Pascal Lorenz (Eds.)

Ad Hoc Networks

4th International ICST Conference
ADHOCNETS 2012
Paris, France, October 16-17, 2012
Revised Selected Papers

 Springer

Volume Editors

Jun Zheng
Southeast University
Nanjing 210096, China
Nanjing 210096, China
E-mail: junzheng@seu.edu.cn

Nathalie Mitton
INRIA Lille-Nord Europe
59650 Villeneuve d' Ascq, France
E-mail: nathalie.mitton@inria.fr

Jun Li
Canada Research Centre
Ottawa, ON K2H 8S2, Canada
Email: jun.li@crc.gc.ca

Pascal Lorenz
University of Haute Alsace
68008 Colmar, France
Email: pascal.lorenz@uha.fr

ISSN 1867-8211   e-ISSN 1867-822X
ISBN 978-3-642-36957-5   e-ISBN 978-3-642-36958-2
DOI 10.1007/978-3-642-36958-2
Springer Heidelberg Dordrecht London New York

Library of Congress Control Number: 2013935557

CR Subject Classification (1998): C.2.0-6, K.6.5, E.3, F.2.2

Typesetting: Camera-ready by author, data conversion by Scientific Publishing Services, Chennai, India

Printed on acid-free paper

Springer is part of Springer Science+Business Media (www.springer.com)

Preface

Ad hoc networks, which include a variety of autonomous networks for specific purposes, promise a broad range of civilian, commercial, and military applications. These networks were originally envisioned as collections of autonomous mobile or stationary nodes that dynamically self-configure into a wireless network without relying on any existing network infrastructure or centralized administration. With the significant advances in the last decade, the concept of ad hoc networks now covers an even broader scope, referring to many types of autonomous wireless networks designed and deployed for a specific task or function, such as wireless sensor networks, vehicular networks, home networks, and so on. In contrast to the traditional wireless networking paradigm, such networks are all characterized by sporadic connections, highly error-prone communications, distributed autonomous operations, and fragile multi-hop relay paths. The new wireless networking paradigm necessitates reexamination of many established concepts and protocols, and calls for developing new understanding of fundamental problems such as interference, mobility, connectivity, capacity, and security, among others. While it is essential to advance theoretical research on fundamental and practical research on efficient policies, algorithms and protocols, it is also critical to develop useful applications, experimental prototypes, and real-world deployments to achieve immediate impact on society for the success of this wireless networking paradigm.

The annual International Conference on Ad Hoc Networks (AdHocNets) aims at providing a forum to bring together researchers from academia as well as practitioners from industry and government to meet and exchange ideas and recent research work on all aspects of ad hoc networks. As the fourth edition of this event, AdHocNets 2012 was successfully held in Paris, France, during October 16–17, 2012. The conference featured two keynote speeches, one on "User Friendly WSN Development and Deployment with FLEXOR" by Silvia Giordano from UPSI, Switzerland, and the other on "Adaptive Efficient Neighborhood Discovery Service in Mobile Ad-Hoc Networks" by David Simplot-Ryl from INRIA, France. The technical program of the conference included 18 regular papers that were selected out of 43 submissions through a rigorous review process and six invited papers contributed by leading researchers in the area.

This volume of LNICST includes all the technical papers that were presented at AdHocNets 2012. We hope that it will become a useful reference for researchers and practitioners working in the area of ad hoc networks.

Jun Zheng
Nathalie Mitton
Jun Li
Pascal Lorenz

Organization

General Chair

Pascal Lorenz   University of Haute Alsace, France

Steering Committee

Imrich Chlamtac   Create-Net, Italy
Jun Zheng   Southeast University, China
Shiwen Mao   Auburn University, USA

Technical Program Committee Co-chairs

Jun Zheng   Southeast University, China
Nathalie Mitton   INRIA Research Center, France

Workshop Co-chairs

Marcelo Dias de Amorim   CNRS and UPMC Sorbonne Universities, France
Miguel Mitre Elias Campista   Universidade Federal do Rio de Janeiro, Brazil

Publication Chair

Jun Li   Communications Research Centre, Canada

Publicity Co-chairs

Melike Erol-Kantarci   University of Ottawa, Canada
Marwan Fayed   University of Stirling, UK

Conference Coordinator

Erica Polini   European Alliance for Innovation

Local Arrangements Co-chairs

Claude Chaudet   Institut Telecom, Telecom Paristech, France
Hakima Chaouchi   Institut Telecom, Telecom Sud Paris, France

Technical Program Committee

Ian F. Akyildiz	Georgia Institute of Technology, USA
Chadi Assi	Concordia University, Canada
Jalel Ben-Othman	University of Paris 13, France
Claude Chaudet	Telecom ParisTech, France
Edgar Chavez	Universidad Michoacana de San Nicolas de Hidalgo, Mexico
Abdellah Chehri	University of Ottawa, Canada
Stefano Chessa	University of Pisa, Italy
Jun-Hong Cui	University of Connecticut, USA
John Daigle	University of Mississippi, USA
Essia Hamouda Elhafsi	University of Riverside, USA
Marwan Fayed	University of Stirling, UK
Antoine Gallais	University of Srasbourg, France
Leenta Groble	North-West University, South Africa
Francesca Guerriero	University of Calabria, Italy
Mesut Gnes	Freie Universitat Berlin, Germany
Abdelmajid Khelil	Technical University of Darmstadt, Germany
Jun Li	Communications Research Center, Canada
Chung-Horng Lung	Carleton University, Canada
Melike Kantarci	University of Ottawa, Canada
Srdjan Krco	Ericsson Dublin, Ireland
Shiwen Mao	Auburn University, USA
Pedro Ruiz Martinez	University of Murcia, Spain
Leonardo Militano	Universita Mediterranea di Reggio Calabria, Italy
Pascale Minet	Inria Rocquencourt, France
Jelena Misic	Ryerson University, Canada
Nathalie Mitton	INRIA Lille - Nord Europe, France
Enrico Natalizio	Universite technologique de Compiegne, France
Symeon Papavassiliou	National Technical University of Athens, Greece
Martin Reisslein	Arizona State University, USA
Loren Schwiebert	Wayne State University, USA
Gaotao Shi	Tianjin University, China
Aaron Striegel	University of Notre Dame, USA
Fabrice Theoleyre	University of Strasbourg, France
Takashi Watanabe	Shizuoka University, Japan
Kui Wu	University of Victoria, Canada
Baoxian Zhang	Chinese Academy of Sciences, China
Jun Zheng	Southeast University, China

Table of Contents

MAC and PHY Layers

Substitution Networks: Performance Collapse Due to Overhead in
Communication Times 1
    Thiago Abreu, Nghi Nguyen, Thomas Begin,
    Isabelle Guérin-Lassous, and Bruno Baynat

Handheld Analyzer of IEEE 802.15.4 PHY and MAC Frames 17
    Milan Simek, Jiri Pokorny, Miroslav Botta, and Lubomir Mraz

Distributed Medium Access Control with Dynamic Altruism 29
    Panayotis Antoniadis, Serge Fdida, Christopher Griffin,
    Youngmi Jin, and George Kesidis

Providing Throughput Guarantees in IEEE 802.11 Wireless Networks –
An Experimentally-Driven Study 43
    Christos Stathopoulos, Georgios Aristomenopoulos, and
    Symeon Papavassiliou

Localization and Position-Based Protocols in WSNs

Node Discovery and Replacement Using Mobile Robot 59
    Kalypso Magklara, Dimitrios Zorbas, and Tahiry Razafindralambo

Dynamic Tracking of Composite Events in Wireless Sensor Networks ... 72
    Giuseppe Amato, Stefano Chessa, Claudio Gennaro, and
    Claudio Vairo

Revisiting Planarity in Position-Based Routing for Wireless
Networks 87
    David Cairns, Marwan M. Fayed, and Hussein T. Mouftah

Localization in Wireless Sensor Networks by Cross Entropy Method 103
    Mohammad Abdul Azim, Zeyar Aung, Weidong Xiao, and
    Vinod Khadkikar

Resource Allocations and Cognitive Radio

Auction-Based Agent Negotiation in Cognitive Radio Ad Hoc
Networks 119
    Asma Amraoui, Badr Benmammar, Francine Krief, and
    Fethi Tarik Bendimerad

Asynchronous Rendezvous Protocol for Cognitive Radio Ad Hoc
Networks 135
   *Sylwia Romaszko, Daniel Denkovski, Valentina Pavlovska, and
   Liljana Gavrilovska*

DISON: A Self-organizing Network Management Framework
for Wireless Sensor Networks 149
   Trang Cao Minh, Boris Bellalta, and Miquel Oliver

Key, Service and Caching Management

A Flexible Deterministic Approach to Key Pre-distribution in Grid
Based WSNs 164
   Sarbari Mitra, Sourav Mukhopadhyay, and Ratna Dutta

LPKM: A Lightweight Polynomial-Based Key Management Protocol
for Distributed Wireless Sensor Networks 180
   Xinxin Fan and Guang Gong

Cross-Layer Interception Caching for MANETs 196
   F.J. González-Cañete, E. Casilari, and A. Triviño-Cabrera

Below Cross-Layer: An Alternative Approach to Service Discovery
for MANETs 212
   Warren Kenny and Stefan Weber

Network Architectures and Frameworks

Modeling the Spontaneous Reaction of Mammalian Cells to External
Stimuli (Invited Paper) 226
   John N. Daigle, Mauro Femminella, and Zia Shariat-Madar

Substitution Networks Based on Software Defined Networking
(Invited Paper) 242
   *Daniel Philip Venmani, Yvon Gourhant, Laurent Reynaud,
   Prosper Chemouil, and Djamal Zeghlache*

A Modular Architecture for Reconfigurable Heterogeneous Networks
with Embedded Devices 260
   José Cecílio, João Costa, Pedro Martins, and Pedro Furtado

CiNetStrain - Wireless Strain Gauge Network - Calibration and
Reliability Measurements 275
   Timo Hongell, Jukka Ihalainen, and Ismo Hakala

Mobility and Disconnection Management

Design Challenges and Solutions for Multi-channel Communications in
Vehicular Ad Hoc NETworks 289
  Claudia Campolo and Antonella Molinaro

Prefix Delegation Based Route Optimisation in Cooperative Ad Hoc
Interconnected Mobile Networks 302
  Rehan Qureshi and Arek Dadej

Movement Speed Based Inter-probe Times for Neighbour Discovery in
Mobile Ad-Hoc Networks 316
  Matthew Orlinski and Nick Filer

Online Algorithms for Adaptive Optimization in Heterogeneous Delay
Tolerant Networks 332
  *Wissam Chahin, Francesco De Pellegrni, Rachid El-Azouzi, and
  Amar Pazad Azad*

Implementation and Analysis of FMIPv6, an Enhancement of MIPv6 ... 351
  Johan Pieterse, Riaan Wolhuter, and Nathalie Mitton

Author Index 365

Substitution Networks: Performance Collapse Due to Overhead in Communication Times

Thiago Abreu[1], Nghi Nguyen[2], Thomas Begin[1],
Isabelle Guérin-Lassous[1], and Bruno Baynat[2]

[1] Université Lyon 1 - LIP (UMR ENS Lyon, CNRS, INRIA, UCBL), Lyon, France
{thiago.wanderley,thomas.begin,isabelle.guerin-lassous}@ens-lyon.fr
[2] Université Pierre et Marie Curie - LIP6, Paris, France
{nghi.nguyen,bruno.baynat}@lip6.fr

Abstract. A substitution network is a wireless solution whose purpose is to bring back connectivity or to provide additional bandwidth capacity to a network that just suffered a failure or a dramatic surge in its workload. We analyze the performance of the simplest possible multihop topology for a substitution network, i.e., the *multihop chain* subject to traffic transmitted in both directions. Clearly, the potential capacity of a substitution network, whose technology should be embedded in mobile routers, is very likely to be far much smaller than the prior base network. We investigate the actual performance attained by such a substitution network under various conditions of the chain length and the carrier sensing range. Our results show that the capacity, viz. its maximum attainable throughput, reaches a peak at a given workload and then, for larger values of workload, decreases towards an asymptote which value can be drastically lower than the peak value. We give insights into this performance collapse and show the need for a suitable admission control.

Keywords: Substitution networks, Multihop chain, Performance collapse, IEEE 802.11.

1 Introduction

A *substitution network* stands for a wireless solution whose purpose is to bring back connectivity or to provide additional bandwidth capacity to a network that just suffered a failure or a dramatic surge in its workload (e.g., flash crowd effect). This latter network is called the *base network*, and it can be based on wired or wireless technologies. It is worth pointing out that, unlike other ad hoc and mesh solutions, a substitution network does not seek to provide new services to customers. Its goal is rather to restore and/or maintain at least some services that were available prior to the base network troubles. As a matter of fact, a substitution network is not a stand-alone network.

Two types of nodes are involved in a substitution network: (i) *Bridge routers*, which are basically gateways interconnecting the base network and the substitution network; (ii) *Mobile routers*, which are the core piece of the substitution

J. Zheng et al. (Eds.): Adhocnets 2012, LNICST 111, pp. 1–16, 2013.
© Institute for Computer Sciences, Social Informatics and Telecommunications Engineering 2013

network. Their positionning should be done so as to give rise to path(s) that will route the traffic delivered by the base network through the substitution network. Obviously, bridge routers require a wireless interface to connect to the subsitution network, and mobile routers require motion capabilities to move towards their expected position. Wifibots[1] or micro-drones, like for instance AR.Drone 2.0[2], can be used as mobile routers. Last but not the least, an algorithm should decide where mobile routers should move to.

The concept of a substitution network has been initially proposed in [1] and it is also the core focus of the ANR VERSO RESCUE project (ANR-10-VERS-003)[3]. In this context, the base network is assumed to operate through wired technologies or through a wireless technology requiring large and fixed facilities. So it is very likely that the attained capacity of the substitution network, whose technology should be embedded in mobile routers, is far much smaller. Such a drop in the available bandwidth has clear implications with regard to the control policy to be implemented on the traffic at bridge routers. However, prior to these operations, it is crucial to position the mobile routers in the best possible way and so to investigate the performance behavior of a substitution network. For instance, investigated factors may include its available bandwidth with regard to the deployed topology, transmission power assigned to router antennas, and buffer size on the wireless interfaces.

The scope of this paper is restricted to the performance analysis of the simplest possible multihop topology for a substitution network, namely the *multihop chain*. The case of a multihop network arranged as a chain topology has been extensively studied, especially when IEEE 802.11 technology in DCF mode is used as MAC protocol. Virtually all, if not all, of these works have dealt with the case of a one-way traffic, viz., traffic transmitted from one endpoint (i.e., bridge routers) of the chain to the other endpoint. Obviously, providing the injected traffic is transported using TCP protocol, then a reverse traffic consisting of ACKs packets is departing from the destination node towards the source node, but its workload is very light and tightly correlated to the data traffic. On the other hand, in the case of a substitution network, the transported traffic is expected to be of roughly equal size in both directions. Therefore, the potential emergence of substitution networks argues the need for new studies that handle the case of a chain topology but subject to a two-way traffic workload and, as far as we know, there is no work providing results and insights for this scenario. In addition, a two-way traffic implies more interferences and collisions in the wireless substitution network that, as shown later, will generate unexpected and critical behaviors.

The paper is organized as follows. Section 2 details the used scenario and the corresponding notation. In Section 3, we discuss the experimental results obtained by simulation. Section 4 brings some insight into the performance collapse potentially exhibted by a substitution network. Section 5 concludes this paper.

---

[1] http://www.wifibot.com
[2] http://ardrone2.parrot.com/
[3] http://rescue.lille.inria.fr/

2   Scenarios

2.1   Description and Assumptions

In this paper, we consider the case of a multihop chain scenario. This is the simplest topology for a substitution network that aims at restoring connectivity to a base network that is in trouble. The number of required hops in the chain depends on the distance in between the two endpoints where the connectivity needs to be brought back. Obviously, performance of the network vary deeply with the number of hops, and hence we consider several lengths of chains. In all tested scenarios, nodes are equidistant (any node is separated from its neighbor(s) by 250 meters).

As said previously, traffic is likely to be exchanged in various directions in the base network. Therefore, it is fair to expect that the traffic sent over the substitution network consists of data transmitted in both directions (from one endpoint of the chain up to the other endpoint). We model the traffic of datagrams in each direction by two independent Poisson processes. The resulting traffic submitted to the substitution network (sum of two independent Poisson processes) is thus also a Poisson process. We refer to the workload as the rate of this resulting process, i.e., the rate of datagrams attempting to access the network at any of the two endpoints. The valued of the workload will be denoted by λ. Hence, at each endpoint, the local workload is of $\frac{\lambda}{2}$. In the aim of assessing the capacity (i.e., the maximum attainable throughput) of a network, UDP traffic appears as a fair choice (unlike TCP, there is no control loop). On top of that, UDP sources may be a suited choice to represent an aggregation of dozens or hundreds of uncorrelated flows. More complex traffic patterns are left for future work.

In our scenario, we rely on-the-shelf wireless technologies for the substitution network. More precisely, we assume that wireless communications are based on IEEE 802.11 and use the DCF mode based on a CSMA/CA approach. Since previous studies has shown that the use of RTS/CTS is ineffective in multihop wireless networks [2,3], we do not include the case of using RTS/CTS in our scenarios.

We also investigate the impact of different carrier sensing ranges on the multihop chain performance. Since the radio environnement may undergo various propagation properties, we consider both the cases of a carrier sensing range greater than the communication range and of equal size. In the last case a node can only sense communications of one-hop neighbors, whereas in the former case it can also sense communication of two-hop neighbors.

Finally, for sake of simplicity we assume that the physical layer is perfect. It means that any frame transmitted on the radio medium is always received successfully if no collision occurs. Of course, this represents a strong assumption that does not match with reality. However the performance analysis under an ideal physical layer assumption is an unavoidable first step in the quest of better understanding the MAC layer behavior in terms of frames collisions, backoff freezes and buffer overflows. In addition, we believe that our qualitative observations will not drastically change with a more realistic physical layer. This will be verified in future work.

2.2   IEEE 802.11 DCF Main Principles

In this section, we remind the main principles of the DCF (Distributed Coordination Function) mechanism of IEEE 802.11 [4], since we rely on precise elements to discuss the obtained results in Section 3. A node that wants to transmit a datagram is required to wait for a fixed period DIFS and another period, called *backoff*, randomly chosen in a contention window. During the backoff period, the backoff is decreased by one whenever the medium is sensed as idle, at the end of a slot duration. If the medium is detected as busy, the backoff counter is frozen, and is resumed as soon as the medium returns to the idle state. When the backoff counter reaches zero, the node starts the transmission of the frame corresponding to the datagram. In 802.11 DCF, (unicast) frames are considered to be successfully transmitted if the sender receives an acknowledgement from the receiver after a fixed and short period SIFS and prior to a given timeout. Otherwise, the sender considers that a collision has occurred. The datagram is then retransmitted by using the same process but with a contention window whose size is doubled (up to a given maximum value).

The maximum number of transmissions for a given datagram is limited to a maximal value defined by the standard. Typically, this value is set to 7. Note that the size of the contention window is reset to its initial value whenever a frame transmission succeeds or when a datagram is dropped because it exceeds the maximal number of retransmissions.

2.3   Notation

We now detail the main notation we use in this paper. Let us a consider a multihop chain with n hops (meaning $n + 1$ nodes labelled from 0 to n).

We let $t_{a,b}$ denote the mean throughput of the traffic sent from node a to node b, which is computed as the number of successfully transmitted datagrams (in bits) per unit of time. $T_{a,b}$ indicates the mean throughput of the aggregate traffic exchanged between nodes a and b (in both directions). By definition, we have:

(1) $T_{a,b} = T_{b,a} = t_{a,b} + t_{b,a}$ $\forall a$ and $b \in [0, n]$

Figure 1 illustrates this notation.

Simple and obvious relations can be established between these latter quantities, and come from the fact that traffic arriving to node n (resp. node 0) corresponds to datagrams that have been sent by node 0 (resp. node n) and that have not been lost in between both:

(2) $T_{0,n} = t_{1,0} + t_{n-1,n}$
(3) $t_{a,a+1} \geq t_{a+1,a+2}$ $\forall a \in [0, n-2]$
(4) $t_{0,n} = t_{n-1,n}$ and $t_{n,0} = t_{1,0}$

By the system symmetry, we also have:

(5) $T_{0,1} = T_{n-1,n}$ and $t_{a,a+1} = t_{n-a,n-a-1}$ $\forall a \in [0, n-1]$

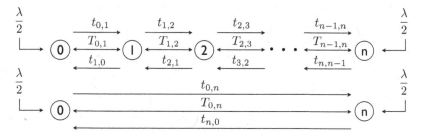

Fig. 1. Notation used in the paper

Similarly, we denote by $p_{a,a+1}$ the probability that a frame transmitted from node a to node $a + 1$ is lost because of a collision. $P_{a,a+1}$ then represents the probability that a frame transmitted between nodes a and $a + 1$ (in both directions) gets corrupted due to a collision. Finally, we let $q_{a,a+1}$ denote the probability that a datagram transmitted from node a to node $a + 1$ is lost because it experienced seven consecutive collisions and $Q_{a,a+1}$ the probability that a datagram transmitted between nodes a and $a + 1$ (in both directions) is lost.

The next two following equations are approximately satisfied:

(6) $q_{a,a+1} \simeq (p_{a,a+1})^7$ $\forall a \in [0, n-1]$
(7) $Q_{a,a+1} \simeq (P_{a,a+1})^7$ $\forall a \in [0, n-1]$

3 Simulation

We assess the performance of the multihop network through extensive discrete-event simulations using Ns2.35 for various lengths of the chain, viz. $n = 3, 4$ and 5. We relate the parameters values we use in Table 1.

3.1 Case of a 3-Hop Chain

A - Carrier Sensing Range Greater Than Transmission Range
We start our analysis with the case of $n = 3$ hops, and a carrier sensing range greater than transmission range. Let us recall that this only means that a node can sense communication of two-hop neighbors, e.g., node 1 can sense communications of nodes 0, 2 and 3, but node 0 can only sense communications of nodes 1 and 2. Figure 2 shows the related results as a function of λ. Remind that a workload of $\lambda/2$ is injected both on nodes 0 and n.

Figure 2(a) indicates the values of $t_{a,a+1}$ for each link, i.e., the mean traffic throughput from node a to node $a + 1$ (viz. in one direction) and $t_{0,n}$, i.e., the mean traffic throughput from node 0 to node n. First, as λ increases from 0.1 up to around 2Mb/s, so do $t_{a,a+1}$ and $t_{0,n}$. Then, the values of $t_{a,a+1}$ and $t_{0,n}$ tend to be flattened at a value often close (sometimes less) to their maximum value. Note that, in this area, we have: $t_{a,a+1} \geq t_{a+1,a+2}$ $\forall a \in [0, n-2]$, which is in line with relation (3) from Section 2.3. This behavior ensues from the combined effect of collision occurences and buffer overflows. As shown in Figure 2(b), $p_{0,1}$,

Table 1. Experimental setup for the simulations

Propagation model	2-Ray Ground
Physical rate	11 Mb/s
Transmision range	399 m
Carrier sensing range	709 m or 399 m
Distance between neighbor nodes	250 m
RTS/CTS	Disabled
Traffic	Two Poisson sources with UDP. One for each direction
Workload λ	From 0.1 to 10 Mb/s with steps of 0.1 Mb/s
Packet size	1500 bytes
SIFS	10 μs
DIFS	50 μs
Backoff time slot	20 μs
Retransmision limit	7
Contention window size (min, max)	32, 1024
Node buffer size	50 packets
Simulation time	150 s

i.e., the probability that a frame transmitted from node 0 to node 1 experiences a collision, is far much larger (around ten times) than $p_{1,2}$ and $p_{2,3}$ because of node 3 that acts as a hidden terminal. However, the values of $q_{0,1}$ and a fortiori those of $q_{1,2}$ and $q_{2,3}$, are almost equal to 0 (consistant with relation (6)), meaning that virtually no datagram will be lost due to consecutive frame collisions. Yet this significant value of $p_{0,1}$ tends to "elongate" the time the node 0 needs to successfully transmit a datagram to node 1 but also the time that nodes 1 and 2 take to forward the datagram due to backoff freezes. Then, given the finite size of buffers at each node, this elongation in the time needed for serving a datagram may ultimately cause datagram losses by overflow. This is in line with the decreasing values of $t_{a,a+1}$ in Figure 2(a). Finally and unsurprinsigly, the values of $t_{0,n}$ match those of $t_{2,3}$ here, which complies with the relation (4).

We turn now to Figure 2(d). Let us remind that $T_{a,a+1}$ denote the mean throughput of the aggregate traffic exchanged between nodes a and $a + 1$ (in both directions). First, $T_{0,1}$ and $T_{2,3}$ are identical due to the intrinsic system symmetry (see relation (5)). Second, as expected, $T_{1,2}$ is slightly less than $T_{0,1}$ since datagram losses occur due to buffer overflow at nodes 1 and 2. By the way, this figure is also in line with relation (1). For instance, $t_{1,2}$ (roughly equal to 1.2 Mb/s from Figure 2(a)) summed up to $t_{2,1}$ (equal to $t_{1,2}$, see relation (5)) comes equal to $T_{1,2}$. Third, $T_{0,3}$ is steadily lower than $T_{0,1}$, $T_{1,2}$ and $T_{2,3}$, which agrees to the fact that $T_{0,3}$ is made up as the sum of the two smallest $t_{a,a+1}$ from Figure 2(a), i.e., $t_{2,3}$ and $t_{1,0}$. Last but not least, it is worth pointing out that the evolution of $T_{0,3}$ hits its top value around $\lambda = 2.1$ Mb/s before decaying slightly. As shown below this unexpected behavior will be accentuated in other examples.

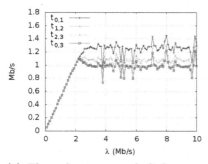

(a) Throughput on each link on ascending nodes direction

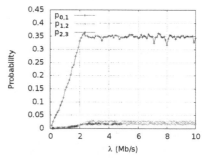

(b) Frame collision probability on each link on ascending nodes direction

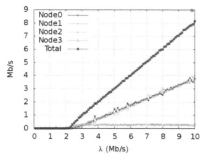

(c) Lost datagrams by buffer overflow at each node and for the overall network

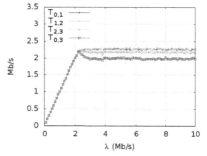

(d) Aggregate throughput on both direction for each link and for the overall network

Fig. 2. $n = 3$ hops and carrier sensing range greater than transmission range

B - Carrier Sensing Range Equal to Transmission Range

We now turn to the case where the carrier sensing range equals the transmission range, i.e., a node cannot sense communication of more than one-hop neighbors. n is kept to 3 hops. We report in Figure 3 the related results (again as a function of λ).

Figure 3(a) shows the obtained results for $T_{0,1}$, $T_{1,2}$, $T_{2,3}$ and $T_{0,3}$. Same remarks can be made here as in the previous case (with a carrier sensing range greater than transmission range). Yet the main difference is quantitative. Obtained values tend to be smaller than previously reported values. The aggregate throughput attained by the network converges towards 1.2 Mb/s with a peak close to 1.6 Mb/s. First, it is worthwhile pointing out that the attained throughput for high traffic is almost half of the one obtained in the previous example (1.2 Mb/s instead of 2 Mb/s). Second, the difference between the asymptote and the peak is also bigger than in the previous example and becomes now significant. It is a consequence of a smaller carrier sensing range that implies more collisions when traffic is high. This behavior may indeed be tied to the rise of the frame collision probabilities $p_{0,1}$ and $p_{1,2}$, which are now laying at much higer

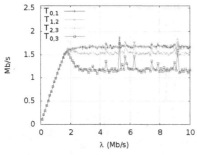

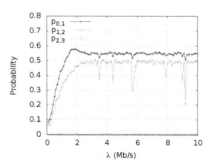

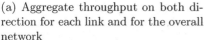

(a) Aggregate throughput on both direction for each link and for the overall network

(b) Frame collision probability for each link on ascending nodes direction

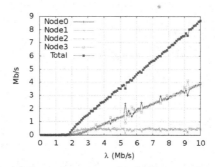

(c) Lost datagrams by buffer overflow at each node and for the overall network

Fig. 3. $n = 3$ hops and carrier sensing range equal to transmission range

values (see Figure 3(b)), since two nodes, viz. nodes 0 and 1, instead of one, are actually subject to hidden terminals. Then, not surprisingly, as frame collision probabilities increase, so do the time needed by a node for serving a datagram which may ultimaty cause datagram losses by buffer overflows. Datagram losses are reported in Figure 3(c).

It thus appears that, at least in this case, it could be worth controlling the workload rates at the input of the network so as to maximize the overall throughput performance of the network.

3.2   Case of a 4-Hop Chain

A - Carrier Sensing Range Greater Than Transmission Range
We carry on our analysis with the case of n = 4 hops, and a carrier sensing range greater than transmission range. Associated results are reported in Figure 4.

Figure 4(a) relates the values of $T_{0,1}$, $T_{1,2}$, $T_{2,3}$, $T_{3,4}$ and $T_{0,4}$. These results somehow differ from those obtained for $n = 3$ (see Figure 2(d)). On the one hand, $T_{0,1}$ and $T_{3,4}$ keep increasing towards an asymptote close to 4 Mb/s. On the other hand, $T_{1,2}$ and $T_{2,3}$ exhibit a peak value around $\lambda = 2.2$ Mb/s and then steadily decrease. Then, not surprisingly, $T_{0,4}$, which represents the aggregate throughput of the network, reaches its peak around $\lambda = 1.9$ Mb/s before decreasing significantly towards 0.5 Mb/s. It is worth noticing that in this case the ratio between the maximum value of $T_{0,4}$ and its asymptotic value is close to 3. (This ratio was only around 1.1 for $n = 3$). In this example, the need for an admission control in order to avoid this huge drop in throughput appears to be crucial.

To go further, we look at the frame collision probability in Figure 4(b). Unlike the case of $n = 3$ (see Figure 2(b)), $p_{0,1}$ exhibits a peak value here around 1.8 Mb/s and then decreases gradually. In addition, again as opposed to the case of $n = 3$, there is another collision probability that is non-null, viz. $p_{1,2}$. This growth of $p_{1,2}$ is mostly due to the presence of a hidden terminal for node 2 when $n = 4$.

The collision probabilities ensue losses of frames, but with such levels of probability, it is very unlikely that a datagram experiences seven consecutive collisions and then gets lost. Datagrams may rather be lost when attempting to access the buffer of nodes when λ is large due to buffer overflows. Figure 4(c) reports these datagram losses at each node as a function of λ. First, as opposed to $n = 3$, losses are now mainly occuring on intermediate nodes, viz. nodes 1 and 3 (though nodes 0 and 4 are still experiencing losses but at a lesser degree). Second, as expected, the total amount of losses in the network, designated by the red curve, exhibits a first regime with no losses going up to around 2 Mb/s, and a second regime with increasing losses. Perhaps more interestingly, on this latter regime, the slope of the curve is greater than 1 and close to 2 when the traffic is slightly higher than 2 Mb/s. This means that, just beyond 2 Mb/s, as the workload of the network is increased by A, then the total amount of losses is roughly increased by $2 \times A$. This somehow counterproductive phenomenon leads to the decay exhibited by $T_{0,4}$ on Figure 4(a).

B - Carrier Sensing Range Equal to Transmission Range

Figure 5 reports the results obtained for $n = 4$ but with a carrier sensing range equal to transmission range. Because of the network symmetry, we get $T_{0,1} = T_{3,4}$ and similarly, $T_{1,2} = T_{2,3}$ as shown by Figure 5(a). This latter figure also shows that $T_{0,4}$, i.e., the aggregate throughput of the network, hits its maximum value around 1.2 Mb/s and then decreases to its asymptotic value. It is worth noting that having carrier sensing range equal to transmission range yields a smaller maximum value of $T_{0,4}$ as compared to having a carrier sensing range greater than transmission range (viz. 0.3 Mb/s), yet the asymptotic value of $T_{0,4}$ for large value of workload λ is slightly higher (viz. 0.2 Mb/s). However the ratio between the peak and the asymptote remains greater than 2 and thus controlling the workload rate at the input of the network would still be very productive.

Here also, datagram losses occur overwhelmingly due to buffer overflows (and not because of seven consecutive collisions). Figure 5(b) relates the amount of

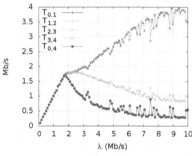
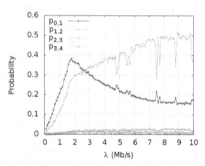

(a) Aggregate throughput on both direction for each link and for the overall network.

(b) Frame collision probability for each link on ascending nodes direction.

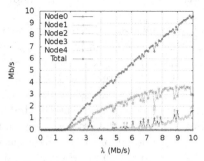

(c) Lost datagrams by buffer overflow at each node and for the overall network.

Fig. 4. $n = 4$ hops and carrier sensing range greater than transmission range

losses at each node. As opposed to previous cases, losses are somehow shared among the nodes (with the exception of node 2). Finally, the total amount of losses in the network, represented by the red curve on Figure 5(b), shows that the network experiences virtually no losses up to a workload $\lambda = 1.5$ Mb/s. Afterwards, the curves starts increasing with a slope starting to 1.5 (for $\lambda <$ 3 Mb/s) and decading to 1. This behavior perfectly complies with Figure 5(a) where one can observe that for increasing values of λ within $[1.5, 3]$ Mb/s, the aggregate throughput of the network, i.e., $T_{0,4}$, tends to decrease. On the other hand, for λ values greater than 3 Mb/s, $T_{0,4}$ holds constant.

3.3 Case of a 5-Hop Chain

A - Carrier Sensing Range Greater Than Transmission Range

Finally we consider the case of $n = 5$ hops. In Figure 6, we represent the aggregate throughput for each link when carrier sensing range is greater than transmission range. As shown on this figure, $T_{2,3}$ plays as the bottleneck link

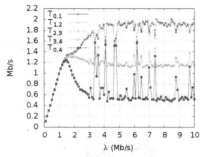

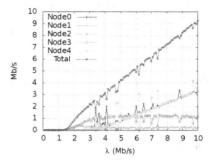

(a) Aggregate throughput on both direction for each link and for the overall network

(b) Lost datagrams by buffer overflow at each node and for the overall network

Fig. 5. $n = 4$ hops and carrier sensing range equal to transmission range

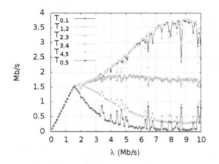

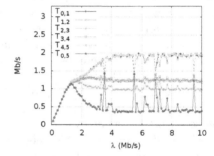

Fig. 6. $n = 5$ hops and carrier sensing range greater than transmission range

Fig. 7. $n = 5$ hops and carrier sensing range equal to transmission range

for this network. Note that the aggregate throughput of the overall network, i.e., $T_{0,5}$, tends to stand below $T_{2,3}$ since datagram losses may still occur after having passed the bottleneck link. This figure also clearly states that $T_{0,5}$ hits its maximum value for a moderate value of λ (around 1.5 Mb/s). Afterwards, $T_{0,5}$ decays gradually towards a drastically small value less than 0.1 Mb/s. Here, more than never, an admission control would be of high productivity.

B - Carrier Sensing Range Equal to Transmission Range

Figure 7 reports the simulation results in the case where carrier sensing range and transmission range match. First, all $T_{a,a+1}$ and $T_{0,5}$ exhibit an asymptotic value for large values of λ. $T_{0,5}$, which represents the aggregate throughput of the overall network, peaks at 1.2 Mb/s for $\lambda = 1.2$ Mb/s, and then decreases gradually towards its asymptotic value of 0.4 Mb/s.

4   Insights into Results

A key result of Section 3 is that for all tested values of n the aggregate throughput of the network, i.e., $T_{0,n}$, always peaks at a given workload value λ. For smaller values of λ, and more surprisingly for greater values of λ, $T_{0,n}$ reaches lower values. Such a performance collapse clearly argues for controlling the rate at which the workload is introduced to the network. Yet before investigating this in more detail, we focus the paper on the reasons that cause this peak to occur.

Overall, the network can be viewed as a black box system that processes datagrams requesting service. Its input corresponds to the datagrams arriving rate, viz. the workload λ, and its output represents the rate of successfully transmitted datagrams through the chain, viz. the aggregate throughput of the network $T_{0,n}$. This

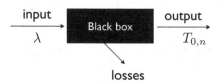

Fig. 8. Network as a black box system

is illustrated by Figure 8. We also represent potential losses on this figure since the network can experience datagram losses if the buffer of a node is found full upon a datagram arrival. Remind that our experiments demonstrated that virtually no datagrams were lost because of 7 consecutive frames collisions.

We denote by t_S the time needed by the network to sucessfully process a datagram, which corresponds to the sojourn time spent by a datagram within the network. This service time includes potential waiting times at buffers, backoff overheads, frames transmissions and retransmissions. Let us emphasize that t_S is not a constant time here, but a function of λ. As λ increases, the waiting time spent by datagrams queueing in buffer nodes tends to increase as well as the backoff overheads, causing ultimately a growth of t_S. The system is said to

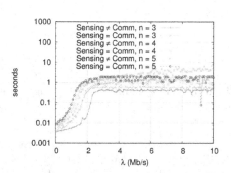

Fig. 9. Evolution of the service time t_S against the workload λ for $n = 5$

undergo an elongation of its service time. Such a feature is quite common for systems where requests need to access a shared ressource to be served. To better understand its evolution, we capture its values in our different simulations. Figure 9 represents the values of t_S against λ for all previous cases (n going from 3 to 5 hops). For $n = 5$ and a carrier sensing range greater than (respectively, equal to) the transmission range, we observe that t_S is close to 0.001 s for low values of λ and then increases steadily, reaching values around 5 s (respectively, 2 s). Similar remarks hold for other values of n.

The capacity of a system usually refers to its maximum attainable throughput. In our case, for a wireless network with n hops, the system capacity varies with λ. This change can be observed in Figures 2(d), 3(a), 4(a), 5(a), 6 and 7 where the network capacity tends to decrease significantly once the peak value has been reached. In a broader way, the system capacity highly depends on its service time but also on other factors. Another key factor is the DOP (degree of parallelism). The parallel processing stems from potential pipelining in the datagram service. For instance, as node a handles its datagram (viz. transmits the corresponding frame on the channel), node $a+4$ can also be in transmission. On top of this, another well-known pipelining effect may occur when two neighboor nodes decrement simultaneously their backoff. We denote by D this degree of parallelism. Typically, we have $D \geq 1$ but it is unclear how to get its exact value. Based on simple queueing theory elements, it follows that the system capacity is equal to $\frac{D}{t_S}$.

The aggregate throughput of the network, i.e., $T_{0,n}$, can obviously not exceed $\frac{D}{t_S}$, neither λ (it can be less than λ due to datagram losses). Hence we have:

$$T_{0,n} \leq \min(\lambda, \frac{D}{t_S})$$

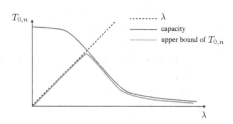

Fig. 10. Schematic view of $T_{0,n}$ against λ

Note that when $\lambda > \frac{D}{t_S}$, then the datagram loss rate increases dramatically. We schematically plot in Figure 10 the evolution of the upper bound of $T_{0,n}$ assuming for t_S an evolution similar to the ones exhibited on Figure 9. The obtained curve for the upper bound of $T_{0,n}$ exhibits a peak value corresponding to the intersection point of the function λ and the one designating the system capacity. This is in line with our simulated experiments (see Figures 2(d), 3(a), 4(a), 5(a), 6 and 7).

5   State-of-the-Art

In [5,6], the authors study, by simulation, the performance of IEEE 802.11 DCF in multihop chains when the injected traffic consists of TCP flows. They point out the TCP instability and the fairness issues that may arise with this topology. Their simulations always include the use of RTS/CTS, and the TCP flows, which compete to access the network ressource, may only go through the network on a segment of the chain (whereas in the case of a substitution networks, it is very likely that the traffic is exchanged from one endpoint to the other). During the same year, the authors of [7] study the capacity of multihop wireless networks based on IEEE 802.11 DCF and, specifically, the capacity of multihop chains. The performance are studied using the simulator Ns2. The authors turn on the RTS/CTS mechanism, set the physical rate of wireless links to 2 Mb/s, and assume that a single flow is sent through this topology (in fact the flow profile is not specified in the article). The simulation results show that, when the flow rate becomes too large, the throughput achieved along a multihop chain tends to decrease with the number of hops of the chain and seems to converge towards a bound. They also show that the capacity of the chain can be attained for a specific flow sending rate and that the the throughput obtained on the chain slightly decreases and becomes smaller than the capacity when the flow sending rate is increased. Other topologies are tested but none of them corresponds to our scenario.

In [8], the authors carry out real experiments on a multihop chain and comment the obtained performance. The chain consists of at most 4 hops and one CBR/UDP flow is transmitted from one endpoint of the chain to the other endpoint at a saturating rate (i.e., there is always a packet to send at the source), with a physical layer of 2 Mb/s and without the use of RTS/CTS. The results show that the obtained throughput on the chain is very low (and smaller than the one obtained by simulation) and very unstable. They also show that the third and fourth links have lower performance than the first and second links. These experiments only consider one saturating one-way flow, which is different from the scenario we consider.

More recently, the multihop chain topology has been investigated in details. In [9], the authors provide a throughput analysis of multihop chains with one transmitted flow. The analysis is carried out both by simulation and analytically and shows that the load injected into the chain must be controlled in order to reach the optimal overall throughput. This analysis focuses on interactions between hidden nodes. A similar study is provided in [10]. In [11], the authors study the performance of a multihop chain under different physical rates, with and without the use of RTS/CTS, and with one-way flow. The results show that using high physical rates do not necessarily lead to the best performance in terms of end-to-end throughput and end-to-end delay, particularly when RTS/CTS are used.

In [12], the authors study potential interactions that can arise between links of a chain. They evaluate, by simulation and with real experiments, the impact of the different possible interactions on the overall chain throughput. The obtained results show that some kinds of interactions give rise to better performance and that the kind of interaction at the beginning of a chain has more impact on the performance than at the end of the chain. The results also show that, beyond a given sending rate of the injected flow, the overall throughput in the chain slightly decreases. This work had been started in [13] with a less realistic model for the packet reception. This study do not consider the targeted scenario of this article. In these works, CBR/UDP flows are transmitted. These studies are extended to TCP flows in [14]. But as explained in Introduction, even though a TCP flow implies two flows at the transport level, one in each direction of the multihop chain, these two flows have dependencies and asymmetric sending rates, as opposed to our work.

6   Conclusion

In this paper, we analyze the performance of the simplest possible multihop topology for a substitution network, i.e., the *multihop chain* subject to traffic transmitted in both directions. Clearly, the potential capacity of a substitution network, whose technology should be embedded in mobile routers, is very likely to be far much smaller than the prior base network. We investigate the actual performance attained by such a substitution network under various conditions of the chain length and the carrier sensing range. Our results confirm that the potential capacity of a substitution network, viz. its maximum attainable throughput, tends to be low. More interestingly, we show that its capacity exhibits a peak value around a given workload rate and then, for larger values of workload, decreases gradually. We provide insights into this performance collapse. Future work will be devoted to automatically detect this optimal running point of the network, and so control the rate at which the workload is introduced to the network.

Acknowledgments. This work was partially funded by the French National Research Agency (ANR) under the project ANR VERSO RESCUE (ANR-10-VERS-003).

References

1. Razafindralambo, T., Begin, T., Dias De Amorim, M., Guérin Lassous, I., Mitton, N., Simplot-Ryl, D.: Promoting Quality of Service in Substitution Networks with Controlled Mobility. In: AdHocNow 2011, Germany (2011)
2. Xu, K., Gerla, M., Bae, S.: Effectiveness of RTS/CTS handshake in IEEE 802.11 based ad hoc networks. Ad Hoc Networks (1), 107–123 (2003)
3. Ray, S., Starobinski, D.: On False Blocking in RTS/CTS-based Multi-hop Wireless Networks. IEEE Transactions on Vehicular Technology 57(2) (March 2007)
4. L.S.Committee, IEEE Computer Society: ANSI/IEEE Std 802.11: Wireless LAN Medium Access Control (MAC) and Physical Layer (PHY) Specifications (2007)
5. Xu, S., Saadawi, T.: Does the IEEE 802.11 MAC protocol work well in multihop wireless ad hoc networks? IEEE Communications Magazine 39(6), 130–137 (2001)
6. Xu, S., Saadawi, T.: Revealing the problems with 802.11 medium access control protocol in multi-hop wireless ad hoc networks. Computer Networks 38(4), 531–548 (2002)
7. Li, J., Blake, C., De Couto, D.S.J., Lee, H.I., Morris, R.: Capacity of Ad Hoc Wireless Networks. In: MOBICOM, pp. 61–69 (2001)
8. Dhoutaut, D., Guérin Lassous, I.: Performance of a multi-hops configuration with 802.11: from simulation to experimentation. In: PIMRC, Barcelona, Spain (2004)
9. Ng, P.C., Liew, S.C.: Throughput Analysis of IEEE 802.11 Multi-Hop Ad Hoc Networks. IEEE Transactions on Networking 15(2), 309–322 (2007)
10. Yoo, J.-Y., Kim, J.: Maximum End-to-End Throughput of Chain-Topology Wireless Multi-Hop Networks. In: Wireless Communications and Networking Conference (WCNC), pp. 4279–4283 (2007)
11. Li, F.Y.L., Hafslund, A., Hauge, M., Engelstadt, P., Kure, O., Spilling, P.: Does Higher Datarate Perform Better in IEEE 802.11-based Multihop Ad Hoc Networks? Journal of Communications and Networks 9(3), 282–295 (2007)

12. Razak, S., Kolar, V., Abu-Ghazaleh, N.B., Harras, K.A.: How do wireless chains behave?: the impact of MAC interactions. In: MSWiM, pp 212-220 (2009).
13. Razak, S., Abu-Ghazaleh, N.B.: Self-interference in Multi-hop Wireless Chains: Geometric Analysis and Performance Study. In: ADHOC-NOW, pp. 58–71 (2008)
14. Majeed, A., Abu-Ghazaleh, N.B., Razak, S., Harras, K.A.: Analysis of TCP performance on multi-hop wireless networks: A cross layer approach. Ad Hoc Networks 10(3), 586–603 (2012)

Handheld Analyzer of IEEE 802.15.4 PHY and MAC Frames

Milan Simek[1], Jiri Pokorny[1], Miroslav Botta[1], and Lubomir Mraz[1]

Brno University of Technology, Czech Republic
simek@feec.vutbr.cz
http://www.vutbr.cz/en/

Abstract. On-site analysis of a radio environment together with a de-coding of transmitted frames is an essential process of wireless networks deployment. We have proposed the PHY and MAC handheld analyzer of IEEE 802.15.4 based communication, which thanks to the wide applica-tion of this standard mainly in the wireless automation domain can find the significant utilization for the testing and troubleshooting of wireless nodes complying with this standard. Within this paper the architec-ture, control and performance of the developed analyzer is introduced in detail.

Keywords: radio analyzer, IEEE 802.15.4, RSSI, LQI, wireless sensor networks, IRIS nodes, MAC, Atmel.

1 Introduction

The most know wireless automation ad-hoc protocols such as Zigbee [1], Wire-lessHART [2], ISA100.11a [3], WIA-PA [4] take advantage of PHY and MAC layer standardized by the IEEE 802.15.4 task group. These protocols define own different upper layers. The Zigbee protocol is fully compatible with the IEEE 802.15.4 standard that defines CSMA-CA access control on predefined channel, which cannot be dynamically be changed. From this reason, the Zigbee protocol is mostly applied in the radio-calm home control systems such as air condition-ing control, lighting control, entertainment control etc. On the other side the WirelessHART, ISA100.11a and WIA-PA protocols are well-suited for the harsh industrial environment thanks to their modified medium access control that al-lows to combine time division (TDMA) and carrier sense (CSMA-CA) methods and thanks to a dynamic channel configuration (known as channel-hopping) when channel interferences becomes intolerable. For the detailed comparison of the industrial wireless protocols we refer to read [5]. All of the introduced proto-cols communicate on the frequency channels and bands specified by the 802.15.4 PHY layer. Whilst the WirelessHART, ISA100.11a and WIA-PA works only on the 2,4 GHz ISM (Industrial Scientific Medical) band, the Zigbee protocols in ad-dition to the 2,4 GHz band can take advantage of subgigahertz band of 916/868 MHz in USA or Europe respectively. The IEEE 802.15.4 PHY layer defines in 2,4 GHz band 16 channels with the width of 2 MHz and 5 MHz separation.

J. Zheng et al. (Eds.): Adhocnets 2012, LNICST 111, pp. 17–28, 2013.
© Institute for Computer Sciences, Social Informatics and Telecommunications Engineering 2013

When deploying wireless network in the harsh environment, it is necessary to observe the ambient channels utilization and carefully plan the channel management with the focus also on the future expansion of the wireless systems in the adjacency. Furthermore, while the wireless network is running one needs to quickly and on-the-spot observe the possible faults in communication caused by the problem of the individual wireless nodes, whose communication can be suddenly disturbed or totally suspended. From these reasons, we have developed prototype of the handheld analyzer that allows to monitor utilization of all 16 channels (11-26)in 2.4 GHz band defined by IEEE 802.15.4 PHY layer and mainly that can perform monitoring of transmission quality from the individual wireless nodes. The designed analyzer reports the quality of the link by means of the *RSSI* (Received Signal Strength Indication) and *LQI* (Link Quality Indication) in the graphical or text list form. The goal of this paper is to describe the hardware and software architecture of the novel analyzer and to describe its suitability for the wireless automation management and control. The rest of the paper is organized as follows: the Section II compares the novel analyzer with the state of art, the Section III introduces the hardware and software used. The following Section IV shows the main characteristics and control items while the Section V presents the measurement results of radio range, the analyzer accuracy and battery lifetime. The paper is concluded by the Section VI, where also the future work is outlined.

2   State of Art

The known IEEE 802.15.4 analyzers can be divided into the two categories: i) channel analyzers and ii) more complex packet analyzers that both can be realized in the handheld or pc-based versions. The channel analyzers mostly work on the physical layer where the energy on the individual channels is detected and reported to the user. Thus this kind of tools is mostly used for coexistence and interference issues. The packet analyzers in addition to the energy detection allow to capture frames and packets from the individual wireless environment and according to the protocol implemented to decode the transmitted information. In the recent years, the Daintree Networks offered powerful pc-based tool known as Sensor Network Analyzer (SNA) allowing commissioning, monitoring and recording of the IEEE 802.15.4 frames together with the packets defined by the Zigbee RF4CE, 6lowPAN, JenNeT, SimpliciTI and Synkro protocols [6]. The SNA analyzer was also the complex visualization software offering to plot the joining and routing behavior what according to our own experience helps in the network troubleshooting. However, the support of the SNA analyzers were discontinued on 2010 and it is no more available for sale. Its place in the market was taken up by the Perytons Packets Analyzers [7] that in contrast to SNA allow multi-antenna operations offering the packet capturing on the several channels simultaneously. The protocols support is restricted only on the Zigbee and 6low-PAN protocols, however the users can easily integrate the packet structures of the demanded protocols. ZENA^{TM} Wireless Network Analyzer from MicroChip [8] is the next known pc-based packet analyzer that in addition to the Zigbee protocol supports also the MiWi protocol. We have recently presented our Open Packet Analyzer [9], which is multi-platform (Windows/Linux) and open-source Zigbee packet analyzer operating in both 2,4 GHz and 868/916 bands. Our Open Packet Analyzer presents the extension of the free Wireshark tool and in addition it allows the web-based access for the remote monitoring and control. In the field of the pc-based IEEE 802.15.4 channel analyzers, the Chanalyzer tool from Metageek is widely used [10]. The Chanalyzer is recording and visualization software capturing signals from the Wi-Spy adapter that is supplied in the 2,4 GHz and 916/868 MHz version. It serves for the signal strength (in dBm) monitoring and recording of the selected frequency bands and channels. The graphical output and channel separation can be modified according to the IEEE 802.15.4 or IEEE 802.11 standard. Chanalyzer can be very helpful during wireless network testing when the interferences from another wireless networks working in the same band needs to be effectively controlled. However, it works only with the PHY layer with the strength of signal and thus do not decode addressing information about the individual IEEE 802.15.4 nodes. Furthermore, as it was already mention Chanalyzer is pc-based application that using in terrain requires some kind of mobile station such as laptop or tablet. From this reason some effort is devoted to the development of the handheld channel analyzers that can be quickly and easily used during network deployment and testing while guarantying optimized battery lifetime. Telegesis has developed the wireless on-site survey kit referred to as Z-HAN (Zigbee-Home Area Network) Range Finder kit [11]. Its main objective is to perform the energy scan of all 2,4 GHz channels and to report $RSSI$ values in both transmission directions from the analyzer to wireless node and vice versa. From this reason the introduced kit contains two wireless nodes supporting these tests. The $RSSI$ values are separately reported through the two test. The test A monitors channels 11, 14, 15, 19 whilst the test B monitors channels 20, 24, 25. This separation of the channel tests together with the static list of some selected channels is the minor drawback of the presented solution. On the other side the "Z-HAN" kit mediates the packet error rate tests together with the configurable transmission power what is very suited during network deployment and troubleshooting. The Deeter Group ® presents the handheld Wireless Site Survey Tool (WSST) for measurement of LQI and data transmission status in 2,4 GHz band mainly prior to network deployment. Thats why also one wireless node acting as a sender is supplied within the tool. The WSST applicability is slightly restricted by its LCD 16x2 display containing only two lines for reported information. The both "Z-HAN" and "WSST" handheld analyzers are powerful tools for the signal strength and the link quality monitoring, however their monitoring function is restricted at the information provided by the 802.15.4 PHY layer only and thus do not report the quality of connection with the individual addressable nodes. From this reason we have decided to develop own handheld channel analyzer that can provide characteristics mentioned above and in addition can work with the information specified at the IEEE 802.15.4 MAC layer. Thanks to the added feature of the

MAC frames decoding we have developed the powerful tool that can be referred to as IEEE 802.15.4 channel and MAC frame analyzer. We have already used the first prototype of our analyzer during the signal propagation and energy analysis research [12], [13], [14].

3   Analyzer Features and Architecture

The main capabilities of the developed channel analyzer can be listed as follows:

- Operation in 2,4 GHz band
- Textual and graphical scan of $RSSI$ through the 16 channels with the results scrolling possibility
- Configurable dBm resolution in the graphical mode
- Selection of the individual channel for analysis
- For each wireless node the analyzer records: MAC address, $RSSI$, LQI, activity
- Results sorted alphabetically or according to the best link
- Configurable time spent in the sniffing mode per each channel
- Power supply by the four AA accumulators

For the analyzer operation we have used the Memsic Iris node that is controlled by the 8-bit ATmega1281 microprocessor with the AT86RF230 radio chip connected through the SPI to the microprocessor [15], see Fig. 1 for detailed picture of Iris node mounting inside of the analyzer.

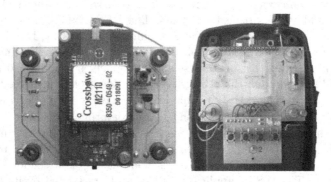

Fig. 1. Assembled Iris node and its mounting inside of the analyzer

The assembled radio chip is compatible with the 802.15.4 standard and supports communication in the 2,4 GHz band. Through the standard 51 extended pin the LCD 16x4 display is connected (type MC41605B6W-SPTLY) together with the control peripheries such as four buttons and two leds. The original $\lambda/4$ monopole antenna of IRIS node was substituted by the $\lambda/2$ dipole antenna with the 3dBi gain. The analyzer is supplied by the four AA NiMH accumulators.

For the communication and the 802.15.4 frames decoding we have implemented "IEEE 802.15.4 MAC" stack from Atmel [16]. IEEE 802.15.4 MAC is portable and very comprehensive software implementing the features of PHY and MAC layer defined by the IEEE 802.15.4 standard. As was already mentioned the proposed analyzer can parse the received MAC frames, especially it decode the addressing field and parse the source address that can be size of 0, 16 or 64 bits. The structure of the MAC frame with the source address field highlighted is illustrated in the Fig. 2.

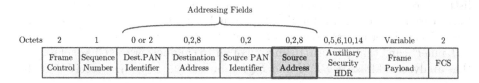

Fig. 2. Structure of MAC frame with the source address field

Information about the source address size is stored in the Frame Control field. After performing Frame Control Sequence checking (CRC control) the result is stored in the 8th bit of the PHY_RSSI register of the radio chip. In the same register, the first five bits are used for the storing of the $RSSI$ value, which is during frame reception updated every $2\mu s$. The range of the stored $RSSI$ parameter is 0-28. To get the the received power level in dBm (P_r) the $RSSI$ value must be converted by means of the $RSSI\_BASE\_VAL$ parameter as follows: $P_r = RSSI\_BASE\_VAL + 3 \times (RSSI - 1)$, where $RSSI\_BASE\_VAL$ = -91 dBm. For the reading of $RSSI$ value from the PHY_RSSI register, the MAC command `pal_trx_bit_read(RG_PHY_RSSI,0x1F,0)` is used.

The LQI parameter (0-255) is automatically derived from the ED (energy detection) and the $RSSI$ value and it is stored in the `ppduLinkQuality` parameter.

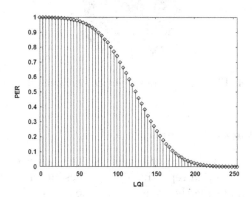

Fig. 3. The Packet Error Rate and LQI mapping, taken from [17]

The *LQI* value can be applied for the representation of the Packet Error Rate (PER), where the high *LQI* value denotes the low PER and thus high quality link. The statistically measured dependency of *PER* on *LQI* is illustrated in Fig. 3.

4   Analyzer Control and Performance

The photography of the developed channel analyzer is depicted in the Fig. 4. The analyzer is controlled through the four buttons that serve for the UP/DOWN listing (first two buttons from the left), confirming of the selected choice (third button from the left) and for the display lightning (last button on the right). Once the analyzer is turned on user can select in the main menu either automatic "Channel Scan" that perform dBm scan of all 16 channels or to "Channel Select" that analyzes addresses, *RSSI* and *LQI* values of all the frames received at the configured channel.

Fig. 4. Photography of developed channel analyzer

4.1   Automatic Channel Scan

The main objective of the "Channel Scan" is the energy detection at the 16 channels of 2.4 GHz band and reporting dBm values either in Graphical or Text list form, see Fig. 5b). During the channel scan the radio chip spends the specific time in the receiving mode at each channel. The time spent in the receiving mode

(a) Configuration of scan
time per each channel

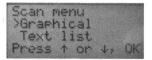

(b) Selection of graphical
or text output

Fig. 5. Scanning configuration

can be before scanning optionally configured in the steps of 1, 2, 3, 5, 10, 30, 60, 120, 300, 600, 1800, 3600 seconds, see Fig. 5a).

If the graphical output is selected, the measured dBm values are represented in the form of bars, which height corresponds with the measured dBm levels. The resolution of each part of the bar can be optionally configured in steps of 5, 10, 15, 20 dBm per mark of the bar. The graphical output together with the dBm values corresponding with the configured resolution can be seen in Fig. 6. Since the LCD display used contains exactly 16 symbols per line, we can effectively visualize the 16 channels (11-26) through the entire display.

If the Text list form is selected, the measured dBm levels are displayed in the form of list sorted by the channel numbers. The analyzer is also capable to identify if the frames are sourced from the 802.15.4 node and to display this

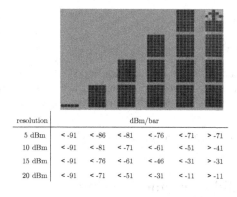

resolution	dBm/bar					
5 dBm	< -91	< -86	< -81	< -76	< -71	> -71
10 dBm	< -91	< -81	< -71	< -61	< -51	> -41
15 dBm	< -91	< -76	< -61	< -46	< -31	> -31
20 dBm	< -91	< -71	< -51	< -31	< -11	> -11

Fig. 6. Graphical outputs in the bar form

Fig. 7. Text list of measured dBm levels

identification by reporting "15.4" characters upon the detected channel, see Fig. 7. By means of this function, the user can observe what channels are occupied by the IEEE 802.15.4 nodes and which are occupied by another wireless system such as IEEE 802.11.

4.2 Analyzing Communication on Selected Channel

In the submenu of the Channel Selection the user can select specific channel for the detailed communication analysis. Once the channel is selected (Fig. 8(a)) one can choose whether the results will be sorted according to the node addresses or *RSSI* measured (Fig. 8(b)). The results of the demonstrated experiment with the one coordinator with the address of 0x0000 and four nodes with the address of 0x000A, 0x000B, 0x000C, 0x000D can be seen in Fig. 8(c), (d). Some nodes are not displayed because of restricted size of the LCD display, these can be listed by the UP/DOWN buttons. The analyzer furthermore reports the freshness of the reported data by putting "x" symbol beside the nodes which did not send any frame for more than 60 seconds (Fig. 8(e)).

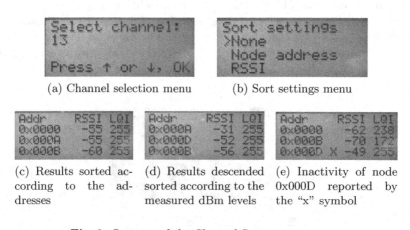

(a) Channel selection menu   (b) Sort settings menu

(c) Results sorted ac-   (d) Results descended   (e) Inactivity of node
cording to the ad-   sorted according to the   0x000D reported by
dresses   measured dBm levels   the "x" symbol

Fig. 8. Outputs of the Channel Scan measurement

5   Analyzer Validation and Testing

As it was already mentioned, the original $\lambda/4$ monopole antenna was substituted by the $\lambda/2$ dipole antenna with the 3dBi gain. The outside light-of-sight range test with the both antennas was conducted in order to evaluate the communication range of the analyzer. From the results depicted in Fig. 9 it is obvious that while using $\lambda/2$ antenna we can achieve distance about 220 meters whilst with the original $\lambda/4$ antenna the communication range is restricted at 160 meters. The received signal strength is in average higher about 4 dBm in contrast to the original antenna.

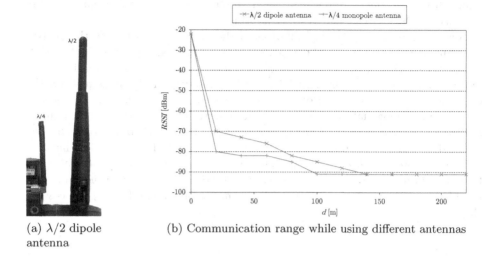

(a) $\lambda/2$ dipole antenna

(b) Communication range while using different antennas

Fig. 9. Communication range testing with $\lambda/2$ and $\lambda/4$ antennas

The accuracy of the $RSSI$ and LQI measurement was validated by means of the SNA analyzer [6], which was already introduced in the State of Art section. The SNA adapter that acts as a sniffer for SNA software is equipped by the similar $\lambda/2$ antenna with the 3dBi gain and thus the values observed by the SNA analyzer could be used as the reference for the accuracy validation. Two IRIS nodes were deployed in the adjacency of the both analyzers, which were placed close to each other. All the antennas of the nodes and the analyzers were angled in vertical direction. The node with address 0x000D set the frame every two second to the coordinator with address 0x0000 that responded with the ACK messages. The $RSSI$ and LQI values from all frames was monitored and results of both analyzers was compared, see Fig. 10.

The $RSSI$ of all the frames was sufficiently high and thus $LQI = 255$ was always reported. The $RSSI$ of the frames sent and received by the node 0x000D fluctuated around $RSSI = -40$ dBm. There can be seen the difference between $RSSI$ values of the ACK frames (black frames) that is observed by the SNA analyzer as -41 dBm and by the novel analyzer as -46 dBm. However this difference is not essential, since the radio chip measures $RSSI$ values with the accuracy of $\pm$ 5 dBm and thus this difference can be caused by the radio chip inaccuracy.

Addr	RSSI	LQI	SNA analyzer						
0x000D	-40	255	239	+00:00:01.995	13	-40 dBm	255	0x000d	0x0000
0x0000	-46	255	239	+00:00:00.003	13	-41 dBm	255		
			240	+00:00:01.992	13	-39 dBm	255	0x000d	0x0000
			240	+00:00:00.003	13	-41 dBm	255		

Fig. 10. Validation of $RSSI$ and LQI measurement by means of the SNA analyzer

However we can conclude that channel analyzer performs measurement sufficient for network deployment and troubleshooting.

According to the theoretical analysis of the lifetime according to the energy consumption of the individual components, we can stated that with the four AA NiMh 1.4 V/2100 mAh accumulators the analyzer should continuously works approximately for 11 hours and 52 minutes. However these values are strictly depended on the duty cycle of wireless nodes and the discharging of the accumulators. To evaluate the estimated lifetime we have used the the configured nodes from the previous experiment and regularly measured voltage of each fully charged accumulator. From the results depicted in Fig. 11 it is obvious that the channel analyzer worked approximately for the 13.5 hours. One can also observe that discharging process is asymmetric for some of the accumulators and thus the lifetime of the analyzer is strongly dependent on the discharging process of the accumulators used.

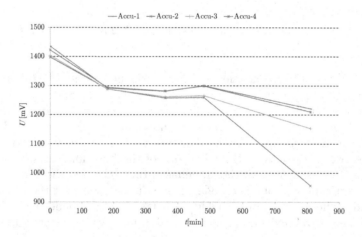

Fig. 11. Measurement of accumulators voltage during network analysis

6   Conclusion and Future Work

Through this paper we have presented development and performance of our novel channel analyzer. At the beginning of the paper we have stated some powerful tools that are applied today for the monitoring and troubleshooting of the wireless automation networks and compared their features with the capabilities of our analyzer. Within the paper we have described the hardware and software used for the development of the analyzer architecture. Due to the low cost peripheries used for the development we can summarize that overall price of the components reaches the 100 EUR. But this price can be significantly reduced at the half if the commercial IRIS node used for analyzer control will be substituted by the individual components such as ATmega1281 microprocessor and AT86RF230 radio chip. In the paper we have further described the main functions and control items and also showed the validation experiments, which validated the performance and accuracy of the proposed channel analyzer. In the future we plan to substitute mentioned IRIS node by the cheaper components and to extend the analyzer capabilities by the radio chip AT86RF212 working also in the subgigahertz band. We also plan to use the graphical display instead of the LCD 16x4 LCD display and to add communication interface such as USART, USB or Ethernet for logging and future analysis. Thanks to the application of the widely used IEEE 802.15.4 standard the proposed architecture can be successfully applied for the analysis of the wireless automation protocols such as Zigbee, 6lowPAN, WirelessHART, ISA100.11a, WIA-PA and others.

Acknowledgment. This paper was prepared within the framework of No. FRTI2/571 grant project of the Ministry of Industry and Trade of the Czech Republic.

References

1. ZigBee Alliance. Zigbee specification (2011),
   http://www.zigbee.org/Specifications.aspx
2. HART Communication Foundation. WirelessHART Technology (2011),
   http://www.hartcomm.org/protocol/wihart/wireless_technology.html
3. ISA 100 Wireless. ISA100.11a Standard (2011),
   http://www.isa100wci.org/Technology/ISA100-11a-Standard.aspx
4. Zhong, T., Zhan, M., Peng, Z., Hong, W.: Industrial wireless communication protocol WIA-PA and its interoperation with Foundation Fieldbus. IEEE Xplore (2010)
5. Gungor, V., Hancke, G.: Industrial wireless sensor networks: Challenges, design principles, and technical approaches. IEEE Transactions on Industrial Electronics 56(10), 4258–4265 (2009)
6. Daintree Networks. Sensor Network Analyzer(SNA),
   http://www.daintree.net/sna/sna.php
7. Perytons Ltd. Perytons-Network Visibility (2012), http://www.perytons.com
8. Microchip Technology Inc. ZENA 3.0 Network Analyzer (2012),
   http://www.microchip.com
9. Mraz, L., Cervenka, V., Simek, M.: Open Packet Analyser for IEEE 802.15.4 Networks. In: Poster and Demo Proceedings of 9th European Conference on Wireless Sensor Network, EWSN 2012, pp. 48–51 (2012)
10. MetaGeek, LLC. Chanalyzer (2012),
    http://www.metageek.net/products/chanalyzer/
11. Telegesis, Ltd. Z-HAN Range Finder (2012), http://www.telegesis.com/
12. Moravek, P., Komosny, D., Simek, M., Jelinek, M., Girbau, D., Lazaro, A.: Signal Propagation and Distance Estimation in Wireless Sensor Networks. In: Telecommunications and Signal Processing, TSP 2010 (August 16, 2010)
13. Moravek, P., Komosny, D., Simek, M., Girbau, M., Lzaro, A.: Energy Analysis of Received Signal Strength Localization in Wireless Sensor Networks. Radioengineering 10(4), 937–945 (2011)

14. Hosek, J., Molnar, K., Jakubek, P.: Map-Based Direct Position Control System For Wireless Ad- Hoc Networks. In: Proceedings of the 34th International Conference on Telecommunication and Signal Processing, TSP 2011, pp. 195–200. Asszisztencia Szervezo Kft. (2011)
15. Memsic Technology Inc., IRIS XM2110CA Data Sheet, http://www.memsic.com
16. Atmel Corporation, IEEE 802.15.4 MAC,
    http://www.atmel.com/tools/IEEE802_15_4MAC.aspx
17. Atmel Corporation, AT86RF230 Datasheet: Low Power 2.4 GHz Transceiver for ZigBee, IEEE 802.15.4, 6LoWPAN, RF4CE and ISM Applications, Rev. 04/09, http://www.atmel.com

Distributed Medium Access Control
with Dynamic Altruism[*]

Panayotis Antoniadis[1,2], Serge Fdida[1], Christopher Griffin[3],
Youngmi Jin[4], and George Kesidis[3]

[1] UPMC Sorbonne Universités
{panayotis.antoniadis,serge.fdida}@lip6.fr
[2] ETH Zurich
antoniadis@tik.ee.ethz.ch
[3] ARL, CS&E and EE Depts, Penn State University
{cxg286,gik2}@psu.edu
[4] EE Dept, KAIST, South Korea
youngmi_jin@kaist.ac.kr

Abstract. In this paper, we consider medium access control of local
area networks (LANs) under limited-information conditions as befits a
distributed system. Rather than assuming "by rule" conformance to a
protocol designed to regulate packet-flow rates (as in, *e.g.*, CSMA win-
dowing), we begin with a non-cooperative game framework and build a
dynamic altruism term into the net utility. Our objective is to define a
utility model that captures more closely the expected behavior of users,
which according to recent results from behavioral and experimental economics should include a conditionally altruistic dimension. The effects
of our proposed dynamic altruism are analyzed at Nash equilibrium in
the quasi-stationary (fictitious play) regime. We consider either power
or throughput based costs, and the cases of identical or heterogeneous
(independent) users/players.

Keywords: MAC, game theory, altruism.

1 Introduction

Flow and congestion control are fundamental networking problems due to the
distributed, information-limited nature of the decision making process in many
popular access technologies. Various distributed mechanisms have been implemented to cooperatively desynchronize demand, *e.g.*, TCP, ALOHA, CSMA.
Typically, when congestion is detected, all end-devices are expected to slow down
their transmission rates and then increase again slowly hoping to find a fair and
efficient equilibrium.

---

[*] The work was supported by NSF CISE grants 0524202 and 0915928, by EINS, the
Network of Excellence in Internet Science EC's FP7 grant 288021, and by a Cisco
Systems URP gift.

J. Zheng et al. (Eds.): Adhocnets 2012, LNICST 111, pp. 29–42, 2013.

The fact that this process is not incentive compatible (a user/player could self-ishly benefit by not following the prescribed protocol) raises an important issue. Since users could have access to alternative implementations of the prescribed ("by rule") protocols, *e.g.*, ones that slow down less than they should, the result could be an unfair allocation or even congestion collapse (see *e.g.*, [11, 38]).

Note that experience with TCP has shown that developers do create versions of the protocol that depart from the standard, cooperative (by-rule) congestion-avoidance algorithm, like Turbo TCP. The fact that non-cooperative devices at the MAC level have not been as widespread is perhaps due to the increased difficulty of modifying lower-level networking drivers by users or third parties, but such modifications are possible. As more network "players" behave selfishly and thereby more significantly reduce the performance of the rest, the other players are increasingly incentivized to adopt selfish strategies themselves, potentially leading to deadlock.

To address this threat, there is a steadily growing literature that analyzes the equilibria of different distributed network resource allocation *games* [2,11,13,21–23,27,29,30,34,43]. Such models provide useful insights on the expected equilibria when users do have the option to choose alternative implementations of the MAC protocol and constitute a framework for devising and analyzing incentive mechanisms to encourage the behavior that would lead to the most desirable equilibria. For example, in a Markovian setting without fictitious play[1], [30] introduces a cooperation parameter (a probability to stop transmitting), and then follows a detection and punishment methodology regarding selfish behavior.

In addition, even when users do follow the prescribed protocol, game theoretical models could be used as analytical frameworks that enable more informed choices in the implementation of the corresponding flow and congestion control protocols (*e.g.*, by associating a utility function to end-devices, which can then be the basis of actions by rationally selfish players). To this end, for a random-access LAN, several authors have recently considered the problem of distributed optimization of a global objective (total throughput, social welfare) subject to a fairness constraint. For example, in [13], a utility function design problem is studied considering estimation errors of the network state.

Our work falls into the first category of game theoretic models, but is different than the typical approach in addressing potentially selfish behavior at the MAC layer. Our objective is to formulate a more realistic utility model that captures the dynamics of altruistic motivations, which do play an important role in shaping human behavior as demonstrated by research in the fields of behavioral and experimental economics. Our analysis could then lead to advanced incentive schemes, which instead of attempting to punish selfish behavior, it will aim to encourage altruistic behavior under certain conditions. For example, a possible realistic outcome could be the design of a high-level user interface which will allow users to set the urgency of their communication, and which will encourage them to assign lower priority to their traffic when there is evidence that other users generally are doing the same. If successful, such a mechanism will not only

---

[1] *i.e.*, without steady-state estimates of certain quantities.

improve performance at any given moment but it will also allow certain users to increase their own throughput only when they really need it, improving this way also the efficiency of the system over time without the need for complex and unattractive pricing schemes (e.g., [21]).

As our main contribution, we formulate and analyze a novel CSMA medium access control game with conditionally altruistic players. Altruistic tactics in evolutionary/mean-field games have long been considered, see [19] as a recent reference. In networking, altruism has been modeled as a user's *statically* personalized weight on the utility of others in games of: network formation [3], packet forwarding in delay tolerant networks [20], routing [5, 42], and medium access control by us in [25].

However, as we argue in detail in the next section, such static altruistic models, although theoretically interesting, fail to capture important realistic attributes of altruistic behavior studied in the behavioral and experimental economics literature. In this paper, we formulate a fictitious play model where altruism by one user is based on perceived mean throughput of the other players modulated (*i.e.*, made "dynamic") by factoring the estimated mean total channel idle time. Unlike Heusee et al. [17], who propose a window-update algorithm that tries to directly minimize the average idle time of the channel, in our model users will use less than their "fair" share when they do not really need it, but under the constraint that others do the same. For example, large idle time may be a signal that competing devices are also behaving in a socially sensitive manner, expressing a cooperative "social norm." In this case, excessive altruism would result in an underused channel.

Note also that our system with heterogeneous users will respond similarly to a selfish user with low throughput demand and a more altruistic one with high throughput demand. Interestingly, as shown in previous studies for the same problem [25] and in more general settings [32] the existence of altruistic motivations among users does not always result in a better outcome. But we should stress that our objective is not to optimize the overall throughput of the system but to study the stable equilibria that altruistic devices could reach. Finally, we do not assume that the users share information and act in a coordinated fashion, *i.e.*, so as to form a player coalition.

This paper is outlined as follows. In Section 2, we give a brief background on altruistic behavior. A fictitious-play model with dynamic altruism for a slotted-ALOHA LAN is given in Section 3. In Section 4, variations of the LAN model are considered. Numerical studies are given in Section 5. Finally, in Section 6, we conclude with a summary and discussion of future work.

2 Background on Altruistic Behavior

Economists are often criticized for the common assumption that humans are "rational" (*i.e.*, purely self-interested), which leads to a pessimistic view of the outcome of various formulated game-theoretic models. In reality, many people act "altruistically", defined as an "unselfish concern for or devotion to the welfare of others" [2]. In fact, despite this selfishness stereotype certain branches of economics, such as behavioral and experimental economics, do incorporate social, cognitive, and psychological factors in their models of human behavior (see [12] for a historical overview), in a way not typically captured in cooperative game-theoretic frameworks.

Two common scenarios in which altruistic behavior consistently appears in experiments with real users is in ultimatum bargaining and public-good contribution games [26, 28]. Ultimatum bargaining reveals the altruistic instincts of humans in a resource-sharing problem in which one player decides how to share a fixed amount of money and the other decides whether to accept or reject sharing: here rejection leaves both with zero profit. Experiments show that people altruistically sacrifice their own profit to punish unfair decisions by others. Analysis of more traditional public-good experiments, where players determine their individual contribution toward the construction of a pure public good, similarly challenges the assumption that free riding is always the dominant strategy.

An important lesson of experimental economics is that altruism does not seem to be a static and hardwired characteristic of humans but depends on many aspects of the environment. In other words, the level of altruism of an individual is *dynamic* and could change over time depending on the context and the behavior of the group. Indeed, the cooperation rate in many experiments has been proven to be much higher if subjects know that there is a possibility of meeting the same partners again in future periods [15], when their perception on the overall level of altruism in their group is high [9], or even just by a positive framing of the experiment [14].

From these and many other contextual factors that can affect the cooperation levels in a group, social norms is perhaps the most influential (see [8, 36]) but complex to incorporate in a simple economic model. To this end, Fehr and Schmidt [16] have proposed a utility function to model the altruistic behavior of people in ultimatum experiments, which incorporates a measure of fairness (or "inequity aversion") in a static way, *i.e.*, its main parameters are indifferent to the dynamics of the system. As a more realistic but less tractable alternative, H. Margolis argues in favor of a more dynamic and complex model, called "neither selfish nor exploited" [31], which proposes a dual utility model which takes into account the history of one's actions, the current overall behavior, the effect of altruistic action, and the developed norms in a society.

When altruism can bring future concrete benefits, one could also see altruistic behavior as a long-term net utility optimization. A characteristic example is the notion of direct and indirect reciprocity and the related work in evolutionary game theory that tries to explain the source of cooperative behavior in nature [4, 35]. We leave to future work the study of such evolutionary extensions of the LAN systems we formulate below.

---

[2] See http://dictionary.reference.com/browse/altruism

3   Slotted-ALOHA Random-Access LAN with Dynamic Altruism

3.1   Altruistic Framework with Power Based Cost and Concave Utility of Throughput

In our scenario, the high complexity of human nature and the surrounding social environment plays a less important role since the cooperation game that we study is limited in time, the identity of the players are hidden, the stakes are relatively low, and the decisions of users are mediated through a programmed device. So, we propose to incorporate in a simple utility function the effect of the external manifestation of altruistic behavior, that is a *statistical norm* as termed in [31], or simply "what others do" [9]. To perceive this, the availability of reliable information about the group's statistical behavior is critical. Our use of the mean idle time per active player to determine the level of altruism in the system is realistic in terms of information availability since it can be easily measured by the different users, though, again, low demand could be mistakenly taken for altruistic behavior and vice versa.

Consider a slotted ALOHA random-access LAN wherein the $N \geq 2$ participating nodes control their access probability parameter, q. A basic assumption is that nodes' control actions are based on observations in steady-state, *i.e.*, "fictitious play" [10], resulting in a quasi-stationary dynamical system [21,43] based on the mean throughputs:

$$\gamma_i(\underline{q}) = q_i \prod_{j \neq i}(1 - q_j).$$

Another basic assumption in the following is that the source of a successful transmission is evident to all other participating nodes. We further assume that the degree of altruism α_i of each node i depends on the activity of the other users as:

$$\alpha_i(\underline{q}_{-i}) = \prod_{j \neq i}(1 - q_j) = \frac{\gamma_i(\underline{q})}{q_i}$$

$$= \gamma_i(\underline{q}) + \prod_j(1 - q_j),$$

where the second term is just the mean idle time of the channel; thus, every node can easily estimate its (dynamic) altruism. By using its control action (strategy), q_i, each i seeks to maximize its *net* utility:

$$V_i(\underline{q}) = C_i \log(\gamma_i(\underline{q})) + A_i \alpha_i(\underline{q}_{-i})\overline{\gamma}_{-i}(\underline{q}) - M_i q_i \tag{1}$$

where: the dynamic altruism factor α modulates the contribution of the mean service of all other players to the net utility of player i,

$$\overline{\gamma}_{-i}(\underline{q}) = \frac{1}{N-1}\sum_{j \neq i}\gamma_j(\underline{q}); \tag{2}$$

the utility derived by one's own throughput is modulated by a concave function [21,22] as modeled here in the form of a logarithm (for tractability); and we have assumed a power based cost[3] Mq. Note that because we assume that the source of each successfully transmitted packet is evident to all nodes, each node i can easily estimate $\bar{\gamma}_{-i}$. Again, though each player i optimizes V_i in a non-cooperative fashion, the game is called altruistic to reflect the second term in (1).

In the following, we consider an *iterated* game where players pursue mixed strategies based on observations of throughput γ_i observed in steady-state. Note that if we further assume that nodes are aware of the C, M parameters of other nodes, then we can replace $\bar{\gamma}$ with the net utility of the other players as in [25] (particularly for throughput based costs $M\gamma$).

Proposition 1. *If the game is synchronous-play and all users i have the same (normalized) parameters*

$$c := C_i/M_i \; < \; 1 \; and \; a := A_i/M_i,$$

then there is a symmetric Nash equilibrium $\underline{q}^* = q^*\underline{1}$, where $0 < q^* < 1$ is a solution to

$$f(q) \; := \; aq^2(1-q)^{2N-3} + q - c = 0. \tag{3}$$

Proof. When $q_i = q$ for all i, the first-order necessary conditions of a symmetric Nash equilibrium,

$$0 = \frac{\partial V_i}{\partial q_i}(q\underline{1}) \; = \; -\frac{M}{q}f(q),$$

i.e., equivalent to (3). Note that $f(0) = -c < 0$ and $f(1) = 1 - c > 0$, the latter by hypothesis. So, by the continuity of f and the intermediate value theorem, a root of f exists in $(0, 1)$.

All such solutions $q^*\underline{1}$ correspond to Nash equilibria because $\partial^2 V_i(\underline{q})/\partial q_i^2 = -C_i/q_i^2 < 0$ for all $i, \underline{q}$.

The following corollary is immediate.

Corollary 1. *There is a unique symmetric Nash equilibrium point (NEP) if $\min_{q \in (0,1)} f'(q) > 0$ (i.e., f is strictly increasing), a condition on parameters N and a.*

Note that there may be non-symmetric Nash equilibria in these games, even for the case of homogeneous users, *e.g.*, [24]. Also, it is well known that Nash equilibria of iterative games are not necessarily asymptotically stable, *e.g.*, [1,40, 44]. In [21] for a slotted-ALOHA game with throughput based costs $M\gamma$, using a Lyapunov function for arbitrary $N \geq 2$ players, a non-cooperative two-player ALOHA was shown to have two different interior[4] Nash equilibria only one of which was locally asymptotically stable (see also [33]).

---

[3] Power based costs are borne whether or not the transmission is successful.

[4] *i.e.*, not including the stable boundary deadlock equilibrium at $\underline{q} = \underline{1}$.

For the stability analysis of our altruistic game, consider the discrete-time (n), synchronous-play gradient-ascent dynamics,

$$q_i(n) = \arg\max_{q_i} V_i(q_i; \underline{q}_{-i}(n-1)) \quad \forall i. \tag{4}$$

In a distributed system[5], the corresponding continuous-time Jacobi iteration approximation is:

$$\dot{q}_i(t) = \frac{\partial V_i}{\partial q_i}(\underline{q}(t)) \quad \forall i, \tag{5}$$

and is motivated when players take small steps toward their currently optimal response, i.e., better-response dynamics [41]. That is, for positive step-size $\varepsilon \ll 1$ (5) approximates the discrete-time better-response dynamics,

$$q_i(n) = q_i(n-1) + \varepsilon \frac{\partial V_i}{\partial q_i}(\underline{q}(n)) \quad \forall i, \tag{6}$$

which is a kind of distributed gradient ascent. The Jacobi iteration is also motivated by the desire to take small steps to avoid regions of attraction of undesirable boundary NEPs, particularly those corresponding to the capture strategy ($q_i = 1$ for some i). Note that when more than one player selects this strategy, the result is a deadlocked "tragedy of the commons." Additionally the players avoid the opt-out strategy ($q_i = 0$ for some i). In summary, (6) represents a repeated game in which players adjust their transmission parameters q_i to (locally) maximize their net utility V_i.

To find conditions on the parameters of net utilities (1) for local stability of the equilibria, we can apply the Hartman-Grobman theorem [37] to (5), i.e., check that the Jacobian is negative definite. The following proposition uses the conditions of [39] for stability (and uniqueness) for a special case.

Proposition 2. *In the case where players have the same parameters C and A, the symmetric NEP $q^*\underline{1}$ is locally asymptotically stable under the dynamics in (5) when the normalized parameters satisfy*

$$C > 2(N-1)A. \tag{7}$$

Proof. By [39], the result follows if the symmetric $N \times N$ matrix $H(\underline{q})$ is negative definite, where

$$H_{ij} = \frac{\partial^2 V_i}{\partial q_i \partial q_j} + \frac{\partial^2 V_j}{\partial q_j \partial q_i}.$$

First note that, for all i,

$$H_{ii}(\underline{q}) = -\frac{C}{q_i^2} < -C.$$

---

[5] *cf.* Section 4.3 for a discussion of asynchronous play.

For $l \neq i$,

$$\frac{\partial^2 V_i}{\partial q_i \partial q_l} = \frac{\partial}{\partial q_l}\left(\frac{C}{q_i} - A\alpha(\underline{q}_{-i})\frac{1}{N-1}\sum_{j\neq i}q_j\prod_{k\neq i,j}(1-q_k)\right)$$
$$= A\prod_{j\neq i,l}(1-q_j)\frac{1}{N-1}\sum_{j\neq i}q_j\prod_{k\neq i,j}(1-q_k)$$
$$+ A\alpha(\underline{q}_{-i})\frac{1}{N-1}\left(\sum_{j\neq i,l}q_j\prod_{k\neq i,j,l}(1-q_k) - \prod_{k\neq i,l}(1-q_k)\right).$$

Now because $0 < q_i < 1$ for all i and the triangle inequality,

$$|H_{ij}(\underline{q})| \leq 2A \quad \forall j \neq i.$$

So, by the Gershgorin circle (disc) theorem (see p. 344 of [18]), all of $H(\underline{q})$'s eigenvalues are less than $-C+(N-1)2A$. So, if (7) holds, then all the eigenvalues of $H(\underline{q})$ are negative, and so $H(\underline{q})$ is negative definite.

3.2   The Marginal Effect of Altruism

In this section, we will write q^* (of the symmetric NEP $q^*\underline{1}$ in symmetric users case) as a function of the normalized altruism parameter $a := A/M$, $q^*(a)$. Note that $q^*(0) = c := C/M$.

Recall that the total throughput for slotted ALOHA, $Nc(1-c)^{N-1}$, is maximal when $c = 1/N$. The maximum total throughput is $(1-1/N)^{N-1} \approx e^{-1}$ for large N, i.e., the maximum throughput per player is $1/(Ne)$ in this *cooperative* setting *without* networking costs accounted for.

So, if $c > 1/N$, i.e., total throughput is less than e^{-1} because of excessive demand (overloaded system), then a marginal increase in altruism from zero $(0 < a \ll 1)$ will cause a marginal decrease in $q^* \downarrow 1/N$, resulting in an increase in throughput per user $\gamma \uparrow 1/(Ne)$. Also, if $c < 1/N$, i.e., total throughput is less than e^{-1} because of low demand (underloaded system), then a marginal increase in altruism from zero will again cause a marginal decrease in q^*, but here resulting in a decrease in throughput γ (further away from the optimum e^{-1}).

4   Model Variations

In this section, we discuss model variations, which we subsequently analyze.

4.1   Throughput Based Costs

In [25] we considered throughput based costs with a static altruism parame-ter and with utility proportional to throughput. Instead of (1), for throughput based costs with dynamic altruism and utility being a concave (log) function of throughput, we can model the net utility as:

$$\tilde{V}_i(\underline{q}) = C_i \log(\gamma_i(\underline{q})) + A_i \alpha_i(\underline{q}_{-i}) \bar{\gamma}_{-i}(\underline{q}) - M_i \gamma_i(\underline{q}). \tag{8}$$

Proposition 1 can easily be adapted for power based costs. Instead of (3), the first-order necessary condition for a symmetric Nash equilibrium $q\underline{1}$ under throughput based cost is

$$\tilde{f}(q) := aq^2(1-q)^{2N-3} + q(1-q)^{N-1} - c = 0. \tag{9}$$

All solutions q for (9) correspond to NEPs $q\underline{1}$ because $\partial^2 \tilde{V}_i(\underline{q})/\partial q_i^2 = -C_i/q_i^2 < 0$ for all i, q (as for power based cost). Note that $\tilde{f}(0) = \tilde{f}(1) = -c < 0$, so we cannot simply use the intermediate value theorem as we did for Proposition 1 to establish existence of a symmetric Nash equilibrium when $c < 1$. Here, existence requires

$$\max_{0 < q < 1} \tilde{f}(q) \geq 0, \tag{10}$$

a condition on N, c, a. Note that if the inequality in (10) strictly holds then there will be an even number of symmetric NEPs, again by the intermediate value theorem. If the maximum equals zero then there may be a unique symmetric NEP.

4.2 Proportional Throughput Utility

Suppose that utility is simply proportional to throughput and cost is power based, i.e., the net utility is

$$\hat{V}_i(\underline{q}) = C_i \gamma_i(\underline{q}) + A_i \alpha_i(\underline{q}_{-i}) \bar{\gamma}_{-i}(\underline{q}) - M_i q_i. \tag{11}$$

Note that the net utility $\hat{V}_i$ is *linear* in q_i (this would also be the case if throughput based costs were involved). This normally leads to candidate "bang-bang" Nash equilibrium play-actions, $q_i \in \{0, 1\}$ for all players i; i.e., the players are either out of the game ($q_i = 0$ if $\partial \hat{V}_i/\partial q_i < 0$) or are *all in* ($q_i = 1$ if $\partial \hat{V}_i/\partial q_i > 0$). Note that the latter play action, potentially leading to the deadlock of "tragedy of the commons", is *not* an equilibrium here because if $q_j = 1$ then $\partial \hat{V}_i/\partial q_i = -M < 0$ for all $i \neq j$.

It turns out that for our scenario, there is a symmetric interior equilibrium $q\underline{1}$ for the identical players case with $0 < q < 1$, i.e., where

$$\hat{f}(q) := \frac{\partial \hat{V}_i}{\partial q_i}(q\underline{1})$$
$$= c(1-q)^{N-1} - aq(1-q)^{2N-3} - 1 = 0. \tag{12}$$

If $c > 1$, $\hat{f}(0) = c - 1 > 0$ and $\hat{f}(1) = -1 < 0$ and so there is a solution to $\hat{f}(q) = 0$ for $0 < q < 1$ by the intermediate value theorem. It should be noted, however, that such an interior Nash equilibrium $q\underline{1}$ is not stable, i.e., it's a saddle point in the domain $[0, 1]^N$.

4.3 Asynchronous/Multirate Players

Asynchronous players were considered previously in [22] using the ideas from [6,7]. A very similar approach can be used to extend the results herein to account for the effects of asynchronous play. Numerical results for this case are given in Section 5.3 below.

5 Numerical Studies

We performed numerical experiments for scenarios with power based costs, log-utility of throughput, and normalized utility parameter $c = 0.5$.

5.1 Comparing Altruism and Non-cooperation under Identical Users

We compare here the Nash equilibria under altruistic player action with equilibria in purely non-cooperative scenarios. For the purely non-cooperative scenario, $i.e.$, $a = 0$, the symmetric Nash equilibrium $q = c = 0.5$ is simply obtained by solving (3). For the scenarios with altruism, the normalized altruism parameter was taken to be $a = 20$. Recall that for static altruism, $\alpha \equiv 1$. At Nash equilibrium $\underline{q}^* = q^*\underline{1}$, the throughput ($\gamma^* = q^*(1-q^*)^{N-1}$) and utility (1) performance per user is given in the following table, in decreasing order of throughput.

Scenario	N	q^*	γ^*	V^*/M
Dynamic Altruism	4	.22	.1044	-0.36
Static Altruism	4	.16	.0935	0.53
Non-cooperative	4	.50	.0625	-1.89
Static Altruism	8	.28	.0277	-1.52
Dynamic Altruism	8	.50	.0039	-3.27
Non-cooperative	8	.50	.0039	-3.27

An interesting observation from this simple numerical study is that our dynamic altruism model does not perform well when contention is high, as it is the case for $N = 8$, under the assumed parameters. This is so because high contention is perceived as non-cooperation and is punished.

To improve the estimation of the altruism levels in the system, we could include in our model a measure on the expected congestion levels based on the number of users sharing the same channel and then estimate the current altruism level of the system as the deviation of this expected average idle time. Finally, if the level of altruism is too high, under either the static or dynamics mechanisms, the channel may be underused; in this case, the altruism parameters could be adjusted via an "evolutionary" process to avoid the waste of resources.

5.2   Players with Different Altruism Parameters

Consider the game with power based costs. In this section, we consider players with different normalized altruism parameters a for $N = 3$ otherwise identical players with normalized parameter $c = 0.5$ associated with power-based cost. Specifically, the first player has a_1 ranging from 30 to 70, while the other two players both have $a = 50$. Note that changing a in this manner will result in changes in the NEP q^* and corresponding throughputs γ^* (and utilities V^* per user, as shown in the following table):

a_1	$q_1^*, q_2^* = q_3^*$	$\gamma_1^*, \gamma_2^* = \gamma_3^*$	$V_1^*, V_2^* = V_3^*$
30	$0.15, 0.10$	$0.13, 0.074$	$0.754, 2.37$
40	$0.12, 0.10$	$0.10, 0.080$	$1.40, 2.24$
50	$0.10, 0.10$	$0.083, 0.083$	$2.10, 2.10$
60	$0.091, 0.11$	$0.073, 0.087$	$2.79, 1.83$
70	$0.079, 0.11$	$0.063, 0.090$	$3.56, 1.82$

Following intuition, increased altruism, $a_1 > 50$, by player 1 resulted in lower throughput for him and higher throughput for the other two players. Similarly, decreased altruism by player 1, $a_1 < 50$, resulted in higher throughput for him and lower throughput for the other players.

5.3   Sizes of Regions of Attractions under Different Play-Rates

In this section, we study how the volume of the regions of attractions of different equilibria are sensitive to players adopting different play-rates, while retaining our assumption of fictitious/quasi-stationary play. Consider the case of $N = 3$ players two of whom have the same play rate while the other adopts a play rate that is a multiple, r, of the other two. We consider the case of throughput based costs, *i.e.*,

$$\dot{\underline{q}}_i(t) = r_i \frac{\partial \tilde{V}_i}{\partial q_i}(\underline{q}(t)) \quad \forall i, \tag{13}$$

where $r_i = r$ for player $i = 1$, otherwise $r_i = 1$ and $\tilde{V}$ is given in Section 4.1. Numerically simulating (13) from different initial points chosen from a grid in the hypercube $[0, 1]^3$, we counted the number of initial points converging to a given NEP so as to estimate the volume of its region of attraction. Note that the introduction of such play-rate parameters r_i does not change the position of the NEPs. Using normalized parameters $a = 50$ and $c = 0.5$, the function $\tilde{f}$ whose roots are the NEPs is depicted in Figure 1. As can be seen from the following table, the region of attraction is very sensitive to r in the range 0.1 to 10.

Volume	NEP $= (0.1)\underline{1}$	NEP $= (0.75)\underline{1}$
$r = 0.1$	0.502	0.498
$r = 0.25$	0.507	0.493
$r = 1$	0.556	0.444
$r = 4$	0.839	0.161
$r = 10$	0.841	0.159

The results are again intuitive: a lower r effectively corresponds to a reluctance to be altruistic and thereby results in a smaller domain of attraction for the more altruistic Pareto equilibrium $(0.1)\underline{1}$ (corresponding to throughputs of $\gamma = 0.081$ and utilities $V = 1.94$, respectively compared to $\gamma = 0.047$ and $V = -1.43$ corresponding to $(0.75)\underline{1}$).

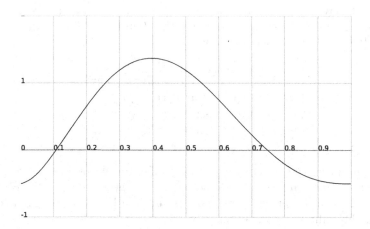

Fig. 1. Power based costs with $N = 3$, $a = 50$ and $c = 0.5$

6   Summary

In this paper, we extended a non-cooperative game framework for information-limited MAC of a LAN by adding an altruism term that depended on both the mean throughput of the other players and the mean channel idle time. The cases of heterogeneous or homogeneous users, and of power or throughput based costs, were considered for a quasi-stationary model of the game.

Our numerical studies produce intuitive results which means that our model is self-consistent and could form the basis for more sophisticated extensions. To this end, we plan to improve its realism, for example by departing from ideal quasi-stationary/fictitious-play dynamics and consider the effects of measurement error (as in [13, 33]), and study mechanisms that could motivate the users to adjust their behavior over time and reach better equilibria in terms of performance and/or efficiency. For example, the altruism parameter of a given user could be allowed to be configured according to the current mode of operation (*e.g.*, urgent versus low priority communication); then, an interesting evolutionary version of our game could be considered.

References

1. Al-Nowaihi, A., Levine, P.L.: The stability of the Cournot oligopoly model: A reassessment. Journal of Economic Theory 35, 307–321 (1985)
2. Alpcan, T., Basar, T., Srikant, R., Altman, E.: CDMA uplink power control as a noncooperative game. Wireless Networks 8 (November 2002)

3. Avrachenkov, K., Elias, J., Martignon, F., Neglia, G., Petrosyan, L.: A Nash bargaining solution for Cooperative Network Formation Games. In: Proc. Networking, Valencia, Spain (May 2011)
4. Axelrod, R.: The Evolution of Cooperation. Basic Books, New York (1984)
5. Azad, A.P., Altman, E., Elazouzi, R.: From Altruism to Non-Cooperation in Routing Games. In: Proc. Networking and Electronic Commerce Research Conference (NAEC), Lake Garda, Italy (October 2009)
6. Basar, T., Olsder, G.J.: Dynamic noncooperative game theory, 2nd edn. Academic Press (1995)
7. Bertsekas, D.P., Tsitsiklis, J.N.: Convergence rate and termination of asynchronous iterative algorithms. In: Proc. 3rd International Conference on Supercomputing (1989)
8. Bicchieri, C.: The Grammar of Society: the Nature and Dynamics of Social Norms. Cambridge University Press, New York (2006)
9. Bicchieri, C., Xiao, E.: Do the right thing: but only if others do so. Journal of Behavioral Decision Making 22, 191–208 (2009)
10. Brown, G.W.: Iterative solutions of games with fictitious play. In: Koopmans, T.C. (ed.) Activity Analysis of Production and Allocation. Wiley, New York (1951)
11. Cagalj, M., Ganeriwal, S., Aad, I., Hubaux, J.P.: On Selfish Behavior in CSMA/CA networks. In: Proc. IEEE INFOCOM (2005)
12. Camerer, C.F., Loewenstein, G.: Behavioral Economics: Past, Present, Future. In: Camerer, C.F., Loewenstein, G., Rabin, M. (eds.) Advances in Behavioral Economics. Princeton Univ. Press (2003)
13. Cui, T., Chen, L., Low, S.H.: A Game-Theoretic Framework for Medium Access Control. IEEE Journal on Selected Areas in Communications 26(7) (September 2008)
14. Dufwenberg, M., Gächter, S., Hennig-Schmidt, H.: The framing of games and the psychology of play. Games and Economic Behavior 73 (2011)
15. Fehr, E., Fischbacher, U.: The nature of human altruism. Nature 425 (2003)
16. Fehr, E., Schmidt, K.: A theory of fairness, competition, and cooperation. Quarterly Journal of Economics 114(3) (1999)
17. Heusse, M., Rousseau, F., Guillier, R., Dula, A.: Idle sense: An optimal access method for high throughput and fairness in rate diverse wireless LANs. In: Proc. ACM SIGCOMM (2005)
18. Horn, R.A., Johnson, C.R.: Matrix Analysis. Cambridge Univ. Press (1988)
19. Huang, M., Caines, P.E., Malhame, R.P.: Social dynamics in mean field LQG control: egoistic and altruistic agents. In: Proc. IEEE CDC, Atlanta (December 2010)
20. Hui, P., Xu, K., Li, V.O.K., Crowcroft, J., Latora, V., Lio, P.: Selfishness, Altruism and Message Spreading in Mobile Social Networks. In: Proc. IEEE International Workshop on Network Science For Communication Networks (2009)
21. Jin, Y., Kesidis, G.: A pricing strategy for an ALOHA network of heterogeneous users with inelastic bandwidth requirements. In: Proc. CISS, Princeton (March 2002)
22. Jin, Y., Kesidis, G.: Dynamics of usage-priced communication networks: the case of a single bottleneck resource. IEEE/ACM Trans. Networking (October 2005)
23. Jin, Y., Kesidis, G.: Distributed contention window control for selfish users in IEEE 802.11 wireless LANs. IEEE JSAC Special Issue on Non-Cooperative Networks (August 2007)
24. Jin, Y., Kesidis, G.: A channel-aware MAC protocol in an ALOHA network with selfish users. IEEE JSAC Special Issue on Game Theory in Wireless Communications (January 2012)

25. Kesidis, G., Jin, Y., Amar, A., Altman, E.: Stable Nash equilibria of medium access games under symmetric, socially altruistic behavior. In: Proc. IEEE CDC, Atlanta, December 15-17 (2010); technical report available at, http://arxiv.org/abs/1003.5324
26. Ledyard, J.O.: Public goods: A Survey of Experimental Research. Social Science Working Paper 861 (1994)
27. Lee, J.W., Chiang, M., Calderbank, R.A.: Utility-optimal random-access protocol. IEEE Transactions on Wireless Communications 6(7) (July 2007)
28. Levitt, S.D., List, J.A.: What Do Laboratory Experiments Measuring Social Preferences Reveal about the Real World? The Journal of Economic Perspectives 21(2), 153–174 (2007)
29. Long, C., Zhang, Q., Li, B., Yang, H., Guan, X.: Non-Cooperative Power Control for Wireless Ad Hoc Networks with Repeated Games. IEEE Journal on Selected Areas in Communications 25(6) (August 2007)
30. Ma, R.T.B., Misra, V., Rubenstein, D.: An Analysis of Generalized Slotted-Aloha Protocols. IEEE/ACM Transactions on Networking 17(3) (June 2009)
31. Margolis, H.: Cognition and extended rational choice. Routledge, New York (2007)
32. Milchtaich, I.: Comparative Statics of Altruism and Spite. Games and Economic Behavior 75(2), 809–831 (2012)
33. Menache, I., Shimkin, N.: Fixed-rate equilibrium in wireless collision channels. In: Proc. Network Control and Optimization (NET-COOP), Avignon, France (June 2007)
34. Meshkati, F., Chiang, M., Poor, H.V., Schwartz, S.C.: A Game-Theoretic Approach to Energy-Efficient Power Control in Multicarrier CDMA Systems. IEEE JSAC 24(6) (June 2006)
35. Nowak, N.: Five Rules for the Evolution of Cooperation. Science 314 (2006)
36. Ostrom, E.: Collective Action and the Evolution of Social Norms. The Journal of Economic Perspectives 14(3) (2000)
37. Perko, L.: Differential Equations and Dynamical Systems, 3rd edn. Springer, New York (2011)
38. Raya, M., Aad, I., Hubaux, J.-P., El Fawal, A.: DOMINO: Detecting MAC Layer Greedy Behavior in IEEE 802.11 Hotspots. IEEE Transactions On Mobile Computing 5(12) (December 2006)
39. Rosen, J.B.: Existence and uniqueness of equilibrium points for concave N-person games. Econometrica 33(3), 520–534 (1965)
40. Seade, J.: The stability of Cournot revisited. Journal of Economic Theory 23, 15–27 (1980)
41. Shamma, J.S., Arslan, G.: Dynamic fictitious play, dynamic gradient play, and distributed convergence to Nash equilibria. IEEE Trans. Auto. Contr. 50(3), 312–327 (2005)
42. Sharma, Y., Williamson, D.P.: Stackelberg thresholds in network routing games or the value of altruism. Games and Economic Behavior 67(1), 174–190 (2009)
43. Wicker, S.B., MacKenzie, A.B.: Stability of Multipacket Slotted Aloha with Selfish Users and Perfect Information. In: Proc. IEEE INFOCOM (2003)
44. Zhang, A., Zhang, Y.: Stability of Nash equilibrium: The multiproduct case. Journal of Mathematical Economics 26(4), 441–462 (1996)

Providing Throughput Guarantees in IEEE 802.11 Wireless Networks – An Experimentally-Driven Study

Christos Stathopoulos, Georgios Aristomenopoulos, and Symeon Papavassiliou

Institute of Communications and Computer Systems (ICCS)
School of Electrical and Computer Engineering,
National Technical University of Athens, Athens 15780, Greece
christos.stathopoulos@gmail.com, aristome@netmode.ntua.gr,
papavass@mail.ntua.gr

Abstract. In this paper the experimental evaluation of the most critical operational QoS enabling parameters for IEEE 802.11e, with respect to service differentiation and throughput provisioning, over pragmatic conditions, is realized, exploiting the NETMODE wireless testbed. Capitalizing on the guidelines and observations that stem from this experimental study, a novel, asynchronous policy based resource allocation mechanism aiming at network's aggregate throughput maximization and stations' throughput prerequisites satisfaction for inelastic traffic is proposed. The operational effectiveness of the proposed method under pragmatic networking conditions is evaluated and tested for various scenarios implemented over the considered wireless testbed.

Keywords: 802.11e, QoS, experimentation, realistic testbed evaluation, throughput guarantees and maximization.

1 Introduction

The growing demand for high data rates and support for multiple services with diverse Quality of Services (QoS) requirements over wireless local area networks has led to the introduction of 802.11e [1], an approved amendment to the IEEE 802.11 standard [2] that defines a set of Quality of Service enhancements through modifications to the Media Access Control (MAC) mechanism. Despite its wide acceptance, an efficient resource allocation mechanism that does not only enable service differentiation but also guaranties stations' strict QoS throughput requirements under pragmatic networking conditions remains a challenge. In this paper, extensive evaluation study on the impact of the Enhanced Distributed Channel Access (EDCA) - the basic 802.11e medium access mechanism - on QoS provisioning over a real wireless testbed is initially provided. Among the contributions and importance of the experimentally-verified results, is the derivation of significant observations on the pragmatic effects of service differentiation on real systems, which essentially set the basic design guidelines of novel resource allocation and call admission control schemes. Therefore, based on arguments along with quantitative and qualitative results that are obtained from the above experimentally driven study, a generic policy based resource allocation algorithm is designed and evaluated, promising to maximize network's utilization, while satisfying users' strict throughput requirements.

J. Zheng et al. (Eds.): Adhocnets 2012, LNICST 111, pp. 43–58, 2013.

The rest of this paper is organized as follows. Section 2 illustrates the main IEEE 802.11e QoS enabling features, while in Section 3 a brief presentation of the experimentation wireless testbed used is provided. Section 4 provides an analytical description as well as an extended experimental evaluation of the impact of the most critical operational parameters of IEEE 802.11e with respect to service differentiation (i.e. Contention Window *(CW)* and Arbitration Interframe Space *(AIFS)* parameters). In Section 5 an optimal throughput maximization scheme is described, while in Section 6 we describe the operation of a joint call admission control and throughput maximization mechanism, along with extensive results providing a proof of concept.

2   IEEE 802.11e and EDCA

IEEE 802.11e MAC layer exploits the Enhanced Distributed Channel Access (EDCA), built on the legacy distributed coordination function (DCF) [2] for sharing the medium between multiple stations. EDCA relies on CSMA/CA, while service differentiation and QoS provisioning is achieved by appropriately tuning the following parameters:

1. Arbitration Interframe Space *(AIFS)*: The varying amount of timeslots the channel must be idle before a station could start its backoff contention period. T_{AIFS} refers to the same amount of slots expressed in seconds.
2. Contention Window *(CW)*: The amount of timeslots a station should wait before attempting to transmit (backoff), is a random integer number following a uniform distribution in the interval *[0, CW]*, where $CW = 2^k - 1, k \in \mathbb{N}$.
3. Transmission Opportunity *(TxOP)*: The amount of timeslots a station has contention-free access to the channel, allowing it to transmit a number of data units without having to contend for access to the medium.

Moreover, sets of the above parameters, with predefined values, define different access categories (ACs) or traffic classes for service differentiation, that allow higher priority traffic to spend less time in the backoff state, resulting in more frequent access to the medium.

The effect of the *AIFS* and *CW* parameters on service differentiation and throughput guarantying will be discussed and analyzed in Section 4. On the other hand, TxOP intuitively causes short term frame bursting, making the quantification and analysis of its long term effects difficult, is not be examined in this work.

3   Testbed Configuration

Towards examining and evaluating the effects of the QoS parameters offered by the 802.11e standard under pragmatic conditions, we exploit an experimental wireless IEEE 802.11 testbed, provided by the Network Management and Optimal Design laboratory (NETMODE) of National Technical University of Athens. The testbed allows the realization of actual IEEE 802.11 networks, while also provides the necessary tools and mechanisms for assessing and evaluating the results.

The NETMODE wireless testbed consists of a control server and 10 wireless nodes all interconnected via an Ethernet switch. The testbed control server (Controller) runs a webserver with a GUI (custom GUI) and an SSH server that gives access to the wireless nodes. Each of the 10 nodes consists of the following components:

- alix3d2 board,
- 1 100Mbit Ethernet interface connected to the switch.
- 2 USB interfaces for additional storage support,
- 2 Atheros AR5004 802.11 a/b/g interfaces with MadWifi driver,
- 1GB flash card storage device installed with Voyage Linux [3].

The wireless nodes are scattered around the 3rd floor of the NETMODE premises according to the topology depicted in Fig. 1.

For our experiments we adopt the Basic Service Set (BSS) architecture, in infrastructure mode. Specifically Node 6 operates as an Access Point (AP) while the rest of the nodes connect through the AP to the network as wireless stations (STAs).

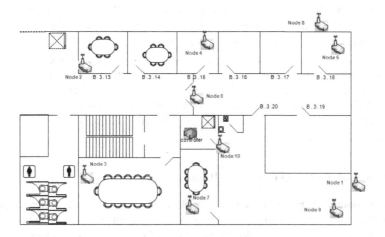

Fig. 1. NETMODE Wireless Testbed Topology

3.1   Software Configuration

Towards examining and analyzing the effects of the QoS mechanisms of 802.11e on service differentiation, we consider one-way UDP traffic from the stations to the AP generated by iperf [4]. Specifically, each station operates an instance of the iperf client, transmitting data to the AP, which, on the other hand, acts as the iperf server. Moreover, the iperf server is responsible for keeping track and logging of all the incoming data streams from the wireless nodes. We also consider, that each station transmits only one continuously backlogged data stream of a specified traffic class, with only one set of EDCA parameters.

Finally, the RTS/CTS and the error and recovery (ACK) mechanisms have been disabled, while the TXOP limit parameter is set to 0, i.e. one frame per transmission. A comprehensive list of all experiment parameters can be found in Table 1.

Table 1. PHY and MAC parameters used in the experiments

Parameter	Value
R (TxRate)	11 Mbps (fixed)
T_I	20 μsec
T_{SIFS}	10 μsec
T_{DIFS}	50 μsec
T_{pre}	96 μsec
T_{phy}	48 μsec
H_{MAC}	34 bytes
L_{DATA}	1470 bytes

4   Evaluation of the EDCA Parameters

As described earlier, the EDCA mechanism offers a variety of parameter configurations to enable QoS differentiation among data streams. Towards providing a clearer understanding of the distinct features and characteristics of each of the EDCA parameters, in the following we will study the effects of CW and $AIFS$ independently. More specifically we will model, study and evaluate the QoS provisioning results obtained by appropriately tuning the CW and $AIFS$ parameters respectively. The ultimate goal of this section is to formalize the behavior of QoS enabled wireless stations, towards devising an efficient resource allocation mechanism capable of providing throughput guarantees in IEEE 802.11e networks (this is analyzed and provided in sections 5 and 6).

4.1   Study of the Effect of the CW Parameter

In the traditional Wi-Fi Multimedia (WMM) model, the CW parameter ranges between CW_{min} and CW_{max} values, following the CW exponential increase scheme [1]. This mechanism contributes to the decongestion of the transmission channel in cases of high collision rates. However, in the special occasion that the occurring load in the channel is known a priori, (i.e. by knowing the number of the transmitting stations and their bandwidth prerequisites), an optimal CW value for each station can be derived, so that an optimal equilibrium occurs among the number of collisions in the channel and the average backoff time for each contenting station. Therefore, we may set $CW=CW_{min}=CW_{max}$, and service differentiation can be achieved by appropriately tuning one single parameter, assuming that for all stations the $AIFS$ parameter is set to its default value, $T_{AIFS}=T_{SIFS}+2*T_I$, where T_{SIFS} is the period of a short inter-frame space and T_I is the duration of an idle timeslot.

4.1.1   Station Throughput Differentiation

Towards devising the channel behavior based on the EDCA parameter settings we model the probability for a station to access the channel at any given timeslot. According to the p-persistent CSMA model [5], any given station j has a constant and independent probability τ_j to attempt transmission in an arbitrary timeslot. Assuming that the number of the timeslot in which a station j will attempt to access the channel is given by a uniform distribution in the interval $[0, CW_j]$, the average back-off time in timeslots will be

$$backoff_j = \frac{CW_j + 1}{2} \tag{1}$$

and consequently, the average transmission attempt probability τ_j by the *jth* station for any given timeslot will be

$$\tau_j = \frac{2}{CW_j + 1} \tag{2}$$

(the interested reader may refer to [5] for a detailed proof of the derivation of this probability).

Having calculated the probability for a station to attempt transmission in a given timeslot, we can now derive the formula for the station throughput as in [5]. Assuming that the collision time is approximately equal to the transmission time [5], and by defining the product

$$\prod_{j=1}^{N}(1 - \tau_j) \triangleq A_N \tag{3}$$

where N is number of connected stations, the calculated average throughput for a station j is:

$$\eta_j = \frac{L_{DATA}}{T_D} \frac{(\tau_j/(1-\tau_j))A_N}{1 - A_N(1 - T_I/T_D)}, (T_C \simeq T_D) \tag{4}$$

while the   average aggregate throughput for all the stations would be:

$$\eta_{total} = \frac{L_{DATA}}{T_D} \frac{(\sum_{i}^{N} \tau_j/(1-\tau_j))A_N}{1 - A_N(1 - T_I/T_D)} \tag{5}$$

where L_{DATA} is the effective frame load in bytes transmitted during a successful time-slot, and the transmission time T_D can be defined in accordance to [7] as

$$T_D = \frac{8 \times (L_{DATA} + H_{MAC})}{R} + T_{pre} + T_{phy} + T_{IFS} \tag{6}$$

with H_{MAC} being the frame header length in bytes, R the transmission rate at the physical layer, and T_{pre}, T_{phy} and T_{IFS} are the duration times for the physical layer preamble, the physical layer header, and the interframe space respectively.

Observing equations (2) and (4), the direct relation between a station's throughput and its *CW* value becomes evident. Specifically, from equation (4) we can derive the ratio of achieved throughput between stations i and j, as a function of their channel access probabilities:

$$\frac{\eta_i}{\eta_j} = \frac{\tau_i(1-\tau_j)}{\tau_j(1-\tau_i)} \tag{7}$$

Moreover, by substituting (2) into (7) and assuming large values of the *CW* parameter, we get:

$$\frac{\eta_i}{\eta_j} = \frac{CW_j + 1}{CW_i + 1} \tag{8}$$

indicating a direct proportional relation between stations' *CW* value and their achieved throughput.

4.1.2 Experimental Evaluation

In this section, the efficacy of the proportional equation (8) is demonstrated by indicative numerical results and insights, providing also a proof of concept of its applicability in a real-life environment. Towards a pragmatic quantification of the achieved proportional fairness we exploit Jain's proportional fairness index Ψ [8] defined as:

$$\Psi = \frac{\left(\sum_{j=1}^{N} s_j/\eta_j\right)^2}{N\sum_{j=1}^{N}(s_j/\eta_j)^2} \tag{9}$$

where N is the number of stations, η_j is the theoretically expected throughput according to equation (4) and s_j is the experimentally measured throughput. This way, we can evaluate the achieved fairness among the theoretical throughput calculated by equation (4) and the observed value. Values close to *1* indicate the correctness and efficacy of the theoretical calculated values.

In our first series of experiments we employ 6 testbed nodes, one acting as an AP and the rest as transmitting stations, which we further divide in two groups, *ClassA* and *ClassB*, containing 1 and 4 nodes respectively. We consider the value of the *CW* parameter for *ClassA* to range from [15, 1023], taking values of the form $CW = 2^k - 1, k \in \mathbb{N}$, while for stations in *ClassB* the *CW* value is fixed to *127* or *31* as depicted in Fig. 2 and Fig. 3 respectively. Finally, all experimental throughput results presented are averaged over a 30 seconds transmission period.

In Fig. 2(a) the normalized values of the theoretically estimated (also referred as estimated) and experimentally observed (also referred as observed) throughput, η_j and s_j, as fractions of the total throughput η_{total} and s_{total} respectively, are illustrated, considering $CW_{ClassB}=127$, while in Fig. 2(b) the estimated and observed achieved aggregated throughput, as well as the proportional fairness index Ψ are presented.

Observing Fig. 2(a) we can conclude that equation (4) is capable of depicting the expected achieved throughput of wireless stations in great accuracy, especially for large values of CW_{ClassA}, as also indicated by the fairness index in Fig. 2(b).

Moreover, examining the observed and estimated (i.e., computed by equation (5)) aggregated throughput, presented in the Fig. 2(b), we notice an unexpected increase of the experimental achieved throughput especially for small values of CW_{ClassA}. However, this unexpected behavior can be explained by the Physical Layer Capture (PLC) effect analytically described in [9] and [10]. In accordance to the PLC effect, even if two or more MAC frames collide on the receiver, the frame with the stronger signal may still be correctly decoded, accounting for some false positive frame collisions and thus increased experimentally achieved throughput values. Moreover, with this behavior being more dominant as the number of collisions increase, the PLC effect can also cause significant unfairness between different transmitters with varying signal strength, leading to a more stochastic behavior of the system.

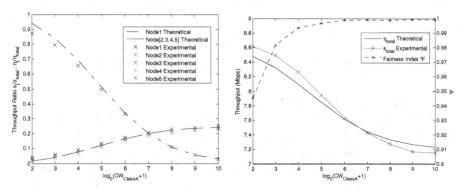

Fig. 2. Experimental results for $CW_{ClassB}=127$. a) Plot of relative rates s_j, η_j as fractions of s_{total} and η_{total} respectively as a function of CW. b) Plot of aggregated estimated and observed throughput and proportional fairness index Ψ.

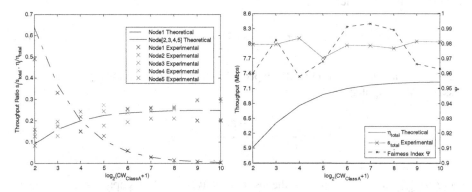

Fig. 3. Experimental results for $CW_{ClassB}=31$. a) Plot of relative rates s_j, η_j as fractions of s_{total} and η_{total} respectively as a function of CW. b) Plot of aggregated estimated and observed throughput and proportional fairness index Ψ.

The results presented in Fig 3, for $CW_{ClassB}=31$, confirm the latter. Specifically, the significantly lower CW value of $ClassB$ stations causes increased channel's congestion, leading to a large number of collisions. Moreover, the increased observed variance in experimental achieved throughput, presented in Fig 3(a), results to lower values of Jain's proportional fairness index Ψ, illustrated in Fig. 3(b). Likewise the achieved aggregated throughput, presented in Fig. 3(b), is constantly higher than the theoretically estimated one, especially for smaller CW_{ClassA} values where collisions are more likely to occur.

4.2   Study of the Effect of the *AIFS* Parameter

Towards completing our EDCA parameters study, the *AIFS* effect on throughput differentiation is examined next. Intuitively, by enabling *AIFS* differentiation among stations of different traffic classes, we allow high priority traffic class stations to start competing for the medium before low priority ones. Modeling channel's behavior in the presence of *AIFS* differentiation is quite complex, and an interested reader can refer to studies such as [11] and [12] for a more detailed description. However, we exploit a simple, yet powerful approach presented in [13], which enables the analytical modeling of only two different traffic classes with the same CW value.

4.2.1   Station Throughput Differentiation

The *AIFS* parameter is defined as $T_{AIFS}=T_{SIFS}+AIFSN*T_l$., where *AIFSN* is the additional number of idle slots a station should wait before starting its contention process, taking integer values in the interval *[0,15]*, while its default value is 2. Moreover, we define two traffic classes, namely *ClassA* and *ClassB*, with N_A and N_B transmitting stations, and $AIFSN_A$ and $AIFSN_B$ AIFSN values respectively, with $AIFSN_A<AIFSN_B$. All stations in both classes use the same CW value, large enough to assume a negligible amount of collisions in the channel.

The transmission probability of each station belonging in any traffic class in any given slot can thus be defined as:

$$\tau_{ClassA} \simeq \tau_{ClassB} \simeq \frac{2}{CW+1} = \tau \qquad (10)$$

Therefore, in accordance to [13], the expected throughput ratio among different traffic classes to be computed by:

$$\frac{\eta_{ClassB}}{\eta_{ClassA}} \simeq \frac{\frac{N_B}{N_A+N_B}(1-\tau)^{N_A\delta}}{1-\frac{N_B}{N_A+N_B}(1-\tau)^{N_A\delta}} = \lambda \qquad (11)$$

where η_{ClassA} and η_{ClassB} denote the estimated average throughput of *ClassA* and *ClassB* respectively and $\delta=AIFSN_B-AIFSN_A$.

Considering also that

$$\eta_{ClassA} + \eta_{ClassB} = \eta_{total} \tag{12}$$

where $\eta_{ClassA} = N_A \cdot \eta_{ClassA,i}$ and $\eta_{ClassB} = N_B \cdot \eta_{ClassB,j}$, with $\eta_{ClassA,i}$, $i=\{1..N_A\}$ and $\eta_{ClassB,j}$, $j=\{1..N_B\}$ denoting the estimated throughput of each station in *ClassA* and *ClassB* respectively.

The estimated throughput of each station can be thus calculated as a fraction of the aggregated throughput as

$$\eta_{ClassA,i} = \frac{1}{N_A} \frac{1}{\lambda+1} \eta_{total} \tag{13}$$

and

$$\eta_{ClassB,j} = \frac{1}{N_B} \frac{\lambda}{\lambda+1} \eta_{total} \tag{14}$$

4.2.2   Experimental Evaluation

To evaluate the behavior of the *AIFS* parameter and derive incentives on its operation and applicability on real-life environment we conduct a new set of experiments. We employ again 6 testbed nodes, one acting as an AP and the rest as stations, which we further divide in two groups, *ClassA* and *ClassB*, containing 1 and 4 nodes respectively. We consider the value of the $AIFSN_A$ parameter to range from [0-15], while for stations in *ClassB* the $AIFSN_B$ parameter is fixed to 7. Finally, all experimental throughput results presented are averaged over a 30 seconds transmission period.

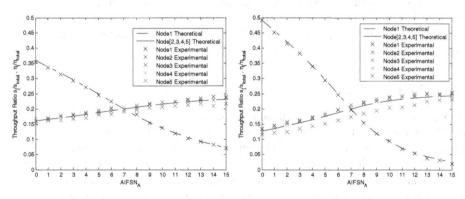

Fig. 4. Plot of relative rates s_j, η_j as fractions of s_{total} and η_{total} respectively as a function of $AIFSN_A$. a) considering $CW=63$, b) considering $CW=31$.

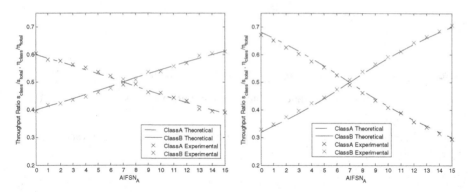

Fig. 5. Plot of relative rates s_j, η_j as fractions of s_{total} and η_{total} respectively as a function of $AIFSN_A$. a) considering $N_A=N_B=1$, b) considering $N_A=N_B=2$.

Fig. 4(a) and Fig. 4(b) illustrate the measured experimental achieved throughput ratio, as well as the theoretically expected one calculated by equations (13)-(14), considering fixed values of CW, 63 and 31 respectively.

Comparing Fig. 4(a) and Fig. 4(b) we conclude to the following observations: Initially and similarly to the results in Section 4.1.2, the larger the value of the CW, indicating a less congested network with less frame collisions, the closer the experimentally observed throughput ratio is to the theoretically estimated one, highlighting the absence of the PLC effect. Moreover, for smaller values of the CW parameter, stronger throughput differentiation is observed, favoring the higher priority traffic classes.

The latter can be further demonstrated in Fig. 5, where the effect of the number of transmitting stations on $AIFS$ throughput differentiation is examined. Specifically, we consider a fixed $CW=63$ for all stations, while we set the number of stations in each traffic class as $N_A=N_B=1$ and $N_A=N_B=2$ illustrated in Fig. 5(a) and Fig. 5(b) respectively. It is obvious that $AIFS$ differentiation favors high priority traffic classes, granting more bandwidth resources, on expense of low priority traffic classes, indicating the great impact of the number of transmitting stations on the achieved throughput ratios among different traffic classes.

4.3   Discussions and Observations

Throughout our experimental evaluation of the EDCA parameters we conclude that the CW is capable of enabling a proficient and reliable throughput differentiation scheme under pragmatic networking conditions, while still following a highly predictable behavior described by equations (4)-(8). Moreover, a trade-off between the degree of achieved proportional fairness among transmitting stations, and overall channel utilization in terms of achieved aggregate throughput, has been observed. The latter is further exploited in Section 5 towards proposing an efficient resource allocation scheme, aiming at throughput maximization.

The effect of the *AIFS* parameter on throughput differentiation appears to be highly complex and difficult to manage, mainly due to the impact of the population of each traffic class on the resource allocation process. Highly competing stations on top priority classes, either as a result of the presence of many stations or low *CW* values, create starving conditions for low priority traffic classes. In this sense, the *AIFS* parameter proves ideal for favoring critical inelastic traffic over best effort CSMA/CA networks.

5 Towards Network's Throughput Maximization

Based on the previous discussions, the *CW* parameter proves to be the most suitable QoS-enabling parameter in 802.11e networks, towards devising an efficient resource allocation mechanism that aims at network's aggregate throughput maximization. Specifically, the latter problem can be efficiently transformed to discovering the optimal *CW* values of transmitting stations [5]. Towards this goal, consider a set of stations' throughput requirements $r = \{r_1,...,r_N\}$ expressed as a relative ratio of station's 1 requirements, i.e., $r_j = \eta_j/\eta_1$, $j = 1,...,N$. Thereupon, via equation (8), an infinite set of *CW* values that can guarantee the required proportional fairness can be derived. Specifically, for every set of *CW* values $\{CW_1, CW_2,...,CW_N\}$ that satisfy (8), there always exist another set $\{a*CW_1, a*CW_2,...,a*CW_N\}$, $a \in \mathbb{R}^+$ also satisfying (8). Therefore, we may arbitrarily choose any such set to achieve the required service differentiation. However, as shown in Section 4.1, small *CW* values lead to increased frame collisions, while large *CW* values increase the presence of idle slots in the channel, both leading to bandwidth waste and thus reduced performance.

Towards pursuing network's throughput maximization, the optimal set $CW^* = \{CW_1^*,...,CW_N^*\}$ which satisfies the proportional fairness equation (8) while also maximizing the overall aggregate throughput, needs to be defined. The latter problem can be formulated as:

$$\max(\eta_{total}) = \sum_{j-1}^{N}\eta_j = \eta_{total}^*(\{CW_1^*,...,CW_N^*\}) \tag{15}$$

Problem (15) is optimally solved in [5], [14], and the optimal *CW* value for the leading station 1 can be thus calculated by:

$$CW_1^* = \sqrt{2\beta T_D'} + 1 \tag{16}$$

while for the remaining stations by:

$$CW_j^* = \frac{\sqrt{2\beta T_D'}}{r_j} + 1 \tag{17}$$

where $\beta = (\sum_{j=1}^{N} r_j)^2 - \sum_{j=1}^{N} r_j^2$ and $T_D' = T_D/T_I$.

5.1   Performance Evaluation and Numerical Results

To evaluate the practical effectiveness of the aforementioned method under pragmatic networking conditions, we employ 6 testbed nodes, one acting as an AP and the rest as transmitting stations, and similarly to Section 4.1 we calculate the estimated theoretical throughput in accordance to (4), measure wireless stations' observed experimental throughput for different choices of CW values, and additionally illustrate the optimal congestion window derived in accordance to equation (17).

In our first set of experiments (Fig. 6) we consider two different traffic classes, *ClassA* and *ClassB*, containing stations {1,2,3} and {4,5} respectively. Furthermore, we assume that stations belonging to *ClassB* request for a service with twice the throughput requirements of *ClassA*, i.e., $\eta_{ClassB}=2*\eta_{ClassA}$ and thus $r_j=\{1,1,1,2,2\}$.

On the other hand, in the second set of experiments (Fig. 7) we define three traffic classes, namely *ClassA*, *ClassB* and *ClassC* assigned to stations {1,2}, {3,4} and {5} respectively. Finally we assume $\eta_{ClassC}=2*\eta_{ClassB}=4*\eta_{ClassA}$, and thus stations' relative throughput requirements are formulated as $r_j=\{1,1,2,2,4\}$. This way, for example, stations of *ClassC* are expected to achieve four times *ClassA* stations' throughput.

Following the previous thread of analysis, we apply different sets of appropriate CW values satisfying equation (8), and measure the achieved stations' throughput over 30 seconds transmission periods.

Observing Fig. 6(a) and Fig. 7(a) and for CW sets with values smaller than the optimal, it is obvious that stations' experimental throughput curve diverges significantly from the theoretically expected behavior. It is the PLC effect, described in Section 4.1 that allows collided frames to be successfully transmitted, increasing stations' actual effective throughput. On the other hand, for larger CW sets the experimental results tightly follow the theoretically estimated behavior. The latter observations are further demonstrated by the proportional fairness index Ψ, comparing the experimental throughput, with the nodes' requirements, illustrated in Fig. 6(b) and Fig. 7(b).

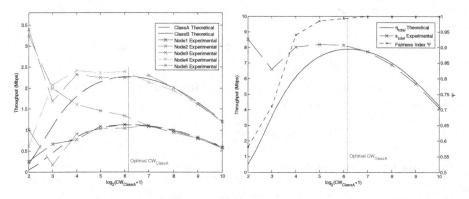

Fig. 6. Experimental results for 2 traffic classes. a) Plot of actual estimated and observed throughput as a function of CW. b) Plot of aggregated estimated and observed throughput and proportional fairness index Ψ.

Moreover, Fig. 6(b) and Fig. 7(b) clearly demonstrate the tradeoff between overall network's achieved throughput and proportional fairness. The smaller the CW values the greater the aggregated throughput, the less the proportional fairness though. However the optimal congestion window set $CW*$ calculated by equation (17), as also confirmed by the experimental results, provides an efficient equilibrium point that guaranties throughput maximization, while also delivering high values of proportional fairness in the medium.

6   Providing Throughput Guarantees in 802.11e networks

The maximum throughput algorithm presented in the previous section, even though achieves proportional fairness among transmitting stations, it fails to provide strict throughput guarantees that will enable the proficient transmission of inelastic data traffic. Towards this goal in this section, and exploiting the previous methodology, we propose a novel joint policy based Call Admission Control (CAC) and resource allocation mechanism that does not only maximize network's aggregate throughput, but also satisfies the QoS throughput requirements of all admitted stations.

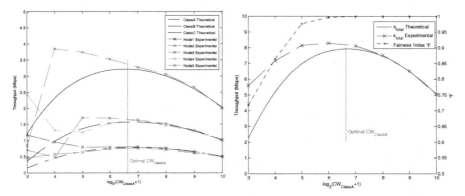

Fig. 7. Experimental results for 3 traffic classes. a) Plot of actual estimated and observed throughput as a function of CW. b) Plot of aggregated estimated and observed throughput and proportional fairness index Ψ.

However, choosing the right admission control policy is not trivial, especially considering the diversity of networks' types, customers' expectations and providers' goals. Therefore, various selection policies could be defined, ranging from already connected stations prioritization, to service classification, i.e., favoring real time traffic over non real time, or pricing plan based selections.

Independently of the chosen policy, Fig.8 illustrates a sequential diagram of the joint operation of the Call Admission Control and Optimal CW selection algorithms, highlighting on their cooperation and flawless integration. In accordance to this, each new station requesting admission also submits its throughput prerequisites to the AP. Then, the AP is responsible for calculating the new set CW' of optimal contention windows that need to be applied taking into account the new station's throughput requirements in accordance to (17). If the estimated stations' throughput rates that will be derived after applying *CW'*, satisfies all connected stations' requirements, then the new station is admitted and *CW'* is broadcasted to all stations. Otherwise and in accordance to the applied CAC policy the selection of those stations that will be rejected may be determined and communicated.

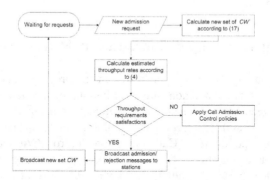

Fig. 8. Sequential diagram of joint CAC and Optimal *CW* selection algorithms

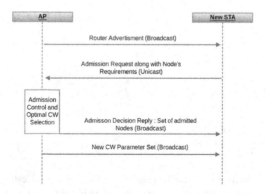

Fig. 9. Signaling diagram of new stations admission

Furthermore, Fig. 9 describes the required signaling information exchange between a new station that requests admission and the corresponding AP. It is important to note that the operation of proposed procedure is fully asynchronous and requires no synchronization among stations, since a) it allows stations to request admission of departure at any time, and b) the operation of the optimal CW algorithm is only performed when needed, i.e. upon a new service request, otherwise the last known set of *CW* values is used. Finally, the imposed signaling overhead introduced by the joint operation of the CAC and optimal *CW* algorithm is minimal, comprising of only one unicast message per new station, and 2 broadcast messages that could possibly be integrated on existing signaling.

Finally we provide some initial, though indicative numerical results demonstrating the applicability and efficacy of the proposed method. Once again we exploit the experimental NETMODE testbed and employ 6 testbed nodes, one acting as an AP and the rest as transmitting stations. We assume 3 types of services, *ClassA*, *ClassB* and *ClassC*, demanding at least *0.512*, *1.024* and *2.048 Mbps* respectively. Initially we consider that stations *{1,2}* request for *ClassA* services, while stations *{3,4}* for *ClassB*. Fig. 10 illustrates the obtained throughput of each station as a function of time, as well as network's aggregate throughput and fairness index in accordance to (9). All results are averaged over 1 sec intervals. At *t=50sec* a new station applies for admission, requesting a service of *ClassC*. The AP, in accordance to Fig. 8, recalculates the new optimal set of CW^* values and examines stations throughput requirements satisfaction. In our case the new user is finally admitted since users prerequisites are satisfied, the new set of CW^* is disseminated and applied, as described in Fig. 10. The major two observations are that a) the proportional fairness index attains high values, indicating the correct operation of the optimal *CW* algorithm, and most importantly, b) network's aggregate throughput achieves high values even with increased number of connected stations. It is the fixed optimal *CW* algorithm that provides an equilibrium operational point that guaranties reduced frame collisions among wireless stations, achieving high network's utilization, proving the efficacy and efficiency of the proposed method.

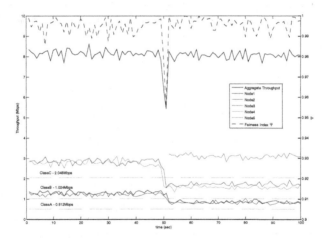

Fig. 10. Experimental results of the joint CAC and throughput maximization algorithm

References

1. IEEE Standard for Information Society, 802.11 Amendment 8: Medium Access Control (MAC) Quality of Service Enhancements (2005)
2. IEEE Standard for Information Society, Part 11: Wireless LAN Medium Access Control (MAC) and Physical Layer (PHY) Specifications, Reference number ISO/IEC 8802-11:1999(E), IEEE Std. 802.11, 1999 edn. (1999)
3. Voyage Linux, http://linux.voyage.hk

4. Iperf, http://iperf.sourceforge.net
5. Hu, C., Kim, H., Hou, J.C., Chi, D., Nandagopalan, S.S.: Provisioning Quality Controlled Medium Access in UltraWideBand-Operated WPANs. In: IEEE INFOCOM 2006, Barcelona (2006)
6. Bianchi, G., Fratta, L., Oliveri, M.: Performance evaluation and enhancement of the CSMA/CA MAC protocol for 802.11 wireless LANs. In: Personal, Indoor and Mobile Radio Communications, PIMRC 1996, Taiwan, vol. 2, pp. 392–396 (1996)
7. Yang, X., Rosdahl, J.: Throughput and Delay Limits of IEEE 802.11. IEEE Communication Letters 6(8), 355–357 (2002)
8. Jain, R.: The Art of Computer Systems Performance Analysis: Techniques for Experimental Design, Measurement, Simulation and Modeling. Wiley-Interscience, New York (1991)
9. Ganu, S., Ramachandran, K., Gruteser, M., Seskar, I., Deng, J.: Methods for restoring MAC layer fairness in IEEE 802.11 networks with physical layer capture. In: REALMAN 2006, pp. 7–14 (2006)
10. Ware, C., Chicaro, J., Wysocki, T.: Modeling of capture behavior in IEEE 802.11 radio modems. In: IEEE International Conference on Telecommunications (2001)
11. Bianchi, G., Tinnirello, I.: Analysis of Priority Mechanisms Based on Differentiated Inter-Frame Spacing in CSMA/CA. In: IEEE VTC – Fall 2003 (2003)
12. Inan, I., Keceli, F., Ayanoglu, E.: Saturation Throughput Analysis of IEEE 802.11e Enhanced Distributed Coordination Function. In: IEEE ICC 2007 (2007)
13. Bing, B.: Emerging technologies in wireless LANs: theory, design, and deployment, Cambridge (2008)
14. Nassiri, M., Heusse, M., Duda, A.: A Novel Access Method for Supporting Absolute and Proportional Priorities in 802.11 WLANs. In: IEEE INFOCOM 2008, Phoenix (2008)

Node Discovery and Replacement Using Mobile Robot

Kalypso Magklara, Dimitrios Zorbas, and Tahiry Razafindralambo

Inria Lille - Nord Europe, France
{Kalypso.Magklara,Dimitrios.Zormpas,Tahiry.Razafindralambo}@inria.fr

Abstract. A critical problem of wireless sensor networks is the network lifetime, due to the device's limited battery lifetime. The nodes are randomly deployed in the field and the system has no previous knowledge of their position. To tackle this problem we use a mobile robot, that discovers the nodes around it and replaces the active nodes, whose energy is drained, by fully charged inactive nodes. In this paper we propose two localized algorithms, that can run on the robot and that decide, which nodes to replace. We simulate our algorithms and our findings show that all nodes that fail are replaced in a short period of time.

1 Introduction

Wireless sensor networks is a collection of a large number of small size, low-cost sensing devices organized into a cooperative network. A sensor network except from the nodes that collect data also consists of a sink (base station). The nodes use their communication range to send the collected data to the base station. This can be succeeded using either a multi-hop architecture or a Connected Dominating Set (CDS) network. The nodes can be deployed in various physical environments to monitor events in the area. Sensor networks can be used in various applications, such as military surveillance, environmental monitoring, health-care and agriculture.

One of the fundamental issues to be addressed in wireless sensor networks is the network lifetime. Due to the device's limited battery lifetime nodes fail, the connectivity is lost and coverage is degraded. This problem can be solved by exploiting the redundant nodes that exist in the terrain. Previous papers have proposed a few strategies that calculate when or if failed nodes should be replaced using mobile nodes or robots [1], [2] and some other algorithms that do not move any of the nodes but activate the ones needed to cover the environment in question [3]. However, most of them assume complete knowledge of the network or the position of redundant/inactive nodes.

We propose two localized solutions, that do not assume any previous knowledge of the network. This means that in an autonomous network, we need to find out the parameters of the nodes, namely the position of the nodes and their energy consumption, in order to replace them with new nodes. We assume that the robot can learn information on the location of the nodes only if they are

J. Zheng et al. (Eds.): Adhocnets 2012, LNICST 111, pp. 59–71, 2013.

within its detection range. The advantages of our solutions are summarized in the following:

1. previous knowledge of the network is not required, namely the position of the nodes or the energy they consume,
2. the robot has the capability to explore the area and detect both active and inactive nodes,
3. both solutions are localized and do not demand a central server to process the network's parameters and
4. we implement a realistic energy consumption model both for the nodes [4] and the robot, for the later specifically we rely on experimental values based on the wifibot [5].

The rest of the paper is organized as follows. In Section 2, we present the related work in the fields of node replacement and sensor network redeployment. In Section 3, we provide a description of our model, while in Section 4 we present our solutions. In Section 5 we evaluate our methods and we compare them. Finally, Section 6 concludes the paper.

2   Related Work

Most of the research literature related to node replacement in wireless sensor networks deal with the problem by assuming they have previous knowledge of the nodes' position or the events' position or even the nodes' energy consumption [1], [6], [7], [8], [9], [10] and others require mobile sensors [2], [11].

In [1] three policies are proposed, each policy determines the importance of each failed node on the coverage and the lifetime of the network, by assigning a weight to each failed node. If the weight is greater than the policy threshold then the node is replaced, otherwise it is ignored. These policies try to maximize the lifetime and simultaneously minimize the redundant resources. Although to evaluate these weights knowledge of the network is needed and a central server to calculate them. In [6] knowledge of the events is needed and also the redundant nodes position is known since they are stored in the sink. The proposed scheme will schedule both the travels of the robot and the duty cycles of the sensors, the goal is to maintain the coverage while minimizing the traveled distance. However it only considers point coverage, so [7] was proposed, that considers area coverage. The nodes are grouped in sets and a staircase-based scheduling model is implemented, a fixed number of backup nodes are also deployed in sets. In this paper the sets are scheduled so that they will not all be exhausted at the same time, so that different sets can be reclaimed and replaced in different time. Still this scheme works under the assumption that active sensors consume energy at the same rate and there is no sensor failure, therefore in [8] an improvement of the staircase-cased scheme was proposed and two other schemes, that minimize the hardware cost and the maintenance labor cost. The recharging time of the nodes is considered non-trivial. In [9] the novel combinatorial problem is introduced, one-commodity traveling salesman problem with selective pickup and delivery and also solved by applying the ant colony optimization meta-heuristic. The inactive nodes report their location to the base station, while the active ones report any adjacent sensing hole. Periodically a robot replaces the failed nodes are replaced by inactive ones. This algorithm tries to minimize the traveled distance and the visited nodes. In [10] a small number of robots to replace failed sensors is proposed, the goal is to minimize the motion and the messaging overhead. Three algorithms are studied, a central and two distributed. Every node knows its own location and needs to know which robot is its manager and the location of the manager.

On the other hand, in [2] a localized solution is proposed, however mobile sensors are required for it to work. This algorithm redeploys nodes from targets that are monitored by a large number of sensors and moves them to other targets that are sparsely covered. The nodes initially know only their own and the targets location. Each node covering a target detects and keeps in its memory other neighboring nodes, that cover only the same target. The nodes covering a target can communicate with the nodes covering 2-hop neighboring targets. A head node in its 2-hop neighbor is selected and that one decides which nodes will be moved towards the most sparsely covered neighboring target. Finally in [11] another localized algorithm is introduced that relocates sensors in a mobile sensor network. It is based on the Distance-Sensitive Node Discovery algorithm. All active nodes send their location to neighboring active nodes but also to redundant nodes. The last send reports to the closest active neighbor. When an active node fails the active neighbors try to find the nearest delegated redundant node.

3   System Description

Since the devices used in wireless sensor networks have a relatively short transmission range and the terrain size can be several thousands of m^2, the nodes are not always close to the sink and they cannot send their messages directly. Therefore, we need to configure the network in a way, so that it will be able to have the messages be relayed through intermediate nodes to reach the destination. Furthermore, using such an approach we also have a way to communicate with the robot even when it is far away from the base station. A multi-hop routing mechanism is required with reduced traffic during communication. Hence, we create a static sensor network and ensure connectivity by using a Connected Dominating Set (CDS).

The main parameters for communication in the energy model of the nodes are the following [13]:

1. the energy consumed by the transmitter α_{11},
2. the energy consumed by the receiver α_{12},
3. the energy for the power amplifier α_2,
4. the energy consumed when inactive α_{idle} and
5. the energy consumed when sensing α_{sense}

All the values are measured per bit. Assuming a $1/d^n$ path loss, the energy consumed is:

$$E_{tx} = (\alpha_{11} + \alpha_2 d^n)r, \tag{1}$$

$$E_{rx} = \alpha_{12}r, \tag{2}$$

and

$$E_{sensing} = \alpha_{sense}r, \tag{3}$$

where E_{tx} is the energy to send r bits, E_{rx} is the energy consumed to receive r bits, d is the distance between the two devices that communicate with each other and n is the path loss exponent, which depends on the distance.

The energy consumed by the robot per time unit can be distinguished in two cases. In the first case, when the robot is not moved, the energy consumption is constant. In the second case, when the robot is moved, the energy cost depends on the traveled distance.

$$E_{robot} = \begin{cases} \alpha_{idle} & \text{if } v = 0, \\ \alpha_{mv}\ dst & \text{if } v > 0. \end{cases} \tag{4}$$

where dst is the distance the robot covered, α_{mv} is a constant value and v is the speed of the robot. We also assume that there is only one available slot on the robot, so it can only carry one node at any time. We assume that the nodes know their own coordinates and send them to the robot when needed, but even if this information is not accurate enough, according to [14] the robot can navigate towards the nodes, then it can pickup and replace them without any knowledge. The received signal strength is used to determine the direction taken by the mobile robot and it is able to move to the destination, using a hop-by-hop approach.

4   Node Replacement Algorithms

In this section we present the two localized solutions, the Reactive and the Proactive algorithm. In both solutions the robot decides which sensing node to pickup and which one to replace based on information that it receives dynamically from the nodes. The robot does not have any knowledge of the network, but it can detect both active and inactive nodes within its sensing range. On the other hand the nodes know their own coordinates. The algorithms never end but the network at some point runs out of inactive nodes.

4.1   Reactive Algorithm

Briefly, in the Reactive algorithm (see Algorithm 1) the nodes send an alarm when their energy falls below a threshold. If there are more than one pending alarms, the robot prioritizes them and decides which one to serve first. The robot stays idle, unless there is a node to serve. The energy threshold of each node depends on the respective consumption rate and the distance between the node and the base station. The messages that the nodes send to the robot contain the following information:

1. the coordinates of the node,
2. the remaining time until it fails

In more details, the algorithm works in rounds. Each round starts by updating the nodes energy according to the energy model described in Section 3. If an alarm has been sent by a node in the previous step or in a previous round, then the robot checks the priority of each outstanding alarm and decides which one is the most important. The weight of an alarm is based on three variables. More important are the nodes that have already failed, the more the time that have passed the higher the priority. If there are no failed nodes then it checks the values of the other two variables, namely the remaining uptime and the distance from the robot. In this case, priority is given to the node that is closer to the robot and has the smallest remaining time until it fails. Subsequently, there are three main cases.

In the first case where there is an alarm to be served, the robot checks if it has enough energy to move towards the node in question and then go back from that point to the base station plus the energy to travel the maximum pickup range. If the robot has enough energy then it sets the node as a target and moves towards it, otherwise it sets the base station as a target and moves towards the sink in order to recharge its battery. In the second case, the robot has no alarm to handle but has set the base station as a target, so it moves towards that direction. In the third case, the robot has absolutely no target. Here, as explained before, it will stay at the point where it last stopped at. At this point we can distinguish two sub-cases. Either the robot is at the base station or it is anywhere else in the terrain. If the first it does nothing, if the second then it has to check if it has enough energy to reach the base station.

When the robot is moving, it performs several tasks. It starts by detecting all active nodes and keeping the information it receives in its memory. It, also, detects any inactive node within its sensing range and keeps them in its memory as well. Next, for each detected inactive node, the robot computes the distance between itself and the node. After it finds the one that is closest to its current coordinates, if that distance is less than or equal to the predefined maximum pickup range, it sets that node as a temporary target. On the other hand, if the target of the robot is the base station, it is moving towards it. Otherwise if it is already there, it starts recharging. However, if there is a temporary target then it moves towards that direction, but if it is already there it picks up the inactive node. Finally, if an alarm was set as a target then the robot moves towards that node, but again if it is there it will try to replace it. The only reason not to succeed in the delivery is when it does not carry any nodes. At this point, it will check one more time the inactive nodes in its memory and set the one closest to itself as a temporary target, without taking into account the pickup range. The robot can have two targets, the main target which is an active node or sensing node that needs replacement and the temporary that is an inactive node, that will be delivered. A temporary target is defined only if the slot on the robot is empty and it is prioritized over the main target, because we need the inactive once we reach the failed node.

4.2 Proactive Algorithm

In a nutshell the Proactive algorithm (see Algorithm 2) does not have the nodes send any alarms and the robot never stops moving. It starts by moving randomly in the terrain and while discovering the active and inactive nodes around, it checks their energy levels and it decides if it needs to take some action.

As in the Reactive algorithm every node has an energy threshold, which depends on the respective consumption rate and the distance between the node and the base station. The information that the nodes send to the robot once they are detected is the following:

1. the coordinates of the node,
2. the remaining time until it fails,
3. the node's current energy,
4. the node's threshold, and
5. the node's maximum consumption rate

More thoroughly, this algorithm likewise works in rounds and starts by updating all nodes' energy levels according to the aforementioned energy model. If no specific target exists or previously chosen coordinates, then a random set of coordinates is calculated. The robot checks if it has enough energy to go to its current destination and back to the base station. If yes it moves towards the coordinates, otherwise it sets the base station as its new target and moves on. The main idea behind the Proactive algorithm is to try to avoid failures, so the robot keeps moving and if it finds an inactive node being close to an active one, and having much more energy than the second, then it will swap them.

When the robot is moving, it performs again various tasks. At the beginning of every move, it detects the active nodes within its range and stores them in its memory. At the same time, it detects the inactive nodes storing them in a different list. It continues by distinguishing four cases. In the first one, the target is the base station and the robot has to move towards it, unless it has reached the sink, in which case it recharges. In the second case, a temporary target exists. If the robot is already at the inactive node then it will pick it up. If not it will move towards it. The third option corresponds to the target being an active node or sensing node. Once again if it has reached the node's coordinates it will try to deliver. If it is not carrying any nodes then as in the Reactive algorithm, the robot will search within its memory for the closest inactive and will go for it. If none of the previous cases are true, then the robot will check the list of detected active nodes and pick the one with the less remaining energy. It will compare that node's remaining energy against its threshold. If it is less than or equal, then the active node will be set as target. After this, it will search in the list of all inactive nodes for the one closest to the robot and will set it as a temporary target. However, if the energy of the active node is greater than its threshold and the robot is not carrying any inactive nodes, then it will search in the list of

---

Algorithm 1: Reactive

---

require: $N_0 \neq \emptyset$, $TN = NULL$, $TC = NULL$, $ALARM = NULL$, $A_0 = NULL$,
$\qquad I_0 = NULL$, $SLOTS = 0$

foreach $n \in N_0$ **do**
$\quad\lfloor$ update n energy;

if $ALARM \neq \emptyset$ **then**
$\quad$**foreach** $a \in ALARM$ **do**
$\quad\quad\lfloor$ check a priority;
$\quad\lfloor$ set $TN = a$, where a with highest priority;

if $TN \neq NULL$ **then**
$\quad$**if** *robot's energy* $\geq$ *needed to go to TN and back to base station* **then**
$\quad\quad$move robot;
$\quad\quad\lfloor$ update robot energy according to traveled distance;

else if $TC = basestation$ **then**
$\quad$move robot;
$\quad$**if** *robot NOT recharging* **then**
$\quad\quad\lfloor$ update robot energy according to traveled distance;

else
$\quad$**if** *robot at base station* **and** *robot energy* $\leq$ *1000* **then**
$\quad\quad\lfloor$ recharge;
$\quad$**else**
$\quad\quad$**if** *robot's energy* $\leq$ *needed to go to base station* **then**
$\quad\quad\quad\lfloor$ set $TC = $ base station coordinates;
$\quad$**if** *robot NOT recharging* **then**
$\quad\quad\lfloor$ update robot energy;

// Tasks performed while updating robot's position
detect active nodes;
insert nodes in A_0;
detect inactive nodes;
insert nodes in I_0;

if $SLOTS = 0$ **and** $TC \neq$ *base station* **then**
$\quad$**foreach** $i \in I_0$ **do**
$\quad\quad$check distance from robot;
$\quad\quad\lfloor$ keep i with minimum distance;
$\quad$**if** *distance(i, robot)* $\leq$ *maximum pickup range* **then**
$\quad\quad\lfloor$ set $TC = i$;

if $TC = $ *base station* **then**
$\quad$**if** *robot is there* **then**
$\quad\quad\lfloor$ recharge;
$\quad$**else**
$\quad\quad\lfloor$ move robot towards TC;

if $TC \neq \emptyset$ **then**
$\quad$**if** *robot is there* **then**
$\quad\quad\lfloor$ pickup;
$\quad$**else**
$\quad\quad\lfloor$ move robot towards TC;

if $TN \neq \emptyset$ **then**
$\quad$**if** *robot is there* **then**
$\quad\quad\lfloor$ deliver;
$\quad$**else**
$\quad\quad\lfloor$ move robot towards TN;

all inactive nodes but this time it will compare the energy between the chosen
active and every detected inactive that is within its pickup range. If the energy
of an inactive node is greater or equal to k times the energy of the active node,
where k is a static integer, then it will set the active as main target and the
inactive in question as temporary target.

5   Evaluation and Discussion of the Results

In this section, we start by presenting the main parameters of the simulations, we
then simulate the proposed algorithms and finally we compute the robot's energy
and the sensing nodes' down time. We assume there are no obstacles in the terrain. The base station is located in the middle of the left side of the terrain and it
is the starting and recharging point of the robot. We use two programs written in
Perl to create the terrain and produce 2-dimensional pictures of the network respectively and we have implemented our own simulation environment written in
Python for the two algorithms. The total number of nodes is 200 and we use two
different terrain sizes, 20K m^2 and 40K m^2 respectively. We assess the algorithms
using six scenarios, by running 30 instances per scenario with random node deployment for each terrain. While the total number of nodes is kept constant, the
percentage of the nodes that act as sensing nodes is changed in each scenario and
the values used are 20, 40, 60 and 80%. This means that in the first scenario (i.e.
20%) there are 40 sensing nodes out of the 200 nodes and from the remaining 160
some are inactive and some are active. The last ones constitute the CDS, while
the sensing nodes constitute the leafs. In the second scenario (i.e. 40%) there are
80 sensing nodes and the remaining 120 are active and inactive and so on. In Figure 1 is depicted an example of a scenario, with 200 nodes in total, while 20 of
them are sensing nodes. The base station is plotted as a big square, the sensing
nodes as small circles, while the rest of the active nodes are drown as big circles
and the inactive nodes as dots. The lines connecting the nodes represent the links
between active and/or sensing nodes. The big circle with the base station in its
center represents the communication range of the nodes.

The communication range of the nodes is $50m$ and their sensing range is
$10m$. The battery of the nodes is initially equal to $20kJ$ (this is a typical energy
capacity of one C-type or two AA-type batteries [4]). The values for the sensing
node's energy model are $\alpha_{11} = 50nJ/bit$ when transmitting, $\alpha_{12} = 100nJ/bit$
when receiving, $\alpha_2 = 100pJ/bit$ for the power amplifier, $\alpha_{idle} = 10nJ/bit$ when
idle and $\alpha_{sense} = 100nJ/bit$ when sensing. Regarding the path loss exponent n,
its value ranges between 2 and 4, depending on the distance d. If $0 <= d < 10$
then $n = 2$, if $10 <= d < 20$ then $n = 2.5$, if $20 <= d < 30$ then $n = 3$, if
$30 <= d < 40$ then $n = 3.5$ and if $40 <= d < 50$ then $n = 4$.

The robot on the other hand, when fully recharged has $388.8kJ$ and it needs
14400 seconds to fully recharge. The values used are $\alpha_{mv} = 24.836J/sec$ when
it moves with $v = 0.9m/sec$ and $\alpha_{idle} = 8.568J/sec$[1]. Finally, the sensing range
of the robot is $50m$ and the maximum pickup range is $100m$.

---

[1] These values were experimentally calculated in our lab.

Algorithm 2: Proactive

---

require: $N_0 \neq \emptyset$, $TN = NULL$, $TC = NULL$, $A_0 = NULL$, $I_0 = NULL$, $SLOTS = 0$
foreach $n \in N_0$ **do**
   | update n energy;

if $TN = \emptyset$ **then**
   | set random coordinates;

if *robot's energy* $\geq$ *needed to go to TC and back to base station* **then**
   | update robot's position;

if *robot not recharging* **then**
   | update robot energy;

`// Tasks performed while updating robot's position`
detect active nodes;
insert nodes in A_0;
detect inactive nodes;
insert nodes in I_0;
if $TC = base\ station$ **then**
    if *robot is there* **then**
      | recharge;

    else
      | move robot;

else if $TC \neq \emptyset$ **then**
    if *robot is there* **then**
      | pickup;

    else
      | move robot towards TC;

else if $TN \neq \emptyset$ **then**
    if *robot is there* **then**
      | deliver;

    else
      | move robot towards TN;

else
    foreach $a \in A_0$ **do**
      if *a remaining energy smaller than all* **then**
        if *a energy* $\leq$ *a threshold* **then**
           set $TC = A$;
           foreach $i \in I_0$ **do**
             check i with minimum distance from robot;
             set $TC = i$;

        else
          if $SLOTS = 0$ **then**
             foreach $i \in I_0$ **do**
               if $distance(i, a) \leq maximum\ pickup\ range$ **then**
                 if $energy\ i \geq k\ *\ energy\ a$ **then**
                   set $TC = i$;
                   set $TN = a$;

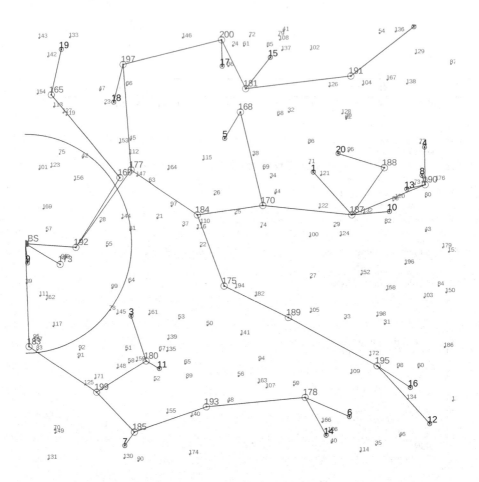

Fig. 1. Terrain with 200 nodes from which the 10% are sensing nodes

5.1   Simulation Results

In the above mentioned scenarios we assess the percentage of the average time of disconnection. For example in the first scenario, we calculate the average time during which the 40 sensing nodes can not send their data to the base station and then we measure the percentage of that time in the total simulation time. The disconnection can either be caused because the sensing node itself failed or because of the failure of an active node on the path between the sink and that sensing node. We also assess the average time needed by the robot to replace the nodes after they have failed, meaning that after we computed the time that passed from the second an active node or a sensing node failed until the second the robot replaced the given node. After that we calculate the average of all nodes and sensing nodes together and then again the percentage of that time in the total simulation time. Finally, another metric that we evaluate is the energy consumption of the robot during the simulation.

The results that are presented in Table 1 refer to the first set of simulations using the smaller terrain of 20K m^2. They show that concerning the time each point of interest in the terrain is not covered, the Reactive algorithm delivered better results than the Proactive. The Reactive algorithm takes advantage of the fact that the nodes are close to each other, since the network density is high, and reacts fast in occurring alarms. Therefore, it needs less time to replace a node. The Proactive algorithm performs well in the scenarios where there are few sensing nodes. In this case, the energy consumption in the network is low, and thus the robot has enough time to travel around the terrain and detect many inactive nodes before the nodes start to fail. Moreover, when the number of sensing nodes is too high, both approaches cannot perform as well as before, because there are less inactive nodes available for the replacements and the robot runs fast out of available nodes.

Table 1. Average Disconnection and Replacement Time for the 4 Scenarios with Terrain 20K m^2

No. of sensing nodes	Reactive			Proactive		
	% of successful replacements	avg % disconnect time	avg % of replace time	% of successful replacements	avg % disconnect time	avg % of replace time
40	100	15.5	3.45	100	18.55	14.05
80	100	26.31	2.77	100	19.46	11.18
120	100	11.46	2.89	100	36.01	6.05
160	100	54.4	11.77	100	69.26	15.89

The results that are presented in Table 2 refer to the second set of simulations using the terrain of 40K m^2. In this case, the network density is low and the distance between the nodes higher, forcing Reactive to travel longer distances when a new alarm appears and, thus, achieving a worse performance. Proactive starts moving from the first second and thus has already discovered a few inactive nodes for the first replacements. In this case, it seems that the trade off between the energy consumption of the robot and the reaction time in case of a failure is better in Proactive algorithm.

In conclusion, we could say that in both terrains – dense and sparse – both algorithms are able to replace all the failed nodes in the field. The Reactive algorithm performs better than the Proactive when the density is low, while Proactive closes the gap in large terrain sizes. We need to stress that Proactive suffers from the long recharging period that occurs more frequently than in Reactive. A representative example is shown in Figure 2. In reference to the robot's energy in the Reactive algorithm the consumption is far slower than that in the Proactive, since in the first case the robot does not need to travel constantly during the simulation and by staying idle it conserves energy.

Table 2. Average Disconnection and Replacement Time for the 4 Scenarios with Terrain 40K m^2

No. of sensing nodes	Reactive			Proactive		
	% of successful replacements	avg % disconnect time	avg % of replace time	% of successful replacements	avg % disconnect time	avg % of replace time
40	100	27.93	4.20	100	28.81	12.33
80	100	36.41	4.24	100	36.19	6.68
120	100	57.83	11.88	100	55.17	9.92
160	100	81.63	41.60	100	85.06	39.37

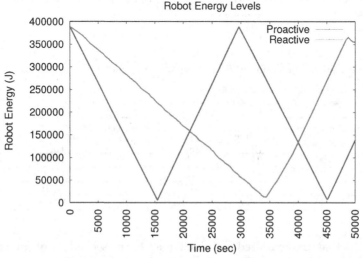

Fig. 2. Robot Energy Consumption for second set (40K m^2), first scenario (20% of sensing nodes)

6   Conclusion and Future Work

In this paper we dealt with node replacement in wireless sensor networks in order to prolong the network's lifetime, while trying to minimize the time a sensing node's data is not able to reach the base station, the time it takes for the robot to replace an active node and the energy of the robot. The nodes are randomly deployed and we do not assume any previous knowledge of the network. To tackle this problem we presented two localized algorithms. In both of them the robot mainly receives information from the nodes that are within its range and uses that to it decides if and which node it should serve. The evaluation results showed that the Reactive algorithm performs better in high-density scenarios, while Proactive closes the gap when the density is low despite the fact that it has to recharge its battery more often. Our future work includes the implementation of a combination of the two algorithms, where the robot evaluates the possible alarm and traveled distance. Moreover, we investigate the use of more than one robot in the field and the use of robots with variable capacity in terms of how many nodes they can carry at the same time.

References

1. Parikh, S., Vokkarane, V.M., Xing, L., Kasilingam, D.: Node-Replacement Policies to Maintain Threshold-Coverage in Wireless Sensor Networks. In: Proceedings of 16th International Conference on Computer Communications and Networks, ICCCN 2007, pp. 760–765 (2007)
2. Zorbas, D., Razafindralambo, T.: Wireless Sensor Network Redeployment under the Target Coverage Constraint. In: 2012 5th International Conference on New Technologies, Mobility and Security (NTMS), pp. 2157–4952 (2012)
3. Sakib, K., Tari, Z., Bertok, P.: Failed node replacement policies for maximising sensor network lifetime. In: 2011 6th International Symposium on Wireless and Pervasive Computing (ISWPC), pp. 1–6 (2011)
4. Battery energy storage,
   http://www.allaboutbatteries.com/Energy-tables.html
5. Wifibots, http://www.wifibot.com/
6. Tong, B., Wang, G., Zhang, W., Wang, G.: Node Reclamation and Replacement for Long-Lived Sensor Networks. IEEE Transactions on Parallel and Distributed Systems 22, 1550–1563 (2011)
7. Tong, B., Li, Z., Wang, G., Zhang, W.: On-Demand Node Reclamation and Replacement for Guaranteed Area Coverage in Long-Lived Sensor Networks. In: Bartolini, N., Nikoletseas, S., Sinha, P., Cardellini, V., Mahanti, A. (eds.) QShine 2009. Lecture Notes of the Institute for Computer Sciences, Social Informatics and Telecommunications Engineering, vol. 22, pp. 148–166. Springer, Heidelberg (2009)
8. Tong, B., Li, Z., Wang, G., Zhang, W.: Towards Reliable Scheduling Schemes for Long-lived Replaceable Sensor Networks. In: 2010 Proceedings IEEE INFOCOM, pp. 1–9 (2010)
9. Falcon, R., Li, X., Nayak, A., Stojmenovic, I.: The one-commodity traveling salesman problem with selective pickup and delivery: An ant colony approach. In: 2010 IEEE Congress on Evolutionary Computation (CEC), pp. 1–8 (2010)
10. Mei, Y., Xian, C., Das, S., Hu, Y.C., Lu, Y.-H.: Sensor replacement using mobile robots. Computer Communications 30, 2615–2626 (2007)
11. Li, X., Santoro, N., Stojmenovic, I.: Mesh-Based Sensor Relocation for Coverage Maintenance in Mobile Sensor Networks. LNCS, pp. 696–708. Springer, Heidelberg (2007)
12. Carle, J., Simplot-Ryl, D.: Energy-efficient area monitoring for sensor networks. Computer 37, 40–46 (2004)
13. Younis, M., Youssef, M., Arisha, K.: Energy-aware management for cluster-based sensor networks. Computer Networks 43, 649–668 (2003)
14. Sheu, J., Hsieh, K., Cheng, P.: Design and implementation of mobile robot for nodes replacement in wireless sensor networks. Journal of Information Science and Engineering 24, 393–410 (2008)

Dynamic Tracking of Composite Events in Wireless Sensor Networks

Giuseppe Amato[1], Stefano Chessa[1,2], Claudio Gennaro[1], and Claudio Vairo[1,2]

[1] ISTI-CNR Via Moruzzi 1, 56124 Pisa, Italy
{giuseppe.amato,claudio.gennaro,claudio.vairo}@isti.cnr.it
[2] Dipartimento di Informatica, Università di Pisa
Largo Pontecorvo 3, 56127 Pisa, Italy
ste@di.unipi.it

Abstract. Tracking moving objects is one important feature of wireless sensor networks. It is of interest in intrusion detection, traffic monitoring, security applications, and environmental monitoring. Current approaches to event tracking either focus on ad-hoc solutions to track specific objects, or address specific sensors or transducers as sources of data. On the other hand, by addressing composite events as source of data, it is possible to obtain higher-level information that is computed cooperatively by the sensors themselves that aggregate and combine the low-level acquired data. To address tracking of composite event we propose a general approach based on query languages. Our proposal allows to express in a simple form the properties of the composite event to be tracked, and the attributes related to the tracked events that have to be reported to the user. We propose and an in-network query processing model that implements the language and that allows the sensors to track and collect data from a moving event in a dynamic and autonomous way. The results of simulation experiments show that the proposed approach allows to successfully track moving events by properly tuning some parameters of the system.

Keywords: wireless sensor networks, tracking, composite events.

1 Introduction

Wireless Sensor Networks (WSN) [1] are a technology suitable for continuous and unattended monitoring of a large variety of environments. A WSN typically consists of a large number of sensors, that are deployed in the environment to be monitored and that self-organize to form a multi-hop wireless network. The sensors can be programmed to sample environmental data, to process sampled data and to forward these information to the user by means of one or more sinks (special sensors that act as gateways between the WSN and other networks). WSN play an important role in many application fields, including environmental monitoring, disaster area monitoring, structure and people health monitoring, ambient assistant living, home applications, surveillance and security.

J. Zheng et al. (Eds.): Adhocnets 2012, LNICST 111, pp. 72–86, 2013.

Tracking moving objects has a great relevance in the WSN context. Such task is typically executed by analyzing, at application level, low-level data acquired by sensors and by submitting interactively specific task in the network to pilot the tracking. Directed Diffusion [2] is the first example of this approach, in which the user submits interests, in the form of queries, to all the sensors of the network. An interest describes an event that sensors can detect. Sensors detecting such events, report the related information to the user, that in turn computes the trajectories of moving event and pilots the tracking by submitting each time a new query.

Paradigms integrating database management systems and WSN are the natural evolution of Directed Diffusion. Some of the most notable approaches of this kind are TinyDB [3], Cougar [4], and MaD-WiSe [5]. With these approaches, the user can inject more structured queries, with semantics inspired to query languages used in databases. Furthermore, the user can specify tasks for the management, filtering and processing of sensed data. On the other hand, such languages do not provide any specific support to tracking tasks and they address specific sensors or transducers as sources of data.

In this paper we present a query language, EQL (Event Query Language), and an implementation model for the dynamic tracking of moving events in WSN. In EQL it is possible to define a composite event to be detected in the form of a set of environmental attributes that can be acquired by the sensors, and it can be specified the information that has to be acquired from the event. An EQL query also specifies a tracking task that instructs the sensors on how to cooperatively and autonomously track a detected event. The simulation results show that our approach successfully tracks composite events defined with EQL with proper configuration of some system, in accordance with parameters of the event such as extension and speed.

The rest of the paper is organized as follows: in Section 2 we report the related work. Section 3 describes the proposed model for dynamic tracking composite events in WSN. Section 4 presents the Event Query Language. In Section 5 we give the implementation details of the proposed approach and we present the results of our simulations. Finally, Section 6 draws the conclusions.

2   Related Work

Several approaches address the tracking of moving objects in WSN. One of the first of these works is ZebraNet [6]. In ZebraNet the sensors operate as a peer-to-peer network that tracks animals in a park. The acquired information is then stored inside the sensors. A base station periodically traverses the network and gathers the acquired data from the sensors when it is close to them. For this reason tracking information is available only witha significant delay, and thus ZebraNet is not suitable for real-time tracking.

In [7] the authors propose a distributed prediction-based algorithm that tracks mobile targets. The protocol uses a predictive mechanism to alert the cluster heads about the approaching targets. Based on this prediction, the cluster heads optimize the execution of the tracking by activating only the interested sensors. A prediction-based approach is also used in [8] and [9].

CODA [10] is an algorithm for the detection and the tracking of continuous phenomena (fires, gas clouds, etc...) based on a hybrid static/dynamic clustering technique. A static backbone is built during the initial network deployment stage. Upon detecting a continuous phenomenon, the cluster heads of the backbone pilot the creation of dynamic clusters by using the information acquired by the sensors at the boundaries of the phenomenon. The dynamic clusters are used to track the phenomena and to acquire data from them.

In [11] the main effort is in reducing the number of environmental readings and, as a consequence, the amount of data delivered outside the network. The proposed solution takes infrequent snapshots of the area and uses a low-quality target tracking algorithm to maintain object identities. The target tracking algorithm adopted is leader-based: the node that is considered to have the best reading for the moving object, is elected as leader. The leadership is passed from a sensor to another (a neighbor of the previous leader) by exploiting probabilistic estimation of the direction of the moving object. When the snapshot period elapses, the leader collects and aggregates the readings of its neighbors to achieve a high-quality belief on the target moving object, and it sends this information to the base station.

The energy consumption of tracking tasks and its optimization is addressed in [12] and [13].

In [14] Calafate et al. present a framework for time-critical event generation in WSN environments that includes tools to model intruder detection events, as well as fire and gas propagation scenarios. The different models developed are integrated into an application optimized for ns-2 compatibility. They also provide a front-end to simplify the interactions with the user and to allow visualizing the different events generated. In [15] the authors use the framework developed in [14] to perform a comprehensive analysis of the performance of IEEE 802.15.4-based WSNs in supporting time-critical applications. In particular, they measure the accuracy and the delay introduced by gas and fire monitoring processes.

Differently than the approaches in the literature, we address the problem of tracking with the purpose of defining a general query language that can express the detection tack of a composite event and the subsequent tracking of the event. This approach is not tailored to a specific event, rather it is general enough to be suitable for a large class of composite events.

3   Tracking Composite Events

A composite event can be defined as the combination of low-level information acquired by a group of sensors in a limited area. It is an abstraction of the transducers used to sample environmental data and provides a high-level of information with respect to the information returned by individual sensors readings. For example, a fire can be characterized by an average high level of light and temperature and an average low level of oxygen in a limited area.

A composite event may cover an area that can also be quite large, and it is characterized by different environmental properties, that are sampled by different transducers. For these reasons, the detection of a composite event usually requires the cooperation of group of sensors, because an individual sensor may not be equipped with all the transducers needed to detect the event and it has a limited view of the environment. For example, a sensor equipped only with a light and temperature transducers may detect high values of light and temperature, but this not sufficient to detect the presence of fire.

The detection of a composite event can be executed by checking proper conditions set on the attributes that define the event, and that are acquired and aggregated by a group of sensors in a given area (see Table 1).

Table 1. Example of definition of a fire event. thT, thL and thO are given threshold values for, respectively, temperature, light and oxygen measurements.

> **Fire:** (avg(Light) > thL) AND (avg(Temperature) > thT)
> AND (avg(Oxygen) < thO)

Once an event occurs, it may evolve during its lifetime. For example an intruder that enters into a building moves and changes his position. Or a gas cloud deriving from an explosion moves into the environment and may change its size and shape. On the other hand the event remains the same, for this reason in our model the user writes the query by addressing the event as source of event, rather than the single transducers or sensors. For example, in the case of the gas cloud it is possible to know where it is located, how fast it is moving, where it is directed, if it is dangerous for people, etc... (see Table 2). However, these information are not produced always by the same transducers or sensors, hence a query that adresses a set of sensors would fail as soon as the event moves or changes shape.

Table 2. The query requests the position and the event speed GasCloud

> **SELECT** Position, Speed, Oxygen
> **FROM**   GasCloud

The tracking of the event should start just after its detection and it should happen in an autonomous way, without any further intervention of the user. In fact, the user query only specifies which information about the event should be reported. The distributed event query processor running on the sensors will handle the transducer activations, the communications and all the operation needed to track the event and to gather the requested data, according to the rules defined in the event specification.

To this purpose we provide a declarative query language (called Event Query Language, or EQL) and in-network query processing strategies, that allow the definition of composite events and the rules for detecting and tracking such events. The language also enables the user to specify the query that uses the tracked event as source of data.

4   Event Query Language

Event Query Language (EQL) is a declarative language that allows the definition of composite events expressed as conditions on values measured by the sensors. When the event occurs, these conditions become true. EQL enables the definition of rules for detecting and tracking the event in a distributed and autonomous way (i.e. without any need for query maintenance by the user), once it has been detected. Also, an EQL query addesses directly the event as data source rather transducers or sensors. This feature enables an EQL query to adapt to events that move or change shape.

A preliminary version of the EQL language was presented in [16]. In the present work we present a refined version of the language and an improved implementation scheme, along with some performance evaluation.

The language is composed of four statement, that address the aspects described above:

- *Event statement* - conditions that define the event and the set of values that can be returned by the event
- *Detection statement* - rules that specify how and where to detect a specified event
- *Tracking statement* - rules that specify how to track a detected event
- *Query statement* - syntax for expressing queries on events

In the next subsections we describe in more details each of these statements.

4.1   Event Statement

The Event Statement specifies the set of attributes that define the event, seen as the environmental parameters that can be measured by the sensor's transducers, and the conditions on these attributes that have to be satisfied in order to detect the event. It also specifies the *Smallest Event Size*, that is, the minimum expected size of the area that is covered by the event when it occurs. The Smallest Event Size also determines the minimum expected number of contiguous sensors that are involved by an event (see Figure 1). In order to detect an event, any set of sensors in any area as big as that expressed by this size, cooperate in computing the aggregate attributes that define the event and check if the condition on these attributes is satisfied.

Table 3 reports the syntax of the Event Statement. We also report an example of the definition of this statement (and of all the other statements) for a sample event of explosion (Table 4) and the deriving event of gas cloud (Table 5). The clause SIZE specifies the extent of the Smallest Event Size in terms of number of hops

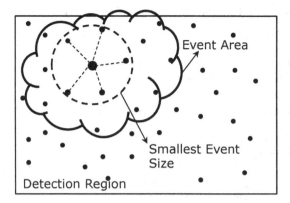

Fig. 1. DETECTION REGION - In the figure the external rectangle represents the Detection Region where the event is monitored, the dotted circle represents the minimum expected size of the event (the Smallest Event Size that in this case is 1 hop) related to the sensor represented with the big black spot, and the cloud represents the actual area covered by the event when it occurs (the Event Area)

Table 3. The Event Statement

```
eventSpecification::=
DEFINE EVENT <eventName>
SIZE:        <length>
AS:          <aggregate_list>
WHERE:       <condition_list>
```

between nodes. A value of SIZE equal to n, means that the event is detected when the values measured by a group of sensors having pairwise hop-distance at least n satisfy the condition of the event. For instance, in the examples of the explosion and the gas cloud, the Smallest Event Size is respectively 3 and 2 hops.

The clause AS specifies the attributes that define the event and that can be read from it. Since these values are acquired by group of sensors in an area of size defined by the Smallest Event Size, they are usually expressed as aggregates. For example, in Table 4, the explosion event is defined by the noise, the average acceleration, and average pressure computed in an area of size 2 hops. In Table

Table 4. The Explosion Event Statement definition

```
DEFINE EVENT Explosion
SIZE:        3 hops
AS:          Avg(Accelerometer) as accelExplAvg,
             Min(Noise) as noiseAll,
             Avg(Pressure) as pressAvg
WHERE:       accelExplAvg > 1000 AND noiseAll > 3000 AND
             pressureAvg > 900
```

5 the gas cloud is defined by the average light, the average temperature, and the average level of oxygen in an area of size 3 hops.

The WHERE clause expresses the conditions that have to be checked to determine whether the event occurred. Either simple transducers readings or the attributes defined in the AS clause can be used here.

Table 5. The GasCloud Event Statement definition

```
DEFINE EVENT GasCloud
   SIZE:        2 hops
   AS:          Avg(Light) as lightGasAvg,
                Avg(Temperature) as tempAvg,
                Avg(Oxygen) as oxygenAvg
   WHERE:       lightGasAvg < 20 AND tempAvg > 80 AND
                oxygenAvg < 50
```

4.2 Detection Statement

The Detection Statement (see Table 6.) defines the rules that the sensors use to perform the detection task for the event defined in the Event Statement.

Table 6. The Detection Statement

```
detectionSpecification::=
DEFINE DETECTION for <eventName_list>
ON REGION:              <area> | <id_list> | <all> |
                        <eventName>
EVERY:                  <rate>
[TIMEOUT:               <time>]
```

In several cases, only a subarea of the whole network is critical for detecting an event, and usually this subarea is known by the user at the moment of defining the detection task. Therefore only the sensors located in this area are requested to monitor for the occurrence of the interested event (in some cases this area can be the entire network as well). For example, only the sensors close to a gas tank need to execute the detection task in order to detect an explosion. We call this subarea the *Detection Region*. The Detection Statement defines the Detection Region in the clause ON REGION. The sensors deployed in this area start executing the detection task. This clause may also specify another event name. This means that the current event depends on a previously occurred event (in the example the gas cloud event is consequence of an explosion). In this case, the Detection Region of the current event corresponds to the Event Area of the previously occurred event.

Different events can have different requirements about the frequency at which the event is monitored. For example the rising or falling of the tides can be measured at a low frequency, while an explosion requires a higher sampling frequency in order to be detected. The clause EVERY specifies the sampling rate at which the attribute that define the event are acquired and the related condition is checked.

Finally, the optional clause TIMEOUT, specifies for how long the detection task is executed.

Table 7. The Explosion Detection Statement definition

```
DEFINE DETECTION for Explosion
ON REGION:         DangerousZone
EVERY:             100
TIMEOUT:           30days
```

Table 8. The GasCloud Detection Statement definition

```
DEFINE DETECTION for GasCloud
ON REGION:         Explosion
EVERY:             5000
```

Tables 7 and 8 report the Detection Statement for the examples of the Explosion and the GasCloud events. We can notice that, since the GasCould event depends from the Explosion event, its clause ON REGION specifies the Explosion event name. This means that the detection task for the GasCould event will start after the Explosion event is occurred, and its Detection Region will be the area where the explosion occurred.

4.3 Tracking Statement

Once an event occurs (that is, the condition on the acquired values results true), the sensors that detect the event initiate its tracking. To this purpose, they start the execution of the tracking task.

An event can evolve in different ways: it may just move while maintaining its shape and size (for example a car moving along a street), or it may expand and change its shape (for example a fire), or it may both move and change its size and shape.

To manage all of these cases, we do not make any assumption on how the tracked events evolve. Rather, we propose a solution in which the sensors that detect the event (those in the Event Area) alert all the sensors around the event. As consequence, the alerted sensors start monitoring for the tracked event. If they also detect the event within a timeout, they join the other sensors in the tracking task and start acquiring data from the event.

The Tracking Statement (see Table 9) specifies the extent of the alert in the clause EVOLUTION. This clause expresses the distance (in number of hops) at which the alert message has to be sent. A value of 2, for example, means that the sensors in the Event Area alert their 1 and 2 hop neighbors about the possible incoming of the event. The clause EVERY specifies the sampling rate for the tracking task, and the clause TIMEOUT specifies for how long the alerted sensors have to sample the event before stop checking for it (if this time expires it is assumed that the event has moved in another direction). Table 10 reports the Tracking Statement for the GasCloud event.

Table 9. The Tracking Statement

```
trackingSpecification::=
DEFINE TRACKING for <eventName_list>
EVOLUTION:          <alert_extension>
EVERY:              <rate>
TIMEOUT:            <sleepTime>
```

Table 10. The GasCloud Tracking Statement definition

```
DEFINE TRACKING for GasCloud
EVOLUTION:       2 hop
EVERY:           2000
TIMEOUT:         120
```

4.4 Query Statement

The Query Statement (Table 11) is used to collect and process information related to a specified event. This statement is similar to a standard SQL query, with the difference that the data are acquired from a composite event rather than from a table in a database.

The clause **SELECT** defines the information that have to be acquired from the event and returned to the user. These can be either simple transducers readings, or some of the aggregated attributes expressed in the Event Statement. We also assume that standard information like position, speed and direction of the event can be expressed as well. The clause **FROM** specifies the event from which the data should be acquired. The clause **WHERE** specifies some conditions that can be expressed on the properties of the event and that have to be satisfied in order to receive the data.

Table 12 reports a query on the GasCloud event. The example requests the position and the speed of the gas cloud only when the average value of the oxygen is below 50.

Table 11. The Query Statement

```
dataSpecification::=
SELECT <attribute_list>
FROM   <eventName>
WHERE  <condition_list>
```

Table 12. The GasCloud Query Statement definition

```
SELECT Position, Speed, oxygenAvg
FROM    GasCloud
WHERE   oxygenAvg < 60
```

Table 13. Parameters used for the simulation

Name	Description
n_x	number of neighbors per sensor
r_x	transmission range
R	Event Area radius
v	event speed
exp	timeout for detecting the event
Δt	sampling rate

5   Evaluation

We implemented a MATLAB simulator to evaluate the performance of EQL in terms of percentage of successfully tracked events. In particular we implemented the tracking task executed by the sensors that are involved in the event during its evolution. The main operation executed by the tracking are:

- leader election
- tree building
- alert
- check inclusion

The first operation executed by the tracking task is the election of a leader for coordinating all the other operations. The leader is elected among the sensors in the Event Area according to one of the distributed algorithms available in literature [17], [18] (the actual algorithm is not relevant to the purposes of this work, it can be based on the sensors' identifiers or it can be a more sophisticated one).

Once elected, the leader builds the data collection tree that spans the whole Event Area. The tree is used by the sensors to collect and aggregate the data to be returned to the user as result of the query.

The sensors that are leaves of the tree (that is, the sensors at the border of the Event Area), alert their neighbors around the event about the possible incoming of the event. As discussed in Section 4.3, we do not perform any kind of prediction on the movements of the event, therefore all the sensors around the event, in a radius specified by the clause EVOLUTION of the Tracking Statement, are alerted. As consequence, these sensors are temporarily added to the data collection tree and they start monitoring for the event. If they detect the event within a time specified by the clause TIMEOUT of the Tracking Statement, they start acquiring data from the event and send them back to the leader through the tree. Otherwise, after the timeout expires, they stop monitoring for the event and they are removed from the tree.

Finally, the sensors belonging to the tree periodically check if they are still included in the event. As soon as a sensor detects that it is not involved in the event anymore, it is removed from the tree and it stops acquiring data.

We implemented all these steps in a MATLAB simulator that models the tracking of generic events with a circular shape that moves with a uniform rectilinear motion, keeping the same shape and size during the evolution. We perform

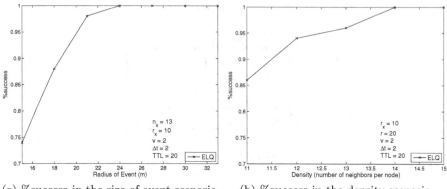

(a) %success in the size of event scenario.   (b) %success in the density scenario.

Fig. 2. Percentage of successful tracking with increasing value of the size of the Event Area (a) and network density (b)

several simulations to study the performance of the system by combining the parameters reported in Table 13. In each experiment we change the value of the analyzed parameters, and we keep the value of the others to a default value, as follows: number of neighbors per node $n_x = 13$, radius of the event $r = 20$, event speed $v = 2Km/h$, sampling rate of the sensors $\Delta t = 2seconds$, transmission range of the sensors $r_x = 10mt$ and TIMEOUT value $exp = 20seconds$.

We focus our evaluation on the percentage of successfully tracked events (hereafter denoted with %success). The event can be lost because of the following reasons:

– the event is too slow and the expiration time is not large enough, so the alerted sensors stop monitoring for the event before it reaches them;
– the event is too fast and the sampling rate too short, hence the sensors do not detect it between two consecutive samplings;
– the event reaches a hole in the network where no sensor can detect it.

We first analyze the percentage of successfully tracked events for some parameters that vary individually, then we analyze combinations of varying parameters.

Figure 2 shows %success with respect to the size of the Event Area and the network density, respectively. In these cases the event may be lost when the event traverses areas of the network in which there are no sensors (network holes). With a bigger Event Area, or a more dense network the probability to lose the event for this reason becomes lower and lower. In fact, we can see in Figure 2(a) that with an event of radius 15 meters the percentage of success is of about 74% over 50 iterations, while the event is not lost at all when the radius of the event becomes bigger than 24 meters. Similarly, Figure 2(b) shows that the percentage of success with a number of neighbors per node equals to 11 is 86%, while it becomes 100% with a number of neighbors per node equals or greater than 14.

In Figure 3(a) is shown the %success for different values of the expiration time. In this case, if the expiration time is too short, the event is lost because the

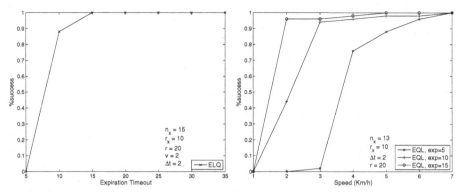

(a) %success in the expiration time sce- (b) %success in the speed-expiration time
nario.   scenario.

Fig. 3. Percentage of successful tracking with increasing value of the expiration time
(a) and with a combination of speed and expiration time values (b)

alerted sensors stop monitoring for the event before it reaches them. We can see
in the figure that with an expiration time of 5 seconds the event is always lost, but
the percentage of success increases as the expiration time grows and the event is
never lost with an expiration time equal or greater to 15 seconds. The expiration
time is strictly related to the event speed. If the event moves with a high speed,
even a low value of the expiration time can be sufficient to successfully track
the event. In Figure 3(b) we analyze %success with a combination of these two
parameters. With an expiration time of 15 seconds, an event speed of 2 Km/h is
enough to guarantee a success rate of almost 100%. With an expiration time of
10 seconds the event should move at at least 3 Km/h in order to be successfully
tracked with a probability of more than 90%, while with an expiration time of
15 seconds the speed grows to 6 Km/h in order to have a success rate greater
than 90%. Therefore the expiration time should be set accordingly to the event
speed, if this information is available.

Figure 4(a) shows the relation between the event speed and the sampling rate
of the sensors. If the event is too fast and the sampling rate is too short, it can
happen that the alerted sensors monitor for the event before it reaches them,
and then they perform the subsequent sampling when the event has already
passed by. Also in this case the event is lost. We can see in the figure that, for a
sampling rate of 2 seconds, the success rate of the tracking is 100% if the event
speed is equal or less than 4 Km/h, while it is always lost if the event moves
at a speed equal or greater than 8 Km/h. With a sampling rate of 4 seconds
the event is successfully tracked with a probability of 100% if it has a speed of
8 Km/h or less, while it is always lost if it moves at 10 Km/h or more. With a
sampling rate of 6 seconds, the event can move at a speed of at most 14 Km/h
and it is still successfully tracked with a probability of 100%, while it is always
lost if it moves at 18 Km/h or more. As the expiration time, also the sampling
rate should be set accordingly to the event speed, if available (and of course to
the application requirements).

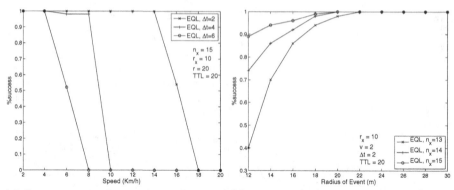

(a) Success rate in the speed-sampling rate scenario.

(b) Success rate in the size of event-density scenario.

Fig. 4. Percentage of successful tracking with increasing values of the event speed and different values of sampling rate of the sensors (a) and with increasing size of Event Area and different values of network density (b)

Finally, Figure 4(b) analyzes the scenario in which the event is lost because it moves to a region of the network with no sensors. This can be avoided if, either the network is more dense, or the event covers a wider area. The figure shows that, with the number of neighbors per node of 13, if the event has radius 12 meters it is successfully tracked only the 40% of times, while this percentage reaches the 100% if the event has a radius of at least 22 meters. With the number of neighbors per node of 14, the successful tracking percentage grows to 74% with an event of radius 12 meters, and it reaches 100% if the event has radius 20. The 100% of successful tracking is reached with an event of radius 20 also in case of number of neighbors per node of 15, but in this case the probability of not losing the event if it has radius 12 is almost 90%.

6   Conclusions

In this paper we presented a query language (EQL) that can define tracking tasks for composite events in WSN. One important feature of EQL is that it addresses events as data sources and not sensors of transducers. We also discussed a distributed query processing mechanism, running on the sensors, for dynamic tracking of such events in an autonomous way. We also implemented a simulator to validate the tracking solution described, and we performed several simulations that confirmed that the proposed approach can successfully track composite events with proper configuration of some system parameters. We believe that this approach has some advantages with respect to other approaches to event tracking. In fact, the usual approach is to define ad hoc strategies for tracking, that cannot be easily adapted to different conditions of the network, environment, and characteristics of the event. On the other hand, our approach builds on a very general model of composite events and it does not make any assumption on event evolution. On going work of this research is the comparison of EQL against classical query languages for WSN (such as TinyDB [3], Cougar [4], and MaD-WiSe [5]). A long term direction of this work is to build functionalities similar to those offered by EQL in form of libraries that can be used by WSN programmers in order to let them use high-level and efficient tracking functionalities in more complex monitoring frameworks.

References

1. Baronti, P., Pillai, P., Chook, V., Chessa, S., Gotta, A., Hu, Y.F.: Wireless Sensor Networks: a Survey on the State of the Art and the 802.15.4 and ZigBee Standards. Computer Communications 30, 1655–1695 (2007)
2. Intanagonwiwat, C., Govindan, R., Estrin, D.: Directed diffusion: a scalable and robust communication paradigm for sensor networks. In: 6th Annual ACM/IEEE International Conference on Mobile Computing and Networking, Boston, MA, USA, pp. 56–67 (2000)
3. Madden, S., Franklin, M.J., Hellerstein, J.M., Hong, W.: Tinydb: an acquisitional query processing system for sensor networks. ACM Trans. Database Syst. 30, 122–173 (2005)
4. Yao, Y., Gehrke, J.: The cougar approach to in-network query processing in sensor networks. SIGMOD Record 31, 9–18 (2002)
5. Amato, G., Chessa, S., Vairo, C.: MaD-WiSe: A distributed stream management system for wireless sensor networks. Software Practice & Experience 40, 431–451 (2010)
6. Juang, P., Oki, H., Wang, Y., Martonosi, M., Peh, L.S., Rubenstein, D.: Energy-efficient computing for wildlife tracking: design tradeoffs and early experiences with zebranet. SIGARCH Comput. Archit. News 30, 96–107 (2002)
7. Yang, H., Sikdar, B.: A protocol for tracking mobile targets using sensor networks. In: 1st IEEE Int. W. on Sensor Network Protocols and Applications, Anchogare, AK, pp. 71–81 (2003)
8. Chong, C.Y., Zhao, F., Mori, S., Kumar, S.: Distributed tracking in wireless ad hoc sensor networks. In: 6th International Conference of Information Fusion, Cairns, Queensland, Australia, pp. 431–438 (2003)
9. Raja, V.S., Mole, S.S.S.: A predictive energy-efficient mechanism to support object-tracking sensor networks. In: IJCA Int. Conf. in Recent Trends in Computational Methods, Communication and Controls (ICON3C), vol. 8, pp. 13–17 (2012)
10. Chang, W.R., Lin, H.T., Cheng, Z.Z.: Coda: A continuous object detection and tracking algorithm for wireless ad hoc sensor networks. In: 5th IEEE Consumer Communications and Networking Conference (CCNC), Las Vegas, NV, pp. 168–174 (2008)
11. Tanin, E., Chen, S., Tatemura, J., Hsiung, W.P.: Monitoring moving objects using low frequency snapshots in sensor networks. In: Int. Conf. on Mobile Data Management (MDM), pp. 25–32 (2008)
12. Lin, C.Y., Peng, W.C., Tseng, Y.C.: Efficient in-network moving object tracking in wireless sensor networks. IEEE Transactions on Mobile Computing 5, 1044–1056 (2006)
13. Olule, E., Wang, G., Guo, M., Dong, M.: Rare: An energy-efficient target tracking protocol for wireless sensor networks. In: Int. Conf. on Parallel Processing Workshops (ICPPW), Xian, China, pp. 76–81 (2007)

14. Calafate, C.T., Lino, C., Cano, J.C., Manzoni, P.: Modeling emergency events to evaluate the performance of time-critical WSNs. In: IEEE Sym. on Computers and Communications (ISCC), Riccione, Italy, pp. 222–228 (2010)
15. Lino, C., Calafate, C.T., Diaz-Ramirez, A., Manzoni, P., Cano, J.C.: Studying the feasibility of IEEE 802.15.4-based WSNs for gas and fire tracking applications through simulation. In: 11th IEEE Int. W. on Wireless Local Networks (LCN), Bonn, Germany, pp. 875–881 (2011)
16. Vairo, C., Amato, G., Chessa, S., Valleri, P.: Modeling detection and tracking of complex events in wireless sensor networks. In: IEEE Int. Conf. on Systems, Man, and Cybernetics (SMC), Istanbul, Turkey, pp. 235–242 (2010)
17. Malpani, N., Welch, J.L., Vaidya, N.: Leader election algorithms for mobile ad hoc networks. In: 4th Int. W. on Discrete Algorithms and Methods for Mobile Computing and Communications (DIALM), pp. 96–103 (2000)
18. Vasudevan, S., Kurose, J., Towsley, D.: Design and analysis of a leader election algorithm for mobile ad hoc networks. In: 12th IEEE Int. Conf. on Network Protocols (ICNP), pp. 350–360 (2004)

Revisiting Planarity in Position-Based Routing for Wireless Networks

David Cairns[1], Marwan M. Fayed[1], and Hussein T. Mouftah[2]

[1] Computing Science & Mathematics, University of Stirling, Stirling, UK
{dec,mmf}@cs.stir.ac.uk
[2] School of Information Technology and Engineering (SITE), University of Ottawa, Ottawa, Canada
mouftah@uottawa.ca

Abstract. In this paper we investigate the limits of routing according to left- or right-hand rule (LHR). Using LHR, a node upon receipt of a message will forward to the neighbour that sits next in counter-clockwise order in the network graph. When used to recover from greedy routing failures, LHR guarantees success if implemented over planar graphs. This is often referred to as face-routing. In the current body of knowledge it is known that if planarity is violated then LHR is guaranteed only to eventually return to the point of origin. Our work begins with an analysis to enumerate all node configurations that cause intersections. A trace over each configuration reveals that left-hand rule is able to recover from all but a single case, the 'umbrella' configuration so named for its appearance. We use this information to propose the Prohibitive Link Detection Protocol (PLDP) that can guarantee delivery over non-planar graphs using standard face-routing techniques. As the name implies, the protocol detects and circumvents the 'bad' links that hamper LHR. The goal of this work is to maintain routing guarantees while disturbing the network graph as little as possible. In doing so, a new starting point emerges from which to build rich distributed protocols in the spirit of CLDP and GDSTR.

Keywords: position-based routing, geographic routing, face routing, wireless routing.

1 Introduction

The construction of network subgraphs appropriate for position-based (or geographic) routing protocols has, to date, remained a complex problem. These subgraphs are needed to recover from the local minima problem (see [3]) that prevents delivery and plagues position-based protocols. Network subgraphs constructed for recovery using only 1-hop information risk inaccuracies that cause routing failures [15,24]. One remedy is to allow nodes to cooperate. If permitted, cooperating nodes may construct a network subgraph that remedies any inaccuracies [14,24,19,25]. Yet the resources needed to power the many rounds

J. Zheng et al. (Eds.): Adhocnets 2012, LNICST 111, pp. 87–102, 2013.
© Institute for Computer Sciences, Social Informatics and Telecommunications Engineering 2013

of communication between nodes, risks being prohibitive in such a resource-constrained environment. The ideal wireless network subgraph would guarantee successful delivery while a) needing only 1-hop information and b) be able to acquire such information passively.

Traditionally, position-based routing protocols construct subgraphs (herein referred to as just 'graph') from available links in somewhat of a bottom-up fashion. Generally the idea is to extract a specific type of graph from the available nodes and links in the network. During the setup of such graphs each node evaluates available links to find those that preserve some global properties. Planar graphs [7] and k-spanners [23] are two such examples. The analogous question would be to ask, "what is the set of edges that must be preserved to guarantee a given feature in the graph?"

Our work is motivated by the opposite question, "What is the minimum set of edges that must be *deleted* while still providing guarantees?" This work is a step in that direction. Without sacrificing the scalability and success of position-based routing, the goal of this work is to disturb the network as little as possible. To this end it is necessary to understand the causes for a position-based routing protocol to fail to recover from local minima and deal with those causes directly.

In this paper we investigate routing according to left- or right-hand rule (LHR). Using LHR, a node, upon receipt of a message, will forward to the neighbour that sits next in counter-clockwise order in the network graph. When used to recover from greedy routing failures, LHR guarantees success if implemented over planar graphs; for this reason it is often called 'face-routing'. We note, however, that if planarity is violated then LHR is only guaranteed to eventually return to the point of origin. Our work seeks to understand and correct the underlying causes of these failures.

We have chosen LHR for three reasons. First, it is most prevalent in position-based routing literature and hence well-studied. Second, it is a simple rule requiring little-to-no overhead. Finally, the ideal network graph remains elusive. To re-iterate, we envision the ideal graph as overcoming the inaccuracies that lead to routing failures; as one that results from knowledge of the 1-hop neighbourhood; and as one where each node transmits a constant number of messages.

We build on a provable enumeration of the possible types of intersections in a unit-disc graph (UDG), within which any two nodes are neighbours if separated by a maximum distance of one unit. Our analysis reveals that only three types of intersections are possible. A trace of face-routing over each intersecting neighbourhood further reveals that in only one of these configurations does LHR fail to recover: We call this the 'umbrella' configuration, so named for its appearance. The umbrella configuration naturally hides links and nodes from a face-routing traversal, partitioning the graph with respect to the traversal. Unless there appears some other non-local route to join these partitions, potential routes will be unavailable to any face-routing technique.

We use this information to propose the Prohibitive Link Detection Protocol (PLDP). PLDP identifies the umbrella configuration and removes from it a single link. In doing so, PLDP provides a graph over which any face-based method may provably guarantee delivery using standard geographic and face-routing rules.

In our evaluation we compare the setup and quality of PLDP graphs with CLDP and GDSTR using Netsim2 [19,20]. Our simulation results demonstrate that PLDP performance is similar to current face-routing schemes. Where PLDP separates itself is in the number of messages required to setup the network: Most nodes will need to generate no setup packets and from those that do, a very small number of packets is needed. Our evaluation will show that the small number of setup packets are indicative of the infrequency of the umbrella configuration, the consequence of which is that PLDP is able to preserve most of the links in the original network graph. In a manner of speaking our evaluations suggest that traditional face-routing schemes may be 'over-solving" the problem by planarizing networks.

On the surface this seems an unfair comparison since both GDSTR and CLDP operate without the unit disc assumption. We emphasize that our goal is to provide a better understanding of the underlying motivations for such distributed protocols and, in doing so, provide a new starting point for distributed protocols that may out-perform those of the current generation. PLDP may be unable to compete directly due to the unit disc assumption, but we will show that it provides a novel direction from which to build.

In summary, this paper seeks to provide a basis that is a lateral shift away from planarity so that better cooperative position-based protocols may be built. By investigating the underlying causes for failure, planarity is shown to be unnecessary in the majority of cases. We propose PLDP as a means to relax constraints on the network graph while preserving the promise of local face-routing techniques.

2   Related Work

Recovery algorithms in Euclidean position-based routing are equivalently known as *face routing* [1,2] and *perimeter routing* [13]. Face routing was first proposed by Bose et al. in [1] with some theoretical bounds. Karp et al. independently proposed an identical mechanism in [13] but with work on a MAC-compatible implementation. Variants have since emerged addressing, for example, theoretical bounds in [17,16,18]. In [11], face-routing is augmented into a "select-and-protest" reactive protocol in order to reduce the information required to planarize the graph.

Wireless network graphs may consist of intersecting edges so it is necessary for planar subgraph methods to prune edges from the network graph so that it is planar while remaining connected. Gabriel Graphs (*GG*) and Relative Neighbourhood Graphs (*RNG*) are planar graphs whose constructions are localised, a characteristic particularly suitable to sensor environments. Intersecting edges are eliminated by connecting pairs of nodes through *witness* nodes, if such a node exists in a common region. It has since been shown that 'Hello' messages may hinder network performance [10]. This is addressed in face-routing directly by [4] and more generally in [6,9,22]. Further work in [26] reduces the path length during the recovery phase.

These distributed constructions are unable to resolve links broken by obstacles or interference [12,21]. Recent breakthroughs have begun to surmount the impracticalities of face-routing while maintaining delivery guarantees [14,19].

The Greedy Distributed Spanning Tree Protocol (GDSTR) algorithm in [19] builds on the fact that any message can be successfully delivered via depth-first search if the network is connected via a spanning tree. This fact alone does not solve the problem: GDSTR provides optimizations to reduce the otherwise inefficient delivery requiring up to $2n - 3$ hops. The authors in [19] describe a new type of spanning tree, the *hull tree*, to route more efficiently. A hull tree is a spanning tree with one added piece of information: each node records the convex hull that contains all of its descendants in the tree. In GDSTR forwarding occurs greedily, as do most position-based protocols. If a message reaches a void, a recovery mode is initiated where convex hulls are used to determine the regions of the network that contain unreachable destinations. This information is used by GDSTR to route along the spanning tree to forward to the appropriate convex hull. If a node is found en route that is closer to the destination than the node where the message was stuck, then GDSTR returns to greedy forwarding. GDSTR is known to scale well as the neighbourhood size grows. Furthermore, the use of multiple hull trees adds fault-tolerance to the network and if multiple trees are rooted at opposite ends of the network, routing efficiency improves.

The Cross-Link Detection Protocol (CLDP) proposed in [14], and later improved in [8], circumvents voids by face-routing. It uses left-hand rule over a planar subgraph of the network; its design however, is motivated by the observation that routing difficulties in planar subgraph methods arise, in part, due to the constructions themselves. (Recall from previous that successful local planar subgraph constructions rely on the unit disc graph.) For this reason, CLDP proposes an alternate construction of planar subgraphs that assumes only that links are bidirectional. CLDP operates in a distributed fashion, exchanging some localised operation for accurate information. The idea behind CLDP is that each node is able to probe the vicinity for intersecting links. A probe packet is initialised with the endpoints of the first link to be probed and forwarded according to left-hand rule. The probe eventually returns to its point of origin with a vector of the path taken. This information is shared with nearby nodes to prune links appropriately. To avoid the slow process of scheduling serial probes by neighbouring nodes, a system for concurrent probing is proposed. Concurrent probing is achieved by implementing a mechanism to 'lock' links so that no more than one link is removed at a time from any vicinity. CLDP is one of very few protocols to have been implemented on testbeds [14]. The associated communication complexities and storage costs revealed in this process (see [15,19]) are motivation to develop alternative approaches to guarantee delivery.

A more recent approach is to think about how the network might embed onto a different physical space. One such work appears in the FaceTrace project [25] which imagines that nodes in the network sit on a high-genus topological surface,

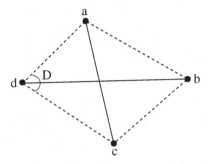

Fig. 1. Intersecting links between two pairs of nodes may impose edges in a 4-gon

such as a torus. It is a novel technique that extracts onto these surfaces faces from the network itself, rather than faces associated with local minima in the network. In doing so, planarity emerges naturally. In simulation FaceTrace exhibits routing quality of a very high order but the setup cost is reported to be similar to those of GDSTR, numbering many orders of magnitude.

Protocols such as CLDP and GDSTR, in order to be feasible for physical networks, sacrifice efficiency for accuracy. CLDP requires high-complexity negotiations within each neighbourhood in order to prune appropriate links. GDSTR reduces the messaging complexity but must broadcast information to construct and maintain its hull trees. It remains an open question whether such trade-offs are a necessity. The work in [11] is a step in the right direction. Its recognition that there are available short-cuts when routing according to LHR is further evidence that the planarity assumption may be excessive.

By contrast, in this work we show that there exists a locally constructed, non-planar graph construction over which face-based protocols guarantee success.

3   Links that Prohibit Routing Success

Left-hand rule (LHR) alone, fails to provide a guarantee of success. Though this fact is well known, the reasons and circumstances under which delivery may fail are poorly understood. In this section we investigate the limits imposed by intersections on face-based recovery.

Our investigation begins with an enumeration of all of the types of intersections that may appear in the UDG. We focus this work on the unit disc graph (UDG), where all communication ranges are normalised. The UDG is appropriate since it limits potential routing options yet still poses a challenge to LHR routing.

3.1   An Analysis of Intersection Types

Consider any two intersecting edges. We provide the edges ac and bd in Figure 1 for reference. The nodes a, b, c, d at the end points of these edges form a 4-gon (shown in Figure 1 using dashed lines). The question we ask is, which of the

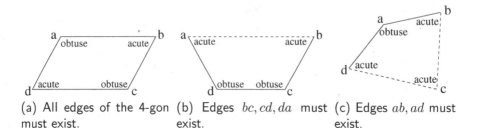

(a) All edges of the 4-gon must exist.   (b) Edges bc, cd, da must exist.   (c) Edges ab, ad must exist.

Fig. 2. Possible 4-gons when edges intersect in the UDG; dashed lines indicating edges that may or may not appear

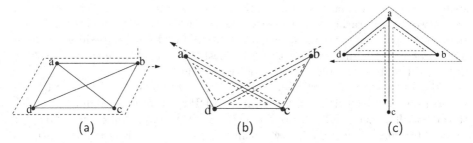

(a)   (b)   (c)

Fig. 3. A unique face emerges from all but the 'umbrella' shape, shown in (c)

edges of the 4-gon may or may not be communicating links in the unit-disc graph? In order for at least one such edge to exist, we need to show that *all four sides cannot be greater than both diagonals.*
Using cosine rule we know,

$$(ac)^2 = (ad)^2 + (dc)^2 - 2(ad)(dc)\cos D. \tag{1}$$

If $|ac|$ is less than or equal to 1, then

$$(ad)^2 + (dc)^2 - 2(ad)(dc)\cos D \leq 1. \tag{2}$$

When $D \geq \frac{\pi}{2}$, then $\cos D \leq 0$. In this case, $(ad)^2 + (dc)^2 \leq 1$, which means $(ad) \leq 1$ and $(dc) \leq 1$. Thus, if an angle of the 4gon is right or obtuse, then both incident edges must exist in the UDG. (By contrast, incident edges when $D < \frac{\pi}{2}$ may or may not exist.)

This implies and restricts the possible configurations that allow intersections to three in number, all shown in Figure 2. The two cases where the nodes of intersecting edges produce a 4-gon with two obtuse angles is shown in Figures 2a and 2b, while the 4-gon containing a single obtuse angle is shown in Figure 2c. (It is impossible for a 4-gon to be constructed with three obtuse edges; and that edges incident to an acute angle may or may not appear in the unit-disc graph.)

3.2   The Prohibitive Link

The finite and small number of possible intersections allows us to carefully examine the behaviour of a left-hand traversal over all possible cases. A left-hand traversal is deemed successful when it can identify a single unique face in an intersecting environment.

We show in Figure 3 the traces corresponding to the three intersections in Figure 2. Traversals are shown using a dotted line. In the first two cases an LHR traversal succeeds in identifying a single face irrespective of the point of entry into the intersecting environment. (We show via inductive proof in [5] that the same holds true when intersections are composed together.)

The 'bad' configuration occurs during a traversal of the intersection shown in Figure 3c. Here the different points of entry reveal that there are two faces with respect to LHR. This means there are two ways in which LHR may fail. The first is demonstrated by the dashed-dot-dash line originating at node d. (Entry at nodes a and b are analogous.) A traversal using left- or right-hand rule will never traverse edge ac while travelling through this intersection. Supposing c must be traversed in order to reach the destination, LHR will fail. The second possible failure occurs when an LHR traversal encounters this intersection first via node c in Figure 3c using the dashed line. LHR traverses the inside of the triangle $\triangle abd$ and exits without ever seeing edges that protrude from the outside of the triangle. As before, any such edges leading to the destination may be overlooked by an LHR traversal.

This represents the case where network node a communicates with b, c, d, and b with d; node c communicates only with a. We call this case the *umbrella* configuration for its appearance.

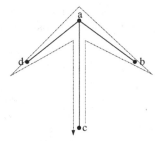

Fig. 4. Removing prohibitive link bd allows LHR to traverse all edges

The cause of both failures lies in the relationship between $\triangle abd$ and ac in Figure 3c: There exists an edge from the triangle that is accessible only from inside the triangle. In other words, a traversal around the inside or the outside of the triangle fails to encounter all edges leading to the triangle. Both failures are solved by removing any of the edges that form the triangle. The easiest of these to identify and remove from the network graph is the edge of the triangle that forms the intersection in the umbrella configuration. In Figure 3c this link is represented by $\overline{bd}$. We call this the *prohibitive link*.

The prohibitive link is most easily identified by the only node that is able to see all four nodes in the umbrella configuration. In Figure 3c this responsibility falls on node a. It looks for intersections consisting of pairs links. The first link is formed by itself and an immediate neighour, with subsequent links formed between two immediate neighbours.

We revisit this subject and build a networking protocol in the next section. Before closing this section the outcome following a removal of the prohibitive link from the umbrella configuration is demonstrated in Figure 4. The intersection that was the umbrella configuration is reduced to a planar set of edges easily navigated by left- or right-hand rule.

4   Prohibitive Link Detection Protocol

We have enumerated all possible intersections in the unit-disc graph and identified the type of intersection with the link that prohibits successful delivery when routing according to right- or left-hand rule. In this section we present a Prohibitive Link Detection Protocol (PLDP). Proofs of correctness may be found in [5].

4.1   PLDP Overview

We assume a static graph where each node is assigned a coordinate in a 2-dimensional Euclidean space. We assume that the graph is connected and that all links are bi-directional. PLDP functions adequately in a mobile space provided that changes in position occur over a greater time-frame than is required to re-evaluate local prohibitive links and transmit local updates. In this work communication range is fixed and uniform across all nodes.

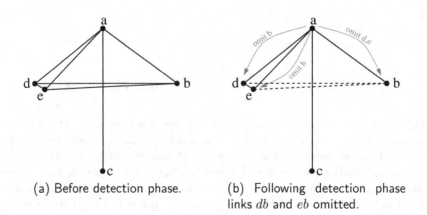

(a) Before detection phase.   (b) Following detection phase links db and eb omitted.

Fig. 5. Local neighbourhood before and after the PLDP detection phase

The face-routing family of protocols preserve their delivery guarantees in PLDP graphs. During their normal operation nodes route in a greedy fashion and forward messages to the neighbour that most reduces the distance to the destination. Where no such neighbour exists a message is deemed 'stuck' in a local minima and is forwarded according to left- (or right-)hand rule. (The node initially selected is the first to appear left, or right, of the line segment from the current location to the destination.) The first node found that sits closer to the destination than the 'stuck' location returns to the greedy forwarding phase. Due to space constraints, we refer our reader to the correctness proof of PLDP and its ability to guarantee delivery to the destination [5].

During the PLDP detection phase each node inspects its neighbourhood using neighbour positions reported in ordinary 'hello' packets. Each node evaluates intersections within range and flags any three neighbours that compose an umbrella configuration, as described in Section 3.2. Once sufficient information is compiled a node sends a notification packet to the neighbours that anchor prohibitive links.

Notification messages exchanged between nodes consist of either a `delete` or an `insert` instruction. As is suggested by its label, a `delete` deactivates a prohibitive link at the anchors of the link. Similarly an `insert` instruction reactivates a link previously deemed prohibitive. This allows for corrections as the network state changes.

We emphasize that PLDP takes a passive approach when looking for the recovery subgraph: In contrast to the 'active' approach taken by protocols such as CLDP and GDSTR, PLDP sends instruction messages only upon witnessing an umbrella configuration, and only to the neighbours that anchor the prohibitive link. The reduction in overall messaging is evaulated in Section 5.3.

The detection phase is demonstrated in Figure 5. In Figure 5a, node a determines that two intersections in its vicinity contain prohibitive links, those links being bd and eb. Nodes b, d, and e have no knowledge of node c's existence. The responsibility falls on node a to inform neighbours of their prohibitive links. Moving to Figure 5b, node a instructs each of d and e to ignore their links to b during recovery; similarly node a instructs b to omit links to d and e.

Alternatively, notifications may be avoided entirely by producing and sending 'hello' notification packets that include neighbour information. Having been provided a 2-hop view of its neighbourhood a node can see all of the information it needs to identify prohibitive links (albeit at the cost of a larger 'hello' packet).

5   Simulation Results

The previous section describes the PLDP protocol. We demonstrate the practical performance of PLDP via simulation in the sections that follow.

5.1   Experimental Design

So that we might better evaluate the performance of PLDP we have implemented PLDP into the netsim platform for geographic routing simulations used to evaluate GDSTR in [19] and GSpring in [20]. We compare PLDP primarily against two protocols. The first is CLDP [15,14], a novel distributed planarization protocol that corrects for real-world events that violate the unit disc assumption. The second is GDSTR [19], also a distributed algorithm that reduces the high communication cost of CLDP but forces the network to cooperate as a whole.

The comparison of PLDP against CLDP and GDSTR may seem somewhat unfair given that CLDP and GDSTR operate outside of the UDG model. Our intention, rather than to 'compete' directly is to question the need for the one assumption on which all face-based routing techniques are based, that planarity is required for correct operation.

For completeness we set our experiments against a backdrop that includes more conventional face-routing schemes. Evaluations of the PLDP and CLDP network graph are made using GPSR [13] and GOAFR [18,16]. GPSR design and accomplishments have served as the foundation on which later efforts have been built; it has long been considered the baseline for benchmark performance, while GOAFR provides some optimal theoretical bounds. Finally, GDSTR is implemented with two trees.

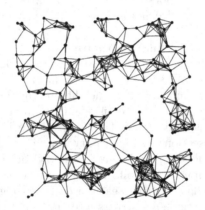

Fig. 6. A sample network containing 250 nodes with an average degree of ~ 8

Simulation networks are composed of nodes placed uniformly in a space that is 1000 units squared; each node having a communication range of 10 units. Node density varies by increasing network size; neighbourhoods ranged from 4 to 16 nodes, on average. Each set of tests consisted of 5 runs, using the same five networks drawn from non-overlapping streams in each set of tests. A sample network with 250 nodes and an average degree of ~ 8 appears in Figure 6.

We test the validity of the CLDP and PLDP subraphs by routing with GPSR and with GOAFR. Our primary performance metrics are hop stretch and message overhead. The latter takes our discussion into an investigation of the frequency of the umbrella configuration.

5.2 Hop Stretch

Hop stretch is defined as the ratio of hops taken vs hops of the minimum path. We consider only those paths over which packets were routed during face-based recovery; this is to avoid the distortion of results that would otherwise occur during the dominant greedy phase.

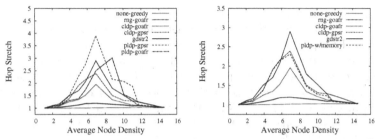

(a) Traditional routing schemes. (b) After memory is added to GPSR packets.

Fig. 7. Hop stretch of face-routing schemes on PLDP-induced graphs

Observations for hop stretch are shown in Figure 7. In this figure we plot for PLDP with no changes to the routing protocols overtop, namely GOAFR and GPSR. The performance of both routing schemes is noticeably worse during the recovery phases over PLDP graphs than it is over planar graphs. In the best case scenario, routing over PLDP graphs during recovery takes 1/3rd greater number of hops than the next best scheme tested. Why is this, and is there anything that can be done?

To understand the cause we refer back to Figure 3b, in which we trace an LHR traversal. In this configuration an LHR traversal that begins at node b and exits at node a requires 7 hops to escape. By contrast, were this region planarized then an LHR traversal requires 3 hops[1].

It is possible to resolve this issue by injecting memory into the routed packet. This memory consists of a record of the links traversed during face-routing so that LHR can avoid next hops that intersect with previous hops. In our evaluations up to this point we have tested unaltered routing protocols over the PLDP graph. Specifically this means that packets have no memory of where they have been. Thus many intersecting links will be traversed, only to return later along the same link in the opposite direction.

So that our readers may clearly understand what is happening we point to Figure 8. A packet enters the intersecting region at node b who, according to LHR forwards to node d, who then forwards to a. Node a sees that the next link in counter-clockwise order $\overline{ac}$ intersects with link $\overline{bd}$, previously seen by this

---

[1] The overall cost to a path stretch is much lower than would appear since the portion of time a packet sends in recovery is much lower than the portion of time that a packet sends in greedy mode.

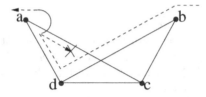

Fig. 8. When packets record traversed links, nodes can substantially reduce hop counts

packet. In this example a packet escapes the intersecting region using 5 fewer hops than if the region had been planarized.

A noticeably different picture emerges if we record the recovery path and allow the routing protocol to skip past those links that would intersect previously traversed links. The effect of this "with memory" approach is demonstrated in Figure 7b, in which we plot GPSR with memory over a PLDP graph. Noting the change in range along the y-axis, we can see that the hop stretch along the PLDP graph has been diminished by roughly 1/2.

In the next we evaluate the messaging cost associated with the setup and maintenance of the PLDP graph.

5.3   Message Cost

It is difficult, though necessary, to compare the setup of PLDP graphs with those setup by CLDP and GDSTR. The difficulty arises because of the difference in assumptions and goals: PLDP in its current form relies on the unit-disc assumption, whereas CLDP and GDSTR make none.

The comparison is necessary since, for all of their achievements, face-based protocols rely on the underlying assumption that some form of planarity is required for guaranteed delivery. PLDP graphs recognise that this assumption is stronger than necessary. Presumably, if we can reduce the set of undesired events then we can create more efficient real-world protocols.

The total number of messages sent in a network, on average, appears on log scale in Figure 9. The results obtained for CLDP and GDSTR are consistent with previous results: CLDP's relatively expensive messaging cost is reduced by

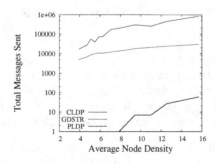

Fig. 9. Packets sent or fowarded per node to achieve stability

an order of magnitude using the GDSTR approach. By contrast the number of PLDP packets produced is three orders of magnitude smaller than GDSTR. In our simulated networks PLDP produced close to zero packets until the average node density reached about 8 nodes. In the densest networks of approximately 16 nodes, 60 PLDP packets are sent.

In our trials these small numbers suggested that the number of prohibitive links is much smaller than we expected. In the next section we validate the small number of messages by investigating the frequency of prohibitive links.

5.4   Umbrella Observations

The very small number of PLDP packets produced implies that the number of prohibitive links is very small. To evaluate this hypothesis we generate large network graphs of varying density, distribution, and topology. Network nodes are distributed in a 200x200 unit space, each node with a fixed range of 8 units. We vary node density by changing the network size. Note that by changing size instead of communication range we can vary the density without affecting the maximum network diameter. Network sizes are 1500, 2500, and 3500 nodes. (In the uniform networks this results in average neighbourhood sizes of ~7, 12, and 17 nodes.) To obtain results unbiased by isolated nodes we tabulate and experiment over the largest connected component of networks where nodes are distributed according to uniform, normal, and pareto distributions.

In each network we count the number of intersecting links. From those we count the number of intersections that form the umbrella configuration. The results are tabulated and averaged in Table 1 with 99% confidence intervals. The ratio of the two numbers appears in the last column, indicating that in all cases the proportion of intersections that form the umbrella configuration is slightly more than 1%. This suggests that the frequency of configurations that might otherwise prevent successful delivery via LHR is quite small.

Table 1. The number of umbrellas in tested networks with 99% confidence intervals

Size (Density)	Node Distribution	Intersections	Umbrellas	Ratio U/I
1500 (7.5)	uniform	119536.4 ± 9563.5	1586.4 ± 96.1	0.013
	norm	2275283.8 ± 226415.4	30521.2 ± 3360.0	0.013
	skew	11577261.2 ± 8833878.2	130028.6 ± 97577.0	0.011
2500 (12.5)	uniform	939384.8 ± 38816.3	12454.6 ± 802.6	0.013
	norm	16631429.2 ± 1775319.2	225528.4 ± 22547.8	0.014
	skew	90216371.2 ± 51567741.3	1007242.4 ± 546546.8	0.011
3500 (17.5)	uniform	3692688.2 ± 124431.4	49094.8 ± 1984.6	0.013
	norm	67160718.8 ± 4266681.4	900722.2 ± 58436.6	0.014
	skew	280116248.2 ± 97476260.3	3199356.0 ± 1024083.1	0.012

6   Conclusions

In this paper we have explored an new approach to graph construction for successful forwarding in position-based routing. It is instructive to compare this approach with previous work.

Traditionally, the success of face-routing schemes relies on the assumption that the underlying graph is planar. This is restrictive; local constructions of planar graphs risk inaccuracies, while co-operative (or global) constructions are resource intensive. In either case there has yet to appear an examination of the challenges that face left-hand rule in the presence of intersections.

By contrast, the approach taken in this work was to enumerate the configurations that form an intersection in the network graph. We then scrutinised each with a left-hand rule traversal so as to isolate the 'bad' configurations from which left-hand rule is unable to recover. In doing so we recognised the existence of a prohibitive link that has the potential to conceal other viable links from a left-hand rule traversal. We then presented PLDP, a protocol that detects and avoids the prohibitive link to successfully deliver packets. It operates locally and, unlike planarization methods, omits only essential links.

Our simulation results demonstrate that routing performance over PLDP graphs is similar to current face-routing schemes. Success rates over all graphs for all schemes is 100%, while the path stretch in PLDP graphs is competitive with other methods. Where PLDP separates itself is in its messaging cost. Messages in PLDP are associated with the removal and maintenance of prohibitive links, which are shown to appear rarely. This suggests that traditional planar schemes may be 'over-solving' the problem.

We are working to release our source code as part of the Netsim2 package. We are pleased to make it available upon request in the meantime. Currently we are working to remove the unit-disc assumption. Then, using the approach presented in this paper we expect to augment PLDP for general case networks where communication error and non-uniform range is commonplace.

Acknowledgment. We thank Ben Leong and Hongyang Li, and for their insightful comments, the reviewers. This work was supported by the Scottish Informatics and Computing Science Alliance, as well as the Natural Sciences and Engineering Research Council of Canada.

References

1. Bose, P., Morin, P., Stojmenović, I., Urrutia, J.: Routing with guaranteed delivery in ad hoc wireless networks. In: Workshop on Discrete Algorithms and Methods for Mobile Computing and Communications (DialM) (1999)
2. Bose, P., Morin, P., Stojmenovic, I., Urrutia, J.: Routing with guaranteed delivery in ad hoc wireless networks. Wireless Networks 7(6), 609–616 (2001)
3. Chen, D., Varshney, P.K.: A survey of void handling techniques for geographic routing in wireless networks. IEEE Communications Surveys & Tutorials 9(1), 50–67 (2007)
4. Chen, D., Varshney, P.K.: On-demand geographic forwarding for data delivery in wireless sensor networks. Elsevier Computer Communications 30(14-15), 2954–2967 (2007)
5. Fayed, M.M., Cairns, D.E., Mouftah, H.T.: An analysis of planarity in face-routing. Technical Report TR-184, Computing Science & Math, University of Stirling (2010)

6. Fler, H., Widmer, J., Ksemann, M., Mauve, M., Hartenstein, H.: Contention-Based Forwarding for Mobile Ad-Hoc Networks. Elsevier's Ad Hoc Networks 1(4), 351–369 (2003)
7. Frey, H., Stojmenovic, I.: On delivery guarantees of face and combined greedy-face routing in ad hoc and sensor networks. In: The 12th Annual International Conference on Mobile Computing and Networking (Mobicom), pp. 390–401 (2006)
8. Kim, Y.-J., Govindan, R., Karp, B., Shenker, S.: Lazy cross-link removal for geographic routing. In: The 4th International Conference on Embedded Networked Sensor Systems (SenSys), pp. 112–124 (2006)
9. Heissenbttel, M., Braun, T., Bernoulli, T., Blr, M.W.A.: Beacon-less routing algorithm for mobile ad-hoc networks. Elseviers Computer Communications Journal (Special Issue) 27, 1076–1086 (2004)
10. Heissenbüttel, M., Braun, T., Wälchli, M., Bernoulli, T.: Evaluating the limitations of and alternatives in beaconing. Elsevier Ad Hoc Networks 5(5), 558–578 (2007)
11. Kalosha, H., Nayak, A., Ruhrup, S., Stojmenovic, I.: Select-and-protest-based beaconless georouting with guaranteed delivery in wireless sensor networks. In: IEEE 27th Conference on Computer Communications (INFOCOM), Pheonix, AZ, USA, pp. 346–350 (April 2008)
12. Karp, B.: Challenges in geographic routing: Sparse networks, obstacles, and traffic provisioning. Presented at DIMACS Workshop on Pervasive Networking (May 2001)
13. Karp, B., Kung, H.: Gpsr: Greedy perimeter stateless routing for wireless networks. In: Proceedings of ACM MobiCom, Boston, MA (September 2000)
14. Kim, Y.-J., Govindan, R., Karp, B., Shenker, S.: Geographic routing made practical. In: Proceedings of the 2nd USENIX Symposium on Networked Systems Design and Implementation (NSDI), Boston, MA, USA (May 2005)
15. Kim, Y.-J., Govindan, R., Karp, B., Shenker, S.: On the pitfalls of geographic face routing. In: Proceedings of the 2005 Joint Workshop on Foundations of Mobile Computing (DIALM-POMC), pp. 34–43 (2005)
16. Kuhn, F., Wattenhofer, R., Zhang, Y., Zollinger, A.: Geometric Ad-Hoc Routing: Of Theory and Practice. In: 22nd ACM Symposium on the Principles of Distributed Computing (PODC), Boston, Massachusetts, USA (July 2003)
17. Kuhn, F., Wattenhofer, R., Zollinger, A.: Asymptotically Optimal Geometric Mobile Ad-Hoc Routing. In: 6th International Workshop on Discrete Algorithms and Methods for Mobile Computing and Communications (DIALM), Atlanta, Georgia (September 2002)
18. Kuhn, F., Wattenhofer, R., Zollinger, A.: Worst-Case Optimal and Average-Case Efficient Geometric Ad-Hoc Routing. In: 4th ACM International Symposium on Mobile Ad Hoc Networking and Computing (MOBIHOC), Annapolis, Maryland, USA (June 2003)
19. Leong, B., Liskov, B., Morris, R.: Geographic routing without planarization. In: Proceedings of the 3rd USENIX Symposium on Networked Systems Design and Implementation (NSDI), San Jose, CA, USA (May 2006)
20. Leong, B., Liskov, B., Morris, R.: Greedy virtual coordinates for geographic routing. In: Proceedings of the IEEE International Conference on Network Protocols (ICNP) (October 2007)
21. Lochert, C., Mauve, M., Fler, H., Hartenstein, H.: Geographic Routing in City Scenarios. ACM SIGMOBILE Mobile Computing and Communications Review (MC2R) 9(1), 69–72 (2005)

22. Sanchez, J., Marin-Perez, R., Ruiz, P.: Boss: Beacon-less on demand strategy for geographic routing in wireless sensor networks. In: IEEE Internatonal Conference on Mobile Adhoc and Sensor Systems (MASS), pp. 1–10 (October 2007)

23. Schindelhauer, C., Volbert, K., Ziegler, M.: Geometric spanners with applications in wireless networks. Computational Geometry: Theory and Applications 36(3), 197–214 (2007)

24. Seada, K., Helmy, A., Govindan, R.: On the effect of localization errors on geographic face routing in sensor networks. In: Proceedings of the 3rd International Symposium on Information Processing in Sensor Networks (IPSN), pp. 71–80 (2004)

25. Zhang, F., Li, H., Jiang, A., Chen, J., Luo, P.: Face tracing based geographic routing in nonplanar wireless networks. In: IEEE 26th Conference on Computer Communications (INFOCOM), Anchorage, AK, USA (May 2007)

26. Zhao, G., Liu, X., Sun, M.-T., Ma, X.: Energy-efficient geographic routing with virtual anchors based on projection distance. Elsevier Computer Communications 31(10) (2008)

Localization in Wireless Sensor Networks by Cross Entropy Method

Mohammad Abdul Azim, Zeyar Aung, Weidong Xiao, and Vinod Khadkikar

Masdar Institute of Science and Technology
Abu Dhabi, United Arab Emirates
{mazim,zaung,mwxiao,vkhadkikar}@masdar.ac.ae

Abstract. Wireless sensor network (WSN) localization technique remains an open research issue due to its challenges on reducing location estimation error and cost of localization algorithm itself. For a large mobile network localization cost becomes increasingly important due to the exponential increment of algorithmic cost. Conversely, sacrificing localization accuracy to a great extent is not acceptable at all. To address the localization problem of wireless sensor network this paper presents a novel algorithm based on cross-entropy (CE) method. The proposed centralized algorithm estimates location information of the nodes based on the measured distances of the neighboring nodes. The algorithm minimizes the estimated location error by using CE method. Simulation results compare the proposed CE approach with DV-Hop and simulated annealing (SA)-based localizations and show that this approach provides a balance between the accuracy and cost.

Keywords: wireless sensor networks, localization algorithms, cross-entropy method.

1   Introduction

Sensor network node location information is important for numerous reasons. Almost always, sensed data has no value without the location information. The location information can be used by routing and other protocols, algorithms and services. Straightforward solution to the localization problem of equipping nodes with GPS receivers is not viable option because GPS receivers require line of sight to GPS satellites. Moreover GPS is costly and power hungry. Therefore for randomly deployed sensor networks various localization algorithms have been introduced where only a small number of sensor nodes are equipped with GPS receivers and other sensor nodes derive their locations by using localization techniques [1,2].

Localization techniques have issues and challenges as some solutions are not cheap and some have unexpected level of errors. WSN localization techniques are largely categorized into **range-free** and **range-based** localizations. The range-free techniques involve in deriving distances from non-anchor nodes to anchor nodes whereas the range-based techniques involve in deriving absolute distances or angles.

J. Zheng et al. (Eds.): Adhocnets 2012, LNICST 111, pp. 103–118, 2013.
© Institute for Computer Sciences, Social Informatics and Telecommunications Engineering 2013

Centroid scheme [14] and DV-Hop scheme [15] are well known range-free schemes in the literature.

In centroid scheme, anchors broadcast their locations. Nodes receive broadcasts and calculate node position by a simple measure of centroid by $(x_{est}, y_{est}) = (\sum x_i/N, \sum y_i/N)$. Here (x_i, y_i) is the coordinate of i_{th} anchor and N is the total number of anchors where the node is receiving beacons. This coarse grain localization algorithm is simple, lightweight and easy to implement. A number of weighted centroid localization is proposed to improve the accuracy by incorporating weights for each neighbor nodes [16,17]. Further improvement of the scheme is made by incorporating the adaptive weight for the centroid algorithm [18].

Well referred DV-Hop algorithm [15] is based on distance vector routing. Nodes calculate the hop distances from the anchors. The distance is measured by multiplying the hop distance to the average hop size where the hop size of the anchor is calculated by $Hopsize_i = \sum \sqrt{(x_i - x_j)^2 + (y_i - y_j)^2} / \sum (h_j)$. Here (x_i, y_i) and (x_j, y_j) are the coordinates of anchor i and j and h_j is the hop distance from anchor j to i.

Well-known range-based localization techniques are based on angle-of-arrival (AoA), time of arrival (ToA) [4,5], time difference of arrival (TDoA) [6,7], or receive signal strength indicator (RSSI) [3], etc.

In time-based methods like ToA and TDoA propagation time is used to derive the distance. But these time-based protocols suffer where the line of sight does not exist. AoA is highly accurate but requires expensive hardware. Due to the specific hardware requirement for the range-based approach a range free approach is considered more appropriate in the context of WSNs to limit the hardware cost of the nodes.

Ideally distances can be measured from transmit and receive signal strengths of radios. If transmit and receive signal strengths are p_i and p_j than the distance can be measured as $d_{ij} = \sqrt[\beta]{p_i/p_j}$. Where β is known as path loss exponent and can be calculated by measuring power at unit distance. But this ideal situation never exists because of the presence of noise. Ref [8] describes the source of noise that can affect the localization estimation from signal strength. Practically, RSS estimation is affected by log-normal shadowing [9]. Where the receive signal varies as $[\mu, \sigma^2]$. Where μ and σ are mean and variance and often taken as 1.0 and 0.0 respectively. The error in signal strength estimation introduces error in measured distances. Therefore RSSI-based algorithms have limitations in accuracy primarily because of multi-path fading. One straight forward solution is taking average (such as auto regressive moving average (ARMA) [10]) of power measurements before calculating the location of the nodes. Unfortunately this approach requires a large number of measurements to get a desired result [11,12,13]. Taking the measurement requires active transmission therefore costly in terms of energy usage.

Two well-known methods that use RSSI are maximum likelihood (ML) estimation technique [19] and simulated annealing (SA)-based localization [22]. The ML technique estimates the position of the node by minimizing the difference between the measured and estimated distances. ML uses well-known minimum mean square error (MMSE) [21] algorithm for this estimation. ML suffers from poor accuracy if the number of neighbors is small [12,20].

An improvement of ML localization technique is proposed in [23] by using cross-entropy (CE)-based method [24]. Note that our approach of CE based localization is totally different an approach where the location estimation error is minimized using the CE method. Ref [23] as well as other ML methods requires multiple samples of the received signals thereby requires a number of energy hungry explicit transmissions undesirable for WSN localization paradigm.

Simulated annealing (SA)-based localization [22] provides similar minimization technique where the minimization is performed by the optimization algorithm known as simulation annealing. But this scheme requires a large computational resource to solve the optimization problem.

Therefore among the localization algorithms in state of the art some are costly in terms of hardware, some are costly in terms of energy and computation, and some are simply too inaccurate to be practically used. Attempt to get a reasonable solution we formulate a localization algorithm that uses CE-based optimization technique while deriving the x, y coordinates of the non-anchor sensor nodes in the network by employing RSSI-based distance measurement.

We compare the performance of our proposed CE-based method with one range-free method, namely DV-Hop, and one range-based method, namely simulated annealing (SA) though simulations. Simulation results show that CE is slower than DV-Hop, but much more accurate. When compared to SA, CE is up to about 4 times faster whilst the accuracy is only negligibly less.

The rest of the paper is organized as follows: Section 2 discusses the proposed CE method of localization that comprises of distance measurement and collection steps, definition of cost function (in our case) along with CE optimization technique. Section 3 presents the simulation results to justify the necessity of such proposal and finally Section 4 concludes the paper along with future directions.

2   Cross-Entropy Algorithm for Localization

Primarily we have N number of nodes randomly deployed in the network; among them A number of nodes are anchor nodes. The localization algorithm needs to determine x and y coordinates of $N - A$ number of nodes. CE-based localization technique is location estimation technique where the location is estimated based on the derived distances of the nodes from its neighborhood. The distance is calculated based on transmit-receive signal strength measures. Fig. 1 shows the steps in detail for the proposed CE-based localization algorithm.

2.1   Collecting Measurements

During the initialization of the protocol each node in the network:

- Creates a neighbor list

- Measures neighbor distances by transmit-receive signal strengths
- Updates central computer with aforementioned information

Upon receiving data the central computer uses CE-based localization algorithm and derive the unknown locations for the non-anchor nodes. Before going into the CE method we first define the cost function used by the optimization algorithm.

2.2 Cost Function

Due to the unreliable nature of the wireless medium the distance measure introduces error. A common approach is to estimate the location of the node by minimizing the estimation error [19,22]. The CE method incorporates the same cost function to be minimized. Let d_{ij} is the measured distance among node i and j. Let $(\hat{x}_i, \hat{y}_i)$ and $(\hat{x}_j, \hat{y}_j)$ are the estimated coordinates of the node i and j by the algorithm. Here the estimated distance is $\hat{d}_{ij} = \sqrt{(\hat{x}_i - \hat{x}_j) + (\hat{y}_i - \hat{y}_j)}$. Therefore the cost function to be minimized can be expressed as

$$cost_i = \sum_{j \in n_i} (\hat{d}_{ij} - d_{ij})^2 \tag{1}$$

where n_i is the set of all neighboring nodes of node i. With the measured distances and the aforementioned cost function CE algorithm solves the localization problem in an iterative learning manner.

2.3 Cross-Entropy Optimization Algorithm

CE localization algorithm attempts to find the best coordinate of the unknown sensor node by minimizing the estimated error. The underlying technique in CE optimization is to generate samples based on the means and variances. Algorithm than selects the best samples as next state while it learns about the next generation samples' means and variances based on the best set of samples in the population. The CE algorithm first generates random states for all nodes. It then generates a set of populations for each state based on the mean and variance of that particular state. Algorithm then finds the cost for all the population based on the cost function. If the minimum cost of the population set is less than the cost function of the current state than the state is updated otherwise a new set of population is generated. In each update of state the algorithm learns about a better sample generation characteristics. Where the characteristics can be defined as the means and variances used to generate the samples. Therefore if there is an instance of an updated state the mean and variance of that state are also updated based on the best population set. CE algorithm updates the states iteratively until the cost or error is within the acceptance limit.

For each unknown node n_i the localization algorithm first randomly generates the coordinates (x_i, y_i) alternatively known as state of the node where n_i is a set of all non-anchor nodes denoted by $n_1 : n_{N-A}$. Algorithm also initializes means μ_i and variances σ_i for all x_i and y_i. Generally the initial means are

Cross-entropy based localization algorithm
N: Total nodes
A: Anchor nodes
μ: Means
σ: Variances
α: Learning rate for means
β: Learning rate for variances
γ: Variance minimum
Node level measurements for all node i
Create neighbor list
Measure distances by Tx-Rx signal strengths
Update central computer with the measured distances
Algorithm at central computer
for all unknown node i
    Randomly initialize (x_i, y_i) coordinates
    Randomly initialize μ and σ for x_i and y_i
    Find cost for (x_i, y_i) and assign to initial $BestCost_i$ by
      $\sum_{j \in N_i} (\hat{d}_{ij} - d_{ij})^2$
end
while $(max(\sigma) < \gamma)$
    for all i
        Generate S samples for x_i and y_i
        Find costs for corresponding samples
        if (min cost of the samples $< BestCost_i$)
        Update state (x_i, y_i) with the best sample
        Update $BestCost_i$
        Update μ and σ
        Select M number of best population
          $(xbest_1, ybest_1) \ldots (xbest_M, ybest_M)$
        Take $\mu best$ and $\sigma best$ of the selected bests
          $x\mu best_i = mean(xbest_1 : xbest_M)$
          $y\mu best_i = mean(ybest_1 : ybest_M)$
          $x\sigma best_i = std(xbest_1 : xbest_M)$
          $y\sigma best_i = std(ybest_1 : ybest_M)$
        Update μ and σ with α and β respectively
          $x\mu_i = \alpha * x\mu_i + (1 - \alpha) * x\mu best_i$
          $y\mu_i = \alpha * y\mu_i + (1 - \alpha) * y\mu best_i$
          $x\sigma_i = \beta * x\sigma best_i + (1 - \beta) * x\sigma_i$
          $y\sigma_i = \beta * y\sigma best_i + (1 - \beta) * y\sigma_i$
        end
    end
end

Fig. 1. Cross-entropy based localization algorithm

set of random numbers and initial variances are set of ones respectively with a length of $N - A$. The cost of all the initialized states of the nodes are determined and subsequently known as initial $BestCost_i$.

After initialization, CE algorithm enters into an iterative mode and updates the states until the desired refinement is achieved. This desired refinement is generally defined by a control parameter known as variance minimum γ. Another important control parameter is the learning rate. Generally two different learning rates are used for the means and variances denoted as α and β respectively.

The iterative method starts with generating a population of S number of samples for all x_i and y_i based on the means and variances of corresponding x_i and y_i. The samples are than evaluated and rated by the cost of a particular sample. If the cost of the best sample is less than $BestCost_i$ then the $BestCost_i$ is replaced by the cost of the best sample. The state (x_i, y_i) is subsequently updated with the best sample for the particular node.

Another parameter of the algorithm is update sample number M. Algorithm selects best M samples and find the mean and variance of the samples by $x\mu best_i = mean(xbest_1 : xbest_M)$ and $x\sigma best_i = std(xbest_1 : xbest_M)$ respectively. The mean of the best samples is used to update the corresponding mean of x_i by $x\mu_i = \alpha * x\mu_i + (1 - \alpha) * x\mu best_i$ for the next generation of samples. Similarly $x\sigma_i = \beta * x\sigma best_i + (1 - \beta) * x\sigma_i$ is used to update the variance of x_i. $y\mu_i$ and $y\sigma_i$ are updated in a similar fashion. The trained means and variances are the key properties of the next generation of samples. Superior samples in successive generations help the algorithm estimating better states (coordinates in our case) in successive iterations.

Alternatively if the cost of the best sample is less than $BestCost_i$ than the population set is discarded and another set of samples are generated. After completion of iterations the final state of i becomes the estimated location of the particular sensor node.

3   Simulation Results

We simulate the CE-based localization algorithm in Matlab using a workstation with 4 Intel Xeon 2.26 GHz 8-core processors, 256 GB main memory, and 3TB RAID 5 hard disk drive.

A total number of 100 nodes are placed in 100m×100m field. Here four anchor nodes are placed in the four corners of the field and rest of the nodes are placed randomly in the whole area. We assume that the network is equipped with radios having uniform transmission range denoted by R. Here radio range R is taken as 20m. We simulate error in distance measurement with log-normal shadowing effect [9] described in Section 1 with mean μ and variance σ as 0.0 and 1.0 respectively. The noise factor of the model is taken as 0.1 for all the experiments. For each distinct experimental setup, we run our simulation 10 times and take the average measurements in order to improve the generality of the results.

CE control parameter variance minimum γ needs to be small enough to run the simulation reasonably long enough to get a good estimation. Then again

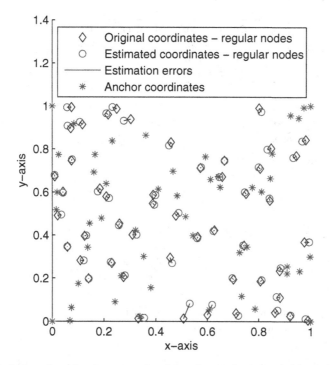

Fig. 2. Node locations in the network where the anchors are 50% of the total nodes. Distances are normalized into the range 0.0 to 1.0.

setting γ too small makes the simulation slow without much improvement. We set $\gamma = 10^{-3}$ in our case. Learning rates α and β are set to 0.7 and 0.9 respectively. Finally sample number S and best sample number M are taken as 100 and 50 respectively.

Fig. 2 shows the sensor field with normalize distances where the anchors are 50% of the total nodes. In this specific arrangement the error is very small. In our results we present two different types of errors: (i) error in each node defined as normalize distance between the original and estimated node coordinates and (ii) average error in the field defined in Equation 2 [22].

$$error = \frac{1}{N-A} * \sum_{i=A+1}^{N} \frac{(x_i - \hat{x}_i)^2 + (y_i - \hat{y}_i)^2}{R^2} \qquad (2)$$

where (x_i, y_i) and $(\hat{x}_i, \hat{y}_i)$ are the absolute and estimated locations of the node i. N and A are total number of nodes and total number of anchors in the network [22].

One common downside of the cost minimization techniques is reported and known as flip ambiguity [25,26,27]. In case the neighborhood of a node is located in such way that some nodes are approximately on a same line then the estimated

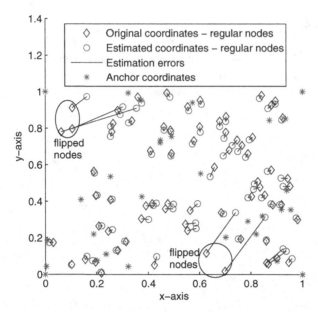

Fig. 3. Node locations in the network where the anchors are 30% of the total nodes. Distances are normalized into the range 0.0 to 1.0.

position may be in the flipped location with respect to the line. Fig. 3 shows a deployment with 30% of anchors with bigger error not only due to the less number of anchor nodes but also due to the aforementioned flip ambiguity. The other source of error is the absence of anchor in a region due to the non-uniform distribution of the anchor nodes. The flipped neighborhood indicated in the Fig. 3 shows the uneven distribution of the anchor in the specified region. In some cases the whole neighborhood is flipped and contributes to upsurge of error. Correcting the flip ambiguity in the CE localization technique necessitates further research and we have intention to contribute to this area in our future works.

Fig. 4 shows the error in successive rounds. The error decays exponentially. Therefore, with a small number of iterations, the algorithm converges to its minimum error. Though the figure demonstrates a single event of error in rounds we observe many instances and almost always this is the case where the convergence is quick and efficient. This is an important criterion of selecting an optimization algorithm. A small number of rounds in convergence demonstrate algorithm efficiency in term of its cost. Fig. 5 displays an example of the changes in estimated locations of a specific node in rounds, alternatively, the searching path of that particular run. Both Fig. 4 and Fig. 5 conform that the search converges to the minimum with exponentially decayed cost.

In order to evaluate the performance of our proposed CE algorithm, we compare it against the two well-known localization algorithms, namely, DV-Hop algorithm [15] and Simulated annealing (SA)-based algorithm [22].

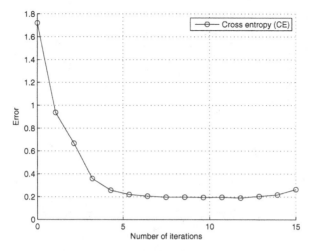

(a) Number of anchors = 30%.

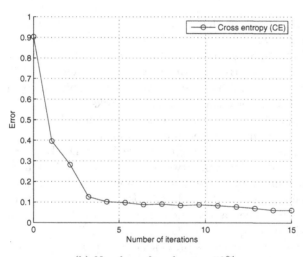

(b) Number of anchors = 50%.

Fig. 4. Error in rounds

It is observed that DV-Hop is much faster but much less accurate than both SA and CE. When compared with SA, CE takes much lesser number of iterations to converge. On the other hand, per iteration of CE takes longer time than that of SA. Therefore to make a fair comparison, Fig. 6 shows the error performance of CE and SA algorithm with respect to time thereby depicts the core algorithmic efficiency of CE over SA. Fig. 6(a) and 6(b) show a trace for such error vs. runtime of the algorithms with 30% and 50% of anchors respectively. It should be noted that the trend shown in Fig. 6(a) is atypical of SA, whose accuracy is

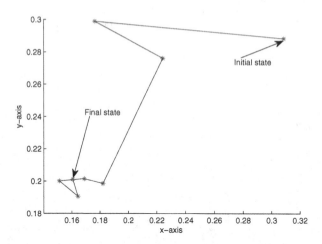

Fig. 5. An example of changes in estimated locations of a specific node in rounds

higher (albeit insignificantly) than that of CE in a majority of cases — as later demonstrated in Fig. 8.

Fig. 7(a) and 7(b) show error performance of individual nodes with 30% and 50% of anchor nodes respectively. Intuitively the big spikes in the CE method are due to the flipped nodes and these can potentially be eliminated by incorporating appropriate measures mentioned in the future works.

Fig. 8 shows algorithm error performance compared with different percentages of the anchor deployments. Here each error point is calculated by averaging 10 measurements. Again, both of the figures reveal that DV-Hop provides a poor performance compared to the other two. When there are less number of anchors the error becomes more and more is a common phenomenon for all the three cases which is quite expected. Though, DV-Hop has the worst increasing rate of error with decreasing percentage of anchors. Especially the performance becomes too poor when the percentage of anchor nodes is small.

On the other hand SA approach provides the best error performance but with a cost of slow algorithmic convergence. Fig. 9 demonstrates the poor efficiency of SA algorithm in terms of its algorithmic runtime. Therefore in case of a large mobile sensor application SA approach of localization can never be justifiable because of its higher processing cost. Alternatively the proposed algorithm becomes a suitable approach of localization with a reasonably low processing cost with a little sacrifice of localization accuracy. One simplest and straight forward way to determine the required number of rounds in algorithm is to track the error in successive rounds. The algorithm exit from the iterative loop, if the current performance compare to the previous performance does not improve more than a predefined threshold. Therefore the runtime is calculated by time stamping the nth round when the $(n+1)^{th}$ round cannot bring the error further down. 10 measurements are taken to get the runtime average for each deployment.

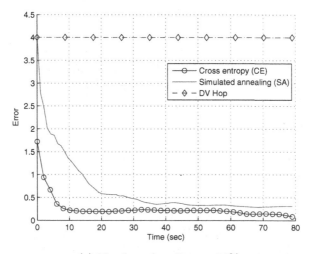

(a) Number of anchors = 30%.

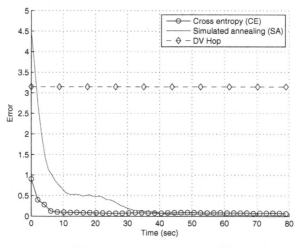

(b) Number of anchors = 50%.

Fig. 6. Error over algorithmic runtime. In both cases, CE requires only about 10 seconds for the error to converge nearly to its minimum whereas SA requires about 40 seconds to achieve this. For mission critical applications with frequently changing node locations, CE has an advantage over SA by allowing the central computer to estimate the nodes' locations about 4 times faster while not much sacrificing the estimation accuracy.

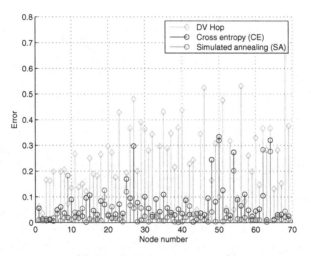

(a) Number of anchors = 30%.

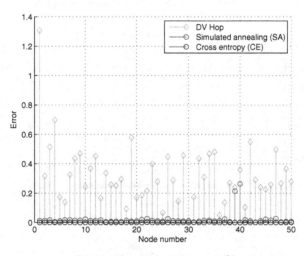

(b) Number of anchors = 50%.

Fig. 7. Error in each node - after convergence to minimum

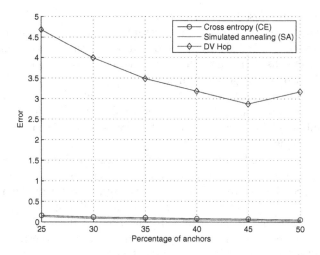

Fig. 8. Average error - after convergence to minimum. It can be observed the two curves for CE and SA are very close, i.e., the differences in minimum errors achieved by CE and SA are rather insignificant.

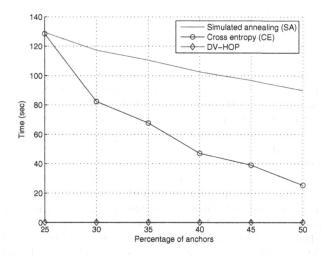

Fig. 9. Simulation runtime required to converge the error to minimum. It can be observed that the running time of CE is about 4 times shorter than that of SA when the number of anchors is 50%.

4   Conclusions and Future Works

A novel cross-entropy-based localization algorithm is devised in the context of wireless sensor networks. The algorithm attempts to estimate the locations of the nodes in the networks centrally from the distance measured based on transmit-receive signal strengths. Error introduced by the unreliable wireless communications is minimized by CE based optimization technique. Simulation results show that the algorithm can estimate the location coordinate of sensor nodes with reasonably good accuracy with low computational costs. Mobile sensor network with large number of nodes can be benefited by this computationally efficient localization technique.

The cost function of CE takes equal weights for all the neighbor distances in the neighborhood. In practice some neighbor information is more reliable than the other [28]. Therefore a possible future improvement of the algorithmic cost function is to incorporate weights base on the reliability of the particular neighbor. We also intend to contribute to the area of flip ambiguity problem in the CE localization approach one common drawback of the error minimizing technique based estimation algorithm for localization.

Acknowledgment. This research was sponsored by the Government of Abu Dhabi, United Arab Emirates through its funding of Masdar Institute of Science and Technology's research project on "Monitoring and Optimization of Renewable Energy Generation using Wireless Sensor Data Analytics" (award number 10XAAA1).

References

1. Bachrach, J., Taylor, C.: Localization in sensor networks. In: Handbook of Sensor Networks: Algorithms and Architectures. Wiley-Interscience (2005)
2. Pal, A.: Localization algorithms in wireless sensor networks: Current approaches and future challenges. Network Protocols and Algorithms 2(1), 45–78 (2010)
3. Rappapport, T.S.: Wireless Communications: Principles and Practice, pp. 50–143. Prentice Hall (1996)
4. Girod, L., Estrin, D.: Robust range estimation using acoustic and n multimodal sensing. In: Proc. IEEE International Conference on Intelligent Robots and Systems, Hawaii, USA, vol. 3, pp. 1312–1320 (2001)
5. Chan, Y., Tsui, W., So, H., Ching, P.: Time-of-arrival based localization under NLOS conditions. IEEE Transactions on Vehicular Technology 55(1), 17–24 (2006)
6. Prorok, A., Tome, P., Martinoli, A.: Accommodation of NLOS for ultra-wideband TDOA localization in single- and multi-robot systems. In: Proc. IEEE International Conference on Indoor Positioning and Indoor Navigation, Guimarães, Portugal, pp. 1–9 (September 2011)
7. Cheng, X., Thaeler, A., Xue, G., Chen, D.: TPS: a time-based positioning scheme for outdoor wireless sensor networks. In: Proc. 23rd IEEE International Conference on Computer Communications, Hong Kong, China, pp. 2685–2696 (March 2004)

8. Patwari, N., Ash, J.N., Kyperountas, S., Hero, A.O., Moses, R.L., Correal, N.S.: Locating the nodes: cooperative localization in wireless sensor networks. IEEE Signal Processing Magazine 22(4), 54–69 (2005)

9. Aitchison, J., Brown, J.A.C.: The Lognormal Distribution. Cambridge University Press (1957)

10. Brockwell, P.J., Davis, R.A.: Time Series: Theory and Methods, 2nd edn. Springer (2009)

11. Zanca, G., Zorzi, F., Zanella, A., Zorzi, M.: Experimental comparison of RSSI-based localization algorithms for indoor wireless sensor networks. In: Proc. Real-World Wireless Sensor Networks, Glasgow, Scotland, UK, pp. 1–5 (April 2008)

12. Chang, C., Sahai, A.: Estimation bounds for localization. In: Proc. IEEE Sensor and Ad Hoc Communications and Networks, Santa Clara, California, USA, pp. 415–424 (October 2004)

13. Langendoen, K., Reijers, N.: Distributed localization in wireless sensor networks: a quantitative comparison. Computer Networks 43(4), 499–518 (2003)

14. Bulusu, N., Heidemann, J., Estrin, D.: GPS-less low cost outdoor localization for very small devices. IEEE Personal Communications Magazine 7(5), 28–34 (2000)

15. Niculescu, D., Nath, B.: DV based positioning in ad hoc networks. Journal of Telecommunication Systems 22(1-4), 267–280 (2003)

16. Blumenthal, J., Grossmann, R., Golatowski, F., Timmermann, D.: Weighted centroid localization in Zigbee-based sensor networks. In: Proc. IEEE International Symposium on Intelligent Signal Processing, Xiamen, China, pp. 1–6 (Octobor 2007)

17. Wang, J., Urriza, P., Han, Y., Cabric, D.: Weighted centroid localization algorithm: theoretical analysis and distributed implementation. IEEE Transactions on Wireless Communications 10(10), 3403–3413 (2011)

18. Behnke, R., Timmermann, D.: AWCL: Adaptive weighted centroid localization as an efficient improvement of coarse grained localization. In: Proc. IEEE Positioning, Navigation and Communication, Hannover, Germany, pp. 243–250 (March 2008)

19. Patwari, N., O'Dea, R., Wang, Y.: Relative location in wireless networks. In: Proc. IEEE Vehicular Technology Conference, Rhodes, Greece, vol. 2, pp. 1149–1153 (May 2001)

20. Nguyen, X., Rattentbury, T.: Localization Algorithms for Sensor Networks using RF Signal Strength. Technical Report, University of California at Berkeley (May 2003)

21. Kay, S.M.: Fundamentals of Statistical Signal Processing: Estimation Theory, pp. 344–350. Prentice Hall (1993)

22. Kannan, A.A., Mao, G., Vucetic, B.: Simulated annealing based wireless sensor network localization. Journal of Computers 1(2), 15–22 (2006)

23. Chen, J.: Improved maximum likelihood localization estimation accuracy in wireless sensor networks using the cross-entropy method. In: Proc. IEEE International Conference on Acoustics, Speech and Signal Processing, Taipei, Taiwan, pp. 1325–1328 (April 2009)

24. Rubinstein, R.Y., Kroese, D.P.: The Cross-Entropy Method: A Unified Approach to Combinatorial Optimization, Monte-Carlo Simulation, and Machine Learning. Springer (2004)

25. Moore, D., Leonard, J., Rus, D., Teller, S.: Robust distributed network localization with noisy range measurements. In: Proc. 2nd International Conference on Embedded Networked Sensor Systems, Baltimore, Maryland, USA, pp. 50–61 (November 2004)

26. Eren, T., Goldenburg, D., Whiteley, W., Yang, Y., Morse, A., Anderson, B.D.O., Belhumeur, P.N.: Rigidity, computation, and randomization in network localisation. In: Proc. 23rd IEEE International Conference on Computer Communications, Hong Kong, China, vol. 4, pp. 2673–2684 (March 2004)
27. Goldenburg, D.K., Krishnamurthy, A., Maness, W.C., Yang, Y.R., Young, A., Morse, A.S., Savvides, A.: Network localization in partially localizable networks. In: Proc. 24th IEEE International Conference on Computer Communications, Miami, Florida, USA, vol. 1, pp. 313–326 (March 2005)
28. Desai, J., Tureli, U.: Evaluating performance of various localization algorithms in wireless and sensor networks. In: Proc. IEEE Personal, Indoor and Mobile Radio Communications, Athens, Greece, pp. 1–5 (September 2007)

Auction-Based Agent Negotiation in Cognitive Radio Ad Hoc Networks

Asma Amraoui[1], Badr Benmammar[1], Francine Krief[2], and Fethi Tarik Bendimerad[1]

[1] LTT Laboratory, University of Tlemcen, Algeria
[2] LaBRI Laboratory Bordeaux 1 University, Talence, France
{amraoui.asma,badr.benmammar,ftbendimerad}@gmail.com,
krief@labri.fr

Abstract. The explosive growth of wireless services in recent years illustrates the growing demand for communications, so the spectrum becomes more congested. We know that static spectrum allocation is a major problem in wireless networks. Generally, these allocations lead to an inefficient use of spectrum. To solve the problem of congestion, cognitive radio networks use dynamic spectrum access. In this paper, we use a technique based on auctions theory known for its simplicity and facilitates the allocation of scarce resources.

Keywords: Cognitive radio, multi agent systems, auctions theory, dynamic spectrum access.

1   Introduction

The Cognitive Radio (CR) is a form of wireless communication in which a transmitter / receiver can detect intelligently communication channels which are in use and those which are not and can move to unused channels. This optimizes the use of available radio frequency spectrum while minimizing interference with other users.

The principle of CR requires an alternative management of spectrum: a user called "secondary" may at any time access to the free channels, i.e., not occupied by the user called "primary" who possess a license on this band. The secondary user (SU) will give way the channel after completing the service or if a primary user (PU) has shown an inclination to login.

To make CR systems practical, CR networks must be able to coexist; this may cause interference to other users. To deal with this problem, the idea of cooperation between users to sense and share spectrum without causing interference is introduced.

The cooperative resolution of problems plays a predominant role in research in DAI[1] (Distributed Artificial Intelligence). A relatively complex area of research derived from the DAI is Multi Agent Systems (MAS). The topic MAS focuses on the study of collective behavior and the distribution of intelligence on autonomous agents able to organize themselves and interact to solve problems.

---

[1] Unlike Artificial Intelligence (AI) which models the intelligent behavior of a single agent, the DAI is concerned with intelligent behaviors that result from the cooperative activity of several agents.

J. Zheng et al. (Eds.): Adhocnets 2012, LNICST 111, pp. 119–134, 2013.
© Institute for Computer Sciences, Social Informatics and Telecommunications Engineering 2013

Cooperation can be considered as an attitude adopted by agents which decide to work together. In the case of CR, before cooperation a step of negotiation is needed because there are many users who want to satisfy their needs. Negotiation plays a fundamental role in the cooperation activities by enabling people to resolve conflicts that could put in danger the cooperative behavior.

In this paper, we start by giving an overview on MAS and then discuss their use in the CR. We will establish a state of the art on the use of auctions in CR networks and then give the network topology and the negotiation algorithms that we propose

2   Multi Agent Systems

2.1   Agent

The concept of agent is used in several disciplines, so there are few compromises when it is question about defining the term "agent". However, one of the most known definitions which is considered as one of the firsts is that of [1]:

> "An agent is an autonomous entity, real or abstract, which can act on itself and its environment, which in a multi agent environment can communicate with other agents, and whose behavior is the consequence of its observations, knowledge and interactions with other agents."

2.2   Multi Agent Systems

MAS are particularly suitable for reactive and robust solutions to complex problems for which there is no centralized control [2] [3]. Indeed, the MAS is a group of agents where each agent has one or more basic skills. The goal is to make work together agents to solve a problem or perform a specific task. Somehow, we distribute intelligence; each autonomous agent has only a local vision of the problem or an elementary task of a job.

2.3   When and Why Choose MAS?

MAS are generally used when the problem is too complex to be solved by a single system because of some software or hardware limitations. In particular, if the component maintains multiple relationships between them. MAS are an excellent tool to ensure an autonomous control system in a widely distributed system and whose characteristics are very dynamic.

For an effective MAS, several agents must work concurrently, which reduces the resolution time considering the used speed which is due to parallelism [19] [20].

When we need a system which must adapt dynamically when adding new components (these components should easily adapt when the environment undergoes modifications); MAS are probably the ideal solution for this kind of scenarios. It should be remembered that one of the most important advantages of

MAS is their modularity that allows making programming easier, i.e. the addition of new agents to the MAS is not a problem which explains their scalability.

The interest of the agent-based solutions lies in the complete absence of central entity governing the operation of agents, which ensures high strength and high reliability (because if an agent fails, the system continues to function).

2.4   Interactions between Agents

One of the main properties of the agent in MAS is interacting with the other agents. These interactions are generally defined as any form of executed action in the system and which causes changing the behavior of another agent.

An interaction is a dynamic linking of two or more agents through a set of reciprocal actions. The interactions are expressed from a series of actions whose consequences exert in return an influence on the future behavior of agents [1].

The interaction can be decomposed into three phases not necessarily sequential:

- Information receipt or the perception of a change,
- Reasoning on other agents from the information acquired,
- A transmitting messages or more actions (action plan) modifying the environment.

Common types of interaction include **cooperation** (working together to solve a common goal), **coordination** (organizing problem solving so that harmful interactions are avoided or beneficial interactions are exploited); and **negotiation** (reaching an agreement acceptable to all parties involved).

3   Multi Agent Systems and Cognitive Radio

3.1   MAS and Spectrum Allocation

The CR offers a balanced solution to the problem of spectrum congestion by giving first priority use to the spectrum owner, then allowing others to use the unused portions of the spectrum. To intelligently manage the CR resources, trading and cooperation algorithms resulting from the field of multi agent are to be exploited in order to ensure a more efficient allocation of spectrum.

In the CR community, we often talk about cooperation between SUs and negotiation between Pus and SUs. Initially we will discuss the second concept (negotiation) assuming that CR nodes are fixed.

Ferber could make a typology of interaction situations through the main components of the interaction (**goals, resources, competences**). Interactions of agents in MAS are motivated by the interdependence of agents according to these three dimensions: their goals can be compatible or not; agents can desire resources that others have, an agent X may have the necessary capacity to an agent Y for the fulfillment of the action plan of Y. **Table 1** summarizes the various possible situations.

Table 1. Classification of interaction situations

Goals	Resources	Competences	Type of situation	Remark
Compatibles	Sufficient	Sufficient	Independence	Situation of indifference
Compatibles	Sufficient	Insufficient	Simple collaboration	Situation of cooperation
Compatibles	**Insufficient**	**Sufficient**	**Congestion**	
Compatibles	Insufficient	Insufficient	Coordinated collaboration	
Incompatibles	Sufficient	Sufficient	Pure individual competition	Situation of antagonism
Incompatibles	Sufficient	Insufficient	Pure collective competition	
Incompatibles	Insufficient	Sufficient	Individual conflicts for resources	
Incompatibles	Insufficient	Insufficient	Collective conflicts for resources	

According to Ferber, the goals are incompatibles if the satisfaction of one causes the dissatisfaction of the other.

In the case of CR, SUs seek to satisfy their application by seeking a free channel and PUs have the opportunity to share their spectrum too. So we can say that the goals are compatibles because there is no contradiction between PUs and SUs goals.

When we speak about resources, we mean the number of available channels (free parts of the spectrum).

In the scenarios we will process, we assume that SUs have sufficient competences, which means that each agent can make the sensing alone (no need to other agents). Based on the classification of interaction situations (Table1), we modeled the scenario that will be encountered in the context of CR through a binary tree in **Fig.1**.

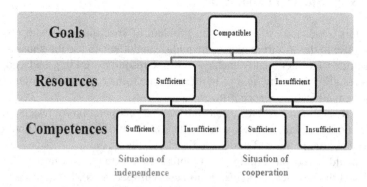

Fig. 1. Binary tree modeling the interactions between agents in the case of CR

In the situation of independence, there is no problem to solve regarding to the interaction of agents because resources and competences are sufficient. This is why we are particularly interested by the situation of cooperation. The goal of researches carried out in the field of cooperation and negotiation between agents is to achieve an overall state of MAS by promoting agents synergy. Thus the objective may be to achieve a better state, to improve the overall result while satisfying all the local results.

When the resources used by the agents are limited and they are in a situation of congestion, we use most often:

- **The law of the strongest** (define a priority according to the strength of the agent), but in the case of CR, SUs have the same goal and want to satisfy their need in spectrum. So setting priorities in this case, returns to favor some types of applications.

- **Techniques of negotiation**, i.e. compromises will be established between the agents. Indeed, it is interesting to use this method because the installation of these mechanisms would make it possible to lead to acceptance by an agent to cooperate with other agents. In the case of CR, we must only verify whether the PU is ready to cooperate or not.

Subsequently, we will use this method (negotiation) to solve the problem of congestion between SUs.

3.2   Negotiation Protocols

A negotiation protocol is the set of rules which direct the interaction. This includes the types of allowed participants, the negotiation states, the events which pass from a state to another and the acceptable and valid actions from participants. In the literature, there are several trading protocols; **Table 2** summarizes the most important protocols.

Table 2. Negotiation protocols

Negotiation protocol	Description
Contract Net	Agents coordinate their activities through the establishment of contracts to achieve specific goals.
Auctions theory	The term "auction" means any technique of establishing a sales competition, which aims to determine the future owner of the article concerned in successive bids.
Heuristic negotiation	The agents must provide useful reactions for the proposals they receive, these reactions can take the form of a criticism or a counter-proposal (refused or modified proposal).
Negotiation by argumentation	An agent may try to persuade another agent to respond favorably to his proposal by looking for arguments that identify new opportunities, create new opportunities or changing the evaluation criteria.

3.3   Protocol Choice

To solve the problem of congestion caused by the lack of resources, and well model the negotiation, a protocol must be selected among those mentioned before. We chose a protocol based on auctions theory because we believe that this is an ingenious approach to allocate resources to a set of agents. It should be understood that the allocation is a difficult problem to the extent that resources are limited compared to the number of requests.

Since an auction restricts negotiating variables to a reduced number of parameters essentially price, this makes it easier for programmers. Finally, an auction leads to a mutually acceptable solution for the seller and buyers (in our case the PU and SUs), markets forces being the only referee of the outcome of the negotiation.

The object of the negotiations in our scenario is the number of free channels proposed by the PU. Initially, we are interested only to the different methods to be used for negotiation between the PU and SUs. These methods will be implemented on the PU side. Interactions between PU and SU will be simulated later using the MAS.

4   Auctions and Cognitive Radio

4.1   Types of Auctions

Currently, there are several auction protocols, only the most frequently used are listed in **Fig.2.** below.

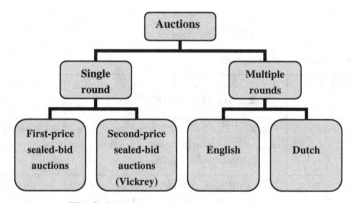

Fig. 2. Organigram showing types of auctions

4.2   Related Works

Generally, an auction consists of several stakeholders; **Table. 3** describes the difference between traditional auctions and what corresponds to each speaker when applying this method to the negotiation in CR networks.

Table 3. Difference between classical auctions and auctions in CR Networks

Traditional auctions	Auctions in CR networks
Objects to sell	Free channels
Bidder	Secondary User (SU)
Seller	Primary User (PU)
Auctioneer	Regulator

Auctions are based on the concept of sale and purchase of goods or services. The main purpose of the use of auctions in CR networks is to provide motivation for SUs to maximize their use of spectrum. To fully utilize the spectrum, dynamic spectrum allocation using auctions has become a promising approach that allows users to rent unused channels by PUs.

In general, the proposed solutions by the different authors working on auctions theory for dynamic spectrum access are based on architecture with infrastructure [7].

In [8], the authors propose a mechanism for an efficient and equitable sharing of spectrum resources where we need a coordinator to manage the operation and model spectrum access in CR networks such repeated auction.

In solutions based on auctions, each channel is assigned to a single network, i.e. there is no notion of SU and PU in the same channel. In the literature, two possibilities are offered:

- Either the regulator allocates channels to PU; they independently allocate unused portions of their channel for SUs [9].

- Either the regulator allocates the right to be SU or PU in the channel [10].

The method of payment is often a major problem when we want to apply auctions in telecommunications networks; this is why some researchers are trying to find adequate solutions. For example the authors in [11] use second price auctions to solve the problem of spectrum allocation and develop an approach which introduces the concept of fictive money for the payment in real time. Another interesting approach is proposed in [12] where the authors think that there is no concept of money for the auction but the price to pay is the waiting time.

However, some researches has been done by [13] and offer a traditional approach based on auctions, and then they do an extension of their approach to a scenario that assumes that there are free unused channels. i.e. the SU will have the choice between paying a good QoS or access to an unused channel for free and encounter risk of interference with the users (if several SU operate simultaneously on these bands).

Another way to use auctions is proposed in [14], where the authors have shown that in some scenarios the spectrum is used efficiently when multiple SU gain access to a single channel, this is what distinguish their method with the traditional auctions where only one user can win.

In these solutions, user behaviors can be false, so the centralized manager can't maximize the utility function of the overall network [15].

4.3   Proposed Network Topology

Several researchers model the auction as a network with infrastructure; otherwise the regulator is required to conduct the sale.

In this paper, we propose to use network architecture without infrastructure or what is generally called an "ad hoc network", because this type of networks differs from the other forms by its ability to organize itself independently without fixed infrastructure. An ad hoc network consists only of a variable number of entities that communicate with each other directly.

In other words, the communication will be directly done between PUs and SUs. **Fig.3** illustrates the network topology that we used:

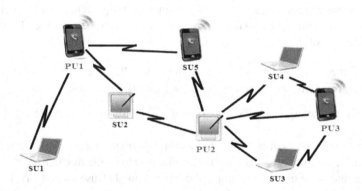

Fig. 3. Network topology (ad hoc mode)

4.4   Scenario

Initially, we focused our attention on a particular type of negotiation "one to many" i.e. there is only one PU who shares its spectrum and several SU who need to ensure free channels for assuring the quality of their application. **Fig.4** illustrates the scenario that we will deal in the paper.

For example, in **Fig.4**, there are 3 SUs (SU1, SU2, SU5) who want to access to the free resources at PU1. However there are only 4 free resources at PU1 which is not sufficient to serve the needs of all SUs (1+2+2 = 5 required resources). So which of SU1 or SU2 or SU5 will access to the spectrum?

To solve this kind of problem, we use dynamic spectrum access techniques, and as mentioned before, we'll use auction theory to manage the spectrum. To be specific, we chose two types of auctions: one taking place in a single round such as First-price sealed-bid auctions and another one taking place in multiple rounds such as English auctions.

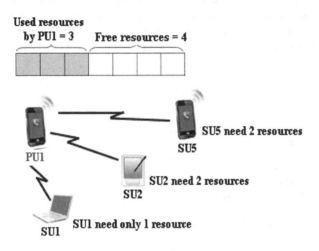

Fig. 4. Proposed scenario

4.5   Proposed Algorithms

To solve the spectrum allocation problem, we propose to use dynamic programming which is an algorithmic technique to optimize the amounts of monotonically increasing functions under constraint. This technique applies to optimization problems whose objective function is described as "the sum of monotonically increasing functions of resources."

We note:

nb : the number of SUs.
m : the number of free channels at PU.
W : array of size nb, W[i] is the number of requested channels by SUi.
C : array of size nb, C [i] is the proposed price for W [i] by SU_i.

The increasing monotonic function to be optimized is: $\mathrm{Max} \sum_{i=0}^{nb-1} C[i]$

The constraint is: $\displaystyle\sum_{i=0}^{nb-1} W[i] \le m$

We therefore proposed and implemented the following algorithms on the PU side.

4.5.1 For First-Price Sealed-Bid Auctions

The initiator starts the auction and each participant submits a bid in an envelope or electronically in a single round (turn), without knowing the bids of the others. The participant who made the biggest bid wins the object and pays the amount of its offer. **Fig.5.** shows the algorithm we have been proposed to solve this type of auction.

```
function COUT(W, C, m)
    n ← C.length
    for j = 0 to m do
        tab[0][j] ← 0
    end for
    for i = 1 to nb do
        for j = 0 to m do
            if j ≤ W[i − 1] then
                tab[i][j] ← tab[i − 1][j]
            else
                tab[i][j] ← max(tab[i − 1][j], C[i − 1] + tab[i − 1][j − W[i − 1]]
            end if
        end for
    end for
    return tab[nb][m]
end function
```

Fig. 5. Algorithm for first-price sealed-bid auctions

4.5.2 For English Auctions

The initiator starts usually the auction by announcing a reservation price (the minimum price for which he is willing to sell the item). Each participant announces publicly its offer in several successive rounds. When no participant wants to increase his bid, the auction ends and the participant who made the biggest offer wins the object at its offer price. **Fig.6** shows the algorithm that was used to solve this type of auction.

```
procedure ANGLAISE
    for i = 0 to nb − 1 do
        max_su[i] ← random * 1000
        if max_su[i] > max then
            max ← max_su[i]
        end if
        C[i] ← random * 100
        C[i] = C[i]/W[i]
        bool[i] ← 1
    end for
while nb_bool ≠ 0 do
    for i = 0 to nb − 1 do
        if bool[i] = 0 then
            continue
        end if
        if C[i] > max_su[i] then
            if bool[i] = 1 then
                C[i] ← max_su[i]
                bool[i] = 0
            end if
            nb_bool ← nb_bool − 1
        end if
        if C[i] > max1 then
            max1 ← C[i]
        end if
    end for
    prix_pu ← max1
    for i = 0 to nb − 1 do
        if bool[i] ≠ 0 then
            C[i] ← random * 100
        end if
    end for
end while
return prix_pu
```

Fig. 6. Algorithm for english auctions

4.6   Comparison between the Two Types of Auctions

We implemented both algorithms on the PU and then compared the obtained results knowing that we tested the two algorithms assuming that there is 10 SUs in the same place.

4.6.1 Comparison in Terms of Running Time

La **Fig.7** shows that the execution time of multiple rounds auction is very large compared to those taking place in a single round.

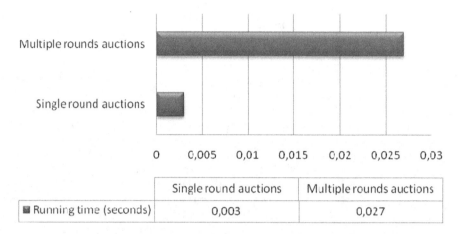

	Single round auctions	Multiple rounds auctions
▨ Running time (seconds)	0,003	0,027

Fig. 7. Comparison between the two algorithms in terms of running time

4.6.2 Comparison in Terms of Efficiency

In our case, when we talk about efficiency, we talk about number of satisfied SUs. For this, we compared the two algorithms and we note that the results are the same.

Fig.8 shows the impact of auctions on the number of satisfied SUs. We clearly see that whatever the number of available channels at the PU, the number of satisfied SUs remains the same with both methods (blue and red curves).

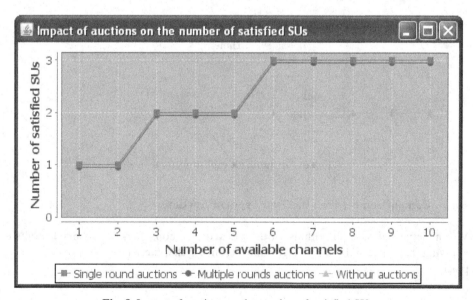

Fig. 8. Impact of auctions on the number of satisfied SUs

We compared also the use of auction with the case where we don't use this technique (PU satisfies the first received demand according to his free channels), we notice that the number of satisfied SUs is always higher compared to that obtained without auctions.

The parameters we used are: nb = 5, C = {10,20,40,120,260} and W = {7,5,3,2,1}.

To determine the number of SU that can be satisfied in a given period of time (1min = 60s), we made a comparison between the use of the two previous algorithms (single round auctions and multiple rounds auctions) with the FIFO method (First In First Out).

For this comparison, we assumed that the operating time of each channel is 10s. In addition to the execution time and operating time, we must also know that the necessary time to exploit a channel (T. establishment) is 5s on average [14] [15].

T. required = T. execution + T. establishment + T. operating

The dataset we used is: m = 4, nb = 4, C = {44, 94, 151, 97} and W = {3, 2, 1, 3}.

Fig.9 shows that in 60s, 3 SUs were satisfied with the use of the two auction methods, however, using the FIFO method only 2 SUs were satisfied.

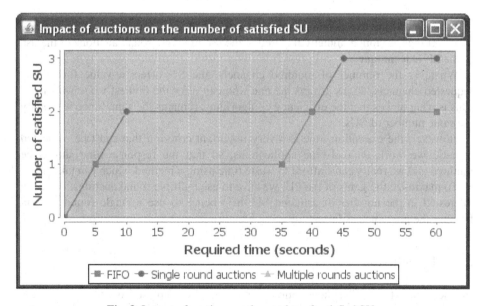

Fig. 9. Impact of auctions on the number of satisfied SUs

Fig.10 below shows the impact of auctions on the gains made by the PU.

The dataset we used is: nb = 10, C (single round) = {39, 51, 160, 59, 64, 145, 177, 53, 42, 106}, C (multiple rounds) = {286, 209, 141, 489, 3, 21, 671, 226, 622, 350} and {W = 3, 2, 1, 3, 2, 1, 1, 2, 3, 1}.

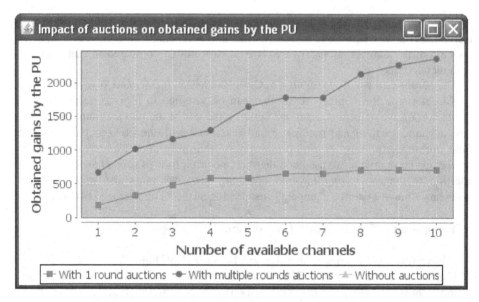

Fig. 10. Impact of auctions on the obtained gains by the PU

We note that the use of multiple rounds auctions is more beneficial for PU because their earnings are much higher compared to the use of single round auctions or the use of the FIFO technique.

Whatever the number of required channels, the SU offers a value for all the requested channels; so it's always the one who can offer the highest value who wins. This is what makes that the efficiency of algorithms remains the same since we satisfy the same number of SUs.

However, the execution time is a very important criterion that can't be neglected because we work on real-time applications, so that the response time should be minimal and we really can't afford to waste time using a method which can take time.

To maximize the gains of the PU, we have to use multiple round auctions. If we are interested in the number of satisfied SU, it is better to use a single round auction because the procedure is faster.

5   Conclusion

In the context of CR, negotiation is one of the simplest solutions to address congestion caused by lack of available resources for SU. We think provide broader view of the negotiation by treating the case where there are several PUs (negotiation many to many).

Our approach has proven that it is preferable to use a single round auction especially if we seek to satisfy applications that require an immediate response, because the use of multiple rounds auctions can make us lose a few seconds since the procedure is slightly longer and slower.

Our method has also proven that to solve the problem of spectrum congestion, we should use one of dynamic spectrum access techniques rather than using nothing and satisfy the first received request.

In our future works, we think we can improve the reliability of wireless links and ensure good QoS to CR mobile terminals [16] [17] [18] by integrating Multi Agent Systems.

References

1. Amraoui, A., Benmammar, B., Bendimerad, F.T.: Accès Dynamique au Spectre dans le Contexte de la Radio Cognitive. In: 2ième édition de la conférence nationale de l'informatique (JEESI 2012), ESI, Oued-Smar (Alger), Algérie (Avril 2012)
2. Ferber, J.: Les systèmes multi-agents. In: Vers une intelligence collective. InterEditions, Paris (1995)
3. Jennings, N.R.: Agent-Oriented Software Engineering. In: Garijo, F.J., Boman, M. (eds.) MAAMAW 1999. LNCS, vol. 1647, pp. 1–7. Springer, Heidelberg (1999)
4. Casteran, J.C., Gleize, M.P.: Des méthodologies orientées multi-agent. In: Hermes, D. (ed.) Actes des Journées Francophones sur les l'Intelligence Artificielle Distribuée et les Systèmes Multi-Agents, JFIADSMA 2000, pp. 191–207 (2000)
5. Chang, H.-B., Chen, K.-C., Prasad, N.R., Su, C.-W.: Auction Based Spectrum Management of Cognitive Radio Networks. IEEE Transactions on Vehicular Technology, 1923–1935 (May 2010)
6. Han, Z., Zheng, R., Poor, H.V.: Repeated Auctions with learning for Spectrum Access in Cognitive Radio Networks. In: Allerton Conference on Communication, Control, and Computing 2009 (2009)
7. Ji, Z., Ray Liu, K.J.: Belief-Assisted Pricing for Dynamic Spectrum Allocation in Wireless Networks with Selfish Users. In: Proc. of IEEE SECON (2006)
8. Kasbekar, G.S., Sarkar, S.: Spectrum Auction Framework for Access allocation in Cognitive Radio Networks. In: MobiHoc (2009)
9. Chen, B., Wu, H.-K., Hoang, A.T., Liang, Y.-C.: Optimizing the second-price auction algorithm in a Dynamic Cognitive Radio Network. In: 11th IEEE Singapore International Conference on Communication Systems, ICCS 2008 (2008)
10. Wu, G., Ren, P., Zhang, C.: A waiting-time Auction Based Dynamic Spectrum allocation in cognitive radio networks. In: GLOBECOM (2011)
11. Chen, L., Iellamo, S., Coupechoux, M., Godlewski, P.: An auction Framework for Spectrum Allocation with Interference Constraint in Cognitive Radio Networks. In: INFOCOM 2010 Proceedings of the 29th Conference on Information Communications (2010)
12. Yongle, W., Wang, B., Liu, K.J.R., Clancy, T.C.: Collusion-resistant multi-winner spectrum auction for cognitive radio networks. In: Proceedings of IEEE GLOBECOM, pp. 1–5 (2008)
13. Mir, U.: Utilization of Cooperative Multiagent Systems for Spectrum Sharing in Cognitive Radio Networks. Thèse 2011 (2011)
14. Busanelli, S., Martalõ, M., Ferrari, G., Spigoni, G.: Vertical Handover between WiFi and UMTS Networks: Experimental Performance Analysis. International Journal of Energy, Information and Communications 2(1) (February 2011)

15. Daia, Z., Fracchiaa, R., Gosteaub, J., Pellatia, P., Viviera, G.: Vertical handover criteria and algorithm in IEEE 802.11 and 802.16 hybrid networks. In: Laboratoire de Motorola Paris
16. Benmammar, B., Amraoui, A., Baghli, W.: Performance improvement of wireless link reliability in the context of cognitive radio. IJCSNS International Journal of Computer Science and Network Security 12(1), 15–22 (2012)
17. Amraoui, A., Benidris, F.Z., Benmammar, B., Krief, F., Bendimerad, F.T.: Toward cognitive radio resource management based on multi-agent systems for improvement of real-time application performance. In: 5th IFIP International Conference on New Technologies, Mobility and Security, NTMS 2012, Istanbul, Turkey (2012)
18. Amraoui, A., Baghli, W., Benmammar, B.: Improving video conferencing application quality for a mobile terminal through cognitive radio. In: Proceedings of the 14th IEEE International Conference on Communication Technology, ICCT 2012, November 9-11, Chengdu, China (2012)
19. Benmammar, B., Krief, F.: La Technologie Agent et les Réseaux Sans Fil. In: Congrès Des Nouvelles Architectures pour les Communications, DNAC 2003, Paris, France (Octobre 2003)
20. Jrad, Z., Krief, F., Benmammar, B.: An Intelligent User Interface for the Dynamic Negotiation of QoS. In: 10th IEEE International Conference on Telecommunications, ICT 2003, Papeete, Tahiti (February 2003)

Asynchronous Rendezvous Protocol for Cognitive Radio Ad Hoc Networks

Sylwia Romaszko[1], Daniel Denkovski[2],
Valentina Pavlovska[2], and Liljana Gavrilovska[2]

[1] Institute for Networked Systems, RWTH Aachen University,
Kackertstr. 9, 52072 Aachen, Germany
sar@inets.rwth-aachen.de
[2] Faculty of Electrical Engineering and Information Technologies
Ss. Cyril and Methodius University in Skopje, Macedonia
{danield,valenpav,liljana}@feit.ukim.edu.mk

Abstract. This paper proposes a rendezvous protocol for Cognitive Radio Ad Hoc Networks, RAC^2E-gQS, which (1) utilizes the asynchronous and randomness properties of the RAC^2E protocol and (2) grid Quorum System-based channel mapping (gQ-RDV) protocol taking into account channel heterogeneity. We show that the combination of the RAC^2E protocol with the grid-quorum based channel mapping can yield a powerful RAC^2E-gQS rendezvous protocol for asynchronous operation in a distributed environment assuring a rapid rendezvous between the cognitive radio nodes.

Keywords: rendezvous, asynchronous, cognitive radio ad hoc networks, quorum systems.

1 Introduction

A common control channel (CCC) in multichannel Cognitive Radio Networks (CRNs) supports the transmission coordination exchange and cooperation between the active CR users. It is aimed to facilitate neighbor discovery, e.g., control signaling, exchange of local measurements, channel sensing etc. However, such CCC existence in CRNs may not be always feasible. When using the CCC notion, a channel needs to be found that is accessible by the majority of CR nodes and it is not interrupted over a long period of time. However, these tasks are not feasible in a CR environment without any imposed assumptions, since CR nodes can have a different view of the channels occupied by incumbents and/or other secondary users. Another issue that arises when all nodes have chosen the same channel is the possibility of single channel bottleneck as well as the single point of failure. Moreover, in Cognitive Radio Ad Hoc Networks (CRANs), the dynamic network topology, distributed multi-hop architecture, and time and location varying spectrum availability are the key factors [1]. Each Cognitive Radio user has a different spectrum availability according to the incumbent (Primary User -PU) activity, as well as it determines its actions based

J. Zheng et al. (Eds.): Adhocnets 2012, LNICST 111, pp. 135–148, 2013.
© Institute for Computer Sciences, Social Informatics and Telecommunications Engineering 2013

on its local observation. Therefore, rendezvous (RDV), the ability of two or more nodes to meet each other and establish a link, is a challenging task in CRANs.

This paper proposes a rendezvous protocol for CRANs that (1) utilizes the asynchronous and randomness properties of the RAC^2E protocol [2], (2) investigates the suitability of two different channel search orders that are based on:

☐ Random selection utilizing weights and utility functions,

☐ Utilizing a grid Quorum System-based channel mapping (gQ-RDV) protocol [3], [4] taking into account channel heterogeneity (in terms of channel quality).

and (3) gives an insight of the performance of the proposed protocol in terms of the Time-To-RDV (TTR) and the probability of RDV for the different channel search orders, as well as the inter-rendezvous time variance.

Section II presents the related work. In Section III we describe a Quorum System (QS) concept and relevant properties. Section IV addresses the gQS mapping algorithm and the RAC^2E protocol followed by the performance evaluation of the RAC^2E-gQS protocol. The last section concludes this study.

2   Related Work

RDV approaches can be divided into three branches, first, non-quorum based solutions representing blind or pseudo-random RDV techniques ([5,6] and more sophisticated [7,8]). To the second branch belong protocols proposed for a multi-channel Medium Access Control (MAC) handling multi -rendezvous [9] (i.e., multiple transmissions pairs can accomplish handshaking simultaneously), missing receiver problem [10] or medium allocation in a hostile and jamming environment [11]. All these protocols are based on cyclic quorum systems. A cyclic QS is proposed in [12] and it is based on the cyclic block design and cyclic difference sets in combinatorial theory [13]. To the last branch belong quorum-based protocols proposed for CRNs ([14,15]). An asynchronous channel view is not handled in quorum-based schemes and the *channel heterogeneity* is not considered in any related work approaches to the best of our knowledge.

The asynchronous operation of the cognitive radio networks and its effect on the rendezvous phase is not well investigated subject. The synchronization establishment in cognitive radio networks, especially in the distributed case, is a time and power consuming task, and therefore, the assumption that the CR nodes operate in time synchronized manner is not always justified. There are only a few papers considering the asynchronism of the CR nodes during the rendezvous phase. Most of them use probabilistic models to generate the channel hopping sequences of the operating CR devices. In the modular clock algorithm (MC) [6] and its modified version MMC [6] each CR node picks a proper prime number P and randomly selects a rate r which is less than P. Based on the two parameters, the user generates its channel search sequence via pre-defined modulo operations. The channel rendezvous sequence (CRSEQ) algorithm [16] uses a method based on triangle numbers and modular operations to calculate the channel hopping order. The ring-walk (RW) algorithm [7] represents each channel as a vertex in a ring. The CR nodes sweep through the ring visiting the vertices (channels) with different velocities and the rendezvous is guaranteed since the nodes with lower velocities will sooner or later be caught by the ones with higher velocities. In [8] the authors propose a jump-stay rendezvous algorithm for blind rendezvous, using jump-pattern and a stay-pattern channel hoping sequences in each round. The CR nodes continuously "jump" on available channels during the jump-pattern and "stay" on a specific channel during the stay-pattern. In the recent study on the blind rendezvous for tactical networks [17], the performances of the MMC [6] and Random Channel Access (RA) [18] algorithms are compared on a testbed using USRP [19]. It is found out that added asynchronization can have a large beneficial effects reducing time to rendezvous.

Up to the best of the authors' knowledge there is only a couple of papers focusing on quorum based asynchronous rendezvous [14,20]. However, these papers as well as the aforementioned works dealing with the asynchronism, do not handle the channel heterogeneity in the generation of channel hopping sequences and do not handle the details of asynchronous operation and rendezvous between the devices. Oppositely, the RAC^{2}E-gQS takes into consideration the *heterogeneity* in terms of the channel priority among the CR nodes. Furthermore, the proposed protocol covers the details of the operation of the nodes *prior the rendezvous* (Sections 4.2 and 4.3) and *after the rendezvous*, i.e. the control channel operation ([2]).

3   Quorum Systems

Quorum-based algorithms become popular as the main asset of these algorithms is their resilience to node and network failures. The usual definition of a quorum system (QS) is given in [21]:

Definition 1. *A quorum system Q under an universal set U, $U = \{0, 1, ..., n - 1\}$ with n being a cycle length (frequently used Z_n symbol referring to $U = Z_n$), is a collection of non-empty subsets of U, called quorums, satisfying the intersection property $\forall A, B \in Q : A \cap B \neq \emptyset$.*

There are different types of QSs, within which a *grid*-based QS proposed by Maekawa [22], is widely utilized, but in power-saving (PS) protocols. In this system, sites (elements) are logically organized in a grid in the shape of a *square*. A quorum for a requesting site contains the union of a row and a column that the requesting site corresponds to. For PS nodes we can divide their beacon intervals into groups, where each group includes n consecutive intervals and is organized in a $\sqrt{n} \times \sqrt{n}$ array array in a row-major manner. Quorum intervals are picked along an arbitrary row and column from this array, where the remaining intervals are non-quorum intervals. Figure 1 depicts an example for 16 beacon intervals and three nodes, A, B, C, selecting different quorum intervals. If the clocks of

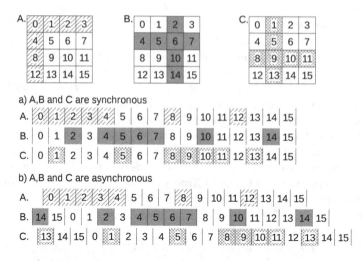

Fig. 1. Grid-based Quorum with 16 beacons [3]

the nodes are synchronized (*case a*) in cycle and slots, the intervals of the nodes overlap twice, e.g., A-B pair in 2 and 4 interval, A-C pair in 1 and 8 interval, and B-C pair in 5 and 10 interval. Moreover, Figure 1.b shows that even when their clocks are not synchronized (neither cycle nor slot alignment) the A's slots still overlap with B's and C's slots.

A quorum system, which satisfies the *Rotation Closure Property (RCP)*, ensures that two asynchronous mobile nodes selecting any two quorums have at least one intersection in their quorums. The grid QS satisfies the RCP:

Definition 2. *For a quorum R in a quorum system Q under an universal set $U = \{0, ..., N-1\}$ and $i \in 1, 2, ..., N-1$, there is defined: $rotate(R, i) = (x + i) mod\ N | x \in R$. A quorum system Q has the Rotation Closure Property if and only if $\forall R', R \in Q, R' \cap rotate(R, i) \neq \emptyset$ for all $i \in 1, 2, ..., N-1$.*

In [3] *Grid-Pair-on-Pair* (PoP) way of forming a grid was proposed as shown in Table 1 (relevant equation can be found in [3]). However, this grid does not satisfy the RCP, hence a node using this grid will encounter problems with RDV when there is no cycle alignment: i.e., selecting a quorum(0,0) as depicted in Table 1 we have $Q1 = \{0, 4, 5, 10, 11, 14, 15\}$. It does not satisfy the RCP, since for $i = 8$ there is no common element: $Q1 \cap rotate(Q1, 8) = \emptyset$, because

Table 1. 4x4 grid: Pair-On-Pair (PoP): quorum (0,0) in bold

0	**5**	**11**	**15**
4	1	7	13
10	6	2	9
14	12	8	3

Table 2. 4x4 grid: Diagonal (Diag): quorum (0,0) in bold

0	4	8	12
13	1	5	9
10	14	2	6
7	11	15	3

of $\{0, 4, 5, 10, 11, 14, 15\} \cap \{8, 12, 13, 2, 3, 6, 7\} = \emptyset$. In all other cases there is at least one common element.

Therefore, *Grid-Diagonal* (Diag) way was also designed in [3] as shown in Table 2. In this method the numbers are ordered according to the positive diagonal rule, i.e., elements are ordered according to

$$f(x, y) = ((y \times n) - ((n - 1) \times x))\%(n \times n) \qquad (1)$$

where $x = 0, ..., n - 1$ and $y = 0, ..., n - 1$. This grid *does* guarantee the RCP. For instance for $Q2 = \{0, 4, 7, 8, 10, 12, 13\}$ from Table 2, there is always at least one common element, i.e., $Q2 \cap rotate(Q2, i) \neq \emptyset$ for all $i \in 1, 2, ..., 15$.

4   RAC²E-gQS

Before going into details of the RAC²E-gQS rendezvous protocol, we describe concepts of two rendezvous approaches, namely the grid-based quorum (gQS) [3,4] and the asynchronous rendezvous RAC²E [2], which the designed protocol is composed of.

4.1   Grid QS Channel Mapping Algorithm

In [3,4] a fully distributed rendezvous (gQ-RDV) protocol has been designed, focusing on both the symmetric and asymmetric channel view (the same and different number, respectively, of available channels in individual sets). The outcome of the algorithm provides an input to the channel hopping sequences called channel maps. Each CR maps its channels according to the channel quality without any exchange of information, where the best channels get *priority*. The best channel is mapped according to the chosen *quorum*. Hence, CRs that allocate a common best channel, while having the *same* number of available channels, will always meet thanks to the quorum intersection property (if satisfying the RCP they also always meet regardless cycle misalignment). The period (cycle) of a channel map depends on the number of channels n and equals n^2 (selected from a $n \times n$ grid). Two channel mapping methods are designed for three or larger number of channels (i.e. $n \geq 3$). In both methods, channels are mapped to grid indexes (channel 1 (C_1) is mapped to index 0, channel 2 (C_2) to index 1 etc.), each channel in a CR network has its own index known by nodes. A CR node

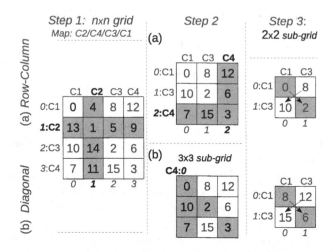

Fig. 2. Three steps of the channel mapping: (a) Row-Column, (b) Diagonal

adopts its map according to the quality of the channels, e.g., node A has the following map $2/4/3/1$, so C_2 is the best, C_4 is the second best etc.

In the first method, *Row-Column* mapping, in the first step (*Step 1* in Figure 2.(a)), a CR selects its map in a row-column manner, where the row number (channel number) is always equal to the column number (channel number). The best A's channel is channel 2, so it selects a quorum (*row=column=C2=index 1*). The set of elements, represented by $(1,1)$ quorum, maps channel 2 to $\{1, 4, 5, 9, 11, 13, 14\}$ slots. Each time when a set of elements is chosen, a grid is cut to a subgrid, together with the already mapped channel, i.e, each sub-grid maintains only the unallocated channels. A set of slots for consecutive channels (according to the quality) is mapped this way till we obtain a 2×2 sub-grid. Note that, each better quality channel has accordingly more mapped slots than a worse quality one. The last two channels are mapped to two slots in a *diagonal* manner. Analyzing the example (map $2/4/3/1$) from Figure 2.(a), channel 4 map (C4, C4) has set of slots: $\{3, 6, 7, 12, 15\}$ (Step 2), channel 3 is allocated in slot 0 and 2 and channel 1 to slot 8 and 10 (Step 3).

The second method, *Diagonal* mapping, is similar to the Row-Column mapping till we obtain a 3×3 sub-grid. The next channel is mapped (and a sub-grid is cut accordingly) in a column-*diagonal* manner, selecting the first column and the main diagonal, e.g., channel 4 is mapped to $\{0, 2, 3, 7, 10\}$ slots (*Step 2* in Figure 2.(b)). The last two channels are allocated as in the first method., i.e, channel 3 is mapped to slots 8 and 6, and channel 1 is mapped to slots 12 and 15 (*Step 3* in Figure 2.(b)). Note that, a channel map with 3 available channels is an exception following the Row-Column mapping, since the first (the best) channel should always follow a quorum concept.

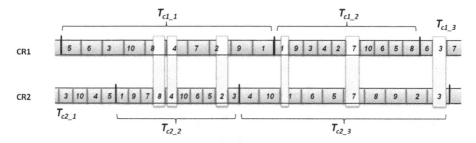

Fig. 3. The random cycle duration and asynchronous operation provides overlapping between the both CRs in the free channels (ch_i, $i = 1, ..., 10$)

4.2 RAC²E Protocol Description

The RAC²E [2] is a MAC protocol for distributed CRN environments. The protocol relies on an asynchronous operation of the nodes, eliminating the need of synchronization establishment, which is a difficult task in the distributed environments. Moreover, it fosters even an additional randomization among the nodes to ensure rapid rendezvous on a particular temporary unused channel from the primary system. The operation of the RDV phase of the RAC²E is illustrated on Figure 3. Each CR aiming to establish a control channel independently selects a random rendezvous cycle duration of Tc_{i_j} (i^{th} cognitive radio, j^{th} cycle). This time duration is selected uniformly in the range $[T_{min}, T_{max}]$, where $T_{min} = T_c - \frac{\Delta T}{2}$, $T_{max} = T_c + \frac{\Delta T}{2}$ and T_c represents the mean rendezvous cycle duration while $\Delta T = kT_c$ is the randomization interval. The chosen Tc_{i_j} interval is further segmented into M time slots, with each slot (having a duration of $\tau_{i\_j} = \frac{Tc_{i\_j}}{N}$) assigned to a particular channel unoccupied by the primary users. As illustrated on Figure 3, the randomization ensures that overlapping at the same channels occurs randomly in wider or narrower time intervals. In each slot interval τ_{i_j}, the CR sends a short beacon message at the beginning and end of the slot to signalize its presence in the channel. These particular times of beaconing are selected since they provide the highest probability of RDV between the CR nodes. In the meantime, between the both beacon messages, the RDV node aims to capture the beacons coming from the other CRs operating on the current channel. As Figure 4 illustrates, the randomization (i.e. asynchronous operation of the both nodes) guarantees that at least one of the beacon messages will be received by other nodes tuned to the same channel at the moment. This justifies the preference of a random Tc_{i_j} duration (Figure 3), which provides a more successful delivery of the beacon messages, in comparison to the synchronous case. A RDV occurs when two nodes are tuned to the same channel and they exchange at least one beacon and one beacon reply message. The condition $\tau' > \tau_{min}$ must be fulfilled for the rendezvous to occur, where τ' is the overlapping duration and τ_{min} is the required time for exchange and processing of both, the beacon and the beacon reply message (Figure 4). Generally, the τ_{min} duration

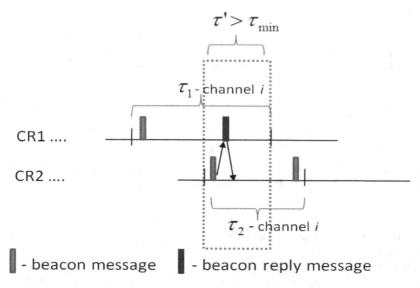

Fig. 4. Rendezvous at channel i event

is influenced by the used sample rates of the CR nodes and the length of the beacon and the beacon reply messages. Since there is not much information to transfer, the length of these messages can be in order of few bytes.

4.3 RAC²E-gQS Protocol Description

The mapping of channels into time slots in the RDV phase of the RAC²E is another important task. This can be done using several methods considering the channel *priorities* based on the channel ranking lists created in the sensing phase by each node independently. The channel mapping can be done utilizing:

☐ grid quorum strategies (gQS),

☐ random selection of channels using utility functions for channels priority-UP.

The combination of the RAC²E protocol with the gQS mapping can yield a powerful RAC^2E-gQS *rendezvous protocol* for asynchronous operation in a distributed environment assuring rapid RDV between the CR nodes. The analyses, in the next section, exploit four grid quorum strategies for channel mapping [3,4] (considering $M = N^2$ number of slots for N available channels): the Row-Column - RC and Column Diagonal - CD channel mapping, for the both grid forming methods: Pair-on-Pair-Grid (PoP) and Grid-Diagonal (GD), as well as the UP approach. The UP method randomly performs the channel mapping with probabilities guarantying that the channels, with respect to their priorities, will statistically be assigned to the same amount of slots per rendezvous cycle as the grid-quorum based methods. This channel mapping strategy is selected as a representative example since it probabilistically maps the channel to slots, oppositely on the regular grid mapping.

5   RAC²E-gQS Performance Evaluation

This section demonstrates the performance of the RAC²E-gQS protocol for the different channel mapping strategies introduced before. The UP based approach is compared with the *grid-quorum* approaches for channel order selection: RC and DC for the both ways of grid forming: PoP and GD.

The simulation analyses envision a scenario with two CRs aiming for a RDV on a certain common channel. Two cases are evaluated:

☐ -when CRs have the same channel ranking lists, e.g. both have 1/2/3/4/5 as a priority map for 5 free channels.

☐ -when both CRs have completely different channel ranking list, e.g. CR1 has 1/2/3/4/5 while CR2 has 5/4/3/2/1 in the case of 5 unoccupied channels.

These two cases are taken as representative examples, since they provide the two extremes of rendezvous performances, i.e. they are the best and the worst case scenarios.

One performance metric of interest in the analysis is the *average number of potential RDVs (channel matchings)* per cycle which is in inverse proportion to the time-to-rendezvous (TTR). The second evaluated performance metric is the *inter-rendezvous time variance*, representing the variance between two potential consecutive rendezvous, calculated with the following formulas:

$$\sigma^2_{irdv} = \frac{1}{N-1} \sum_{i=2}^{N} ((t_i - t_{i-1}) - \mu_{irdv})^2 \tag{2}$$

$$\mu_{irdv} = \frac{1}{N-1} \sum_{i=2}^{N} (t_i - t_{i-1}) \tag{3}$$

where σ^2_{irdv} is the inter-rendezvous time variance, μ_{irdv} is the mean inter-rendezvous time, N is the total number of rendezvous, while t_i is the time of rendezvous i. For the same number of average potential RDVs per cycle, a higher variance means that channel matchings occur in bursts, leaving longer gaps between bursts, while the lower variance represents the case when channel matchings are more regularly distributed in time. The lower variance case is better since it would assure that two CRs going online would not be stuck into the long no-RDV gaps before a successful RDV.

Monte Carlo simulations were made to test the performance of the RAC²E-gQS protocol, for 5, 10 and 20 channels. A total of 10000 trials (RDV cycles) with random start times of the CR nodes were made for each case for statistical correctness. The simulations were performed for a mean rendezvous cycle duration $T_c = 1s$ and duration of $\tau_{min} = 1\mu s$. This τ_{min} duration roughly maps to

Table 3. Minimum (Min), Maximum (Max) and average (Mean) number of potential
RDVs per cycle for gQS schemes in slot synchronized CRNs; No.c/s stands for Number
of channels / slots; List^{Rk} is the channel ranking lists

No.c/s	List^{Rk}	Metr.	PoP^{RC}	GD^{RC}	PoP^{DC}	GD^{DC}
5/25	same	Min	1	3	1	3
5/25	same	Mean	6.52	6.52	6.52	6.52
5/25	same	Max	25	25	25	25
5/25	different	Min	0	0	0	0
5/25	different	Mean	3.56	3.56	3.56	3.56
5/25	different	Max	7	7	7	7
10/100	same	Min	1	3	1	3
10/100	same	Mean	13.28	13.28	13.28	13.28
10/100	same	Max	100	100	100	100
10/100	different	Min	0	0	0	0
10/100	different	Mean	6.74	6.74	6.74	6.74
10/100	different	Max	20	28	30	28
20/400	same	Min	0	3	0	3
20/400	same	Mean	26.645	26.645	26.645	26.645
20/400	same	Max	400	400	400	400
20/400	different	Min	0	0	0	0
20/400	different	Mean	13.36	13.36	13.36	13.36
20/400	different	Max	158	108	160	108

a case when we have 10Msps sampling rate, 1 byte of beacon and beacon reply
message lengths and 4-QAM modulation. Different randomization intervals were
evaluated, for k ($k = \frac{T_c}{\Delta T}$) ranging from 1/4 up to 2 with step size of 1/4.

In order to justify the need of randomization introduced by RAC^{2}E, the grid-
QS mapping schemes were tested for a scenario of slot synchronized CRs aiming
for RDV. Slot shifts are likely to occur since both CRs do not start the RDV
phases simultaneously. Table 3 presents the performances of the grid-quorum
schemes in terms of the minimum, the maximum and the average number of
potential RDVs per cycle with respect to the slot shifts. As evident slot shifts
can cause a high TTR even in the case when both CRs have the same channel
ranking lists. The different ranking lists and several slot shifts between can result
in no RDV between the CRs.

Table 4 presents the average number of potential RDVs per cycle for the
RAC^{2}E-gQS protocol, for the *same channel ranking lists* and *different channel
ranking lists* of the CRs. It is evident that the case of the same channel ranking
lists of the both CRs, results in higher average number of potential RDVs per
cycle than the case with different channel ranking lists. RAC^{2}E improves the
RDV performances of the grid-quorum channel mapping schemes, as evident
comparing Table 3 and Table 4 results.

The channel matching percentage, calculated as the average number of potential
rendezvous per cycle divided by the number of slots, is about 52%, 26% and 13.25%

Table 4. Average Number of potential RDVs per cycle for the RAC^2E-gQS; No.c/s stands for Number of channels / slots; $List^{Rk}$ is the channel ranking lists

No.c/s	$List^{Rk}$	PoP^{RC}	GD^{RC}	PoP^{DC}	GD^{DC}	UP
5/25	same	13.042	13.042	13.037	13.043	13.041
5/25	different	7.1065	7.1207	7.0994	7.1045	3.6729
10/100	same	26.563	26.557	26.554	26.558	26.559
10/100	different	13.409	13.408	13.434	13.356	15.207
20/400	same	53.263	53.243	53.283	53.325	53.296
20/400	different	26.543	26.424	26.515	26.504	31.128

for 5, 10 and 20 number of channels, respectively, for the *same channel ranking lists* case and two times lower for the case with *different channel ranking lists*.

All inspected grid channel mapping methods ($PoP^{RC}, GD^{RC}, PoP^{DC}, GD^{DC}$), for the particular channel ranking cases and the particular numbers of available channels, provide the same average number of potential RDVs per cycle. The UP mapping method provides the same performances as the grid channel mapping methods when the CRs channel ranking maps are the same. In the case of different channel rankings the UP performances differ from the grid-based methods: lower number of free channels results in worse performances compared to the gQS methods; higher number of available channels results in better performances than the gQS schemes.

Although most of the methods experience the same or similar average number of potential RDVs per cycle, they differ in the inter-rendezvous time variance, as demonstrated on Figure 5. It presents the dependence of the variance between consecutive RDVs of the both users from the factor of randomization k ($k = \frac{T_c}{\Delta T}$), for the cases with the same and different channel ranking lists and for 5, 10 and 20 channels. UP achieves a lower variance between potential consecutive RDVs and outperforms the gQS strategies, only for the cases of higher number of free channels and different channel ranking lists, and lower number of free channels and the same ranking lists. The gQS strategies (RC-PoP, RC-GD, DC-PoP and DC-GD) perform better in all other cases. Among the grid quorum strategies, the DC-PoP and DC-DG achieve the lowest variance between RDVs, for the cases with large number of channels, different channel ranking lists and small number of channels, same ranking lists.

Regarding the randomization factor k, it is evident that there is an optimal setting providing the lowest variance between potential RDVs. The optimal k depends on the number of available channels, the difference between the channel ranking lists and the employed channel mapping method (Figure 5).

The fact that gQS strategies encounter somewhat worse performance for the cases of a *larger* number of channels and *different* channel ranking lists (e.g., in the case with 20 channels the UP inter-rendezvous variance is ~ 0.008 better than that of gQS) is as expected, since in gQS each better quality channel has accordingly more mapped slots than a worse quality one, but always in a *regular* distributed manner. Although UP channels are also assigned to the same

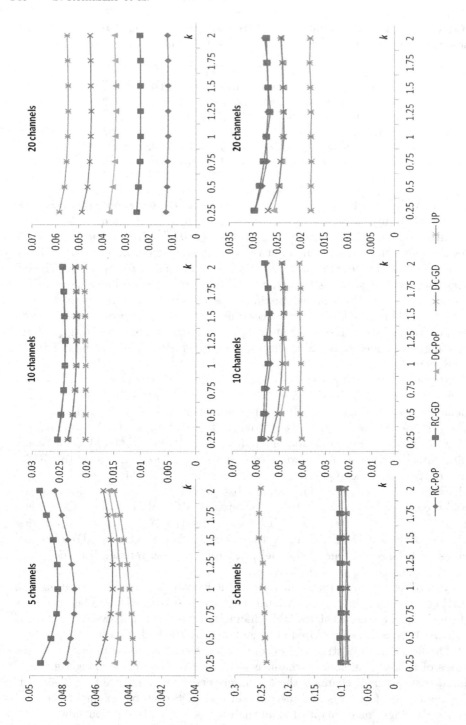

Fig. 5. Inter-rendezvous time variance σ^2_{irdv} [sec^2] vs randomization coefficient k, first row: same channel ranking case, second row: different channel ranking case

amount of slots as in gQS, the *random* mapping increases an amount of RDVs as well as decreases an inter-rendezvous time variance with a larger number of available channels. The opposite behavior, i.e., a *large* number of channels but the *same* channel ranking lists can justify this reasoning, since regularly mapping is noticeable better approach (e.g., in the case with 20 channels the gQS inter-rendezvous variance can be even ~ 0.05 better than that of UP), but it is favorable to have the same amount of assigned slots for the same channel while having a large number of free channels. Moreover, while having a *smaller* number of channels in a set (e.g., 5 channels), the regular grid mapping is definitely better (it decreases the inter-rendezvous variance around 0.15), as a difference of the amount of assigned slots of better quality-channels and worse quality-channels is not so drastic as in scenarios with a large number of free channels.

6   Conclusion

This paper proposes a RDV protocol for CRANs that (1) utilizes the asynchronous and randomness properties of the RAC^2E protocol and (2) the grid quorum channel mapping (gQ-RDV) protocol taking into account channel heterogeneity. We showed that the combination of the RAC^2E protocol with the gQS mapping can yield a powerful RAC^2E-gQS rendezvous protocol for asynchronous operation in a distributed environment assuring rapid RDV between the CR nodes.

In our future work the gQS approach will be enhanced to improve its performance in the case of a large number of channels and different channel ranking lists. An asymmetric channel view (different number of available channels) will also be investigated. Finally, the algorithms will be implemented on a testbed platform with USRP nodes in order to evaluate both approaches in real conditions.

Acknowledgments. We thank Professor Petri Mähönen for fruitful discussions. This work was funded by FP7-ICT NoE ACROPOLIS project [23]. We also thank a partial financial support from Deutsche Forschungsgemeinschaft and RWTH Aachen University through UMIC-research centre.

References

1. Akyildiz, I.F., Lee, W.-Y., Chowdhury, K.R.: CRAHNs: Cognitive radio ad hoc networks. Ad Hoc Networks 7, 810–836 (2009)
2. Pavlovska, V., Denkovski, D., Atanasovski, V., Gavrilovska, L.: RAC2E: Novel Rendezvous Protocol for Asynchronous Cognitive Radios in Cooperative Environments. In: PIMRC, Turkey (2010)
3. Romaszko, S., Mähönen, P.: Grid-based Channel Mapping in Cognitive Radio Ad hoc Networks. In: PIMRC, Canada (2011)
4. Romaszko, S., Mähönen, P.: Quorum-based Channel Allocation with Asymmetric Channel View in Cognitive Radio Networks. In: MSWiM Poster and 6th ACM PM2HW2N Workshop, USA (2011)

5. Silvius, M.D., Ge, F., Young, A., MacKenzie, A.B., Bostian, C.W.: Smart Radio: spectrum access for first responders. In: Wireless Sensing and Processing III, SPIE (2008)
6. Theis, N.C., Thomas, R.W., DaSilva, L.A.: Rendezvous for cognitive radios. IEEE Transactions on Mobile Computing 10, 216–227 (2010)
7. Liu, H., Lin, Z., Chu, X., Leung, Y.W.: Ring-walk based channel hopping algorithms with guaranteed rendezvous for cognitive radio networks. In: International Workshop on Wireless Sensor, Actuator and Robot Networks (WiSARN 2010-FALL), in Conjunction with IEEE/ACM CPSCom, China (2010)
8. Lin, Z., Liu, H., Chu, X., Leung, Y.W.: Jump-stay based channel hopping algorithm with guaranteed rendezvous for cognitive radio networks. In: IEEE INFOCOM, China (2011)
9. Chao, C.M., Tsai, H.C., Huang, K.J.: A new channel hopping mac protocol for mobile ad hoc networks. In: Wireless Communications and Signal Processing, WCSP (2009)
10. Chao, C.M., Wang, Y.Z.: A multiple rendezvous multichannel mac protocol for underwater sensor networks. In: WCNC, Australia (2010)
11. Lee, E.K., Oh, S.Y., Gerla, M.: Randomized channel hopping scheme for anti-jamming communication. In: Wireless Days, Venice, Italy (2010)
12. Luk, W.S., Wong, T.: Two new quorum based algorithms for distributed mutual exclusion. In: 17th International Conference on Distributed Computing Systems, ICDCS, USA (1997)
13. Hall, J.: Combinatorial Theory chapter 1. John Wiley and Sons (1986)
14. Bian, K., Park, J.M., Chen, R.: A quorum-based framework for establishing control channels in dynamic spectrum access networks. In: 15th Annual International Conference on Mobile Computing and Networking, MobiCom, China (2009)
15. Hou, F., Cai, L.X., Shen, X., Huang, J.: Asynchronous multichannel mac design with difference-set-based hopping sequences. IEEE Transactions on Vehicular Technology 60, 1728–1739 (2011)
16. Shin, J., Yang, D., Kim, C.: A Channel Rendezvous Scheme for Cognitive Radio Networks. IEEE Communications Letters 14(10), 954–956 (2010)
17. Robertson, A., Tran, L., Molnar, J., Fu, E.H.F.: Experimental comparison of blind rendezvous algorithms for tactical networks. In: IEEE CORAL 2012 in Conjunction with IEEE WoWMoM 2012, San Francisco, USA (2012)
18. Balachandran, K., Kang, J.: Neighbor discovery with dynamic spectrum access in adhoc networks. In: IEEE 63rd Vehicular Technology Conference, VTC 2006-Spring, vol. 2, pp. 512–517 (2006)
19. Universal Software Radio Peripheral (USRP), http://www.ettus.com
20. Bian, K., Par, J.-M.: Asynchronous Channel Hopping for Establishing Rendezvous in Cognitive Radio Networks. In: IEEE INFOCOM, China (2011)
21. Jiang, J.R., Tseng, Y.C., Hsu, C.S., Lai, T.H.: Quorum-based asynchronous power-saving protocols for IEEE 802.11 ad hoc networks. In: Parallel Processing (2003)
22. Maekawa, M.: A p N algorithm for mutual exclusion in decentralized systems. ACM Trans. Comput. Syst. 3, 145–159 (1985)
23. FP7-ICT NoE ACROPOLIS project, http://www.ict-acropolis.eu

DISON: A Self-organizing Network Management Framework for Wireless Sensor Networks

Trang Cao Minh, Boris Bellalta, and Miquel Oliver

Universitat Pompeu Fabra, Barcelona, Spain
{trang.cao,boris.bellalta,miquel.oliver}@upf.edu

Abstract. Wireless sensor networks have a wide variety of applications in many areas from detecting enemy targets in the military to monitoring patient health or water/gas usage in the civil. However, sensor devices are usually equipped with a limited power battery and deployed at a very high density in inaccessible environments. Therefore, it is impractical to change or maintain manually these sensor networks. In this paper, we have designed and implemented a general and extendable management framework called DIstributed Self-Organizing NEtwork management (DISON) framework to provide an autonomous management mechanism for WSNs. In DISON, sensor nodes exploit local knowledge or cooperate with other nodes to coordinate and adapt management and application tasks effectively according to their capabilities. To verify the efficiency of the proposed framework, we have evaluated DISON in a data collection application scenario, where DISON is used to optimize the number of active nodes. The simulation results show that running DISON reduces the energy consumption up to 30%, and also improves other key parameters such as the packet delivery rate and the end-to-end delay.

Keywords: network management, wireless sensor networks, self organizing.

1 Introduction

With the rapid development of technologies in IC (Integrated Circuit) and MEMS (Microelectromechanical systems), Wireless Sensor Networks (WSNs), networks of tiny sensor devices, have been extensively used nowadays in various applications such as target tracking, habitat monitoring and many others. However, sensor nodes have very limited power and resource constraints. Therefore, they are prone to fail. The sensor failure may cause changes in network topology and affect the quality of offered services. Moreover, sensor nodes can be deployed in a large number of nodes and in inaccessible environments depending on the application. Thus, the manual replacement of failed sensor nodes is impossible or expensive. To cope with these challenges, the development of self-organizing management functionalities in WSNs is desirable.

Due to the limited resource nature of sensor nodes, a management system for WSNs needs to be lightweight, autonomous and scalable. In addition, the

J. Zheng et al. (Eds.): Adhocnets 2012, LNICST 111, pp. 149–163, 2013.
© Institute for Computer Sciences, Social Informatics and Telecommunications Engineering 2013

requirements of WSN applications are expected to evolve over time. Therefore, a WSN management system should be able to adapt the network operations not only to the network state but also to the changes in application requirements. Moreover, it is complex and not efficient to develop an adaptive management system for each application or each hardware platform. Hence, it is required to develop a management system that supports various applications and platforms.

Many network management architectures for WSNs have been designed. Some policy based management approaches are introduced in [2], [5]. In [2], Cha et al. proposed a hierarchical framework in which the base station is responsible for interpreting high level management policies and distributing them to sensor nodes. These policies are applied locally on sensor nodes as soon as the node state matches the policy condition. Therefore, their approach requires the base station to maintain the up-to-date global view of the network which is not always available, especially in large scale networks. Le et al. [5] proposed three level management policies to distribute management tasks to the base station, cluster heads and sensor nodes. However, management policies in their approach are represented in the high level XML language [1] at the base station, and interpreted to the machine code at sensor nodes.

In [8], the authors divided the network into multiple clusters in which each cluster has a gateway node that organizes and manages network operations based on application requirements and the available energy in sensor nodes. However, their approach mainly focus on finding data relay routes and arbitrating medium access. WinMS [6] allows individual sensor nodes to perform management functions locally based on the network state of their neighbors. In addition, the base station works as a central manager to store, analyze the global state of the network and execute management maintenance operations if it detects any interesting event. Other policy-based management systems are also presented in [11], [7]. However, there are some issues which are not covered by the existing approaches. First, there is no work on defining in detail management data models or management mechanisms used in sensor nodes. Second, the capability to adapt to the changes in application requirements is not completely taken into account in current management approaches.

In this paper, we propose a DIstributed Self-Organizing Network management (DISON) framework that provides an autonomous management mechanism to allow sensor nodes to self configure and adapt to the changes in application requirements, resources and network state. In DISON, sensor nodes perform management tasks at different level according to their resources. Sensor nodes with limited resources can exploit their local knowledge to reconfigure their operations and provide management information for other nodes. In case of nodes that have more resources (ex. more powerful battery or larger memory), more complex management tasks can be performed by them. One example is they can coordinate application tasks among a set of nearby nodes. Another example is they collect management data from a set of nodes to detect if there is any problem and reconfigure the operation of these nodes if needed. Sink nodes or base stations which are normally connected to large power suppliers and have strong computing capacity are responsible for global management tasks such as topology management and disseminating new code to support new management tasks. We have implemented and evaluated DISON framework in SENSE simulator [3] to organize active sensor nodes in a data collection application. Our simulation results show that DISON can reduce the energy consumption, up to 30%, and improve other network performance metrics such as the packet delivery rate and the end-to-end delay.

The rest of the paper is organized as follows. In Section 2, we describe the DISON system overall. Section 3 presents the detail of the DISON Management components. Section 4 presents the scenario in which DISON is evaluated. In Section 5 we show and discuss the simulation results. The conclusions are presented in Section 6.

2   DISON Framework

Since wireless sensor networks can be deployed with a large number of nodes, central management systems are not suitable for WSNs due to the delay to take management decisions and distribute them, and the traffic congestion at nodes which are close to the central manager. The distributed management solutions also have drawbacks. Due to the limited energy battery and resources, sensor nodes can not do complicated management functions. Therefore, it is essential to use a hybrid solution, combining both distributed and centralized techniques, for management in WSNs. Every sensor node should have the ability to do simple local management tasks while complex management decisions should be only performed by some powerful nodes.

In this article, we have developed a hybrid self-organizing management framework for WSNs. Nodes in the network can have different roles in performing management tasks according to theirs capabilities. In our framework, we define three types of management roles: Self Manager (SM), Group Manager (GM) and Network Manager (NM). A SM role contains abilities to control, regulate and adapt the node's behavior in accord with the changes in application requirements, the node's resources and the neighborhood information. The GM role is used to achieve an effective utilization of the resources in a set of nodes by coordinating nodes' operations. The GM role is normally performed by nodes that have rich resources and energy. The NM role is used to manage the whole network. For example, it stores the network topology or decides the nodes that have the GM and the SM role. Therefore the NM role should be performed by the base station. The GM role is normally assigned to some sensor nodes which have rich resources while the SM role should be performed by every node. Be aware that a sensor node can have both SM and GM roles if it has enough resources. Figure 1 depicts our proposed framework. The network is divided into multiple sets of nodes. Each set of nodes are managed by a node with the GM role, called Manager node. The whole network is managed by Base Station with the NM role. Every nodes are assigned SM role. If the node only has SM role, it is called Normal node.

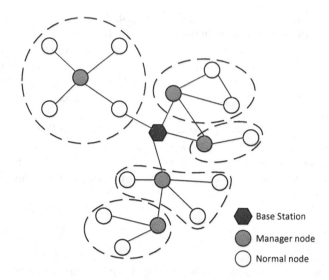

Fig. 1. DISON System Overview

Only the GM role needs to be distributed through the WSN in an efficient way. One distributing approach is using central servers (base stations) to assign the GM role to a certain group of nodes based on the network topology. This approach is efficient for networks which have a fixed topology and a small number of nodes. Another approach is the use of clustering algorithms [4][9]. The chosen cluster heads, which are elected by using a clustering algorithm, are suitable to role as Manager nodes. Since the clustering algorithms do not make any assumptions about the presence of infrastructure, they are useful for networks that do not have a fixed and stable topology, a common case in wireless sensor networks.

In this article, we focus on the design of a WSN architecture that have GM and SM roles. We propose a new protocol stack for the sensor nodes as illustrated in Figure 2. The first element, Hardware APIs, provides access interfaces to

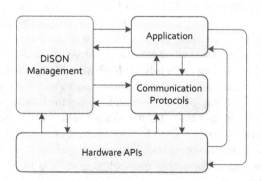

Fig. 2. Protocol Stack of a sensor node in DISON framework

the controller, communication devices, storage resources, sensors and the power supply of the sensor node. Examples of these interfaces are switch on/off the node, read/write the memory, switch on/off the radio. The second element of the DISON node is the Communication Protocols that govern data transmission through wireless channel by using the Hardware APIs interfaces. In the Communication Protocols, several protocols are implemented: MAC, routing, location and time synchronization. The third element is Application. It is responsible for sending sensor data and receiving user requests by using communication protocols. It can also access the interfaces in Hardware APIs component to trigger sensors and receive sensing data. The last element is DISON Management. This element provides mechanisms to analyze the changes in application requirements, node's resources, and network state to reconfigure the communication protocols and the application if needed to ensure the required quality of service or to prolong network lifetime.

3   DISON Management Components

This section presents further details on the DISON Management part of the proposed protocol stack. As illustrated in Figure 3, there are three main components: Context Establishment, Policy based Reasoning and Controlling Response. The Context Establishment component is responsible for extracting meaningful contexts from the raw data such as application requirements, the node's residual energy or the packet error rate. In our framework, a meaningful context is the information that affects node's operations. Based on the meaningful context extracted by the Context Establishment component, the Policy based Reasoning component selects a set of policies that govern node behaviors or network operations. The Controlling Response component is responsible for executing the actions indicated in those policies. It is important to note that only the basic functions of the DISON architecture are implemented in each node at the initialization. When there is a change on a node's resources or in the network state, a node can request to the base station or other nodes to provide it with new functions to ensure that it can complete the management tasks it has assigned.

3.1   Context Establishment

The main goal of the Context Establishment (CE) component is to form the meaningful context from the given current raw data. In order to accomplish this goal, the CE component predefined context formats are stored in the Context Database. Using these formats, the sub component Context Interpreter recognizes the context values, handles missing values, removes redundant data and finally forms the requested context. Then the resulting context is transmitted to the Policy based Reasoning component.

As shown in Figure 3, there are three sources that produce context information: **Node Information** which is the information about sensing capabilities, the residual energy, the memory status, the node location and the radio state;

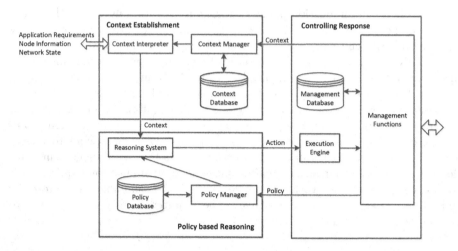

Fig. 3. DISON Components and Process

Application Requirements which include the query information such as what types of sensing data are needed, when it needs to collect data, the data sample rates, and how long data is collected; **Network State** which includes some network performance metrics such as the transmission delay, the packet error rate and the neighborhood information such as the number of neighbors and their information. Due to the limited resources of sensor nodes, the context representation scheme and the context interpreter mechanism need to be simple but efficient. To achieve this, we model the context which are stored in the Context Database as follows

[CONTEXT_ID] [INFORMATION_TYPE] [INFORMATION_ID] [INFORMATION_VALUE]

where CONTEXT_ID is the unique identifier of the context, INFORMATION_TYPE describes the source of the raw information; INFORMATION_ID represents the identifier of each specific information such as the sensing capabilities, the residual energy, etc; and INFORMATION_VALUE is the value of that specific information in bits. This model ensures that the context is stored and queried efficiently based on the characteristic of each source of raw information and the information itself. For example, we represent the sensing capability of the sensor node as in Table 1. It is easy to see that each position in 7 bits corresponds to one sensing ability. Hence, the **"temperature sensor is on"** context is represented as 01 001 0000001 where 01 is INFORMATION_TYPE, 001 is INFORMATION_ID, 0000001 is INFORMATION_VALUE. Similarly, 01 001 0000011 means temperature and light sensors are on.

Another example is the node receives a query that requests to collect temperature during 10 seconds with a frequency of 2 seconds. After analyzing the query, the above context is represented as 10 001 0000001101010 where 10 indicates that the information is an Application Requirement, 001 indicates that

Table 1. Sensing Capability Value

Sensor Type	Bits	Meaning
NO SENSOR	0000000	No sensor is enabled
TEMPERATURE	0000001	Temperature sensor is enabled
LIGHT	0000010	Light sensor is enabled
HUMIDITY	0000100	Humidity sensor is enabled
ACCELEROMETER	0001000	Accelerometer sensor is enabled
MAGNETOMETER	0010000	Magnetometer sensor is enabled
MICROPHONE	0100000	Microphone sensor is enabled
SOUNDER	1000000	Sounder sensor is enabled

the application is a query, the array of bits 0000001101010 contains the sensing type, the query period and the sampling frequency. In order to prevent any waste of memory resources, we limit the number of contexts each node can have according to its management role. Nodes with the SM role will have less contexts than nodes with the GM role. The Context Manager in the CE component is responsible for adding new contexts or removing old contexts if the number of contexts reaches a predefined threshold.

3.2 Policy-Based Reasoning

The second component of DISON Management, Policy-based Reasoning (PBR), is responsible for determining whether, or which respectively, actions should be taken referring to the changes in node's state, network conditions or application requirements. It is essential to see that in this scenario the rule based policy solution appears naturally. In general, a rule based policy system is to decide the set of actions to be executed in a given situation based on rules. The advantage of rule-based solutions is their flexibility. Rules can be modified and added at application runtime with no need for code recompilation. Due to the heterogeneous characteristics of sensor networks, it is beneficial to use a mechanism that offers such flexibility for the reasoning process. Therefore we have built our reasoning mechanism based on a rule-based system. We form a rule based policy in the Policy Database as the following formula:

[SET OF CONTEXTS] [SET OF ACTIONS]

The left hand side of a policy includes identifiers of contexts (CONTEXT_ID) which is combined by conditional elements such as 'AND', 'OR', 'NOT', etc. The right hand side is the set of actions to be executed when the policy is applied. Each action is represented by a couple (ActionID, Parameters) where ActionID is the identifier of the action (e.g. reconfiguring networks, route discovery ...) and Parameters is the list of the parameters used by the action. When receiving the context from the CE component, the Reasoning System queries the list of policies in Policy Database that matches to the context. Utilizing the query results, it chooses which policies have to be activated. If one of the existing policies satisfies completely the context, it extracts the list of actions in the policy and sends them to the Controlling Response. Otherwise, it gets the default policy that includes actions such as ignoring this context or asking support from other nodes. For example, when a node receives a query that requests to collect temperature, it needs to turn on the temperature sensor to collect data and start the communication protocols to transmit the data to the sink. To support that scenario, a policy is defined as 0001 0001 1 0000001 in which, the first 0001 is the identifier of the **"temperature sensor is on"** context, the second 0001 indicates the hardware function that needs to execute is the "switching sensor", 1 0000001 are parameters provided to the switching sensor function (e.g 1 means switch on and 0000001 means temperature sensor).

Similar to the CE component, the PBR component also limits the number of policies and the complexity of the reasoning system according to the node management roles. Nodes with the GM role have more policies and more powerful reasoning systems.

3.3 Controlling Response

As soon as receiving the list of actions to be executed from the PBR component, the subcomponent Execution Engine maps the actions with the management functions it supports and executes them. The Management functions element includes the local functions that control hardware devices and protocols that implement the cooperative management tasks. The Management Database is used to store buffers and variables used in management tasks.

4   A Data Collection Scenario

In this section, we apply the proposed DISON framework to resolve a popular data collection application scenario in WSNs. In this scenario, we consider a WSN in which sensor nodes are randomly deployed in a square or rectangle area. We assume that sensor nodes have different energy and sensing capabilities. For example, some nodes can have both the temperature and the light sensor while other nodes only have the temperature sensor. A sink node (base station) broadcasts a query to network at specific times to collect sensing data. A query includes three parameters: types of sensing data, the sampling frequency and the collecting period. The types of sensing data is encoded based on the Table 1. For example, a query to collect light and temperature every 10 seconds for 1000 seconds is represented by a triple (3, 10, 1000).

Since sensor nodes are densely deployed, there might have more than two nodes at each sensing area unit. It results in the data redundancy and non efficient resources usage if all nodes collect data and transmit it to the sink. Therefore it is necessary to choose some active nodes to collect and transmit data while other nodes are switched to sleeping state to save energy if they do not affect the network connectivity and the full sensing coverage. There are some approaches to handle this issue as in [10]. However their solutions are based on the assumption that sensor nodes know their geographical location. This assumption is not practical and expensive even though we can use location algorithms to find approximately locations of sensor nodes.

In our proposal, we divide the network area into a grid of multiple adjacent cells. The grid is symmetric or asymmetric. Nodes are deployed randomly in each cell of the grid. We assume that each node can know the identifier of the cell where it is located and its sensing radius covers that cell. This assumption is different to the assumption in which the node knows its geographic location. First of all, the network grid is built based on the structure of the deployment area. For example, if sensor nodes are deployed in a building, the network grid will be the room structure of the building and each cell is corresponding to a room. In case sensor nodes are deployed on streets, we can use the GOOGLE map application to build the network grid. Second, the process of building the network grid is performed at the base station before deployment. Therefore, it is not constrained by the energy or resources. After building the network grid, each cell in the network grid is assigned a unique identifier. These identifiers can be assigned to sensor nodes manually before deployment or automatically in run time. For example, we can have a special device moving around the network area. This device has the GPS module and the WIFI/3G connection that allows it to detect its geographic position and communicate with the base station to determine the cell where it is currently located. Then it broadcasts beacons that include the cell identifier to nearby nodes. As soon as sensor nodes receive a beacon, they assign their cell identifier to the one indicated in the beacon.

After deployment, every node broadcasts its presence to neighbor nodes. Then, some random nodes calculate the capability function based on the node resources and decide to start the manager election round. After the round ends, the network is divided into sets of nodes. In each set of nodes there is a Manager node with the GM role. The sink roles as Network Manager. We assume that it knows the cell identifier of every node in network. This assumption is used to calculate performance metrics.

When receiving a query from the sink, each sensor node needs to consider whether or not it performs that task. First of all, it checks the context of the query. If the node has the required sensing capabilities, it executes the corresponding action, the task registering by transmitting a Task Register Message (TREG) to its Manager node. The TREG message includes the unique identifier of the request query, the node capability, the identifier of the cell where the node is located and the cell code. The node capability is calculated based on the battery information, the number of hops to the sink, the number of internal links which are links to nodes in the same cell and the number of external links which are links to nodes in other cells as in the Equation 1.

$$\text{capability} = \alpha_1 \cdot \text{BL} + \alpha_2 \cdot \text{HC} + \alpha_3 \cdot \text{IL} + \alpha_4 \cdot \text{EL} \tag{1}$$

in which BL is the battery level, HC is the number of hops to the sink, IL is the number of internal links, EL is the number of external links, α_1, α_2, α_3, α_4 are the priorities of the battery level, the number of hops to the sink, the number of internal links and the number of external links correspondingly. It it important to note that these parameters are normalized before they are used by dividing for the corresponding maximum value. In our scenario, the priorities of the battery level and the number of external links are setup higher than other ones in order to ensure that if nodes have higher power and more connections to other cells, they will have higher probability of being selected. The cell code is a special value to encode adjacent cells that a node can connect. Figure 4 illustrates how to calculate the 8-bit cell code on the two plane area. The node maps the relative location of the connected cell to a corresponding bit in the cell code. For example, if the node has a link to the north west cell, the bit 1 of the cell code is ON. A cell code 01001001 indicates that the node can connect to the cells: north west, west, and south. Node A has a better cell code than node B if all ON bits of cell code B is ON on cell code A and there is at least a ON bit in cell code A that is not ON in cell code B. For example, if cell code A is 01001001 and cell code B is 00001001, we can infer that the node A has a better cell code than node B. In other words, node A covers all links to other cells of node B, that is, if node B switches to sleeping state, node A can ensure the connectivity of adjacency nodes are not affected.

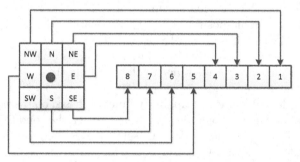

N: North – W: West – E: East – S: South

Fig. 4. Cell code illustration

When the Manager node receives TREG messages from nodes in its managed set, it groups all nodes that have same query request and same cell identifier together. In each group, it chooses nodes which have the highest capability and the best cell code as active nodes. Other nodes are considered as redundant nodes. Then, the Manager node broadcasts a Task Response Message (TREP) message to inform nodes in its managed set. As receiving TREP, the node checks if it is a redundant node. If yes, the node broadcast a SLP (Sleep) beacon to its neighbors to inform it will go to the sleeping state, then it waits a period of time T before going to the sleeping state. Otherwise, it starts performing the requested query task. If a neighbor node receives an SLP beacon and detects that the sleeping node is the unique connection to other cells, it sends a Active Request (AR) beacon to the sleeping node. During the period T, if the sleeping node receives any AR beacon from its neighbor, it ignores the query task but still works as a forwarding node. Otherwise, it changes to the sleeping state to save energy.

5   Evaluation

We have implemented the above scenario in SENSE [3]. For comparison, we have implemented a data collection application where all sensor nodes transmit data to the sink as soon as receiving the query as the baseline, and refer to it as BDC. In BDC, the data relay path is built on the query broadcasting process. Each node setups the node from which it receives the query as the next node to forward data. We also have built the forwarding mechanism in DISON based on the query request similarly to BDC. However, DISON stores the identifier of the cell from which it receives the query instead of the node identifier because DISON could switch off some nodes which can be on the data relay route to save energy. When the node need to send or forward data to the sink, it adds the cell identifier to the data packet and broadcast to its neighbors. If the neighbor nodes are in the indicated cell, they forward the packet. Otherwise, they drop the packet.

In our experiments, we consider one symmetric scenario and one asymmetric scenario. In the symmetric scenario, the network is deployed in a 10x10 grid, in which each cell has a radius of 40m. In the asymmetric one, we use a 10x2 grid, that could be similar to the room structure of an office building floor. Sensor nodes are randomly placed in each cell of the grid with a density from 2 to 4 nodes. Moreover, in order to ensure the reality of the performance results we have also placed sensor nodes randomly through all the area and vary the number of nodes in case of the asymmetric grid. The transmitting radius of a sensor node is 50m. The battery level of each node is generated randomly in the range of $[0, 10^6]$J. We define one special node as the sink and put it randomly in the grid. The sink node is responsible for broadcasting a query at a specific time to collect data from the network. The time to start querying is set randomly in the range $[80, 90]$ seconds. We set the sampling frequency to 10 seconds. The period of collecting sensing data is chosen randomly in the range $[1000, 1200]$ seconds. Every random number in the simulator is generated by using a linear congruential algorithm and 48-bit integer arithmetic. The simulation results are calculated based on the results from running each scenario with 10 different seed numbers. The other parameters are set as in Table 2.

In order to calculate the coverage ratio, we calculate the number of packets including sensing data from each cell at the sink node. We denote $recv_i$ as the number of received packets including the sensing data from i^{th} cell. Assume that each sensor node transmits sensing data to the base station in the interval T seconds with a rate APP_RATE. To make it clearly, T is the query period and APP_RATE is the sensing data sampling frequency. If the condition shown in the Equation 2 is satisfied, the ith cell is considered as transmitting enough data to the sink. In other words, i^{th} cell is covered. The simulation area is fully covered if every cell in the simulation area is covered.

Table 2. Network Settings

Parameters	Value
Tx Power	$24, 75 \cdot 10^{-3}$ J
Rx Power	$13, 5 \cdot 10^{-3}$ J
Channel	Error-free
Tx Rate	125 kbps
MAC layer	IEEE 802.11 (DCF)
Transmitting Radius	50 m
Simulation Time	3000s
Threshold	0.8

$$\text{recv}_i = \text{Threshold} \cdot \left\lceil \frac{T}{\text{APP\_RATE}} \right\rceil \tag{2}$$

We use the following metrics to evaluate our proposal:

- **Average Node Used Energy.** The average used energy of each node.
- **Packet Delivery Rate (PDR).** The percentage of packets generated at the sensor nodes that are successfully delivered to the sink.
- **Coverage Percentage.** The percentage of the number of covered cells per total cells in the grid.
- **End-to-End Delay.** The average time taken for a packet to be transmitted across the network from the node to the sink.

In case of the 10x10 grid scenario (Figure 5), the packet delivery rate is improved significantly for all node density values, up to 30% at node density 4. The

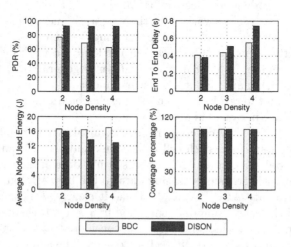

Fig. 5. Grid 10x10

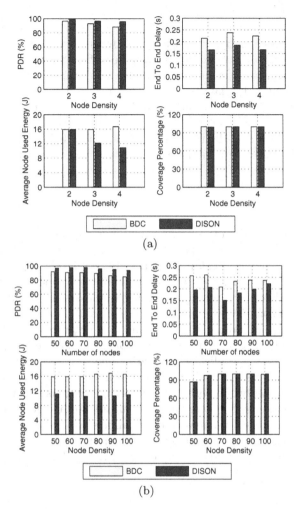

Fig. 6. Grid 10x2: (a) Variable Node density, (b) Variable Number of Nodes

end-to-end delay of the DISON solution is higher than BDC because there are more successfull received packets in DISON, and these packets can be sent from nodes which are far from the sink. Therefore it results in an increase of the average delay. It is important that the used energy is reduced significantly, up to 23% at node density 4.

As shown in Figure 6(a), DISON solution does not improve the used energy comparing to BDC if there are only two nodes in each cell. However it increases the packet delivery rate slightly and reduces the end-to-end delay significantly. It is because the energy that saves from switching off some nodes is approximately the same as the required management overhead in DISON. In addition, as the number of nodes that transmit data to the sink decreases, it results in less traffic in the network. Therefore the packet delivery rate and the end-to-end delay are improved. When the node density increases to 3 and 4, we can see that DISON reduces the power consumption from 18% to 29% because there are more redundant nodes that can be switched off without compromising the network operation. Moreover, it also improves significantly the packet delivery rate and the end-to-end delay. In case nodes are randomply placed in all the area, DISON still achieve better performance than BDC (Figure 6(b)). The used energy and the end to end delay of DISON is much lower than BDC while the packet delivery rate is also slightly higher. In addition, it is easy to see that the sensing coverage is ensured in all scenarios.

6   Conclusion

This article presents a hybrid, self-organizing management framework for wireless sensor networks. In the proposed framework, sensor nodes participate in the self-organizing management process at different levels depending on their resources and the relationship with their neighbors and to the network at large. We have presented a new protocol stack for wireless sensor nodes to support management functions. This protocol stack allows each sensor node to reconfigure its operations according to the application requirements, resources and network state. We have analyzed and have implemented the management framework in a data collection application scenario. The simulation results show that the proposed framework not only reduces the node's energy consumption but also improves other network performance metrics such as the packet delivery rate and the end-to-end delay. In the near future, we are going to implement and evaluate the proposed framework in dynamic scenarios where, for instance, the network topology changes rapidly due to the node mobility and in multiservices WSNs where there are multiple sinks with different types of requests as well.

References

1. Biron, P.V., Malhotra, A.: XML Schema Part 2: Datatypes. W3C Recommendation. W3C, 2nd edn (October 2004)
2. Cha, S.-H., Lee, J.-E., Jo, M., Youn, H.Y., Kang, S., Cho, K.-H.: Policy-based management for self-managing wireless sensor networks. IEICE Transactions, 3024–3033 (2007)
3. Chen, G., Branch, J., Pflug, M., Zhu, L., Szymanski, B.: SENSE: A Sensor Network Simulator. In: Advances in Pervasive Computing and Networking, pp. 249–267 (2004)
4. Chen, Y.P., Liestman, A.L., Liu, J.: Clustering Algorithms for Ad Hoc Wireless Networks. In: Ad Hoc and Sensor Networks. Nova Science Publishers (2004)
5. Le, T.D., Hu, W., Jha, S., Corke, P.: Design and implementation of a policy-based management system for data reliability in wireless sensor networks. In: 33rd IEEE Conference on Local Computer Networks, LCN 2008, pp. 762–769 (October 2008)

6. Lee, W.L., Datta, A., Oliver, R.C.: WinMS: Wireless Sensor Network-Management System, An Adaptive Policy-Based Management for Wireless Sensor Networks. Technical report, School of Computer Science & Software Engineering, The University of Western Australia (2006)
7. Wenbo, Z., Haifeng, X.: A Policy Based Wireless Sensor Network Management Architecture. In: 2010 3rd International Conference on Intelligent Networks and Intelligent Systems, ICINIS, pp. 552–555 (November 2010)
8. Younis, M., Youssef, M., Arisha, K.: Energy-aware management for cluster-based sensor networks. Computer Networks, 649–668 (2003)
9. Younis, O., Fahmy, S.: HEED: A Hybrid, Energy-Efficient, Distributed Clustering Approach for Ad Hoc Sensor Networks. IEEE Transactions on Mobile Computing 3(4), 366–379 (2004)
10. Zhang, H., Hou, J.: Maintaining Sensing Coverage and Connectivity in Large Sensor Networks. Ad Hoc & Sensor Wireless Networks 1(1-2) (2005)
11. Zhu, Y., Keoh, S.L., Sloman, M., Lupu, E.C.: A Lightweight Policy System for Body Sensor Networks. IEEE Transactions on Network and Service Management 6(3), 137–148 (2009)

A Flexible Deterministic Approach to Key Pre-distribution in Grid Based WSNs

Sarbari Mitra, Sourav Mukhopadhyay, and Ratna Dutta

Department of Mathematics
Indian Institute of Technology, Kharagpur, India
{sarbari,sourav,ratna}@maths.iitkgp.ernet.in

Abstract. In this paper we present a key pre-distribution scheme adapting a deterministic approach. The distribution of keys to the nodes precedes a virtual arrangement of the nodes into a rectangular grid structure. Distribution of keys is based on projective planes and pairwise connectivity. If the nodes are mapped to the vertices of a graph then the shortest path between any two nodes (considering key-connectivity) is at most three. With a small memory, the nodes induce a network, which offers a trade-off between connectivity and resilience. The impact of resilience and connectivity can be controlled by choosing the number of rows and columns suitably. Another significant aspect of the proposed scheme is that the key-path between any pair nodes is not unique, which leads to a well-connected network.

Keywords: key pre-distribution, projective planes, pairwise connectivity.

1 Introduction

Wireless Sensor Network (WSN) is a collection of spatially distributed small devices, with limited constraints to transmit data within a specified range, known as wireless sensor nodes. Sensor nodes are supposed to collect data from the environment and then transmit them to the base station by communicating with other nodes within the specified transmission range. This communication, when takes place in a hostile region, is intended to be secret, in which secret keys need to be given to the nodes. One of the most common practice is to store the keys to the nodes before their deployment. The process of assigning keys to the nodes prior to their deployment is termed as key pre-distribution. A key pre-distribution scheme can be deterministic, probabilistic or hybrid (i.e., a combination of both), if the keys are assigned to the nodes in a fixed or random manner.

Random Key Pre-distribution Scheme (KPS) was introduced by Eschenauer and Gligor in 2002 [5], whereas combinatorial designs were first used in KPS by Mitchell and Piper [8]. Since then, combinatorial designs have become one of the most useful mathematical tools for KPS. *Projective planes* are used in [2]. Transversal design based schemes were proposed by Lee and Stinson in [6, 7],

J. Zheng et al. (Eds.): Adhocnets 2012, LNICST 111, pp. 164–179, 2013.

which were extended in [3] by merging blocks to construct nodes. Partially Balanced Incomplete Blocks Designs were used in [10] and Codes in [11] for KPS. Recently, Steiner trades have been used to construct KPS in [13]. Some grid-based KPSs are [1, 12, 14]. For details of other combinatorial design based KPS we refer to the surveys [4, 9].

Our Contribution: We propose a deterministic key pre-distribution scheme considering a network where the nodes are virtually placed at the intersection points on a rectangular grid. The whole key-pool is divided into two parts - one part is used to assign keys to the nodes along the rows and the other part is kept for distributing keys to the nodes along the columns. Row-wise keys are distributed according to a projective plane which ensures a direct connection between any two nodes on the same row, whereas column-wise key distribution allows any node (including the nodes on the boundary) to connect with its immediate neighbors on either side: i.e., above and below that node. This holds for all columns except one in which all the nodes are made pairwise adjacent. This particular column is referred to as the center column. Our network is heterogeneous in the sense that all the nodes are not identical on the basis of resources. The center column nodes are more powerful as they are connected to more nodes in the network compared to other nodes. The network thus obtained is connected with a maximum distance of three. Our analysis shows that the proposed scheme provides consistently better result for resilience − both in node disconnection and link failure. Moreover, given the size of the network, the number of rows and columns can be suitably chosen so as to get a desirable trade-off between the evaluation parameters, e.g., storage, connectivity and resilience. Except the nodes on the center column, the number of keys to be stored at the nodes in the network is very low. Most interesting feature of the network is that there are multiple paths of various lengths between two nodes in the network.

2   Preliminaries

2.1   Definitions

Definition 2.1 A *set-system* is defined as a pair (X, A) such that
(i) X is a set of points or elements,
(ii) A is a subset of the power set of X (i.e. collection of non-empty subsets or blocks of X).
The *degree* (denoted by r) of $x \in X$ is the number of blocks of A containing x; the *rank* (denoted by k) is the size of the largest block in A.
    (X, A) is said to be *regular* and *uniform* if all the points in X have the same degree and all the blocks in A have the same size respectively. A regular, uniform set-system with $|X| = v$, $|A| = b$ is known as a (v, b, r, k)-*design* .
Definition 2.2 A (v, b, r, k)-design in which any set of t points is contained in exactly λ blocks, is known as a t - (v, b, r, k, λ)-*design* which is often denoted as t - (v, k, λ)-*design*.

Definition 2.3 A symmetric $2 - (n^2 + n + 1, n^2 + n + 1, n + 1, n + 1, 1)$-design is known as a *finite symmetric projective plane of order* n. Precisely, it is a pair of a set of $(n^2 + n + 1)$ points and a set of $(n^2 + n + 1)$ lines, where each line contains $(n + 1)$ points and each point occurs in $(n + 1)$ lines.

2.2   Projective Plane Based KPS

When a set of keys is assigned to a set of nodes according to a projective plane, where the points correspond to the keys and the lines are associated with the key-chains of each node, any two nodes in the set share exactly one common key. As a result a network of size N can be designed with only $O(\sqrt{N})$ keys per node such that any two nodes in the network is directly connected. The existence of a projective plane of order p is certain when p is a prime power [15]. Smallest projective plane is of order 2) is a 2-(7, 3, 1)-design. Projective plane of order 3 is a 2-(13, 4, 1)-design consisting of a pair of sets (X, A), where X is the set of 13 points, say, $X = \{1, 2, 3, 4, 5, 6, 7, 8, 9, 10, 11, 12, 13\}$, and A is the set of blocks each of size 4, given by $A = \{(1, 2, 3, 4); (1, 5, 6, 7); (1, 8, 9, 10); (1, 11, 12, 13); (2, 5, 8, 11); (2, 6, 9, 13); (2, 7, 10, 12); (3, 5, 10, 13); (3, 6, 8, 12); (3, 7, 9, 11); (4, 5, 9, 12); (4, 6, 10, 11); (4, 7, 8, 13)\}$. Let the key-pool be X, and the nodes as the blocks of A. Now, initially to accommodate a network of size N, the order of the projective plane p is chosen in such a way that $p^2 + p + 1 \geq N$. Even if all the blocks of the set A are not present in the network, any two nodes in the network will be still directly connected. If we want to develop a network of size 10 and choose any 10 blocks say, $\{(1, 2, 3, 4); (1, 5, 6, 7); (1, 8, 9, 10); (1, 11, 12, 13); (2, 5, 8, 11); (2, 6, 9, 13); (2, 7, 10, 12); (3, 5, 10, 13); (3, 6, 8, 12); (3, 7, 9, 11); (4, 5, 9, 12)$, it will not affect the nature of the connectivity in the network. This is very beneficial, as there is a huge gap between the affordable sizes of the networks when p has to be increased to the next prime power to introduce some new nodes in the network.

3   Proposed Scheme

3.1   Terminologies

A network consists of a set of nodes pre-loaded with keys. The network can be represented by a graph, by mapping the nodes to the vertices. Two vertices in the graph are made adjacent by an edge if their corresponding nodes share at least one common key. A graph is said to be complete if any two vertices in the graph are connected by an edge. We discuss below, the procedures to form two different kinds of complete graphs.

(1) *Pairwise Complete Graph*: It is a very obvious and extreme case. A set of n nodes is considered. Let K be the key-pool. Let 1st node is given a set k_1 of $n - 1$ distinct keys chosen from K and each key from k_1 is given to exactly one from the remaining $n - 1$ nodes. This way, 1st node is made pairwise connected to all the other $n - 1$ nodes. In a similar manner 2nd node is made connected to remaining $n - 2$ nodes by choosing a set k_2 of $n - 2$ distinct keys chosen from $K - k_1$. The process is repeated for the last but one node of the network. The resulting graph thus obtained is complete, we refer to this as a pairwise complete graph. Each node contains $n-1$ distinct keys.

(2) Combinatorially Complete Graph: As the name suggests, here we shall make use of a combinatorial design, namely projective planes, to form a complete graph. A projective plane of order p is used in such a way that the graph representing the network containing n nodes is complete with only $p+1$ keys assigned to each of the nodes, where $n \approx p^2 + p + 1$, for some prime power p, as we discussed in the previous section. The graph thus obtained is referred as a combinatorially complete graph.

The advantage of **(2)** over **(1)** is that **(2)** requires only $O(\sqrt{n})$ keys to be stored in comparison to $O(n)$ keys in case of **(1)**, but when some nodes are compromised, the remaining portion of the network gets affected highly in case **(2)**. On the other hand, although **(1)** is not suitable for assigning keys in a large network, for small values of n it is appropriate to use **(1)** since compromise of one or more nodes has no effect on the rest of the network. Therefore, we shall make use of both the techniques in proper situations. Our network consists of a virtual rectangular grid of nodes. We form combinatorially complete graph in each row using projective plane and a pairwise complete graph in a particular column.

3.2   Notation

r	Number of rows in the network
c	Number of columns on the network
p	Smallest prime power such that $p^2 + p + 1 \geq c$
N	Total number of nodes in the network
$N_{i,j}$	The node belonging to the ith row and j^{th} column of the network, where $i \in \{1, 2, \ldots, r\}$ and $j \in \{1, 2, \ldots, c\}$
R_i	i^{th} row of the grid, for $i \in \{1, 2, \ldots r\}$
C_j	j^{th} column of the grid, for $j \in \{1, 2, \ldots c\}$
C_k	The center column
$d(A, B)$	Distance between the nodes A and B in the virtual network
s	The number of nodes compromised
$V(s)$	The fraction of nodes that become disconnected
$fail(s)$	Probability that the link between two uncompromised nodes is broken

The distance function $d(\cdot, \cdot)$ is different from the conventional distance function. the distance between two nodes depends only on the keys stored at them, not on their physical location. The distance function, on the virtual network, is defined as follows:
Define a graph $G=(V, E)$, where $V=\{$Sensor nodes$\}=\{N_1, N_2, \cdots, N_N\}$, say, with $|V|=N$. $(N_1, N_2) \in E$ if N_1 and N_2 have at least one common key. Define $d(N_1, N_2) = l$, if $\exists$ a path $N_1 N_{u_1} N_{u_2} \cdots N_{u_{l-1}} N_2$ in G where $(N_1, N_{u_1}), (N_{u_1}, N_{u_2}) \in E$ and $(N_{u_i}, N_{u_{i+1}}) \in E$, for $i = 1, 2, \cdots, l-2$.

3.3   Description of the Scheme

- Suppose that there are total N nodes in the network. We distribute the nodes into r rows and c columns such that $rc \geq N$. We choose $c \approx p^2 + p + 1$, for some prime integer p.
- Let $N_{i,j}$ be the node that lies at the intersection point of the ith row and j^{th} column, $i \in \{1, 2, \ldots, r\}$ and $j \in \{1, 2, \ldots, c\}$.
- We form a combinatorially complete graph, in each row using projective plane. The nodes in each row are connected to each other by a single hop path. This ensures that the number of columns c is chosen to be $\approx p^2 + p + 1$, p being prime integer to form row-wise projective planes.
- We make exactly one column to form a pairwise complete graph. Then the nodes lying in that column are pairwise connected to each other. We refer to this column as the *center column* for our convenience. Let k^{th} column $(k \leq c)$ be the center column.
- The nodes lying in columns other than the center column are connected to their two adjacent nodes only, including the boundary nodes, i.e., node $N_{i,j}$ where $j \neq k$ is adjacent to $N_{l,j}$ where $l = (i - 1) \bmod r$, or $l = (i + 1) \bmod r$. Here we mention column-wise adjacency only, as all the nodes lying in a particular row are adjacent by projective plane based combinatorially complete graph.

A virtual network is developed, as shown in Fig. 1, by placing the nodes in a rectangular grid, during the key predistribution phase. Thew nodes are then deployed in the target area in such a manner that the nodes on each of the rows are deployed together and it is also assumed that the neighboring nodes of any node (along the column) lie within its communication range. After deployment, the nodes are scattered within a specified area and thereby the actual network is formed. Two nodes are said to be connected in the actual network in the sense that they share a secret common key and lie within each others communication range so that they can communicate directly.

4   Memory

Let there be $N = rc = r(p^2 + p + 1)$ nodes in the network. All the nodes are distributed in a grid structure with r rows and c columns as described before. The number of keys to be stored in a node for row-wise communication is $p + 1$, i.e., $O(\sqrt{c})$, which follows from the property of the projective planes. The nodes in the center column require $r - 1$ extra keys and that on the other non-center columns require 2 extra keys to be stored to ensure column-wise communication. Thus the number of keys needs to be stored is $(p + 1) + (r - 1) = r + p$ for the node in the center-column and $(p + 1) + 2 = p + 3$ for the other nodes.

A larger network may be established with very less memory requirements. For a fixed value of N, by choosing p suitably such that c gets the maximum possible value and r gets the minimum possible value, we obtain comparatively better storage requirement. For instance, let $N = 2000$ nodes are arranged in

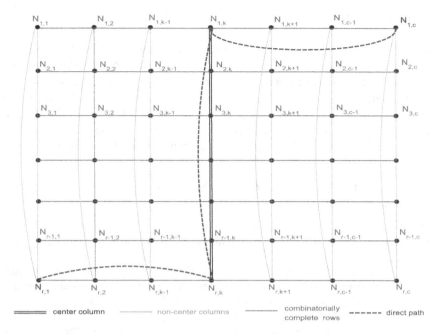

Fig. 1. Our grid structure, with a 3-hop path between nodes $N_{r,1}$ and $N_{1,c}$

$r = 2$ rows and $c = 1000$ columns, then $p = 37$. Thus, a node on the center column stores only $k_c = 39$ keys and a node on a non-center column stores only $k_o = 40$ keys, with an average storage $k_{avg} = 39.999$. Table 1 provides the storage requirements for different possible values of r and c when $N = 2000$. Table 1 indicates that the optimum memory requirement is achieved when the number of columns c is almost equal or just greater than the number of rows r.

Table 1. Memory requirements for different grids with $N = 2000$

r	c	p	k_c	k_o	k_{avg}
2	1000	37	39	40	39.999
4	500	23	27	26	26.002
8	250	17	25	20	20.020
10	200	16	26	19	19.035
20	100	11	31	14	14.170
40	50	7	47	10	10.740
50	40	7	57	10	11.175
100	20	4	104	7	11.850
200	10	3	203	6	25.700
250	8	3	253	6	36.875
500	4	2	502	5	129.250
1000	2	2	1002	5	503.500

5   Connectivity

Connectivity is one of the important feature to measure the efficiency of a scheme. In this section we investigate how well connected our scheme is and how the rest of the network behaves when some of the nodes are captured.

Note that the nodes in the rth row are made adjacent to the 1st row in our virtual grid structure. Therefore, $(i \pm 1)^{th}$ rows mean $((i \pm 1) \mod r)^{th}$ row, i.e. $R_{i \pm j} = R_{((i \pm j) \mod r)}$, and $R_0 \equiv R_r$. However, we do not consider the same operation for columns as all the columns are made virtually adjacent to each other.

Theorem 5.1. *Any two nodes in the proposed network are connected by at least one path of length at most three.*

Proof:
Let the nodes N_{i_1,j_1} and N_{i_2,j_2} wish to communicate. We consider the following cases:
Case (i): Let $i_1 = i_2$ and $j_1 \neq j_2$.
When $i_1 = i_2$, then both the nodes N_{i_1,j_1} and N_{i_2,j_2} will lie on the same row, and since nodes on the same row form a combinatorially complete graph based on projective plane, N_{i_1,j_1} and N_{i_2,j_2} are directly connected, i.e., $d(N_{i_1,j_1}, N_{i_2,j_2}) = 1$.
Case (ii): Let $i_1 \neq i_2$ and $j_1 = j_2 = k$.
According to our construction, nodes lying on the center columns form a pairwise complete graph, hence we must have $d(N_{i_1,j_1}, N_{i_2,j_2}) = 1$.
Case (iii): Let If $i_1 \neq i_2$ and $j_1 \neq j_2$.
Let us consider two nodes $N_{i_1,k}$ and $N_{i_2,k}$. Now, by case (i), $d(N_{i_1,j_1}, N_{i_1,k}) = 1$, and $d(N_{i_2,j_2}, N_{i_2,k}) = 1$. Again, by case (ii) $d(N_{i_1,k}, N_{i_2,k}) = 1$. Therefore, $d(N_{i_1,j_1}, N_{i_2,j_2}) = d(N_{i_1,j_1}, N_{i_1,k}) + d(N_{i_1,k}, N_{i_2,k}) + d(N_{i_2,k}, N_{i_2,j_2}) = 3$.
Case (iv): Let $i_1 = i_2$ and $j_1 = j_2 \neq k$. This case is same as Case (iii).   □

Theorem 5.2. *Let r, c, L_1, L_2, L_3 be the number of rows, number of columns, the total number of one-hop, two-hop and three-hop paths in the proposed network respectively. Then*

(a) $L_1 = \begin{cases} \frac{1}{2}r(r-1) + \frac{1}{2}rc(c-1) + (r-1)(c-1), & \text{if } r \leq 2; \\ \frac{1}{2}r(r-1) + \frac{1}{2}rc(c-1) + r(c-1), & \text{if } r > 2. \end{cases}$

(b) $L_2 = \begin{cases} 0, & \text{if } r < 2; \\ c(c-1), & \text{if } r = 2; \\ 3c(c-1), & \text{if } r = 3; \\ 4(c-1)(c+\frac{3}{2}), & \text{if } r = 4; \\ r(c-1)(r+c-2), & \text{otherwise}. \end{cases}$

(c) $L_3 = \begin{cases} 0, & \text{if } r \leq 3; \\ 2(c-1)(c-2), & \text{if } r = 4; \\ r(c-1)\{(c-2) + \frac{1}{2}(c-1)(r-5)\}, & \text{otherwise}. \end{cases}$

Proof:

(a) Case (i): *Nodes in the center column.*
There are r nodes $N_{1,k}, N_{2,k}, \cdots, N_{r,k}$ in the center column C_k. Since C_k forms a pairwise complete graph, $d(N_{i_1,k}, N_{i_2,k}) = 1$, for all $i_1, i_2 \in \{1, 2, \cdots r\}$. Hence, the

number of the direct paths in C_k is $\frac{1}{2}r(r-1)$.

Case (ii): *Nodes in rows.*

There are c nodes $N_{i,1}, N_{i,2}, \cdots, N_{i,c}$ on R_i, for $i = 1, 2, \cdots r$. Since R_i forms a combinatorially complete graph, we must have $d(N_{i,j_1}, N_{i,j_2}) = 1$ for all $j_1, j_2 \in \{1, 2, \cdots, c\}$. Therefore, one hop paths in R_i is $\frac{1}{2}c(c-1)$. Since, there are r identical rows on R_i, the total number of single hop paths along rows is $\frac{1}{2}rc(c-1)$.

Case (iii): *Nodes in a non-center column.*

There are r nodes $N_{1,j}, N_{2,j}, \cdots, N_{r,j}$ in the non-center column C_j, for $j = 1, 2, \cdots c$, $j \neq k$. The nodes on C_j are connected in such a manner that $d(N_{i_1,j}, N_{i_1+1,j}) = 1$, for $i_1 = 1, 2, \cdots r - 1$, and $(N_{i_1,j}, N_{i_2,j}) \notin E$, if $|i_1 - i_2| \neq 1$, where $G = (V, E)$. When $r = 2$, there are $r - 1$ one-hop paths (i.e., only one link) in C_j, and hence there are $(r-1)(c-1)$ single hop paths in the network.
When $r \geq 2$, there are r one-hop paths in C_j. Therefore, the number of single -hop paths obtained in this case is $r(c-1)$.

Since the above three cases provide disjoint sets of direct links, sum of them will give the total number of single hop paths.

(b) Note that each node on the center column are connected to the nodes that lie neither on the same row nor on the center column. It can also be noted that this fact is independent of the number of rows whenever $r \geq 2$. The number of two-hop paths from a node on the center column is $(c-1)(r-1)$. Since there are r identical nodes on the center column, the number of two-hop paths from the center column is $t' = r(r-1)(c-1)$.

Let t denotes the number of two-hop paths between two nodes neither of which lies on the center column. Then, $L_2 = t' + t$. We further assume that t_1 denotes the number of 2-hop paths from a particular non-center column node, n_1 denotes the number of such nodes present in the network so that $t = \frac{1}{2}t_1 n_1$. The factor $1/2$ included since each path is counted twice.

Now we compute the two-hop paths in the network where no node from the center column is involved. The number of paths depends on the number of rows present in the network.

Case (i): *Let the number of rows be less than two.*

Since all the nodes lie on the same row, there will be no two hop path. Therefore, $L_2 = t' + t = 0$.

Case (ii): *Let there be exactly two rows in the network.* We observe that each node is connected to the non center column nodes of the other row in 2-hop. Therefore, we have in this case, $t_1 = (c-2)$, $n_1 = r(c-1)$ and hence, $t = \frac{1}{2}t_1 n_1 = \frac{r}{2}(c-1)(c-2)$. Thus, $L_2 = t' + t = r(r-1)(c-1) + \frac{r}{2}(c-1)(c-2) = r(c-1)(r + \frac{c}{2} - 2) = c(c-1)$.

Case (iii): *Let there be exactly three rows in the network.*

We observe that each node is connected to $c-2$ non center column nodes (excluding the node along the same row) of both of the remaining rows. Therefore, we have in this case, $t_1 = 2(c-2)$, $n_1 = r(c-1)$ and hence, $t = \frac{1}{2}t_1 n_1 = r(c-1)(c-2)$. Thus we have, $L_2 = t' + t = r(r-1)(c-1) + r(c-1)(c-2) = r(c-1)(r+c-3) = 3c(c-1)$.

Case (iv): *Let there be exactly four rows in the network.*

It can observed that, each node on a non-center column is connected to all the $(c-2)$ non-center column nodes (excluding the node on the center column along the same row) of two rows and exactly one node in the remaining row. Therefore, in this case, $t_1 = 2c - 3$, $n_1 = r(c-1)$ and hence, $t = \frac{1}{2}t_1 n_1 = \frac{r}{2}(c-1)(2c-3)$. Hence, we have $L_2 = t' + t = r(r-1)(c-1) + \frac{r}{2}(c-1)(2c-3) = r(c-1)(r+c-\frac{5}{2}) = 4(c-1)(c+\frac{3}{2})$.

Case (v): *Let there be more than four rows in the network.*
It can be noted the node $N_{i,j}$ is connected by two-hop paths to
• $(c-2)$ nodes in the neighboring rows R_{i+1} and R_{i-1}.
• Exactly one node from each of the rows R_{i+2} and R_{i-2}.
• No node from the remaining $(r-5)$ rows.
Therefore, we have in this case, $t_1 = 2(c-2)+2 = 2(c-1)$, $n_1 = r(c-1)$ and hence, $t = \frac{1}{2}t_1 n_1 = r(c-1)^2$. Thus we have, $L_2 = t' + t = r(r-1)(c-1) + r(c-1)^2 = r(c-1)(r+c-2)$.

We observe that each node is connected by a 2-hop path to $(c-2)$ non-center column nodes (excluding the node along the same row) of two rows and all the $(c-1)$ non center column nodes in the remaining $(r-5)$ rows. Hence, combining the expressions obtained in each of the above five cases we get the desired result as stated in the theorem.

(c) Case (i): *Let the number of rows be at most three.*
The distance between two rows is one, i.e., two nodes in the same column but different row must be connected by at most 1-hop path. From the construction, it follows that any two nodes on the same row are connected directly. All the columns in this network behaves as the center column. This implies that in this case, any two nodes in the network are connected by a path of maximum length two. Therefore, there are no 3-hop paths in this case.

Case (ii): *Let the number of rows be exactly four.*
In this case we observe that the nodes in the center column are connected to rest of the nodes on the network by a path of maximum length two. Therefore, we will not consider the center column in this evaluation. Let us assume that the rows are numbered as R_1, R_2, R_3 and R_4. We observe that the nodes in the row R_i are connected to the nodes in the rows $R_{((i+1) \mod 4)}$ and $R_{((i+3) \mod 4)}$ by 2-hop paths, for $i = 1, 2, 3, 4$. Thus, nodes on the row R_i may have a three-hop paths with some of the nodes in the row $R_{(i+2) mod4}$, for $i = 1, 2, 3, 4$. Note that the node $N_{i,j}$ (with $j \neq k$) is connected to $N_{i+2,j'}$ for $j' = \{1, 2, \cdots, c\} \setminus \{j, k\}$. Therefore, each node on R_i are connected to $(c-2)$ nodes. This holds true for all the $(c-1)$ non-center nodes in each row, and since all the rows are identical, we have the total number of three-hop paths $= \frac{1}{2}r(c-1)(c-2) = 2(c-1)(c-2)$. The factor $1/2$ comes as each path is counted twice corresponding to each end of the path.

Case (iii): *Let the number of rows be more than four.*
Following the similar arguments as in the above cases, the paths originated from the nodes lying on the center-column are not considered. We consider any arbitrary node $N_{i,j}$ (for $j \neq k$) and calculate the number of paths originated from this point. We observe that the node $N_{i,j}$ is connected by three-hop paths to
• No nodes in the neighboring rows, i.e., $R_{(i+1) \mod r}$ and $R_{(i-1) \mod r}$.
• $(c-2)$ nodes in rows $R_{(i+2) \mod r}$ and $R_{(i-2) \mod r}$ as out of total c nodes on each of these two rows, one node lies on the center column and one node is connected to $N_{i,j}$ by a 2-hop path.
• $(c-1)$ nodes (excluding that on the center column) in all the remaining $(r-5)$ rows.
Hence, by three-hop path, the node $N_{i,j}$ is connected to $2(c-2)+(c-1)(r-5)$ nodes. The similar result holds for the nodes of the form $N_{i,j}$ for all $i = 1, 2, 3, \cdots, r$ and all $j = 1, 2, \cdots, k-1, k+1, \cdots, c$. But considering the summation of the three-hop

paths for all the $r(c-1)$ nodes will count each path twice (corresponding to each extreme of the path). Thus, the total number of three hop paths in the network is given by $\frac{1}{2}r(c-1)\{2(c-2) + r(c-1)^2(r-5)\}$. Rearranging the terms we obtain the desired result.   □

It follows from Theorem 5.1 that all the nodes in the network are connected by at least a path of distance at most three. It can also be observed that the path between two nodes is not unique, instead there are a number of routes between two nodes, so that two nodes will be able to communicate until all the paths between them are destroyed, which involves compromise of a huge number of nodes. Although it is very unlikely, even if all the nodes on the center column are destroyed, the network will be still connected by row-wise communication and that along the non-center columns.

The expressions obtained in Theorems 5.2(a), 5.2(b) and 5.2(c) adds up to give $\frac{1}{2}rc(rc-1)$, which is the total number of possible links in the network, as there are total rc nodes present in the network. This also verifies the validity of Theorem 5.1 alternatively.

Theorems 5.2(a), 5.2(b) and 5.2(c) give the number of single-hop, 2-hop and 3-hop paths in the network. Therefore, the average path-length between two nodes in the network is $d = (L_1 + 2L_2 + 3L_3)/(L_1 + L_2 + L_3)$. The connection probability of the proposed network is $p(c) = \frac{L_1}{L}$.

5.1   Key Path Establishment

It is mentioned earlier that two nodes communicate securely provided they share a common key or, can establish a key-path based on keys distributed following our Key PreDistribution scheme in the virtual rectangular grid network.

We discuss the key path establishment phase between two randomly chosen nodes, $A : N_{i_1,j_1}$ and $B : N_{i_2,j_2}$, from the network. Let C_k be the center column.
Step 1: The nodes A and B will broadcast their node-identifiers (which is their location on the virtual rectangular grid) (i_1, j_1) and (i_2, j_2). On receiving the other node's identifier each of A and B compare the received identifier with its own and check the following conditions.
Step 2: Direct Path
• If $i_1 = i_2$ or $j_1 = j_2 = k$ then both of the two nodes A and B lie on a combinatorially complete or a pairwise complete graph and hence they share a common key. This implies that the nodes are directly connected.
• If $\mid i_1 - i_2 \mid = 1$ and $j_1 = j_2 \neq k$ i.e., the nodes are adjacent on the same non-center column and thus share a common key.
Step 3: Two-hop Path
• Let exactly one of the two nodes A and B lie on the center column. Without loss of generality, let us assume that $j_1 = k$ and $j_2 \neq k$, then the 2-hop key-path between A and B is $N_{i_1,k} \longrightarrow N_{i_2,k} \longrightarrow N_{i_2,j_2}$.
• If $\mid i_1 - i_2 \mid = 1$ and $j_1 = j_2 \neq k$, then the nodes A and B establish a two-hop key path $N_{i_1,j_1} \longrightarrow N_{i',j_1} \longrightarrow N_{i_2,j_1}$, where $R_{i_1}, R_{i'}$ and R_{i_2} are three consecutive rows on the virtual grid.

Step 4: Three-hop Path
When none of the above conditions is satisfied, the nodes establish a three-hop path as $N_{i_1,j_1} \longrightarrow N_{i_1,j_k} \longrightarrow N_{i_2,j_k} \longrightarrow N_{i_2,j_2}$.

It may happen that two nodes that are adjacent in the virtual network do not lie in each others communication range in the actual network. In that scenario, the nodes look for any intermediate node in the virtual network (nodes lying on the same row as them) which lie within the communication range of both of the above two nodes. Since all the nodes on each row are pairwise connected, the existence of such a node can be ensured with high probability. Similarly if two adjacent nodes on a column are not within communication range, then they reach to each other by any alternative multi-hop path. Hence it can be noted that since the key-path between any two nodes is not unique as shown in the virtual network, we can always find a key-path between any two nodes in the network, with high probability. Hence the induced network is well-connected.

6   Resilience

We adapt the random node capture model. The adversary captures nodes randomly from the network and thereby extracts all the secrets stored at those compromised nodes. We analyze the effect on both nodes and links when a few nodes are compromised by the adversary. We discuss both the cases in the following subsections.

6.1   Node-Disconnection

Theorem 6.1. *Minimum number of nodes to be compromised to disconnect a node $N_{i,j}$ completely from the network is given by*

$$\begin{cases} r + p, & \text{if } N_{i,j} \text{ lies in the center column, i.e., } j = k; \\ p + 3, & \text{otherwise.} \end{cases}$$

Proof: A node $N_{i,j}$ gets disconnected from the network if all the connections from $N_{i,j}$ are destroyed, i.e., all the nodes having a common key with $N_{i,j}$ get captured. We consider the following two cases:
Case (i): Let the node $N_{i,j}$ be a center column node, i.e., $j = k$.
Now, it can be noted that, all the nodes lying in the same column and same row of $N_{i,j}$ should be captured in order to disconnect $N_{i,j}$. There are $r - 1$ nodes in the column. From the property of the projective plane of order p, which has $p^2 + p + 1$ nodes, it follows that in order to disconnect one node, at least $p + 1$ nodes should be destroyed. Therefore, one node on the center column will be disconnected provided $r - 1$ nodes along this column and $p + 1$ nodes along the row of $N_{i,j}$ get captured.

Case (ii): Let the node $N_{i,j}$ be a non-center column node.
It can be observed observe that to disconnect $N_{i,j}$, all the nodes along the same row of $N_{i,j}$ and the two adjacent nodes of $N_{i,j}$ along the same column as $N_{i,j}$ should be destroyed. Therefore, total number of nodes to be captured to disconnect $N_{i,j}$ completely is $(p + 1) + 2 = p + 3$ nodes.   □

Corollary 6.2. *Average number of nodes disconnected when s nodes are captured is given by* $v_1(s) = \frac{s}{p+3+\frac{r-3}{c}}$.

Proof: The number of nodes in center column is r. To disconnect each of them, $r+p$ nodes have to be compromised. Again, $p+3$ nodes required to be captured to disconnect any one node from the rest of the $rc-r = r(c-1)$ nodes. Therefore, the average number of nodes required to be compromised to disconnect one node completely from the network is $\frac{(r+p)r+(p+3)r(c-1)}{rc} = p+3+\frac{r-3}{c}$.

Hence, the average number of nodes disconnected when s nodes are captured is given by $v_1(s) = \frac{s}{p+3+\frac{r-3}{c}}$. □

The fraction of nodes that become disconnected when s nodes are compromised is $V(s) = \frac{v_1(s)}{N-s} = \frac{s}{(N-s)\{p+3+\frac{r-3}{c}\}}$

6.2   Link-Failure

The anti-resilience of a scheme is measured using the expression [6]:

$$fail(s) = 1 - \left(1 - \frac{m-2}{N-2}\right)^s \tag{1}$$

where $fail(s)$ denotes the probability that a link between two uncaptured nodes is broken when s nodes are compromised in a network of size N and each key is assigned to m number of nodes. Since our grid-based scheme is neither regular nor uniform, i.e., the number of nodes to which each key is assigned varies in our case. Therefore, in our analysis m stands for the average number of nodes to which each key is assigned. Let us now find an expression for m. Note the followings:

Keys in Rows : Keys are assigned to each of the rows according to a projective plane of order p, i.e., a set of $c = p^2 + p + 1$ keys are distributed to a set of $p^2 + p + 1 = c$ nodes $N_{i,1}, N_{i,2}, N_{i,3}, \cdots, N_{i,c}$ in a row R_i such that each key is assigned to $p+1$ nodes in R_i. Total number of keys required to ensure row -wise key distribution is $r(p^2 + p + 1) = rc$.

Keys in Center Column : All the r nodes $N_{1,k}, N_{2,k}, N_{3,k}, \cdots, N_{r,k}$ on the center column C_k, are made pairwise connected so that each key is assigned to exactly two nodes, to form a pairwise complete graph. Total number of keys used in this case is $\frac{1}{2}r(r-1)$.

Keys in Non-Center Columns : Let C_j be a non- center column. Keys are distributed to the r nodes $N_{1,j}, N_{2,j}, N_{3,j}, \cdots, N_{r,j}$ in such a manner that $N_{i,j}$ is made adjacent to (i.e., shares distinct common keys with each of) $N_{i-1,j}$ and $N_{i+1,j}$, for $i = 1, 2, 3 \cdots, r$. Thus each key is assigned to exactly two nodes. The total number of keys used in assigning keys to $c - 1$ non-center columns $C_j, j \in \{1, 2, \cdots, k-1, k+1, \cdots c\}$, is $r(c-1)$. Therefore,

$$m = \frac{(p+1)rc + 2\frac{1}{2}r(r-1) + 2r(c-1)}{rc + \frac{1}{2}r(r-1) + r(c-1)} = \frac{(p+2)(p^2+p+1)+r-3}{2(p^2+p+1)+\frac{1}{2}(r-3)}$$

Table 2 shows how the network collapses with increasing number of compromised
nodes considering a network with 11 rows and 183 columns..

Table 2. Link failure of a particular network with $r = 11, c = 183$

s	$fail(s)$	s	$fail(s)$	s	$fail(s)$
10	0.029124	20	0.057400	30	0.084853
40	0.111506	50	0.137383	60	0.162506
70	0.186898	80	0.210579	90	0.233570
100	0.255892	150	0.358120	200	0.446303
250	0.522371	300	0.587989	350	0.644593
400	0.693420	500	0.771871	600	0.830247
700	0.873686	800	0.906008	900	0.930060

7 Efficiency

7.1 Overall Performance

We provide the overall performance of our scheme in Table 2 on the basis of
comparison among the parameters. In the table, we have chosen different sets
of values for the number of rows and the number of columns in the grid so that
the total number of nodes in the network is close to 2000.

The table gives the measures for connectivity such as L - the total number of possible links, L_1, L_2, L_3 - the number of one-hop, two-hop and 3-hop
paths respectively in the network, d - average path length and $p(c)$ - connection
probability. Moreover, the measure for resilience is also provided in the table by
$V(100)$ and $fail(10)$ where $V(100)$ is the fraction of disconnected nodes when

Table 3. Performance of the proposed scheme

r	p	c	N	L	L_1	L_2	L_3	d	$p(c)$	$V(100)$	$fail(10)$
2	31	993	1986	1972097	987041	985056	0	1.499497	0.500503	0.000816	0.073102
3	27	757	2271	2577585	860709	1716876	0	1.666079	0.333921	0.000808	0.055839
5	19	381	1905	1813560	363860	729600	720100	2.196400	0.200600	0.001351	0.046241
6	19	381	2286	2611755	436635	877800	1297320	2.329500	0.167180	0.001116	0.038638
8	16	273	2184	2383836	299228	607104	1477504	2.494277	0.125524	0.001371	0.033693
10	13	183	1830	1673535	168395	347620	1157520	2.591039	0.100622	0.001993	0.032040
15	11	133	1995	1989015	133755	289080	1566180	2.720168	0.067247	0.002111	0.024265
22	9	91	2002	2003001	92301	219780	1690920	2.798112	0.046081	0.002504	0.018846
27	8	73	1971	1941435	73251	190512	1677672	2.826410	0.037730	0.002813	0.018846
35	7	57	1995	1989015	58415	176400	1754200	2.852570	0.029369	0.003104	0.013122
65	5	31	2015	2029105	34255	183300	1811550	0.875901	0.016882	0.003481	0.006604
95	4	21	1995	1989015	26315	216600	1746100	2.864641	0.013230	0.003518	0.003587
154	3	13	2002	2003001	25641	304920	1672440	2.822166	0.012801	0.002629	0.001280
286	2	7	2002	2003001	48477	499356	1455168	2.702290	0.024202	0.001095	0.000225

100 nodes are compromised and $fail(10)$ is the same for links when 10 nodes are compromised from the network.

Table 3 indicates that better connectivity (i.e., smaller average path length, greater connection probability) and better node-disconnection can be achieved by decreasing the number of rows and increasing the number of columns while keeping the total number of nodes in the network unchanged. On the contrary, a better link failure is obtained for less columns and large number of rows.

Table 4. Comparison of node disconnection

	N	s	$V(s)$	N	s	$V(s)$
[11]	2041	100	0.0003867	2041	150	0.0981
Ours	2013	100	0.001803	2013	150	0.002776
[11]	5041	150	0.00283	5041	200	0.0762
Ours	5040	150	0.000706	5040	200	0.000950

7.2 Comparison

Comparison of node-disconnections of our scheme with [11] is given in Table 4. Note that for a smaller network of size just above 2000, initially the scheme in [11] provides better value for node disconnection when the number of compromised nodes is 100, but as the value of compromised nodes is increased to 150 then better value of $V(s)$ is obtained in our scheme. This shows that our scheme is consistent compared to the scheme mentioned above. Moreover, for a larger network consisting of almost 5040 nodes, our scheme outperforms [11].

In Table 5, we provide the comparison based on the performance of our scheme with Lee-Stinson linear scheme [6], Chakrabarti et al. Merging scheme [3], Ruj-Roy scheme PBIBD [10] and Lee-Stinson quadratic scheme [7], where N denotes the total number of nodes in the network and k denotes the total number of keys present in each node. To keep up N in our scheme comparable with other schemes, we consider a network with 11 rows and 183 columns ($p = 13$), i.e., total number of nodes in the network being 2013. Therefore, the nodes in the center-column need to store 24 keys and 16 keys are stored at each node in non center-columns.

In Fig. 4 we provide the comparison of our scheme's link failure with Lee-Stinson linear scheme [6] and Lee-Stinson quadratic scheme [7] for a large number (i.e., 10 - 200) of compromised nodes. It is very evident from the figure that the networks incorporated on other schemes collapses in no time when compared to ours.

Table 5. Comparison of memory and link-failure with the existing schemes

	Linear [6]	Quadratic [7]	Merging [3]	PBIBD [10]	Ours
N	1849	2197	2550	2415	2013
k	30	30	≤ 28	136	≤ 24
$fail(10)$	0.201070	0.297077	0.213388	0.0724	0.02914

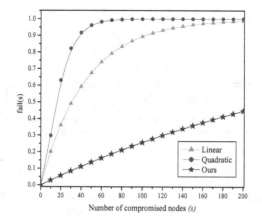

Fig. 2. Comparison of link-failure with the existing schemes for large number of compromised nodes

8   Conclusion

Our deterministic KPS places the nodes virtually on a rectangular grid and key distribution is done row-wise and column-wise from two disjoint sets of key-pools. Keys are distributed along the rows on the basis of projective planes and pairwise connectivity is ensured along the columns. The induced network enables any two nodes to be connected by at least one path of length less than or equal to three. Additionally, there are multiple paths between any two nodes chosen randomly from the network. Our experimental results support the fact that our grid based scheme provides better resilience (for both node disconnection and link failure) against random node capture attack when compared to the existing combinatorial design based schemes.

Acknowledgement. We thank the anonymous reviewrs for their valuable comments in improving our paper.

References

1. Blackburn, S.R., Etzion, T., Martin, K.M., Paterson, M.B.: Efficient Key Pre-distribution for Grid-Based Wireless Sensor Networks. In: Safavi-Naini, R. (ed.) ICITS 2008. LNCS, vol. 5155, pp. 54–69. Springer, Heidelberg (2008)
2. Camptepe, S.A., Yener, B.: Combinatorial Design of Key Distribution Mechanisms for Wireless Sensor Networks. ACM Trans. Netw. 15(2), 346–358 (2007)
3. Chakrabarti, D., Maitra, S., Roy, B.: A Key Pre-distribution Scheme for Wireless Sensor Networks: Merging Blocks in Combinatorial Design. In: Zhou, J., López, J., Deng, R.H., Bao, F. (eds.) ISC 2005. LNCS, vol. 3650, pp. 89–103. Springer, Heidelberg (2005)
4. Chen, C.Y., Chao, H.C.: A survey of Key Predistribution in Wireless Sensor Networks. Security Comm. Networks (2011)
5. Eschenauer, L., Gligor, V.D.: A Key-management Scheme for Distributed Sensor Networks. In: ACM CCS, pp. 41–47. ACM (2002)
6. Lee, J., Stinson, D.R.: A Combinatorial Approach to Key Predistribution for Distributed Sensor Networks. In: IEEE WCNC, pp. 1200–1205 (2005)
7. Lee, J., Stinson, D.R.: On The Construction of Practical Key Predistribution Schemes for Distributed Sensor Networks Using Combinatorial Designs. ACM Trans. Inf. Syst. Secur. 11(2) (2008)
8. Mitchell, C.J., Piper, F.: Key Storage in Sensor Networks. Discrete Applied Mathematics 21, 215–228 (1988)
9. Paterson, M.B., Stinson, D.R.: A Unified Approach to Combinatorial Key Pre-distribution Schemes for Sensor Networks. In: IACR Cryptology ePrint Archive (2011)
10. Ruj, S., Roy, B.: Key Predistribution Using Partially Balanced Designs in Wireless Sensor Networks. In: Stojmenovic, I., Thulasiram, R.K., Yang, L.T., Jia, W., Guo, M., de Mello, R.F. (eds.) ISPA 2007. LNCS, vol. 4742, pp. 431–445. Springer, Heidelberg (2007)
11. Ruj, S., Roy, B.: Key Predistribution Schemes Using Codes in Wireless Sensor Networks. In: Yung, M., Liu, P., Lin, D. (eds.) Inscrypt 2008. LNCS, vol. 5487, pp. 275–288. Springer, Heidelberg (2009)
12. Ruj, S., Roy, B.: Key Predistributions Using Combinatorial Designs for A Grid-group Deployment Scheme in Wireless Sensor Networks. ACM Transactions on Sensor Networks 6(4) (2009)
13. Ruj, S., Nayak, A., Stojmenovic, I.: Fully Secure Pairwise and Triple Key Distributions in Wireless Networks Using Combinatorial Designs. In: IEEE INFOCOM, pp. 326–330 (2011)
14. Sadi, M.G., Park, J.S., Kim, D.S.: Randomized Grid Based Scheme for Wireless Sensor Network. In: Molva, R., Tsudik, G., Westhoff, D. (eds.) ESAS 2005. LNCS, vol. 3813, pp. 91–101. Springer, Heidelberg (2005)
15. Stinson, D.R.: Combinatorial Designs: Constructions and Analysis. Springer (2003)

LPKM: A Lightweight Polynomial-Based Key Management Protocol for Distributed Wireless Sensor Networks

Xinxin Fan and Guang Gong

Department of Electrical and Computer Engineering
University of Waterloo
Waterloo, Ontario, N2L 3G1, Canada
{x5fan,ggong}@uwaterloo.ca

Abstract. Due to the critical resource constraints of wireless sensor nodes such as processing speed, memory size and energy supply, implementing security mechanisms, in particular key management schemes, is quite challenging. Motivated by the conference key establishment scheme proposed by Harn and Gong in [11], we propose **LPKM** (Lightweight Polynomial-based Key Management Protocol), a key management scheme for distributed WSNs. LPKM enables sensor nodes to establish different types of keys to bootstrap trust and secure one-to-one and one-to-many communications in a flexible, reliable, and non-interactive way. Moreover, LPKM can effectively mitigate or thwart the most common attacks to WSNs such as node clone attacks, node impersonation attacks, etc. In addition, LPKM can tolerate changes of network topology and incurs little computational and communication overhead. Our experimental results on MICAz motes show that LPKM can be efficiently implemented on low-cost sensor nodes. In particular, a MICAz mote running at a frequency of 8MHz can generate required group keys of 128-bit in a few milliseconds, at a cost of 6.12 KBytes ROM and 68 Bytes RAM.

Keywords: Wireless Sensor Networks, Security, Authentication, Key Management.

1 Introduction

Wireless sensor networks (WSNs) are integrations of low-cost and resource-constrained sensor nodes into sophisticated sensing, computational and communication infrastructures. In WSNs, all sensor nodes collaborate towards the common goal of collecting and processing certain physical information such as temperature, light, radiation, etc. from their environment. The sensed data is then sent through multi-hop communication to base stations. These new networks are having a significant impact (and promises to have even more) on a wide range of applications in both civilian and military domains, such as target tracking, medical care and environment monitoring [15, 16, 21].

Many applications require sensor nodes to be deployed in unattended and even hostile environments and thus security becomes important issues in these

J. Zheng et al. (Eds.): Adhocnets 2012, LNICST 111, pp. 180–195, 2013.

applications. In WSNs, sensor nodes unicast, multicast, or broadcast messages to each other, which makes them vulnerable to a host of attacks, such as eavesdropping, impersonation, malicious modification or injection of unauthorized data. Hence, an efficient key management scheme together with strong encryption and authentication mechanisms need to be deployed for establishing the trust and protecting a network from various attacks. Unfortunately, due to the low-cost nature and resource constraints of sensor nodes, it is a quite challenging task for implementing security mechanisms in WSNs.

Designing a sound key management scheme for WSNs depends on specific applications and typical requirements might include supporting in-network processing and passive participation as well as facilitating self-organization of data, among others [24, 25]. A host of key management schemes for WSNs have been proposed during the past few years to address the tradeoff between security and performance, which are either symmetric-key based schemes [6,8,10,14,20,23–26] or public-key based mechanisms [9, 17]. While public-key based schemes can provide more strong security features like non-repudiation through the usage of certificates, symmetric-key based solutions have advantages in terms of computational and computation cost as well as energy consumption. Most symmetric-key based key management schemes are based on preloading keying materials into sensor nodes before deployment. In those schemes, two sensor nodes can establish a pairwise key either in a deterministic way [20, 23–25] or in a probabilistic fashion [6,8,10,14,26]. We notice that most of the previous work only consider the pairwise key establishment and the problem of establishing a shared key for arbitrary groups of sensor nodes did not receive much attention[1]. A more general key management scheme that is able to establish different types of keys for arbitrary groups of nodes in WSNs is high desirable.

In this paper, we present LPKM (Lightweight Polynomial-based Key Management Protocol), a key management scheme for distributed WSNs. LPKM enables sensor nodes to form a group and establish a shared key on the fly. Three types of keys can be established for each sensor node – a *pairwise key* shared with another senor node or the base station, a *cluster key* shared with multiple neighboring nodes, and a *group key* shared within certain group of nodes. With different types of keys, LPKM is able to support in-network processing and passive participation. Furthermore, LPKM also includes a probabilistic local broadcast authentication protocol that supports source authentication through *collaboration* among neighboring nodes. To mitigate node compromise by adversaries and protect WSNs in the long run, distributed node revocation and share updating protocols have been proposed. Our node revocation protocol can evict compromised nodes from a certain group by generating a new group key only shared by legitimate nodes, whereas the share updating protocol updates the preloaded keying materials periodically. Besides various salient features provided by LPKM, the key establishment procedure can be efficiently implemented on MICAz motes and required group keys can be generated in a few milliseconds.

---

[1] The group key establishment scheme proposed in [24, 25] only deals with the case of establishing a key shared by all the nodes in the network.

The remainder of this paper is organized as follows. Section 2 gives a brief overview of a recently proposed conference key establishment protocol, followed by the description of system, network and adversary models in Section 3. The LPKM design is detailed in Section 4. Section 5 reports the performance of group key generation on MICAz motes. Finally, Section 6 concludes this contribution.

2   An Efficient Conference Key Establishment Protocol

Harn and Gong [11] recently proposed a polynomial-based conference key establishment protocol which enables a group of m users to establish common keys in a non-interactive and flexible way. To initialize a system, a key distribution center (KDC) first chooses a prime p, a group size m such that either $(m-1)^{-1}$ or m^{-1} modulo $p-1$ exists. It is assumed that a group of m users is indexed as $S_m = \{1, 2, \cdots, m\}$ and an integer h is defined by

$$h = (m-1+\delta)^{-1}, \quad \delta = \begin{cases} 0 \text{ for } m \text{ even} \\ 1 \text{ for } m \text{ odd} \end{cases}.$$

In the share distribution phase, KDC randomly generates an integer $b \in \mathbb{F}_p$ and a univariate k-degree polynomial $f(x) = a_k x^k + \cdots + a_1 x + a_0 \in \mathbb{F}_p[x]$, where $\mathbb{F}_p$ is finite field with p elements and p is a prime that is large enough to accommodate a cryptographic key. For a user with a unique identity i, KDC computes a share of $f(x)$, that is $f_i(x) = bf(i)^h f(x) \in \mathbb{F}_p[x], i = 1, 2, \cdots, m$. KDC then sends the share $f_i(x)$ to user i through a secure channel. To establish a group key for a t-subset $I = \{i_1, i_2, \cdots, i_t\} \subseteq S_m = \{1, 2, \cdots, m\}$, each user calculates the conference key non-interactively as follows:

$$K_i = \prod_{j \in I \setminus \{i\}} f_i(j) f_i(0)^{m-t+\delta},$$

where $I \setminus \{i\}$ is the set consisting all the elements in I but i. The shared conference key is given by $K_i = K$ for all $i \in I$ where

$$K = \begin{cases} b^{m-1} f(0)^\delta \prod_{j=1}^m f(j) & \text{for } t = m \\ b^{m-1} f(0)^{m-t+\delta} \prod_{j \in I} f(j) & \text{for } t < m \end{cases}.$$

In the above approach, each user i only needs to store $(k+1)$ coefficients of the polynomial $f_i(x)$, which requires $(k+1) \log p$ memory space. To establish a common key for a subgroup of size t, each user i needs to evaluate the polynomial $f_i(x)$ at $(t-1)$ identities in $I \setminus \{i\}$. Furthermore, there is no communication overhead during the process of group key establishment. The security analysis in [11] shows that the proposed conference key establishment protocol is information-theoretic secure and can resist to the known shares and known conference keys attacks. Consequently, the coalition of t users in I can recover neither the conference keys and secret shares for users in $S_m \setminus I$, nor the master key of the KDC.

A salient characteristic of the protocol in [11] is that the storage cost for a polynomial share is $(k + 1)$ coefficients, which is independent of the group size. This feature overcomes the disadvantage of the previous key distribution protocol proposed by Blundo *et al.* [4] (i.e., the storage cost for a polynomial share is exponential in terms of the group size) and makes the conference key establishment protocol in [11] an ideal solution for bootstrapping the trust and securing both one-to-one and one-to-many communications in distributed WSNs.

3 System, Network and Adversary Models

System Model: We assume that sensor nodes have constrained resources in terms of computational capabilities, memory, bandwidth, and power supply (see MICAz motes [7] for example). A typical MICAz mote running TinyOS operating system features a low-power 8-bit microcontroller ATmega128L from Atmel and provides a throughput up to 8 MIPS. We assume that sensor nodes are not equipped with tamper-resistant hardware and can be compromised by adversaries. However, the system bootstrapping phase is secure and sensor nodes cannot be compromised during this stage.

Network Model: We consider a large-scale, distributed, and densely deployed WSN consisting of a base station and a large number of sensor nodes. Due to the limited communication capabilities, devices communicate in a multi-hop fashion using bidirectional wireless links. We assume that the base station, acting as a key distribution centre, is responsible for assigning and preloading keying materials into a sensor node before it is deployed. Sensor nodes can be deployed through aircraft scattering or by physical installation. We further assume that a compromised node can eventually be detected by most of its neighboring nodes within a certain time period (e.g., using a watchdog mechanism). We also assume that sensor nodes are loosely synchronized.

Adversary Model: With respect to the key management in the WSN, the main goal of an adversary is to inject bogus commands or queries into the network for deceiving sensor nodes and obtaining the information of his interest. Due to the nature of wireless communication in sensor networks, the adversary may also overhear, intercept, or alter any messages during the multi-hop forwarding. In addition, we assume that the adversary can capture and compromise a small fraction of sensor nodes and therefore exploit those compromised nodes to mount various attacks. We also assume that if a sensor node is compromised, all the keying materials it hold will be known by an adversary.

4 LPKM Description

In this section, we present a lightweight polynomial-based key management protocol for WSNs, which provides non-interactive and flexible group keying mechanisms for establishing the trust and securing communications in WSNs.

4.1   Network Initialization

The KDC conducts the following steps to initialize a sensor network:

1. The KDC generates the system parameters $(p, m, h, b, f(x))$, as described in Section 2. While parameters (p, m, h) are public knowledge, parameters $(b, f(x))$ are secret information.
2. For a sensor node with a unique identity i, the KDC calculates a share of $f(x)$ (see Section 2), which is a $(k+1)$-dimensional vector $v_i = (by_i a_0, by_i a_1, \ldots, by_i a_k) \in \mathbb{F}_p^{k+1}$, where $y_i = f(i)^h$.
3. The KDC preloads public parameters (p, m, h) and the share v_i into the sensor node i.

4.2   Pairwise Key Establishment

In WSNs, a pairwise key is used to secure one-to-one communications, which are either between sensor nodes and their immediate neighbors (i.e., one-hop neighbors) or between two sensor nodes that are multiple hops away. We discuss these two cases separately below.

Pairwise Keys for Neighboring Nodes: Before sensor nodes start establishing pairwise keys with their immediate neighbors, they need to run a *neighbor discovery* phase. More specifically, after sensor nodes are deployed, node i locally broadcasts a HELLO message containing its identity. Every node j receiving the HELLO message responds with an ACK message that includes j's identity. The ACK message from node j can be authenticated by the pairwise key $K_{i,j}$ that is computed as follows:

$$K_{i,j} = f_i(j)f_i(0)^{m-1+\delta} = f_j(i)f_j(0)^{m-1+\delta} = b^{m-1}f(0)^{m-1+\delta}f(i)f(j).$$

The neighbor discovery phase is illustrated below:

$$i \longrightarrow * : \ i.$$
$$j \longrightarrow i : \ j, \mathbf{MAC}(K_{i,j}, i\|j),$$

which is similar to the neighbor discovery procedure described in LEAP [24] and LEAP+ [25]. However, our scheme employs a polynomial-based approach for generating a pairwise key. Moreover, the pairwise key is used to authenticate the ACK message that is also served as a pairwise key confirmation message. After a sufficient amount of time, node i will add all the legitimate neighbors into its neighbor list and the neighbor discovery phase is completed.

During the above neighbor discovery phase, each node needs to compute a pairwise key and verifies a **MAC** for every neighbor, whereas each neighbor node has to derive a pairwise key followed by the generation of a **MAC**. The communication overhead includes a HELLO message (i.e., sender's identity) and an ACK message (i.e. receiver's identity concatenated with a **MAC**), which can be transmitted with one packet.

Pairwise Keys for Non-Neighboring Nodes: Establishing pairwise keys for non-neighboring nodes is desirable in applications like data aggregation, where a sensor node needs to report its readings to an aggregation node, which is usually multiple hops away, in a secure way. A multi-hop pairwise key between a sensor node i and an aggregation node a can be efficiently computed on the fly:

$$K_{i,a} = f_i(a)f_i(0)^{m-1+\delta} = f_a(i)f_a(0)^{m-1+\delta} = b^{m-1}f(0)^{m-1+\delta}f(i)f(a).$$

After obtaining the pairwise key $K_{i,a}$, node i broadcasts a QUERY message containing its identity i, aggregation node's identity a, and a **MAC** which allows the aggregation node a to verify the validity of $K_{i,a}$. If the verification succeeds, the aggregation node a will respond with a REPLY message that includes identities a and i as well as a **MAC** for authenticating itself to node i and confirming the establishment of the pairwise key $K_{i,a}$. The entire pairwise key establishment and confirmation procedure is shown below:

$$i \longrightarrow a : \; i, a, \mathbf{MAC}(K_{i,a}, i\|a).$$
$$a \longrightarrow i : \; a, i, \mathbf{MAC}(K_{i,a}, a\|i).$$

The computational overhead of establishing a pairwise key for non-neighboring nodes includes the calculation of pairwise key (i.e., evaluate the polynomial share) and the generation of a **MAC** for both entities. Furthermore, our pairwise key establishment scheme incurs the following communication overhead. Both QUERY and REPLY messages consists of two identities as well as a **MAC**, which can be easily fit into one packet.

Securing Pairwise Key Establishment against Node Clone Attacks: A node clone attack (also known as a node replication attack) [5,19,24] is a typical threat against the security of WSNs, in which an adversary introduces his own sensor nodes and deceives the network into accepting them as legitimate nodes. To this end, the adversary first physically captures one sensor node and extracts its secret information. The adversary then reproduces the node in large quantity and deploys the replicas into the network. It is not difficult to find that without additional protection our pairwise key establishment schemes are also vulnerable to node clone attacks. Here we propose a few *two-factor* authentication mechanisms to mitigate or thwart potential node clone attacks. In our scheme, we require that each new sensor node must provide two pieces of authentication information in order to join the network, one of which is a proof of knowledge about the polynomial share and the other of which is obtained from the KDC. We differentiate the following two cases:

Case I: Using the Deployment Knowledge. We assume that the KDC knows the area in which a new sensor node is going to be deployed. In other words, the KDC knows all the neighbors of the new node before deployment. This assumption is reasonable because in many WSN applications the KDC usually deploys new sensor nodes at certain strategic positions to collect data of interest. For a new sensor node with identity i_τ, we assume that its l neighbors are indexed by a set $S_{i_\tau} = \{i_{\tau_1}, i_{\tau_2}, \ldots, i_{\tau_l}\}$. The KDC first computes a group key shared by $\{i_{\tau_1}, i_{\tau_2}, \ldots, i_{\tau_l}\}$ as follows:

$$K_{i_{\tau_1},\ldots,i_{\tau_l}} = \prod_{j \in S_{i_\tau} \backslash \{i_{\tau_1}\}} f_{i_{\tau_1}}(j) f_{i_{\tau_1}}(0)^{m-\tau_l+\delta} = b^{m-1} f(0)^{m-\tau_l+\delta} \prod_{j \in S_{i_\tau}} f(j).$$

The KDC then generates a message authentication code $mac_1 = \mathbf{MAC}(K_{i_{\tau_1},\ldots,i_{\tau_l}}, T, i_\tau \| i_{\tau_1} \| \cdots \| i_{\tau_l})$, where T is a time stamp, and preloads it into the new sensor node i_τ. Before joining the network, node i_τ first calculates a group key shared by $\{i_\tau, i_{\tau_1}, \ldots, i_{\tau_l}\}$ as follows:

$$K_{i_\tau, i_{\tau_1},\ldots,i_{\tau_l}} = \prod_{j \in S_{i_\tau}} f_{i_\tau}(j) f_{i_\tau}(0)^{m-(\tau_l+1)+\delta} = b^{m-1} f(0)^{m-(\tau_l+1)+\delta} \prod_{j \in S_{i_\tau} \cup \{i_\tau\}} f(j).$$

Node i_τ then computes a message authentication code $mac_2 = \mathbf{MAC}(K_{i_\tau, i_{\tau_1},\ldots,i_{\tau_l}}, T', i_\tau \| i_{\tau_1} \| \cdots \| i_{\tau_l})$ and locally broadcasts a REQUEST message containing identities $\{i_\tau, i_{\tau_1}, \ldots, i_{\tau_l}\}$, two time stamps T and T', and two message authentication codes mac_1 and mac_2. Upon receiving the REQUEST message from node i_τ, each neighboring node checks two time stamps and verifies two message authentication codes. If time stamps are valid and verifications succeed, the neighboring nodes will add node i_τ into their neighbor lists. Moreover, each neighboring node sends back an ACK message that consists of its identity and a message authentication code for authenticating itself to node i_τ and confirming the establishment of the pairwise key. The entire procedure for a new node i_τ joining into the network is demonstrated below:

$$i_\tau \longrightarrow * : \{i_\tau, i_{\tau_1}, \ldots, i_{\tau_l}\}, mac_1, mac_2.$$
$$i_{\tau_j} \longrightarrow i_\tau : i_{\tau_j}, i_\tau, \mathbf{MAC}(K_{i_{\tau_j}, i_\tau}, i_{\tau_j} \| i_\tau), j = 1, 2, \ldots, l.$$

In order to introduce a cloned sensor node i_τ into the network, an adversary should be able to generate a valid message authentication code mac_1. To this end, the adversary needs to compromise one more node from $\{i_{\tau_1}, i_{\tau_2}, \ldots, i_{\tau_l}\}$. Therefore, the above symmetric-key based two-factor authentication scheme increases the difficulty for the adversary launching node clone attacks. While symmetric-key based countermeasure is efficient in terms of computation speed and energy consumption, it is only able to mitigate node clone attacks to a certain degree. A more secure mechanism is to exploit public-key certificates, as detailed below.

Case II: Using a Public-Key Certificate. If the KDC does not have the exact deployment knowledge about new sensor nodes (e.g., new nodes might be deployed through scattering from an aircraft across an area of interest.) or a more secure node join procedure is needed, the KDC can issue public-key certificates for those new sensor nodes. For a sensor node i_τ, the KDC preloads a special certificate $cert_{i_\tau}$ into node i_τ. Such a certificate, to its simplest form, consists of the following contents:

$$cert_{i_\tau} = i_\tau, ExpT, \mathbf{SIG}_{SK_{KDC}}\{h(i_\tau \| ExpT)\},$$

where $ExpT$ denotes expiration time of the certificate, $h(\cdot)$ denote a cryptographic hash function, and $\mathbf{SIG}_{SK_{KDC}}\{h(i_\tau\|ExpT)\}$ is a signature signed over $h(i_\tau\|ExpT)$ with the KDC's private key SK_{KDC}. Upon joining the network, node i_τ locally broadcasts the certificate $cert_{i_\tau}$, which serves as a short-lived admission ticket for node i_τ. If node i_τ's neighbors verify $cert_{i_\tau}$ successfully, they will respond with an ACK message as described in *Case I*. After node i_τ authenticates all its neighbors, it generates a message authentication code mac_2 as described in *Case I* to prove the knowledge about the polynomial share to its neighbors. The neighboring nodes will add node i_τ into their neighbor lists upon a successful authentication. The above public-key certificate based node join process is shown below:

$$i_\tau \longrightarrow *: \ i_\tau, cert_{i_\tau}.$$
$$i_{\tau_j} \longrightarrow i_\tau: \ i_{\tau_j}, i_\tau, \mathbf{MAC}(K_{i_{\tau_j}, i_\tau}, i_{\tau_j}\|i_\tau), j = 1, 2, \ldots, l.$$
$$i_\tau \longrightarrow *: \ \{i_\tau, i_{\tau_1}, \ldots, i_{\tau_l}\}, mac_2.$$

Using a public-key certificate as a piece of authentication information is able to thwart node clone attacks since an adversary cannot generate a valid certificate without knowing the secret key of the KDC. However, each neighboring node needs to verify a digital signature, which is more expensive when compared to the symmetric-key based mechanism.

Comparison with Other Pairwise Key Establishment Schemes: Our pairwise key establishment protocol is a deterministic scheme. In Table 1 we compare a couple of pairwise key establishment schemes with respect to several desired properties, where ProbK denotes random key predistribution based pairwise key establishment schemes like [6, 10, 26] and ProbP denotes random polynomial predistribution based pairwise key establishment schemes like [8, 14]. Since the random perturbation based pairwise key establishment scheme in [23] has been broken, we did not include it in the table. The Table 1 shows that our scheme is able to establish a pairwise key for sensor nodes in a deterministic and non-interactive way with little performance overhead. Moreover, our scheme can scale well with the network size and also tolerate the dynamic topology of network. With certain node admission mechanism in place, potential node clone attacks can be mitigated or prevented.

4.3   Cluster Key Establishment

Cluster key is useful for securing the broadcast messages sent by a sensor node to its neighbors. Assuming that a node i's immediate neighbors are denoted by a set $I = \{i_1, i_2, \ldots, i_t\}$, the cluster key $K_{i,i_1,\ldots,i_t}$ can be computed on the fly as follows:

$$K_{i,i_1,\ldots,i_t} = \prod_{j\in I} f_i(j)f_i(0)^{m-t+\delta} = b^{m-1}f(0)^{m-t+\delta}\prod_{j\in I\cup\{i\}} f(j).$$

Table 1. Comparison of Different Pairwise Key Establishment Schemes

Scheme	LPKM	SPINS	LEAP/LEAP+	ProbK	ProbP	Blundo et al.
Property	(this work)	[20]	[24, 25]	[6, 10, 26]	[8, 14]	[4]
Deterministic Key Establishment	Yes	Yes	Yes	No	No	Yes
Direct Key Establishment	Yes	No	No	No	No	Yes
Non-Interactive Key Establishment	Yes	No	No	No	No	Yes
Resilience to Node Clone	Partial	No	Partial	No	Yes	No
Resilience to Dynamic Network Topology	Yes	No	No	No	No	Yes
Computation Overhead	Modular + MACs	MACs + Enc	PRF + MACs	MACs + Enc	Modular + MACs + Enc	Modular + MACs
Communication Overhead (hops)	1	≥ 2	1	≥ 1	≥ 1	1
Storage Overhead (keys/coefficients)	$k + 1$	1	1	hundreds	hundreds	$\binom{m+k}{k}$

After obtaining the cluster key $K_{i,i_1,\ldots,i_t}$, node i locally broadcasts a CLUSTER_FORMATION message containing $(t+1)$ identities $\{i, i_1, \ldots, i_t\}$ and a message authentication code $\mathbf{MAC}(K_{i,i_1,\ldots,i_t}, i\|i_1\|\cdots\|i_t)$. Upon receiving the CLUSTER_FORMATION message, each neighboring node i_j $(j = 1, 2, \ldots, t)$ calculates the cluster key in a similar way as node i does and responds with a CLUSTER_DONE message that includes identities i_j and i as well as a message authentication code $\mathbf{MAC}(K_{i,i_1,\ldots,i_t}, i_j\|i)$ to confirm the establishment of the cluster key. The communication flows for establishing a cluster key is demonstrated below:

$$i \longrightarrow * : \{i, i_1, \ldots, i_t\}, \mathbf{MAC}(K_{i,i_1,\ldots,i_t}, i\|i_1\|\cdots\|i_t).$$
$$i_j \longrightarrow i : i_j, i, \mathbf{MAC}(K_{i,i_1,\ldots,i_t}, i_j\|i), j = 1, 2, \ldots, t.$$

The computational overhead for establishing a cluster key in our scheme involves evaluating a polynomial share at t identities and computing a $\mathbf{MAC}$. Furthermore, only one CLUSTER_FORMATION message needs to be locally broadcast in order to form a cluster and establish a cluster key. Note that for the cluster key establishment scheme in LEAP [24] and LEAP+ [25] a cluster initiator needs to send an encrypted cluster key to each neighboring node individually, which incurs a computational overhead of t encryptions and a communication overhead of t messages. Therefore, our cluster key establishment scheme has much smaller performance overhead when compared to those in [24, 25].

4.4   Local Broadcast Authentication

In WSNs, a local broadcast is a typical one-to-many communication mode for disseminating routing control packets and reporting sensor readings. Due to a wide range of attacks to WSNs, those locally broadcast messages must be authenticated before they are forwarded or processed. A sound local broadcast authentication mechanism should be lightweight with respect to computation in order to thwart potential Denial-of-Service attacks. Hence, a symmetric-key based scheme becomes a natural option. As noticed in [24, 25], μTESLA [20] is not suitable for local broadcast authentication because of the nature of delayed message authentication. Although the cluster key established in Section 4.3 can be used to secure a broadcast message, a cluster-key based scheme does not provide source authentication and therefore is vulnerable to node impersonation attacks. To mitigate those attacks, we propose a lightweight probabilistic local broadcast authentication scheme in this section, which utilizes a cluster key for message authentication and a subset of pairwise keys for source authentication.

A Probabilistic Local Broadcast Authentication Scheme: In this scheme, node i first forms a cluster with t neighboring nodes and establishes a cluster key $K_{i,i_1,\ldots,i_t}$ as described in Section 4.3. Node i then selects s out of t neighboring nodes $\{i_{\tau_1}, i_{\tau_2}, \ldots, i_{\tau_s}\}$ as *witnesses*, where each node is chosen with probability q_1. To locally broadcast a message M, the following packet is transmitted:

$$i \longrightarrow * : \{i, i_{\tau_1}, \ldots, i_{\tau_s}\}, M, \mathbf{MAC}(K_{i,i_1,\ldots,i_t}, M),$$
$$\mathbf{MAC}(K_{i,i_{\tau_1}}, M), \ldots, \mathbf{MAC}(K_{i,i_{\tau_s}}, M),$$

where $\{i_{\tau_1}, \ldots, i_{\tau_s}\}$ is called a *witness list*, $\mathbf{MAC}(K_{i,i_1,\ldots,i_t}, M)$ is generated using the cluster key $K_{i,i_1,\ldots,i_t}$, and $\mathbf{MAC}(K_{i,i_{\tau_1}}, M), \ldots, \mathbf{MAC}(K_{i,i_{\tau_s}}, M)$ are generated using pairwise keys $K_{i,i_{\tau_1}}, \ldots, K_{i,i_{\tau_s}}$, respectively. For those nodes whose identities belong to the witness list, the corresponding message authentication code $\mathbf{MAC}(K_{i,i_{\tau_u}}, M)$ for some $i_{\tau_u} \in \{i_{\tau_1}, i_{\tau_2}, \ldots, i_{\tau_s}\}$ is verified, whereas other nodes only need to check the validity of $\mathbf{MAC}(K_{i,i_1,\ldots,i_t}, M)$. If any verification fails, an INVALID message will be locally broadcast. Furthermore, non-witness nodes will wait for a short time period λ to see whether an INVALID message is broadcast from a witness node. If no any INVALID message is received during the time period λ, non-witness nodes will accept the message M as an authenticated one sent from node i. Otherwise, the message M will be discard.

The above authentication scheme partially provides source authentication through the *cooperation* among neighboring nodes (i.e., non-witness nodes indirectly authenticate the source node through witness nodes). Our scheme is able to thwart node impersonation attacks unless all the selected witness nodes get compromised by an adversary. The probability that an adversary can launch a node impersonation attack against the authentication scheme is as follows:

$$p_{imper} = \sum_{s=1}^{t} \binom{t}{s} (q_1 q_2)^s (1 - q_1)^{t-s},$$

where q_2 is the probability that a sensor node is compromised by an adversary. Figure 1 shows that under a typical setting (e.g., $t = 30, q_1 = 0.4 \sim 0.9$, and $q_2 = 0.5 \sim 0.9$) the successful probability for an adversary launching a node impersonation attack is small. Therefore, given a certain network environment (i.e., q_2 is determined), our scheme can effectively mitigate node impersonation attacks by an appropriate selection of q_1.

The computational overhead for authenticating a broadcast message involves the verification of a **MAC**, which is similar to the one-way key chain based authentication scheme in LEAP [24] and LEAP+ [25]. While the one-way key

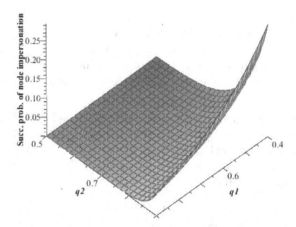

Fig. 1. The successful probability p_{imper} of a node impersonation attack

chained based authentication provides stronger protection against node impersonation attacks than ours, each node needs to transmit an encrypted commitment (i.e., the first authentication key in the one-way key chain) to all its neighbors, which incurs a lot of computational and communication overhead. In this aspect, our scheme is superior because it enables a system administrator to make trade-offs between security and performance of the network.

4.5   Group Key Establishment

In WSNs, a group key is useful in applications where a base station or a mobile sink disseminates queries/commands to a certain area or even the entire network. While a group key shared by a base station and all the nodes in the network can be precomputed and preloaded into each node, a group key shared by a mobile sink and a small group of nodes can be generated on the fly. Establishing a group key between a mobile sink g and a group of sensor nodes $\{g_1, g_2, \ldots, g_t\}$ follows the same procedure as the establishment of a cluster key (see Section 4.3). Basically, the mobile sink g first broadcasts a GROUP_FORMATION message containing the target group identities $\{g_1, g_2, \ldots, g_t\}$ and a **MAC** calculated with the group key $K_{g,g_1,\ldots,g_t}$. After the mobile sink g receives GROUP_DONE messages from all the group members, the group key is established and ready to use. Due to the high similarity between the group and cluster key establishment process, we omit the details here.

A more challenging issue about group key management is to deal with *group rekeying*, namely to refresh a group key in a secure, reliable, and timely fashion upon detecting a compromised node [24, 25]. The group rekeying problem has been extensively investigated in the context of secure multicast in wired or wireless networks. Recently proposed group rekeying schemes for WSNs [24, 25] have improved previous solutions [2, 12, 22] significantly in terms of communication overhead and rekeying delay. Unfortunately, those group rekeying schemes still need interactions between a KDC and sensor nodes [24, 25] or among a group of sensor nodes. In this section, we propose two efficient, distributed, and non-interactive group key management schemes, including a *distributed key revocation scheme* and a *distributed share updating scheme*.

Distributed Key Revocation: Let $K_{g,g_1,\ldots,g_t}$ be the shared key between the mobile sink g and a group of sensor nodes indexed by a set $G = \{g_1, g_2, \ldots, g_t\}$. Then we obtain

$$K_{g,g_1,\ldots,g_t} = \prod_{j \in G} f_g(j) f_g(0)^{m-(t+1)+\delta} = b^{m-1} f(0)^{m-(t+1)+\delta} \prod_{j \in G \cup \{g\}} f(j).$$

Without loss of generality, we assume that the first l sensor nodes $g_1, g_2, \ldots, g_l \in G$ were compromised by an adversary and have been detected by all the other group members at a certain time instant. To secure the subsequent communications between the mobile sink g and sensor nodes in $G \backslash \{g_1, \ldots, g_l\}$, a new group key $K_{g,g_{l+1},\ldots,g_t}$ should be established. To this end, the mobile sink g performs the following computation to refresh the group key:

$$K_{g,g_{l+1},\ldots,g_t} = K_{g,g_1,\ldots,g_t} \cdot \left(\prod_{j \in \{g_1,\ldots,g_l\}} f_g(j) \right)^{-1} \cdot f_g(0)^l$$

$$= b^{m-1} f(0)^{m-(t-l+1)+\delta} \prod_{j \in \{g,g_{l+1},\ldots,g_t\}} f(j).$$

Other sensor nodes in $G \backslash \{g_1, \ldots, g_l\}$ will independently conduct the similar calculations to generate the new group key $K_{g,g_{l+1},\ldots,g_t}$. In this way, the compromised nodes $g_1, g_2, \ldots, g_l$ are evicted from the group automatically. Note that in our scheme all the sensor nodes refresh a group key in a distributed and non-interactive fashion. Furthermore, no any rekeying delay has been introduced in our scheme.

Distributed Share Updating: To mitigate the effect of node compromise in WSNs and provide backward secrecy, an effective approach is to periodically update the key share preloaded into sensor nodes. In our scheme, a polynomial share for node i has a form of $(by_i a_0, by_i a_1, \ldots, by_i a_k)$, where $b \in \mathbb{F}_p$ is a random mask. In order to refresh polynomial shares, one can employ a secure and lightweight pseudorandom number generator (see [18] for example) to generate new random masks $b_u \in \mathbb{F}_p, u = 1, 2, \ldots$ periodically. With the random masks b_u's, the new polynomial share of node i at the time interval u becomes $((\prod_{j=1}^u b_j) by_i a_0, (\prod_{j=1}^u b_j) by_i a_1, \ldots, (\prod_{j=1}^u b_j) by_i a_k)$. If an adversary compromises a node at the time interval u, he cannot obtain the polynomial share used in previous time intervals and therefore cannot decrypt any communication in previous sessions. Furthermore, each node independently refreshes the share according to its own timer and the entire share updating procedure is distributed and non-interactive.

5   Performance Evaluation

Evaluating a k-degree polynomial at multiple node identities is essential for generating required keys in the LPKM, which involves performing modular operations (i.e., modular addition, modular squaring, modular multiplication, etc.) over a finite field $\mathbb{F}_p$. In order to demonstrate the feasibility and performance of the LPKM for wireless sensor nodes, we address efficient implementation of the polynomial-based conference key establishment protocol on MICAz motes below.

5.1   Selection of System Parameters

We first notice that the shared key is used to compute a message authentication code that is usually generated using AES-CBC-MAC [3] described in IEEE 802.15.4 security suites [13]. Hence, the characteristic p should be 128-bit long to accommodate a cryptographic key for AES. Taking into account both security and efficiency, we choose $p = 2^{127} - 1$, which enables us to conduct fast finite field arithmetic. According to [11], m should be chosen such that either $(m - 1)^{-1}$ or m^{-1} modulo $p - 1$ exists. Moreover, m should also be large in order to provide security services for large WSNs. In our implementation, we choose $m = 2^{16} + 1$, which can support up to $65,536$ sensor nodes and is large enough for most applications. Since m is odd, we have $\delta = 1$ and $h = m^{-1}$ mod $p = $ 0x5555AAAA5555AAAA5555AAAA5555AAA9 (in hexadecimal representation) in this case. The selection of the degree k for the polynomial $f(x)$ is determined based on a system administrator's evaluation about potential threats to the network. While choosing a larger k is helpful to improve the security of the entire network, the computational and storage overhead will also be increased accordingly. In Section 5.2, we will further study the effect of different k's on the performance and storage.

5.2   Implementation Results

To generate required keys using LPKM, a sensor node i needs to evaluate its polynomial share $f_i(x) = c_0 + c_1 x + \cdots + c_k x^k$ at different identities $id \in \mathbb{F}_{p'}$, where $p' = 2^{16} + 1$ and $c_j = b y_i a_j, j = 0, 1, \ldots, k$ are preloaded into node i. As noticed by Liu and Ning in [14], computing $f_i(id)$ only involves modular multiplications between an integer in $\mathbb{F}_p$ and another integer in $\mathbb{F}_{p'}$, which is more efficient than multiplying two integers in $\mathbb{F}_p$. The performance of finite field arithmetic over $\mathbb{F}_{2^{127}-1}$ on MICAz motes is summarized in Table 2, where Multiplication (F) denotes a full modular multiplication with two operands in $\mathbb{F}_p$ and Multiplication (P) represents a partial modular multiplication with one operand in $\mathbb{F}_p$ and the other in $\mathbb{F}_{p'}$.

When node i wants to establish a shared key with a group of nodes indexed by a set $I = \{i_1, i_2, \ldots, i_t\}$, it needs to compute

$$K_{i,i_1,\ldots,i_t} = \prod_{j \in I} f_i(j) f_i(0)^{m-t+\delta}.$$

Table 2. Performance of Finite Field Arithmetic over $\mathbb{F}_{2^{127}-1}$ on MICAz Motes

Operation	Addition	Multiplication (F)	Multiplication (P)	Squaring	Inversion
Time (ms)	0.027	0.562	0.075	0.375	8.475

To accelerate the computation, we can rewrite $K_{i,i_1,\ldots,i_t}$ as

$$K_{i,i_1,\ldots,i_t} = \prod_{j \in I} f_i(j) f_i(0)^{m+\delta} \left(f_i(0)^{-1} \right)^t .$$

Hence, after the initial polynomial share is preloaded into node i, it can precompute both $f_i(0)^{m+\delta}$ and $f_i(0)^{-1}$. Those precomputation results can be repeatedly used by node i to calculate group keys with different nodes in the network until the polynomial share $f_i(x)$ is updated. The aforementioned trick has been used in our implementation. Figure 2 illustrates the performance of establishing a group key when the group size t increases from 2 to 30 and the polynomial degree k is taken as $30, 50$ or 100. One can notice that establishing a group key in LPKM does not incur significant computational overhead for sensor nodes.

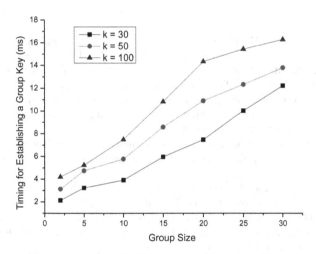

Fig. 2. The performance of establishing a group key for different group size t and polynomial degree k on MICAz motes

Regarding to the storage cost, the LPKM inherits the salient feature of the polynomial-based conference key establishment protocol in [11]. Therefore, each node only needs to store $(k + 1)$ coefficients of its polynomial share. Table 3 summarizes the storage overhead of the LPKM when the degree of the polynomial $f(x)$ increases from 30 to 100. The code size of our implementation is around 6.12 Kbytes and the RAM usage is 68 bytes. Considering the sizes of RAM and Flash ROM in MICAz are 4 Kbytes and 128 Kbytes, respectively, the storage cost of the LPKM is negligible.

Table 3. Storage Overhead of the LPKM for Different Polynomial Degree k (in Bytes)

k	30	40	50	60	70	80	90	100
ROM	496	656	816	976	1136	1296	1456	1616

6   Conclusion

Designing a lightweight key management protocol for WSNs is a critical issue that has attracted a lot of attention in recent years. In this paper, we proposed a lightweight key management scheme called LPKM, which enables an arbitrary group of sensor nodes to establish a shared key on the fly in a distributed and non-interactive way. LPKM can support in-network processing and is able to secure different communication patterns. Through extensive analysis and implementation, we showed that the LPKM can mitigate or prevent the most common attacks to WSNs and achieve good performance on current generation of wireless sensor nodes.

References

1. Albrecht, M., Gentry, C., Halevi, S., Katz, J.: Attacking Cryptographic Schemes Based on "Perturbation Polynomials". In: The 16th ACM Conference on Computer and Communication Security - CCS 2009, pp. 1–10. ACM Press (2009)
2. Balenson, D., McGrew, D., Sherman, A.: Key Management for Large Dynamic Groups: One-Way Function Trees and Amortized Initialization. In: IETF Internet Draft (August 2000), http://tools.ietf.org/html/draft-irtf-smug-groupkeymgmt-oft-00
3. Bellare, M., Kilian, J., Rogaway, P.: The Security of the Cipher Block Chaining Message Authentication Code. Journal of Computer and System Sciences 61(3), 362–399 (2000)
4. Blundo, C., De Santis, A., Herzberg, A., Kutten, S., Vaccaro, U., Yung, M.: Perfectly-Secure Key Distribution for Dynamic Conferences. In: Brickell, E.F. (ed.) CRYPTO 1992. LNCS, vol. 740, pp. 471–486. Springer, Heidelberg (1993)
5. Chan, H., Perrig, A.: Security and Privacy in Sensor Networks. IEEE Computer Magazine 36(10), 103–105 (2003)
6. Chan, H., Perrig, A., Song, D.: Random Key Predistribution Schemes for Sensor Networks. In: The 2003 IEEE Symposium on Security and Privacy - S&P 2003, pp. 197–213. IEEE Computer Society (2003)
7. Crossbow Technology Inc., MICAz – Wireless Measurement System, http://bullseye.xbow.com:81/Products/Product_pdf_files/Wireless_pdf/MICAz_Datasheet.pdf
8. Du, W., Deng, J., Han, Y., Varshney, P.: A Pairwise Key Pre-Distribution Schemes for Wireless Sensor Networks. In: The 10th ACM Conference on Computer and Communication Security - CCS 2003, pp. 42–51. ACM Press (2003)
9. Du, X., Guizani, G., Xiao, Y., Chen, H.-H.: A Routing-Driven Elliptic Curve Cryptography Based Key Management Scheme for Heterogeneous Sensor Networks. IEEE Transactions on Wireless Communications 8(3), 1223–1229 (2009)

10. Eschenauer, L., Gligor, V.: A Key-Management Scheme for Distributed Sensor Networks. In: The 9th ACM Conference on Computer and Communication Security - CCS 2002, pp. 41–47. ACM Press (2002)
11. Harn, L., Gong, G.: Conference Key Establishment Using Polynomials, Centre for Applied Cryptographic Research (CACR). Technical Reports, CACR 2012-10, http://cacr.uwaterloo.ca/techreports/2012/cacr2012-10.pdf, 2012.
12. Hung, H., Muckenhirn, C., Rivers, T.: Group Key Management Protocol (GKMP) Architecture, Request for Comments (RFC 2094), Internet Engineering Task Force (July 1997), http://tools.ietf.org/html/rfc2094
13. IEEE Standard 802.15.4: Wireless Medium Access Control (MAC) and Physical Layer (PHY) Specification for Low-Rate Wireless Personal Area Networks (WPANs). IEEE Computer Soceity (June 2006)
14. Liu, D., Ning, P.: Establishing Pairwise Keys in Distributed Sensor Netowrks. In: The 10th ACM Conference on Computer and Communication Security - CCS 2003, pp. 52–61. ACM Press (2003)
15. Liu, D., Ning, P.: Security for Wireless Sensor Networks. Advances in Information Security Series. Springer (2006)
16. López, J., Zhou, J.: Wireless Sensor Network Security. Cryptology and Information Security Series. IOS Press (2008)
17. Malan, D., Welsh, M., Smith, M.D.: Implementing Public-Key Infrastructure for Sensor Networks. ACM Transactions on Sensor Networks 4(4), Article No: 22 (2008)
18. Mandal, K., Fan, X., Gong, G.: A Light weight Pseudorandom Number Generator for EPC Class 1 Gen 2 RFID Tags. In: West European Workshop on Research in Cryptography - WEWoRC 2011, Conference Record, pp. 91–95 (2011)
19. Parno, B., Perrig, A., Gligor, V.: Distributed Detection of Node Replication Attacks in Sensor Networks. In: The 2005 IEEE Symposium on Security and Privacy - S&P 2005, pp. 49–63. IEEE Computer Society (2005)
20. Perrig, A., Szewczyk, R., Wen, V., Culler, D., Tygar, J.: SPINS: Security Protocols for Sensor Netowkrs. In: The 7th Annual ACM International Conference on Mobile Computing and Networks - Mobicom 2001, pp. 189–199. ACM Press (2001)
21. Ren, K., Lou, W.: Communication Security in Wireless Sensor Network, VDM Verlag Dr. Müller (2008)
22. Wallner, D., Harder, E., Agee, R.: Key Management for Multicast: Issues and Architectures, Request for Comments (RFC 2627), Internet Engineering Task Force (June 1999), http://tools.ietf.org/html/rfc2627
23. Zhang, W., Tran, M., Zhu, S., Cao, G.: A Random Perturbation-Based Scheme for Pairwise Key Establishment in Sensor Netowkrs. In: The 8th ACM International Symposium on Mobile Ad Hoc Networking and Computing - MobiHoc 2007, pp. 90–99. ACM Press (2007)
24. Zhu, S., Setia, S., Jajodia, S.: LEAP: Efficient Security Mechanisms for Large-Scale Distributed Sensor Networks. In: The 10th ACM Conference on Computer and Communication Security - CCS 2003, pp. 62–72. ACM Press (2003)
25. Zhu, S., Setia, S., Jajodia, S.: LEAP+: Efficient Security Mechanisms for Large-Scale Distributed Sensor Networks. ACM Transactions on Sensor Networks 2(4), 500–528 (2006)
26. Zhu, S., Xu, S., Setia, S., Jajodia, S.: Establishing Pairwise Keys for Secure Communication in Ad Hoc Networks: A Probabilistic Approach. In: The 11th IEEE International Conference on Network Protocols - ICNP 2003, pp. 326–335. IEEE Computer Society (2003)

Cross-Layer Interception Caching for MANETs

F.J. González-Cañete, E. Casilari, and A. Triviño-Cabrera

Dpt. Tecnología Electrónica, University of Málaga
Campus de Teatinos, ETSI Telecomunicación, Málaga, Spain
+34 952 13 71 76
{fgc,ecasilari,atc}@uma.es

Abstract. In this work we study the interception of the requests performed by the mobile nodes in a wireless network. This interception can be achieved because a local cache is implemented in each wireless device. In that way, the nodes can serve the documents instead of forwarding the requests to the data servers. In our proposal, the interception is enhanced so it is also implemented when the mobile nodes create the route to the data servers. Using cross-layer information, the routing algorithm can discover the location of the documents disseminated across the network. By means of simulations, we evaluate the performance of the proposed interception mechanism. We study the effect of the network load, the expiration time of the documents, the requests pattern and the cache size on these cache mechanisms. Under all the assumptions the proposed scheme reduces the delay, the network traffic and the amount of timeouts when the servers are not reachable.

Keywords: MANET, local caching, interception caching, AODV.

1 Introduction

In the mobile computing paradigm, devices are expected to demand the access to the Internet anywhere and anytime. Some geographic and economic constraints may limit the access through infrastructure networks. In order to overcome this restriction, the MANET (Mobile Ad hoc NETwork) technology outstands as a feasible solution. Mobile ad hoc networks are composed of wireless devices that communicate among themselves without any specific router. Actually, routing tasks are transferred to the mobile nodes so two distant devices (not directly connected by a wireless link) can exchange packets through the collaboration of intermediate nodes that retransmit and route the packets to the final destination. As packets traverse multiple links or hops, these networks are also known as multihop wireless networks.

One member of the MANET can be an Internet Gateway [1] through which the network can access some external hosts, DHCP (Dynamic Host Configuration Protocol.) servers or HTTP (Hyper Text Transfer Protocol) servers. However, the use of the Internet Gateway must cope with the peculiarities of mobile devices in a MANET. Firstly, the Internet Gateway may not be permanently available for the MANET as the mobility of the nodes may lead to situations where this element is not reachable. Additionally, the wireless medium has restricted bandwidth. In particular, the links to the Gateway will be notably saturated when mobile nodes inject traffic to

J. Zheng et al. (Eds.): Adhocnets 2012, LNICST 111, pp. 196–211, 2013.

the Internet. This could provoke a bottleneck effect in the Internet Gateway. Therefore, web technologies in a MANET must take into account the temporary connection to the Internet while they should also reduce the signalling and the traffic load through the Internet Gateway.

Taking into account these new requirements, the traffic could benefit from caching techniques. When using caching, devices store some documents which were previously requested to a server. Mobile devices in a MANET can take advantage of others' storage so that the documents can be served without accessing the server and, in turn, without occupying the wireless links to the Gateway. Furthermore, the requests can be satisfied even when the Gateway is not reachable. In addition, the traffic generated to get the document is reduced as an intermediate node serves it. This operation is called interception caching. Although interception caching is not exclusively conceived for ad hoc networks, the technique has been adapted and optimized for a MANET context. Specifically, this paper evaluates a cross-layer technique by which interception caching uses some routing resources to expand the use of the caches.

The paper is structured as follows. Section 2 presents the related work. In section 3, the caching scheme that intercepts the requests is described. This scheme exchanges some cross-layer information using the routing protocol in order to know where the documents are located in the MANET. Section 4 details the simulation model. Section 5 studies the performance of a MANET when the interception scheme proposed in Section 3 is employed. The study takes into account the time between requests, the expiration time of the documents, the cache size and the distribution of the requests. Finally, section 5 outlines the main conclusion and suggests possible future work.

2   Related Work

Although there are many works devoted to caching technology in the wired environment the particular literature about caching in MANETs is not so abundant.

Some caching schemes employ broadcast message as the first choice in order to find the documents in the network. These broadcast messages can be sent to the entire network, as in the case of MobEye [2] or following a more restrictive approach that limits the distance of the messages as used in SimpleSearch [3]. Similarly, the caching scheme proposed by Moriya in [4] sends the broadcast messages to the neighbourhood so that, if the document is not found, the request is transmitted to the server.

Other caching schemes employ information of the location of the documents in the network. Nodes obtain this information by analysing the messages that they forward. As examples of this kind of caching schemes we can mention: DGA (Distributed Greedy Algorithm) [5], Wang [6], Cho [7], CacheData, CachePath, HybridCache [8] and GroupCaching [9].

Some caching schemes assign a predefined role to every node in the wireless network. In that way, they can perform as caching nodes, requesting nodes, coordinator nodes, gateway nodes, etc. CC (Cluster Cooperative) [10] and Denko [11] are examples of this kind of caching policy.

However, some caching schemes follow a hybrid policy. Thus, the caching schemes COOP [12] and IXP/DPIP (IndeX Push/Data Pull/Index Push) [13] employ network information and broadcast requests. On the other hand, COACS (Cooperative and Adaptive Caching System) [14] and GROCOCA (Group-based Cooperative Caching) [15] are role-based caching schemes that also utilize information obtained from the network.

3   Caching in MANETs

In this section we define the formulation of caching in MANETs following a modified version of the notation presented in [16].

For a mobile node in a MANET that requests information to a data server or to the Internet through a Gateway, the first strategy to reduce the traffic in the network is by implementing a local cache for the requested documents. This cache allows that future requests to the same documents will be served by the local cache even if the Gateway is not available, thus they will not produce any traffic in the ad hoc network.

Formally, let $MN = \{w_1, w_2, ..., w_w\}$ be the set of w mobiles nodes in a MANET. Let $U = \{1, 2, ..., n\}$ be the universe of n documents that can be requested by the mobile nodes, where $s(i)$ represents the size of the document i with $1 \leq i \leq n$. $TTL(i)$ is defined to be the time when the document i expires and becomes obsolete. Let $R_j = \{r_{j1}, r_{j2}, ..., r_{jm}\}$ be the sequence of requests performed by the node j, where r_{jk} denotes the request of mobile node j in the k instant taking into account that $r_{jk} \in U$. The destination of the requests in R_j is a fixed node w_{DS} (Data Server) in the Internet that has access to all the documents in U. The data server is supposed to be accessed through the Internet Gateway.

Let us implement a local cache in each mobile node in the MANET. B_{jk} denotes the set of documents stored in the cache of node j at time k, where $B_{jk} \subset U$. The set of documents stored in the caches must satisfy the properties (1) and (2):

$$\sum\nolimits_{i \in B_{jk}} s(i) \leq S_j \tag{1}$$

$$\forall i \in B_{jk} \Rightarrow TTL(i) > k \tag{2}$$

where S_j is the size of the cache in node j. Property (2) states that the documents stored in the caches cannot be obsolete. Therefore, the sequence of states $(B_{j0}, B_{j1}, ..., B_{jm})$ indicates the states of the cache in node j as the requests in R_j are resolved. B_{j0} is the initial state when the cache is empty and B_{jm} is the state when all the requests have been served.

Let $p_{k,ij} = \{w_i, w_u, w_v, ..., w_j\}$ be the active route between node i and node j at instant k, defined as the set of mobile nodes that are necessary to reach node j from node I at the instant k. Only two consecutive nodes in a path are directly connected, that is, a wireless link between them is available. If $p_{k,ij} = \varnothing$ then there is no route created to reach node j from node i, otherwise $card(p_{k,ij}) \geq 2$, where $card(p_{k,ij})$ is the cardinality of the set $p_{k,ij}$. We can define the distance between node i and j at the instant k as (3):

$$dist(w_i, w_j)_k = card(p_{k,ij}) - 1 \tag{3}$$

This distance defines the number of hops needed to reach node j from node I at the instant k. When the distance between nodes i and j is one, the nodes are neighbour. On the other hand, we consider that $dist(w_i, w_j)_k = \infty$ if there is not a route created between the nodes i and j at the instant k ($p_{k,ij} = \emptyset$).

We define the local cache hit sequence in node j to be $(h'_{j1}, h'_{j2}, ..., h'_{jm})$ where h'_{jk} is defined in (4).

$$h'_{jk} = \begin{cases} 1 & \text{if } r_{jk} \in B_{j(k-1)} \\ 0 & \text{if } r_{jk} \notin B_{j(k-1)} \end{cases} \tag{4}$$

When h'_{jk} equals I a local cache hit is considered in node j, otherwise a local cache miss is assumed as the document required is not in the local cache at that moment.

The cache replacement policy decides which documents must be evicted from the cache in order to make room for the new ones. The goal of the caching scheme is to retain in the cache the documents that have a high probability to be requested again near in time.

Given a request sequence R_j in node j, a cache of size S_j and an initial state B_{j0}, the replacement policy produces a cache state sequence $(B_{j1}, ..., B_{jm})$, we have for $k=1,...,m$ the equation (5):

$$B_{jk} = \begin{cases} (B_{j(k-1)} - \varepsilon_{jk}) \cup \{r_{jk}\} & \text{if } r_{jk} \notin B_{j(k-1)} \\ B_{j(k-1)} & \text{otherwise} \end{cases} \tag{5}$$

In the first case considered in the previous equation, the document requested is not stored in the cache of node j (cache miss). The term ε_{jk} (with $\varepsilon_{jk} \subset B_{j(k-1)}$) denotes the set of documents that have to be evicted from the cache in order to make room for the new one in the request r_{jk}. If there is enough room for the new document, ε_{jk} is an empty set. In the second case there is a local cache hit and the cache remains unchanged.

The next step compels the mobile nodes to cooperate between them in order to respond to the requests of the other nodes using their local caches. As an example, Fig. 1 shows a snapshot of a MANET where DS indicates a Data Server node, that is, the node that physically stores all the documents. This node is accessed through a Gateway (GW). Nodes $1, 2, 3$ and 4 are user nodes that request documents to DS. The connections between the nodes indicate the existing wireless links created by the routing protocol.

Let us suppose that node 2 requests the document A. The request will be forwarded using the routing protocol to the Gateway. The data server will respond with the document A using the reverse route and the node 2 will store A in its local cache. In the case that node 3 requests the same document A to DS, the request will reach node 2, which can respond to node 3 with the copy of the document A stored in its local cache. The interception of the requests reduces the number of hops necessary to obtain the document and hence the number of forwarding messages along the network.

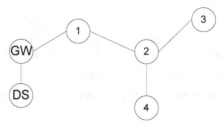

Fig. 1. Example of a MANET connected to a Data Server (DS)

We define the interception cache hit sequence in node j to be $(h^i_{j1}, h^i_{j2}, ..., h^i_{jm})$ where h^i_{jk} is defined in (6):

$$h^i_{jk} = \begin{cases} 1 & \text{if } r_{jk} \notin B_{j(k-1)} \wedge r_{jk} \in B_{i(k-1)} \mid i \neq j \wedge i \neq DS \wedge w_i \in p_{k,jDS} \\ 0 & otherwise \end{cases} \tag{6}$$

where w_i indicates an intermediate wireless node that has a copy of the document requested in its local cache. The node w_i is located in the route of the request r_{jk} from the node j to the server node DS. When $h^i_{jk}=1$ an interception cache hit is considered in node j. As $dist(w_j, w_i)_k < dist(w_j, w_{DS})_k$, the number of hops needed to satisfy the request r_{jk} is diminished as well as the time to serve the request.

The proposed interception caching procedure works in the cases when the routing paths from the source of the requests to the data servers are created. However let us suppose the situation presented in Fig. 2 (which follows a similar network topology of the example in Figure 1): Node *1* has moved outside the coverage area of *DS* and hence node *2* cannot access *DS* directly. Nodes *3* and *4* are located in the coverage area of node *2* but there is no route created between them. When node *4* proceeds to request the document *A* to *DS*, it detects that there is no path to the Gateway and therefore, DS is unreachable. The request is not served even when node *2* has a valid copy of the document *A* in its local cache.

This problem can be solved if the routing algorithm is involved in the process of looking for the documents in the MANET. Let us suppose that the AODV protocol [17] is utilized. The broadcast RREQ (Route Request) message sent in order to create the route to the gateway could include information about the demanded document, that is, a field with the document identification is 'piggybacked' (inserted) into the RREQ message. In our example, node *4* will broadcast a RREQ in order to create the route to *DS* with the information of the document *A*. When node *2* receives the RREQ, it checks if a document request is piggybacked in the routing message. If this is the case, the node extracts the information and verifies if there is a copy of the document in its local cache. If so, node *2* responds to node *4* using a RREP (Route Reply) message including the piggybacked identification of the document. As the node *4* receives the RREP and hence the route between node *4* and *2* is created, node *4* directly sends the document request to node *2*.

By using this procedure nodes in the MANET can access to the disseminated documents even if the data server is inaccessible.

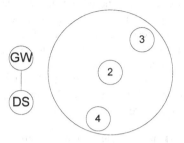

Fig. 2. Example of an isolated MANET

We define the route creation interception cache hit sequence in node j to be $(h_{j1}^{rci}, h_{j2}^{rci}, ..., h_{jm}^{rci})$ where h_{jk}^{rci} is defined in (7):

$$h_{jk}^{rci} = \begin{cases} 1 & \text{if } r_{jk} \notin B_{j(k-1)} \wedge r_{jk} \in B_{i(k-1)} \mid i \neq j \wedge i \neq DS \wedge p_{k,jDS} = \varnothing \\ 0 & \text{otherwise} \end{cases} \tag{7}$$

where w_i indicates a wireless node that replies to the request of a route from node j to the server node DS because it has a copy of the document requested in its local cache when it receives the RREQ message. When $h_{jk}^{rci}=1$ a route creation interception cache hit is considered to have occurred in node j. Again, as $dist(w_j, w_i)_k < dist(w_j, w_{DS})_k$ the amount of hops required to satisfy the request r_{jk} (and consequently the delay perceived to obtain the document) is diminished.

In order to implement the proposed piggyback method using AODV routing protocol, the RREQ and RREQ messages must be modified. Fig. 3 shows the modified version of the RREQ message. The idea is that RREP packets also includes the identifier of the document.

0	7	8				13	23	24	31
Type		J	R	G	D	U	Reserved	hop count	
RREQ id									
destination IP address									
destination sequence number									
originator IP address									
originator sequence number									
document id									

Fig. 3. Modified AODV RREQ message

Typical AODV RREQ message contains a field reserved for future use but, unfortunately, they are 11 and 9 bits long respectively. That space is not enough to handle the identifier of a document, so we propose, for simulation purposes, to add a 32 bit field including the identification (e.g. the URL) of the document to be requested compressed using Bloom Filters [18].

4   Simulation Model

By means of simulations, we have evaluated the performance benefits of the caching techniques proposed in section 2, especially the cross-layer interception scheme. The simulations are based on the network simulator NS-2.33 [19] which is the most popular simulator for the researches on ad hoc networks [20].

Table 1 summarizes the main simulation parameters. We will consider W=50 mobiles nodes distributed in a 1000 meters by 1000 meters area. The mobile nodes follow the Random Waypoint mobility pattern [21] moving at a constant speed of 1 m/s with no pause time when they reach the destination.

Table 1. Simulation parameters

Parameter	Default	Tested values
Simulation area (meters)	1000x1000	
Number of nodes	50	
Number of Documents	1000	
Documents size (bytes)	1000	
Number of requests per node	10000	
Simulation time (s)	20000	
Timeout (s)	3	
TTL (s)	2000	250-500-1000-2000-∞
Mean time between requests (s)	25	5-10-25-50
Traffic pattern (Zipf slope)	0.8	0.4-0.6-0.8-1.0
Replacement policy	LRU	
Cache size (number of documents)	100	25-50-100-200
Warm-up (requests)	2000	
Ad hoc routing protocol	AODV	
MAC protocol	802.11b	
Propagation model	Two Ray Ground	
Coverage radio (meters)	250	
Mobility pattern (Random WayPoint)	Min. and max. speed: 1m/s Pause time: 0 s	

We consider n=1000 different documents (identified by a specific number) distributed between two fixed (immobile) servers. Those servers are located at positions (x,y)=(0,500) and (x,y)=(1000,500) in the simulation area respectively. Each server is directly connected to a Gateway. For our study, we assume that the Gateway and the servers are the same nodes. With this assumption, we avoid that the effects of the connection between these two elements alter our analysis. To distribute the traffic, documents with an odd identifier are placed in a server while even-numbered documents are located in the other one. In addition, each document has an associated TTL time that determines the instant when the document expires and it is considered obsolete. The expired documents stored in the local caches are evicted in order to make room for fresh documents. We have considered an exponential distribution with a mean between 250 and 2000 seconds for the TTL of the documents. In that way we model both a high and low variability of the documents. In addition we also consider the case of an infinite TTL for the documents, that is to say, the case where the documents never expire. The size of all the documents is constant and set to 1000 bytes.

Each node that is not a server is programmed to generate requests to the servers along the simulation time. When a request is served another request is generated by the same node. The idle time between the reception of a response and the next request follows an exponential distribution with a mean between 5 and 50 seconds. Using this variety of values we evaluate a wide range of patterns for the node activity (and consequently for the networks load). A document is requested again if the response of the present request is not served before a defined timeout is triggered.

The pattern of requests of the documents follows a Zipf-like distribution that has been demonstrated to properly characterize the popularity of the Web documents in the Internet [22]. The Zipf law asserts that the probability $P(i)$ for the i-th most popular document to be requested is inversely proportional to its popularity ranking as shown in eq. (8)

$$P(i) = \frac{\beta}{i^{\alpha}} \qquad (8)$$

The parameter α is the slope of the log/log representation of the number of references to the documents as a function of its popularity rank (i) while the β parameter is the displacement of the function. In our simulations, the slopes selected to generate the requests are 0.4, 0.6, 0.8 and 1.0.

Finally, every node implements a local cache that employs the Least Recently Used (LRU) replacement policy. This replacement policy evicts the documents that were referenced longest ago. All nodes have the same cache size, which has been configured to fit 25, 50, 100 and 200 documents. In order to avoid cold start influences, that is to say, cache misses because the cache is empty, the local caches are "warmed up" using the first 20% of the requests.

The simulation time (k) has been set to 20000 seconds.

5   Performance Evaluation

Each scenario has been executed five times using the same TTL and time between requests but using a different request distribution. The performance evaluation presented is the mean of the results obtained for the five simulations. All the figures of this section include the 95% confidence interval for every measured parameter.

As performance metrics we utilise:

- Delay: Defined as the time elapsed between the request of a document and the reception of the response.

- Percentage of timeouts: Defined as the proportion of requests that must be requested again because the response does not reach the destination before a timeout.

Also, we define the local hit ratio (LHR), interception hit ratio (IHR) and AODV interception hit ratio (RCHR) in (9), (10) and (11) respectively:

$$LHR = \frac{1}{w} \sum_{j=1}^{w} \frac{\sum_{k=1}^{m} h_{jk}^{l}}{card(t_j)} . \qquad (9)$$

$$IHR = \frac{1}{w}\sum\nolimits_{j=1}^{w} \frac{\sum\nolimits_{k=1}^{m} h_{jk}^{i}}{card(t_j)} \tag{10}$$

$$RCHR = \frac{1}{w}\sum\nolimits_{j=1}^{w} \frac{\sum\nolimits_{k=1}^{m} h_{jk}^{rci}}{card(t_j)} \tag{11}$$

where $t_j \subset R_j$ represents the subset of requests that the node j has performed until the end of the simulation time t with $t \leq m$.

We will compare the performance of a MANET in four situations: 1) the nodes do not implement any cache mechanism (No cache), 2) the nodes only use the local cache (LC), 3) the nodes implement local cache whilst the intermediate nodes can also intercept the requests (I) and 4) the nodes implement the previous schemes as well as the route creation interception using AODV (AODV Interception).

5.1   Effects of the Mean Time between Requests

Fig. 4 represents the mean delay, timeouts and cache hits as a function of the mean time between requests. As it can be observed in Fig. 4 a) the delay is decreased if a local cache is used and this reduction is greater as we implement the interception and AODV interception caching. The delay reduction is independent of the mean time between requests and is about 40% for the last case, in which all caching schemes are utilised. On the other hand Fig. 3 b) shows that for highly loaded networks (low time between requests) the timeouts are slightly diminished using the local cache while they are drastically reduced (almost 50% in high loaded networks) if the interception is implemented. This is due to the fact that with the interception mechanism the number of access to the highly saturated servers is dramatically reduced. As the network load decreases (high time between requests) the interception techniques also outperform the local caching approach, although the reduction in the percentage of timeouts is less meaningful. Finally, Fig. 3 c) illustrates that the local cache hits are reduced as the time between requests increases. This is due to the expiration time of the documents. As the nodes perform fewer requests, the documents stored in their local caches expire and they have to be requested again. The interception caching is also reduced as the time between requests increases because the routes to the servers expire and they must be created again, that is, the AODV interception can operate and that is why the number of AODV interception increases as the network load diminishes.

This study reveals that our proposal of routing interception outperforms the standard interception for medium and low loaded networks. In the best case, the reduction of the delay is about 14% and the number of timeouts is reduced by 5%. For high loaded networks the improvement is not very significant.

5.2   Effects of the TTL

Fig. 5 illustrates the delay, timeouts and cache hits as a function of the TTL of the documents. As the mean TTL increases the documents can be stored longer in the local caches because they are considered to be obsolete later. Fig. 5 a) and b) show that the delay and percentage of timeouts are reduced as the TTL increases if we use any of the caching techniques proposed. As in the case when traffic load is varied, results indicate that the combination of caching schemes outperforms the local and interception caching. Fig. 5 c) reveals that all the cache hits are increased as the mean TTL increases. Supposing that documents do not expire the percentage of cache hits almost reach 65%, i.e. 65% of the requests are served by the local caches or other nodes instead of by the servers. In that way the servers load is dramatically reduced.

This study demonstrates that the proposed routing interception outperforms the standard interception scheme for a low variability of the documents. If the documents do not expire the reduction of the delay is about 20% and the number of timeouts is reduced by 10%. As the TTL of the documents is decreased the difference between the standard interception and our proposal is reduced. For high variable documents the improvement is not significant.

5.3   Effects of the Zipf Slope α

Fig. 6 displays the delay, timeouts and cache hits as a function of the Zipf slope (α parameter) selected for the pattern of the requests. As the Zipf slope is close to 1.0 there is a small set of documents that are requested more times and hence the local cache will also hit more frequently. Fig. 6 c) confirms this behaviour. On the other hand the interception and AODV interception hit rate remain practically unchanged as we vary the Zipf slope. As in the previous studies, Fig. 6 a) and b) show that the policy using all the techniques outperforms the other methods, considering both the delay and the percentage of timeouts. As the Zipf slope raises, the benefits of employing a caching scheme is increased compared to the scheme without cache.

We can conclude that the use of the routing interception outperforms the standard interception for all the studied Zipf slopes. In fact, the interception mechanism reduces the delay by 10% and the number of timeouts by 5%. Only the local cache hits are incremented as the Zipf slope is increased.

5.4   Effects of the Cache Size

Fig. 7 illustrates the delay, timeouts and cache hits as a function of the cache sizes. These figures show that for a cache size greater than 50KB (50 documents – 5% of the documents) there is not any relevant improvement in the network performance. The delay, timeouts and cache hits remain constant for cache sizes greater than 50 documents. Further studies will be needed in order to evaluate the behaviour with smaller caches. Anyway the routing interception caching outperforms the standard interception for all the cache sizes studied, reducing the delay by 10% and the number of timeouts by 7%.

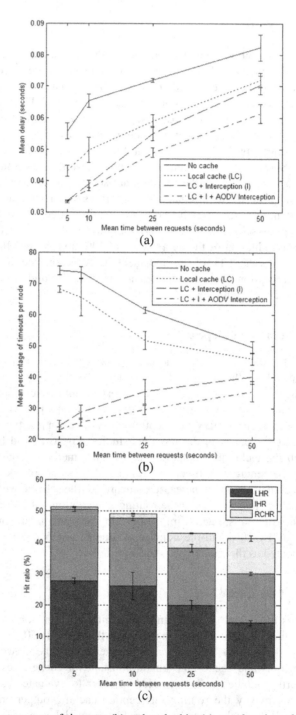

Fig. 4. Delay (a), percentage of timeouts (b) and cache hits (c) as a function of the mean time between requests

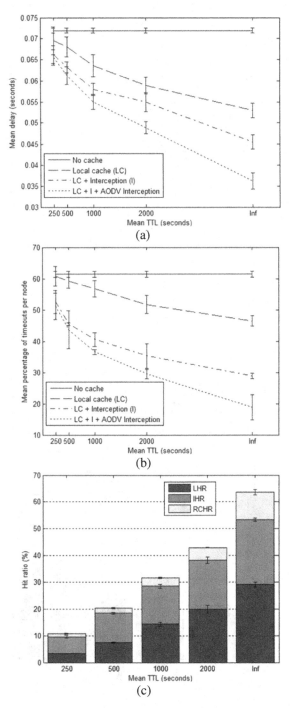

Fig. 5. Delay (a), percentage of timeouts (b) and cache hits (c) as a function of the mean TTL of the documents

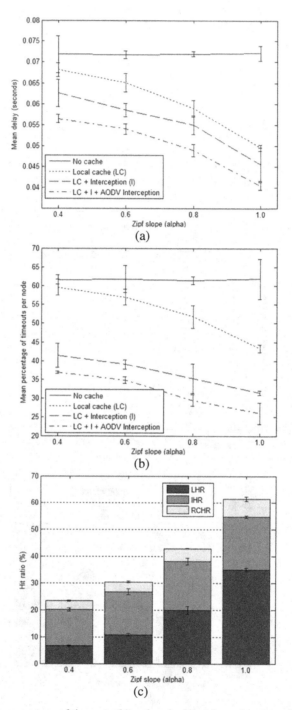

Fig. 6. Delay (a), percentage of timeouts (b) and cache hits (c) as a function of the Zipf slope

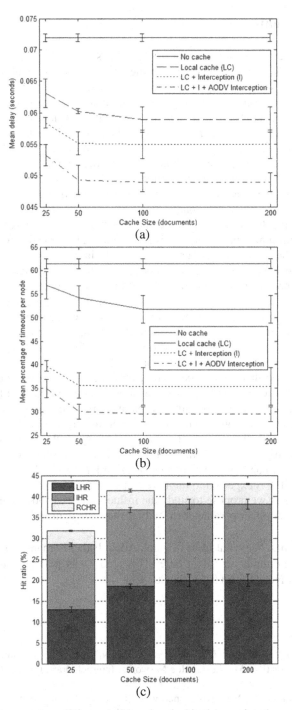

Fig. 7. Delay (a), percentage of timeouts (b) and cache hits (c) as a function of the cache size

6   Conclusions

We have evaluated a caching scheme for MANETs that includes the implementation of a local cache in each mobile device in the ad hoc network. With this scheme, the mobile nodes also have the ability to intercept the requests from other nodes. By using cross-layer information the routing protocol can also piggyback the requests information in the routing protocol messages, so that other nodes can respond with the location of the document when the route to the data source is being created.

By means of simulations, we have studied the influence in performance of the cross-layer interception caching technique of the mean time between requests (the network load), the mean document lifetime, the requests pattern and the cache sizes. Taking into account the network load, the benefits of using the interception caching are more significant for highly loaded networks. Results show that as the network load decreases the local caches reduce their performance although the amount of AODV interception hits increases. In this sense, the TTL of the documents is a crucial parameter for the cache behaviour. As the TTL increases all the cache hits are incremented and hence there is a progressive reduction of the delay and number of timeouts. As expected, results are also proved to be very dependent on the popularity of the document. In particular, if the popularity of the documents is modelled by a Zipf distribution and the Zipf slope is close to 1.0, the cache hits increase because fewer documents are requested more often provoking more cache hits. Finally, the cache size also influences the delay and timeouts but for cache sizes greater than 5% of the document, the performance is not improved.

We can conclude that the interception of the requests when the route between the source node of the request and the server is already created obtains a reduction of the delay and timeouts for all the studied parameters. On the other hand, AODV interception, specially designed when there is not an active route between the source of the requests and the server, in conjunction with the previous interception techniques reduces even more the delay and the occurrence of timeouts. As a consequence of the cache hits the server load is widely reduced. The reduction of the load in the MANET is expected to improve its performance.

As a future work we propose to study the influence of the node speed as well as the mobility pattern. Another parameter to study is the node density in the network.

Acknowledgments. We would like to thank Adela Isabel Fernandez Anta for revising the syntax and grammar of this article. This study was partially supported by the National Project No. TEC2009-13763-C02-01.

References

1. Wakikawa, R., Malinen, J.T., Perkins, C.E., Nilsson, A., Tuominen, A.J.: Global Connectivity for IPv6 Mobile Ad Hoc Networks. Internet Draft, Internet Engineering Task Force (2006)
2. Dodero, G., Gianuzzi, V.: Saving Energy and Reducing Latency in MANET File Access. In: 26th International Conference on Distributed Computing Systems Workshops (ICDCSW 2006), pp. 16–20 (2006)

3. Lim, S., Lee, W.C., Cao, G., Das, C.R.: A novel caching scheme for improving Internet-based mobile ad hoc networks performance. Ad Hoc Networks 4(2), 225–239 (2006)
4. Moriya, T., Aida, H.: Cache Data Access System in Ad Hoc Networks. In: 57th IEEE Semiannual Vehicular Technology Conference (VTC 2003), vol. 2, pp. 1228–1232 (2006)
5. Tang, B., Gupta, H., Das, S.R.: Benefit-Based Data Caching in Ad Hoc Networks. IEEE Transactions on Mobile Computing 7(3), 289–304 (2008)
6. Wang, Y.H., Chen, J., Chao, C.F., Chuang, C.C.: A Distributed Data Caching Framework for Mobile Ad Hoc Networks. In: 2006 International Conference on Wireless Communications and Mobile Computing, pp. 1357–1362 (2006)
7. Cho, J., Oh, S., Kim, J., Lee, K.H., Lee, J.: Neighbor Caching in Multi-Hop Wireless Ad Hoc Networks. IEEE Communications Letters 7(11), 525–527 (2003)
8. Yin, L., Cao, G.: Supporting Cooperative Caching in Ad Hoc Networks. IEEE Transaction on Mobile Computing 5(1), 77–89 (2006)
9. Ting, Y., Chang, Y.: A Novel Cooperative Caching Scheme for Wireless Ad Hoc Networks: GroupCaching. In: International Conference on Networking, Architecture and Storage (NAS 2007), pp. 62–68 (2007)
10. Chand, N., Joshi, R.C., Misra, M.: Cooperative Caching in Mobile Ad Hoc Networks Based on Clusters. International Journal on Wireless Personal Communications (43), 41–63 (2007)
11. Denko, M.K.: Cooperative Data Caching and Prefetching in Wireless Ad Hoc Networks. International Journal of Business Data Communications and Networking 3(1), 1–15 (2007)
12. Du, Y., Gupta, S.: COOP – A cooperative caching service in MANETs. In: Joint International Conference on Autonomic and Autonomous Systems and International Conference on Networking and Services (ICAS-ICNS 2005), pp. 58–63 (2005)
13. Chiu, G., Young, C.: Exploiting In-Zone Broadcast for Cache Sharing in Mobile Ad Hoc Networks. IEEE Transactions on Mobile Computing 8(3), 384–397 (2009)
14. Artail, H., Safa, H., Mershad, K., Abou-Atme, Z., Sulieman, N.: COACS: A Cooperative and Adaptive Caching Systems for MANETs. IEEE Transactions on Mobile Computing 7(8), 961–977 (2008)
15. Chow, C.Y., Leong, H.V., Chan, A.: Group-based Cooperative Cache Management for Mobile Clients in a Mobile Environment. In: 33rd International Conference on Parallel Processing (ICPP 2004), pp. 83–90 (2004)
16. Hosseini-Khayat, S.: Optimal solution of off-line and on-line generalized caching. Technical Report WUCS-96-20 (1996)
17. Perkins, C.E., Belding-Royer, E.M., Das, S.: Ad Hoc On Demand Distance Vector (AODV) Routing. IETF RFC 3561 (2003)
18. Bloom, B.: Space/time Trade-offs in Hash Coding with Allowable Errors. ACM Communications 13(7), 422–426 (1970)
19. NS-2 Home page, http://isi.edu/nsnam/ns/
20. Kurkowski, S., Camp, T., Colagrosso, M.: MANET Simulation Studies: The Incredibles. ACM's Mobile Computing and Communications Review 9(4), 50–61 (2005)
21. Broch, J., Maltz, D., Johnson, D., Hu, Y., Jetcheva, J.: Multi-Hop wireless ad hoc network routing protocols. In: ACM/IEEE International Conference on Mobile Computing and Networking (MOBICOM 1998), pp. 85–97 (1998)
22. Adamic, L.A., Huberman, B.A.: Zipf's law and the Internet. Glottometrics 3, 143–150 (2002)

Below Cross-Layer: An Alternative Approach to Service Discovery for MANETs

Warren Kenny and Stefan Weber

Trinity College, College Green, Dublin, Ireland
{kennyw,sweber}@scss.tcd.ie

Abstract. Service discovery protocols for mobile ad hoc networks attempt to overcome the inability to locate resources presented by networks in which prior knowledge of node identity and capability is not available. Existing approaches continue to rely on underlying address-based routing protocols in order to communicate with discovered services. These two-tier approaches generate routing overheads which negatively impact on performance and network scalability.

As high-powered mobile computing devices with wireless connectivity become increasingly ubiquitous, the need for routing protocols which can operate at increased network densities becomes more acute. Cross-layer approaches to service discovery in MANETs have attempted to optimize the discovery process through direct integration with underlying routing protocols, however additional steps are necessary to improve service discovery performance, network scalability and application throughput.

This paper describes the Service Discovery and Routing Protocol (SDRP), a novel service-oriented routing protocol for MANETs. This protocol eschews the use of network-wide unique addresses or underlying address-based routing protocols and focuses instead on routing only to and from nodes which provide services. A comparison with existing approaches demonstrates that this approach improves discovery success rates and application throughput at higher node densities.

Keywords: MANET, Routing, Service Discovery.

1 Introduction

MANETs are characterised by variable topologies, unreliable connections between nodes and limited resources [6]. It is assumed that nodes have limited battery life and communication capacity, thus it is important to minimise unnecessary overheads in order to maximise performance.

Existing research in the area of routing for mobile ad hoc networks (MANETs) has focused on a particular set of deployment scenarios; disaster zones, battlefields and wireless sensor deployments. As high-powered mobile devices with wireless capability become increasingly ubiquitous, new scenarios involving drastically greater network densities and sizes are set to emerge; particularly those in urban environments. Such scenarios involve network scales far beyond those traditionally studied [1].

J. Zheng et al. (Eds.): Adhocnets 2012, LNICST 111, pp. 212–225, 2013.
© Institute for Computer Sciences, Social Informatics and Telecommunications Engineering 2013

Current approaches to routing are designed to replicate the functionality of infrastructure networks [14], particularly facilitating arbitrary connections between nodes based on addresses. Infrastructure networks are capable of supporting reliable communications between arbitrary nodes with routing based on optimal paths over dedicated routers along high-bandwidth links. However, providing this functionality in MANETs has an adverse effect on communication in terms of the overheads that are generated and the interference that this causes [4,9] and may not be well suited to typical MANET deployment scenarios such as those mentioned above.

Facilitation of arbitrary connections between nodes also makes little sense in the above MANET deployment scenarios, where the capabilities and identities of nodes are unlikely to be known ahead of network deployment. Service-oriented routing protocols [20] attempt to solve this problem by allowing services provided by nodes in the network to be discovered or advertised to peers. However, these approaches assume that arbitrary connections between nodes are already facilitated in the network by an underlying routing protocol and thus attempt to provide nodes with connections to services by mapping service requests to network addresses, creating a two-tier routing approach which generates unnecessary overheads and suffers from the same problems as address-based approaches.

In this paper we present a highly-scalable and flexible service-oriented routing protocol for MANETs called Service Discovery Routing Protocol (SDRP). SDRP does not use an underlying address-based routing protocol, but was instead designed to provide routing only to services rather than to arbitrary node addresses. This approach, combined with a novel use of Bloom Filters [2] for the purpose of optimizing service advertisement, results in a routing protocol which exhibits favourable characteristics in a variety of scenarios; particularly in large-scale, high-density networks.

The rest of the paper is organized as follows: Section 2 will discuss protocols which implement service-discovery architectures mentioned above. Section 3 discusses the design and implementation of SDRP. Section 4 presents an analysis, through simulation, of SDRP and a number of service-oriented protocols. Sections 5 will discuss the results of this analysis and the conclusions that can be drawn from the performance of the protocol.

2   Related Work

The following section discusses a number of service-oriented routing protocols for MANETs. These protocols may be classified as either service coordinator, distributed query-based or hybrid architectures [17].

Service-coordinator protocols designate a subset certain nodes as Service-Coordinators (SCs) or directories which are responsible for tracking the services provided by Service Agent (SA) nodes [15]. User Agent (UA) nodes connect to SCs in order to request services. SCs then respond with a list of SAs which provide that service. Directories advertise their presence either through direct advertisement flooding through a cross-layer approach based on the piggy-backing advertisements onto routing protocol packets.

Such protocols have been shown to perform well with large numbers of service agents and user agents, as advertisement flooding is restricted to service coordinators which can be distributed in optimal numbers during deployment. Directory placement is, however, a key concern as service location delay and success rates depend on distance between service requesters and service directories [7].

Hybrid approaches solve this problem by falling back on direct query flooding or service advertisement when service coordinators are unavailable [12], thus improving service availability in networks with high node failure rates or frequent partitioning.

Distributed query protocol operate in a purely peer-to-peer fashion; with clients querying the network for servers or with servers advertising their services to the network depending on the specific protocol mechanism [21,3]. These approaches may generate high overheads when compared to service coordinator approaches, as queries and advertisements are directly flooded throughout the network by user agents or service agents.

These categories can be further sub-divided into cross-layer and application-layer architectures [19]. Cross-layer approaches attempt to optimize communications by integrating with an underlying routing protocol [18], piggy-backing service discovery messages or advertisements onto routing messages. Application layer protocols operate independently of the installed routing protocol, advertising or flooding service requests and advertisements directly in order to discover the addresses of servers. This disconnect results in some inefficiency due to redundant broadcasts and transmissions, however application-layer approaches can operate on top of any routing protocol, unlike cross-layer approaches.

Mercury [5] is a cross-layer protocol integrated with OLSR [11]. OLSR attempts to optimize dissemination of link state information using its multi-point relay (MPR) algorithm, which reduces flooding by selectively rebroadcasting topology control message based on link-state data received from neighbours in periodically broadcast HELLO messages. OLSR attempts to determine the subset of neighbour nodes required to reach all two-hop neighbours. Those neighbours are then selected as multi-point relays and rebroadcast topology control messages containing the source's link-state information. This approach improves on naive flooding mechanisms be eliminating redundant rebroadcasts. Mercury piggybacks service advertisement messages onto OLSR's topology control messages and takes advantage of the OLSR's extensible messaging format by appending a *Service Filter*; a bloom filter [2] containing service descriptor strings for local and neighbour node services.

Service descriptors are encoded using the MD5 digest algorithm [16], producing a 128-bit hash value. This hash value is split into k groups of r bits, resulting in offsets into the bloom filter to be set in order to encode the service descriptor. When a service advertisement is received, the receiving node adds the source node's address and associated service filter to its service routing table. When an application requests a service, this routing table is checked by first encoding the requested service's descriptor and checking it against stored filters. If an associated address can be found, the message is then forwarded using OLSR.

Mercury is designed to reduce the overheads associated with service discovery. Mercury's use of a cross-layer design reduces messaging overheads as service advertisements are attached to routing protocol packets instead of being sent separately. The use of bloom filters as service descriptors acts as an optimization in terms of header size when compared with direct linear serialization of service information, particularly when service information is in the form of variable-length strings or complex data structures. As OLSR is a proactive routing protocol, its generated overheads can be expected to increase with increasing network size as additional nodes send HELLO and topology control messages.

The Lightweight Service Discovery protocol (LSD) is a cross-layer service coordinator discovery mechanism designed to adapt to changes in the underlying network and reduce messaging overheads through direct interaction with an underlying proactive routing protocol [12]. Nodes in an LSD network are designated as either clients, service nodes or directories. Service nodes register their network addresses and a description of their services with available directories in order to allow client nodes to locate them. These registrations are refreshed periodically in order to avoid false positives during service requests. Directory nodes periodically advertise their presence in the network by piggybacking advertisement messages onto routing protocol topology control messages. Client nodes cache addresses for directory nodes and may query them in order to locate service nodes as required.

LSD integrates with OLSR, allowing it to attach directory advertisements to OLSR topology control message broadcasts. This approach reduces overheads by combining route and service information into a single packet rather than multiple separate packets. LSD is designed to adapt to changing network conditions by falling back on a direct query broadcast approach when no directory node is available. Client nodes piggyback a query for a service onto topology control messages as described above, allowing clients to locate services without the assistance of an intermediate directory node. However, as with Mercury, the use of OLSR as an underlying routing protocol can be expected to result in higher overheads as network density increases. In addition, optimal distribution of directory nodes is required in order to avoid the use of direct query flooding; a difficult task in large-scale or highly mobile networks [7].

SMF [21] is a cross-layer distributed-query protocol based on AODV [13] which combines aspects of advertisement and query protocols; advertisements are piggybacked onto AODV HELLO messages and distributed to 1-hop neighbours while AODV's route request messaging mechanism is extended to include a service request function. SMF uses received HELLO and route response packets to calculate a metric called the service magnetic field. This metric is used for route selection and is based on the number of hops to the server as well as the density of servers providing the same service in a given area. SMF's reactive query-based approach performs well in networks where the number of clients is expected to be low, as AODV's flooding approach to route discovery can overwhelm available bandwidth when there are many service or route requests [8].

The Pervasive Discovery Protocol (PDP) is an example of an application-layer protocol. PDP does not integrate with the underlying routing protocol, instead assuming that a multicast-capable routing protocol is available. PDP uses a hybrid pull-push service advertisement feature that delays advertisements for services until they are first requested; thus ensuring that only service which are in demand use network resources. PDP's application-layer design allows it to be deployed in any MANET with a multicast-capable routing protocol installed, however this lack of integration may result in additional overheads and poor mobility adaptation when compared to the cross-layer approaches described above.

2.1 Discussion

The above approaches attempt to map services to network addresses which are then be used by an underlying routing protocol to direct packets to a discovered server. By tightly coupling services to network addresses, existing protocols reduce potential redundancy and add an unnecessary additional step in the routing process.

Once the described protocols have mapped service identifiers to network addresses, their role in the process is finished. At this point, the underlying routing protocol is responsible for routing traffic to and from the selected server. In the case where the server is no longer available, due to network partitioning or battery depletion for example, the path between the client and server is lost and the discovery process must be restarted at the source. In addition, the overheads generated by the address-based routing step can negatively affect application throughput, particularly in high-density networks [1].

These factors combine to reduce the usability of service-oriented networks based upon such protocols. The next section will detail how SDRP addresses these issues.

3 Service Discovery Routing Protocol

Service Discovery Routing Protocol (SDRP) is designed to provide robust, low-overhead routing to and from servers in MANETs. It accomplishes this through a combination of header size reduction through extensive use of bloom filters, the use of a mechanism similar to OLSR's MPR [11] for proactive service advertisement, the removal of support for arbitrary node-to-node routing and by decoupling network addresses from service descriptors.

3.1 Overhead Reduction and Robustness

SDRP reduces overhead generation and improves scalability when compared to alternative approaches which rely on an underlying routing protocol. In a network based upon an address-based routing protocol, nodes generate control overheads regardless of their role or functionality. In the case of OLSR, all nodes generate periodic HELLO messages, while topology control messages are flooded by MPR nodes. Reactive protocols such as AODV flood route requests [13]. In an SDRP-based network, only server nodes act as sources of advertisements. This approach retains the advantage of a proactive protocol, such low end-to-end delay and prior knowledge of existing services, while reducing overheads by restricting message flooding to a subset of network nodes based on role.

SDRP adds redundancy to the routing process by decoupling network addresses from service identifiers. At each hop in a multi-hop client-server connection, packet headers are inspected in order to ascertain the target service. Each node on the route sends the packet to the next hop on the shortest route to the target service, as recorded in its service routing table. This approach allows service requests to follow shortest paths to an available server and be re-routed by intermediate nodes when that server is no longer available.

Bloom filters are used extensively by SDRP in order to reduce network overheads. However unlike Mercury, which uses them only for optimizing the transmission of service descriptors, SDRP also uses them to convey link state information in order to optimize service advertisement distribution.

Bloom Filters [2] are space-efficient probabilistic data structures used to represent sets, against which membership queries may be performed. A bloom filter is a bit array of m bits initially set to 0. Insertion is performed by executing k hash functions on elements in order to obtain array offsets. These offsets are then set to 1.

A membership query is performed by using the same process to generate array offsets and then checking whether each offset is set to 1. If any of the produced offsets are set to 0, the element is definitely not in the filter. If the offsets are set to 1, it is assumed that the element is present in the filter, although there is a probability that this is incorrect.

The probability of incorrect membership queries increases as more elements are inserted into the filter and more filter bits are set. Eventually, a filter may have all of its bits set, in which case all membership queries will succeed and the filter becomes functionally useless. The probability of a false positive query occurring is a function of the array size m, number of inserted elements n and number of hashes used k. The probability that a specific bit is still 0 after n elements have been inserted into the filter may be expressed as

$$\left(1 - \tfrac{1}{m}\right)^{kn} \approx e^{-kn/m}$$

Thus there are tradeoffs between the computational effort in terms of calculation of k hashes per element, bit array size and the probability of a false positive occurring. Bloom filters have a strong space advantage over other data structures for representing sets. A bloom filter with an optimal hash count and a 1% false-positive rate requires approximately 9.6 bits per element, regardless of the size of the elements. Compared to direct serialization of network addresses or service descriptors, bloom filters represent a space-efficient method for containing set data; OLSR's linear serialization of network addresses, for example, requires 32 bits per address, as well as the space required to convey link-state. Thus the use of bloom filters for conveying information in protocol messages provides a significant advantage in terms of control overheads reduction.

3.2   SDRP Advertisement Mechanism

Servers in an SDRP network advertise their services using an algorithm called Reduced MPR (RMPR). RMPR is is designed to further reduce messaging overheads when compared to the MPR approach used by OLSR by avoiding the broadcast of HELLO packets and using bloom filters for neighbourhood description instead of direct neighbour link-state serialization. The reduced MPR algorithm attempts to select a subset of a message source's neighbours as message rebroadcasters based on their distance from the source.

Servers periodically broadcast service advertisements containing a bloom filter describing the identifiers of the nodes in their local area and another filter, the MPR filter, containing the identifiers of those nodes that should rebroadcast the message. Nodes receiving this advertisement will rebroadcast if their address is contained in the MPR filter or if their address is not contained in the neighbourhood filter. Thus the role of HELLO messages in describing the link state of all neighbouring nodes is replaced using service advertisement messages. Highly mobile nodes will tend to rebroadcast messages frequently, as they move into range of nodes that are not aware of their presence, while immobile non-MPR nodes will tend to remain silent.

The use of variable-length bloom filters for neighbourhood description means that bitwise comparison of filters for the purpose of MPR selection cannot be used. Instead, a probabilistic approach is used to calculate MPR nodes using the following steps:

1. Enumerate over all stored neighbours
2. Generate a bloom filter with the same parameters as the current node's neighbour filter
3. Insert the addresses of all neighbours except the current neighbour into the generated filter
4. Perform a difference operation on the filters and insert the result into an ordered container

The above algorithm produces a set of neighbours ordered by how different their neighbourhood is from the source node's. This difference may be interpreted as a measure of how distant a neighbour is from the source and how many nodes are in the neighbour's local area which are not also in the source's local area.

Neighbour nodes with a distance metric higher than a configured value are then added to the MPR set. The set is further filtered by determining which of the chosen nodes are likely to be near to eachother through comparison of their neighbour filters. Nodes which are determined to be in close proximity to eachother based on comparison of their neighbour filters are then removed from the MPR set.

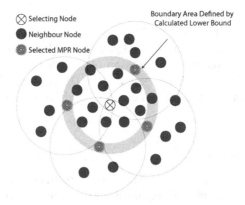

Fig. 1. Nodes are selected for the rebroadcasting of service advertisement based on their probable distance from the source determined by comparison of neighbour filters

These steps remove nodes on the boundary of the local node's coverage which are within close proximity to eachother as illustrated in figure 1. Unlike OLSR's MPR mechanism, RMPR cannot reliably choose MPR nodes with unique connections to second-hop neighbours or an optimal set of MPR nodes to achieve full coverage due to the probabilistic nature of bloom filters. However, the control overhead reduction achieved through the use of variable-length bloom filters, removal of HELLO messages and selective rebroadcasting allow for greater scalability and throughput when compared to existing approaches. Calibration of the distance metric limit can increase MPR selection reliability at the expense of control overhead increase due to more frequent rebroadcasting.

Reduced MPR mode is designed to operate well in very high-density networks with low mobility, such as networks composed of pedestrian mobile devices in urban areas. The reduction in control overheads achieved by the removal of HELLO broadcasts and the size reduction in advertisement due to the use of dynamically-size bloom filters results in lower medium contention and improved application throughput.

4 Evaluation

SDRP is implemented as a shared library, written in C++, to allow for possible deployment on node hardware in the future. For the purpose of evaluation, it was linked with the NS-2 simulator [10]. Mobility was simulated using the random waypoint mobility model generator *setdest* which is distributed with NS-2. Comparison was performed against a number of alternative service discovery protocols. Mercury, PDP and SMF were included in the evaluation.

As an LSD NS-2 agent implementation was unavailable, it was reimplemented as an application-layer protocol operating on top of both AODV and OLSR. This implementation was named Service Coordination and Discovery Protocol (SCDP). SCDP operates similarly to LSD. Directory nodes store the addresses of registered servers in the network and broadcast their presence periodically.

User agents which cannot locate a directory node adapt by flooding requests for services as needed. However, SCDP does not integrate with the underlying routing protocol using a cross-layer design as LSD does. This design decision was made in order to expand the evaluation to include more protocols based on reactive routing mechanisms. The version of SCDP integrated AODV is called SCDPRA (Reactive) while the version integrated with OLSR is named SCDPPA (Proactive).

4.1 Experiment Setup

Client applications were simulated using a request-response agent designed specifically for this evaluation. Limitations in NS-2's scripted agent connection mechanism mean that spontaneous connections between application agents at runtime are not well supported. This poses a problem in a network based on dynamic service discovery, thus the use of NS-2's built-in FTP and CBR agents was not possible. This may also be the reason for the lack of application throughput analysis in previous evaluations of the above protocols. The client application attempts to discover a service at set intervals and, if available, attempts to send packets to the located server.

When the server application receives a request packet, a response packet is returned to the client. The client then immediately sends another request until the server can no longer be reached and the periodic request process begins again. The number of discovery attempts, requests sent, requests received, responses sent and responses received are recorded. The application's total data throughput is also measured.

Nodes are configured with a single wireless interface and omnidirectional antenna. Maximum wireless reception range was set to 160m, matching wireless interface parameters detailed in the technical specifications of an Orinoco 802.11b PC Card.

The evaluation aims to measure the overheads generated by the above protocols and measure the throughput the may be achieved by client nodes utilizing services in the network. Overheads are defined as the number of bytes of messaging traffic sent by the discovery protocol and, if applicable, its underlying routing protocol, per second. Throughput is defined as the number of bytes of application data received by servers in the network per second. Both overheads and throughput are measured as a combined total across all nodes and servers.

Service availability and service request message success rates are also measured. Service availability may be defined as the fraction of service discovery attempts which succeed. Service discovery involves the client application querying the discovery protocol for a route to a particular service. Depending on the protocol used, this may produce a flooded query or a check against a stored table. Service request success rate is defined as the number of application packets sent to the discovered server which are successfully received. Static simulation parameters are detailed in table 1.

Table 1. Static Simulation Parameters

Simulation Time	300s
Topography	Flat 1000m x 1000m
Mobility Model	Random Waypoint
Node Pause Time	5s
HELLO Message Interval	1s
Advertisement Cache Period	30s
TC/SA Interval	3s
Client Discovery Interval	1s
Service Count	3
Server Count	3
Client Count	5
Bloom Filter False Positive Probability	0.01

4.2 Experiment Results

Effect of Network Density. The node count was varied between 10 and 200 nodes in order to measure protocol performance with increasing network density. Nodes are configured to move at 5m/s using the random waypoint model. A total of 3,200 simulation runs were used, with 20 runs performed per protocol-node count combination in order to reduced the effects of random variation. The number of client and server nodes remain static in this evaluation so that the effects of node and client/server density variations are not conflated in the results.

A comparison of application throughput with node count can be seen in figure 3. It can be observed that SDRP performs well in this scenario, with protocols based on application-layer or a proactive design experiencing a large drop in throughput with increasing node count. This may be attributed to the large increase in overheads experienced by such protocols with increasing network density, as illustrated in figure 2.

It is observed that the overheads generated by protocols based on OLSR are similar and increase greatly with increasing network density. This may be attributed to the increased number of HELLO and topology control messages sent as new nodes are added to the network. At a node count of 200, the overheads generated by these protocols dominate the medium and leave no bandwidth for application traffic. NS-2 is also designed to prioritize routing traffic over agent traffic, thus contributing to this effect. SDRP's overheads primarily increase as more servers are added to the network, thus allowing it to scale well when compared to address-based protocols. Reactive protocols such as SMF also perform well here as they only generate traffic in response to service requests. SDRP is observed to produce significantly lower overheads than all other protocols due to the lack of HELLO broadcasts and the reduced size of service advertisements due to the use of dynamic bloom filters.

Service availability is illustrated in figure 5. Here we see the protocols which use a cross-layer design such as Mercury and SMF perform best due to NS-2's

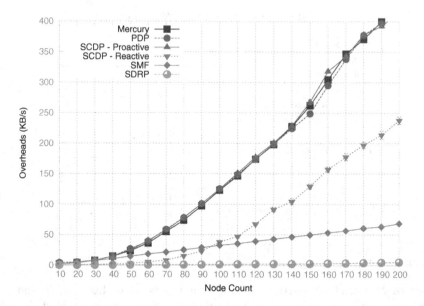

Fig. 2. Control Overheads vs. Node Count. As the network density increases, approaches based on an underlying routing protocol experience a significant increase in control overheads, while SDRP's remains low.

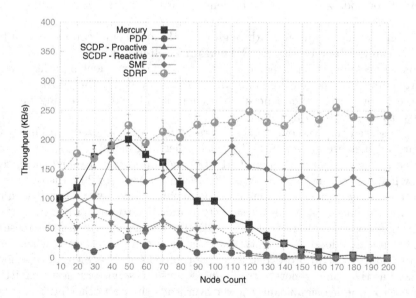

Fig. 3. Application Throughput vs. Node Count. The control overhead increase experienced by other approaches tends to have a corresponding negative impact on application throughput due to medium contention and interference. Here it can be seen that SDRP's low control overheads result in higher application throughput.

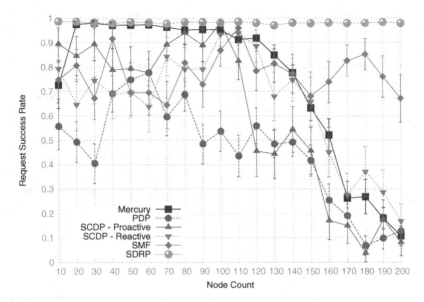

Fig. 4. Request Success Rate vs. Node Count. Medium contention and interference caused by control overheads have a marked effect on the success of service requests. SDRP's low control overheads and robust service advertisement approach maintain consistently high success rates.

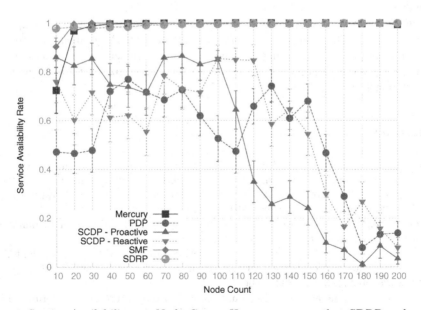

Fig. 5. Service Availability vs. Node Count. Here we can see that SDRP and cross-layer approaches maintain a high availability rate due to NS-2's prioritization of routing traffic and SDRP's lower control overheads.

prioritization of routing traffic while application-layer protocols such as PDP and SCDP experience a drop in availability as medium contention increases. SDRP also performs well due to its lower messaging overheads.

Figure 4 shows the request success rate compared with node count. Here it can be seen that proactive and application-layer protocols experience sharp drops in success rates which correlate with the high overheads produced at greater network densities. As medium contention increases, the probability that an application packet will experience collisions or delays during transit increases. Due to the lower overheads produced by the reactive protocols and SDRP, success rates remain high. It is observed that protocols which achieved high availability rates, such as Mercury, suffer from low success rates; this is due to NS-2's prioritization of routing protocol traffic above data traffic. As service advertisements are carried in routing protocol messages, those messages are more likely to traverse the network than the data packets sent by client-server communication.

5   Conclusions

In this paper we presented a new service discovery protocol for MANETs called SDRP. SDRP was designed to maximise network scalability by reducing overheads through the use of compressed data structures and by avoiding reliance on an underlying routing protocol. SDRP is designed to provide routing only to and from servers in MANETs, rather than between arbitrary nodes, and incorporates additional optimizations which enhance network robustness and communication reliability.

SDRP was evaluated against existing service discovery protocols using the NS-2 simulator. The evaluation demonstrates that SDRP significantly reduces overheads compared to existing approaches without affecting the success rates of service requests, thus improving application throughput; particularly at high network densities.

References

1. Arora, D., Millman, E., Neville, S.: Assessing the expected performance of the olsr routing protocol for denser urban core ad hoc network deployments. In: IEEE 26th International Conference on Advanced Information Networking and Applications, AINA 2012, pp. 406–414 (March 2012)
2. Bloom, B.: Space/time trade-offs in hash coding with allowable errors. Communications of the ACM 13(7), 422–426 (1970)
3. Campo, C., García-Rubio, C., López, A., Almenárez, F.: Pdp: a lightweight discovery protocol for local-scope interactions in wireless ad hoc networks. Computer Networks 50(17), 3264–3283 (2006)
4. Corson, S.: Mobile ad hoc networking (manet): Routing protocol performance issues and evaluation considerations. In: IETF RFC 2501 (1999)
5. Flathagen, J., Øvsthus, K.: Service discovery using olsr and bloom filters. In: Proceedings of the 4th OLSR Interoperability Workshop (October 2008)

6. Giordano, S.: Mobile Ad Hoc Networks, pp. 325–346. John Wiley and Sons, Inc. (2002)
7. Gonzalez-Valenzuela, S., Vuong, S., Leung, V.: A mobile-directory approach to service discovery in wireless ad hoc networks. IEEE Transactions on Mobile Computing 7(10), 1242–1256 (2008)
8. Haerri, J., Filali, F., Bonnet, C.: Performance comparison of aodv and olsr in vanets urban environments under realistic mobility patterns. In: Proceedings of the 5th IFIP Mediterranean Ad-Hoc Networking Workshop, pp. 14–17 (February 2006)
9. Hekmat, R., Van Mieghem, P.: Interference in Wireless Multi-Hop Ad-Hoc Networks and Its Effect on Network Capacity. Wireless Networks 10, 389–399 (2004)
10. Issariyakul, T., Hossain, E.: Introduction to Network Simulator NS2. Springer (2008)
11. Jacquet, P., Muhlethaler, P., Clausen, T., Laouiti, A., Qayyum, A., Viennot, L.: Optimized link state routing protocol for ad hoc networks. In: Proceedings of the IEEE Multi Topic Conference on Technology for the 21st Century, INMIC 2001, pp. 62–68 (February 2001)
12. Li, L., Lamont, L.: A lightweight service discovery mechanism for mobile ad hoc pervasive environment using cross-layer design. In: Third IEEE International Conference on Pervasive Computing and Communications Workshops, pp. 55–59 (March 2005)
13. Perkins, C., Belding-Rowyer, E., Das, S.: Ad hoc on-demand distance vector (aodv) routing. In: Proceedings of the 2nd IEEE Workshop on Mobile Computing Systems and Applications, WMCSA 1999, pp. 90–100 (February 1999)
14. Rahman, M., Anwar, F., Naeem, J., Abedin, M.: A simulation-based performance comparison of routing protocols in mobile ad-hoc networks (proactive, reactive and hybrid). In: 2010 International Conference on Computer and Communication Engineering, ICCCE, pp. 1–5 (May 2010)
15. Raychoudhury, V., Cao, J., Wu, W., Lai, Y., Chen, C., Ma, J.: Fast track article: K-directory community: Reliable service discovery in manet. Pervasive and Mobile Computing 7(1), 140–158 (2011)
16. Rivest, R.: Rfc1321: The md5 message-digest algorithm. RFC Editor United States (1992)
17. Toh, C., Guichal, G., Kim, D., Li, V.: Service location protocols for mobile wireless ad hoc networks. International Journal of Ad Hoc and Ubiquitous Computing 2(4), 250–262 (2007)
18. Varshavsky, A., Reid, B., de Lara, E.: A cross-layer approach to service discovery and selection in manets. In: Proceedings of IEEE International Conference on Mobile Adhoc and Sensor Systems Conference, pp. 466–474 (November 2005)
19. Ververidis, C., Polyzos, G.: Routing layer support for service discovery in mobile ad hoc networks. In: Proceedings of the Third IEEE International Conference on Pervasive Computing and Communications Workshops, PerCom 2005, pp. 258–262. IEEE (2005)
20. Ververidis, C., Polyzos, G.: Service discovery for mobile ad hoc networks: A survey of issues and techniques. IEEE Communications Surveys & Tutorials 10(3), 30–45 (2008)
21. Zhou, X., Ge, Y., Chen, X., Jing, Y., Sun, W.: Smf: A novel lightweight reliable service discovery approach in manet. In: 7th International Conference on Wireless Communications, Networking and Mobile Computing, WiCOM 2011, pp. 1–5 (September 2011)

Modeling the Spontaneous Reaction
of Mammalian Cells to External Stimuli
(Invited Paper)

John N. Daigle[1], Mauro Femminella[2], and Zia Shariat-Madar[1,*]

[1] The University of Mississippi, University MS 38677
{wcdaigle,madar}@olemiss.edu
[2] University of Perugia, via G. Duranti 93, 06125 Perugia
mauro.femminella@diei.unipg.it

Abstract. We argue that the potential benefits of developing high-fidelity models of biological communication systems has enormous potential in terms of enhancing the understanding of biological systems and that such understanding is a major step towards detection and treatment of disease. By focusing on lysosomal enzyme response to stimuli, we demonstrate that the understanding of the protocols governing cellular communications is far from complete. We discuss some major challenges and outline promising approaches to reaching the next level.

Keywords: lysosomal PRCP, nano-bionetworks, modeling, platelet-endothelial cell interaction, cellular state transition diagrams.

1 Introduction

The objective of this paper is to discuss research challenges in developing high-fidelity communication models for bio-nanomachine networks for the purpose of supporting research into the diagnosis and treatment of mammalian diseases. It is argued here that high-fidelity mathematical and simulation models can complement laboratory experimentation and analysis in order to facilitate both cost reduction and lead time for understanding the origins, diagnosis and treatment of diseases.

In order to elucidate the environment in which the communications takes place, two distinct threads of research are described, both involving endothelial cells. The main trust of this research is to increase the understanding of how cells work, which is a crucial step in diagnosing diseases and in developing drugs or other procedures for treating diseases. The immediate objective of the first thread, discussed in section 2, is to understand the production and function of the lysosomal prolylcarboxypeptidase (PRCP). Its long-term objective is the understanding of the means of regulating PRCP production and of the relationship between PRCP production and diseases such as diabetes, high blood pressure,

---

* This work was supported by SBAHQ-10-1-0309 to ZSM.

J. Zheng et al. (Eds.): Adhocnets 2012, LNICST 111, pp. 226–241, 2013.
© Institute for Computer Sciences, Social Informatics and Telecommunications Engineering 2013

and obesity. The second thread, described in section 3 targets the diagnosis and treatment of cardiovascular diseases. The question of immediate concern addressed in the experiment has to do with the role of platelets in the production of vascular adhesion molecules (VCAM-1), which facilitates coagulation.

In each case, the main idea of the communications research is to develop a system level communication model that helps to explain the biological processes that are happening at the nanoscale. In section 4, the discussions and results of sections 2 and 3 are used as a basis for discussing the current state of the art. Areas where further investigation with regard to communication system modeling are discussed. In section 5, shortcomings of the current state of the art are discussed, and it is pointed out that a major shortcoming is the lack of definitive communication models for cells. It is suggested through discussion of a specific example, that joint development of state machine and experiment planning may serve to develop more productive experimentation and modeling.

2   Endothelial Cell Reactions to Angiotensin III

High Level Problem Description. Prolylcarboxypeptidase (PRCP) has been identified as a regulator of blood vessel homeostasis [1] and represents a promising multifunctional cardiovascular disease target. Recent studies[2,3,4] have shown that PRCP modulates a variety of biochemical and physiological systems, including the regulation of proliferation and signal transduction pathways of angiotensin 1-7 (Ang_{1-7}), des-Arg^9-bradykinin (des-Arg^9-BK), and alpha-melanocortin stimulating hormone (α-MSH). Indeed, PRCP deficiency has been identified as a regulator of food intake [5], significant elevation of blood pressure and increased risk of blood clotting due to increased production of reactive oxygen species (ROS) and uncoupling of endothelial nitric oxide synthase (eNOS) [1,6]. Moreover, genetic and pharmacological reduction of PRCP markedly increases energy expenditure, reduces food-intake, and thrombus formation in carotid artery model of thrombosis. Observations linking PRCP to hypertension, obesity, and diabetes are consistent with its reported effects on the renin-angiotensin, kallikrein-kinin and proopiomelanocortin systems.

The enzyme PRCP is found in abundance in the endothelial cells and in the kidneys. Although PRCP is primarily known as a lysosomal enzyme based on its structural properties, it is detected in various cellular compartments including cytoplasm, plasma membrane and extracellular compartments. Based on these observations, two independent mechanisms for PRCP trafficking are possible. An explicit and plausible mechanism has been suggested that PRCP contains a potential targeting signal resides in its amino terminal end that can facilitate PRCP to gain access to the lysosomes. Since pools of PRCP are found in plasma, an alternative mechanism for the trafficking of PRCP can be considered which support the idea that PRCP is a membrane-bound trans-Golgi network resident enzyme. The aforementioned hypotheses have not yet been scientifically explored.

Lysosomes play an integral role in cellular catabolism but also a source of PRCP [7]. The dogma was that lysosomes are responsible for killing cells. Although lysosomes may be involved in cell death, an emerging body of evidence supports the idea that the lysosomes appear to have the ability to be involved in protecting cells against overstimulation and harmful proteins and metabolites [8]. Permeabilization of lysosomes is dangerous to the cell [9,10], but selective translocation of lysosomal proteases across lysosomal membrane have been reported by numerous independent investigators beginning in the mid 90s [8,11,12]. For this reason, we propose that the release of lysosomal protease such as PRCP might be highly regulated by the external environmental input.

Most studies have demonstrated the importance of PRCP expression and function but the lysosomal molecular machinery involved in the secretion of PRCP is still uncharacterized. The goal of this study is to determine the life cycle of PRCP. Since upregulation of PRCP is associated with diabetes [13] and rheumatoid arthritis [14], mathematical modeling and simulating the experimentation results can be used to improve our understanding and prediction of the behavior of PRCP under physiological and pathophysiological conditions.

Mechanisms of generation of Ang_{1-7} and kinins at the membrane surface have been always a subject matter of controversy. According to one hypothesis, des-Arg^9-bradykinin (des-Arg^9-BK, BK_{1-8}) and angiotensin II (Ang II) are translocated across the lysosome membrane, where PRCP metabolizes BK_{1-8} to bradykinin 1-7 (BK_{1-7}) and Ang II to Ang_{1-7} [7]. However, recent findings by independent groups have shown that PRCP metabolizes its substrate at the cell surface [15,16,17]. This unusual observation prompted us to propose that PRCP participates in membrane-bound substrate peptide cleavage. This observation has profound implications. First, the release of PRCP from lysosomes is a highly orchestrated process at the cellular level. Secondly, PRCP translocation is a dynamic process. At any given time, the cellular expression and distribution of PRCP are heavily influenced by the environmental heterogeneity and the diversity of substrates of PRCP at one or several membrane sites.

In the present experiments, the focus is on the steady state distribution and trafficking of PRCP between lysosome, cytosol, plasma membrane and endosome compartments. Our data supports the hypothesis that substrates of PRCP influence the expression of PRCP. Thus, the lysosomal pathway of PRCP may represent potential target for both obesity and diabetes therapies [18].

Fig. 1 depicts the possible flow of PRCP within the cell environment, which, as stated above, has not been thoroughly explored scientifically. External stimuli are presented to the cell and begin interaction at the cell with conformal receptors, which are protein on the cell plasma membrane. The stimulant, in the case shown, Ang III, forms a complex with a receptor, in this case AT1 or AT2. This signaling mechanism, denoted by S in Fig. 4, that results in the generation PRCP mRNA from the nucleus and released. The PRCP mRNA is picked up by ribosomes on the endoplasmic reticulum, formed into the PRCP protein and sent on to the Golgi apparatus.

Each PRCP protein, denoted by P in Fig. 1, contains targeting information that is used to guide the PRCP to its intended destination. Some PRCP are intended to leave the cell; these are transported to the cell's plasma membrane in vesicles called exosomes. Some are bound for lysosomes; those are transported

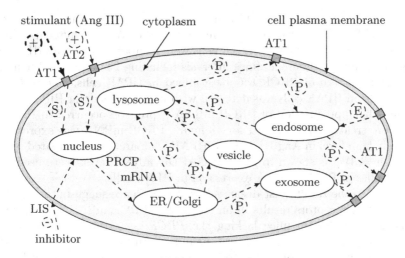

stimulant (Ang III)   cytoplasm   cell plasma membrane

$\langle \underline{S} \rangle \Rightarrow$ stimulus signaling; $\langle \underline{P} \rangle \Rightarrow$ PRCP; $\langle \underline{E} \rangle \Rightarrow$ non stimulus signaling;

Fig. 1. Communication paths relevant to PRCP trafficking in the human pulmonary artery endothelial cell in response to external stimuli

in specialized vesicles that circulate between the lysosomes and Golgi apparatus [19, see Fig. 10.12]. Still others are intended to move about in the cytoplasm and are enclosed in cytoplasmic vesicles. Such vesicle encapsulated PRCP may eventually attach to the cell's plasma membrane or lysosome. Additional PRCP circulation may result from other external signaling that does not specifically encourage the production of PRCP directly. Such signaling may result from complexes binding on the cell's plasma membrane and producing protein specifically bound for the lysosome, in which case the protein is transported in an endosome [19]. In addition, PRCP may be dispatched from the lysosome to perform a function at the cell's plasma membrane, such as metabolizing its substrate, and then possibly exit the cell directly or return to an endosome. From the endosome, the protein may return to the lysosome or exit the cell via a vesicle. Again, it is emphasized that the exact mechanisms of PRCP trafficking are not completely understood at this time.

Again, as stated above, over the long term, the objective is to completely understand the entire life cycle of PRCP. A set of experiments in that direction is now described.

Laboratory Experiments. In these experiments, we wished to identify receptor-dependent or -independent mechanisms responsible for lysosomal-mediated secretion of PRCP in human pulmonary artery endothelial (HPAE) cells. PRCP has a low Michaelis-Menten kinetic constant, K_m, and a very high catalytic efficiency for angiotensin III (Ang III). Furthermore, angiotensin II type 1 (AT1) and angiotensin II type 2 (AT2) receptors have a similar affinity for Ang III.

To elucidate the importance of AT1 and AT2 receptor signaling in the regulation of PRCP secretion, we first determined whether Ang III influences the function and expression of PRCP. HPAE cells were incubated with Ang III (100 μM)[1] over a number of different times intervals including 24, 48, and 72 hours. The expression pattern of PRCP was determined in HPAE cells. The mRNA signal for PRCP in HPAE cells was detected with use of primers for PRCP, and it was found that upregulation of PRCP mRNA expression occurred in HPAE cells that were treated with Ang III for 48 hours. PRCP mRNA was expressed at a relatively high level in Ang III–treated HPAE compared to non-treated cells ($^*P = 0.05, n = 3$)[2], as shown in Fig. 2a. GAPDH mRNA levels were used as control in studies of PRCP mRNA expression in HPAE cells.

With regard to the results just discussed, recent evidence suggests that overexpression of AT2 receptors results in an increase in PRCP mRNA [20]. It has been demonstrated that in mice lacking the *PRCP* gene, there is a reduced food intake along with increased energy expenditure. In theory, elevated PRCP mRNA might be inversely correlated to an increased appetite and reduced energy expenditure in experimental models of obesity. Further investigations are necessary to determine if there is an association.

Next, investigations were performed to determine whether Ang III influences PRCP trafficking. HPAE cells were incubated with Ang III (100 μM) for 48 hours at 37 °C. At the end of incubation period, the cell bathing growth medium (known as conditioned growth medium) was collected, concentrated, and assayed for PRCP activity. The activity of PRCP was detected using Ala-Pro-para-nitroanalide (APpNA), a chromogenic substrate. Although the immunological quantification of PRCP was not determined in the conditioned growth medium, there was no significant change in PRCP activity between the control (untreated) and Ang III-treated cells, Fig. 2b.

Recently, we showed that upregulation of PRCP is accompanied by an increase in endothelial nitric oxide (eNOS) mRNA expression in lipopolysaccharide treated cells. Thus, the effect of Ang III on eNOS mRNA expression was quantified in HPAE cells. As shown in Fig. 2c, contrary to our hypothesis, eNOS mRNA expression was not significantly increased in Ang III-treated cells compared with untreated HPAE cells.

Angiotensin converting enzyme (ACE) is one of several enzymes that catalyze Ang III. In this series of experiments, we tested the hypothesis that PRCP expression and function might be regulated by a receptor-independent pathway. We determined whether lisinopril (an ACE inhibitor) influences the function and expression of PRCP. PRCP mRNA increased in a time-dependent manner after lisinopril (100 μM) treatment, Fig. 3a. The most profound upregulation of PRCP expression occurred when HPAE cells were treated for 48 hours. PRCP activity was consistently higher in the conditioned growth medium of lisinopril-treated HPAE cells than in the controls, Fig. 3b. Then, we hypothesized that lisinopril might contribute to the expression and production of eNOS via PRCP dependent

---

[1] Notation: 100 μM denotes the molar concentration.

[2] Notation $^*P = 0.05, n = 3$ means a confidence level of 95% with 3 samples.

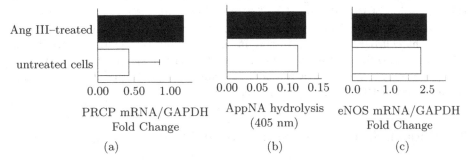

Fig. 2. Angiotensin III induces PRCP gene expression in cultured human pulmonary artery endothelial cells. (a) PRCP mRNA expression levels of HPAE cells were determined in the presence and absence of angiotensin III (Ang III), a PRCP substrate, at 48 h. (b) Enzymatic activity was measured in conditioned media of untreated and Ang III-treated cells. PRCP activity in HPAE cells were determined by quantifying the hydrolysis of pNA from Ala-Pro-para-nitroanalide (APpNA) at 405 nm. (c) Endothelial nitric oxide synthase (eNOS) mRNA expression levels in HPAE cells at 48 h. The results are presented as mean SEM of two or three independent experiments. Ang III $^*P \leq 0.05$ vs untreated group.

pathway. As shown in Fig. 3c, lisinopril caused an increase in eNOS mRNA at 48 h. Although its mechanism of action is not yet determined, lisinopril appears to stimulate eNOS expression via PRCP. Further investigations are required to establish this association. In conclusion, these studies provide the first evidence that PRCP expression and activity is inducible after lisinopril treatment.

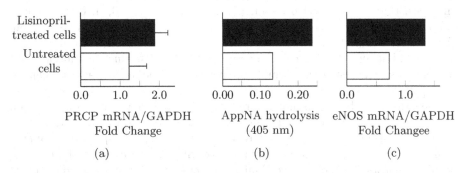

Fig. 3. Lisinopril induces PRCP gene expression in cultured human pulmonary artery endothelial cells. HPAE cells were treated Lisinopril. (a) PRCP mRNA expression levels of HPAE cells were determined in the presence and absence of lisinopril, an angiotensin converting enzyme inhibitor, at 48 h. (b) Enzymatic activity was measured in conditioned media of untreated or lisinopril-treated cells. PRCP activity in HPAE cells were determined by quantifying the hydrolysis of pNA from Ala-Pro- paranitroanalide (APpNA) at 405 nm. (c) Endothelial nitric oxide synthase (eNOS) mRNA expression levels in HPAE cells at 48 h. The results are presented as mean SEM of two or three independent experiments. Lisinopril, $^*P < 0.05$ vs, untreated cells.

Taken together, we established that the stimulation of endothelial cells triggers the expression of PRCP. These studies provide the first evidence that PRCP is inducible after lisinopril or Ang III treatment. We developed a fairly rapid and convenient cell-based assay for studying the cellular trafficking of PRCP. In addition, this cell-based assay combined with microscopy based assays will be used to develop a mathematical model and computational simulation describing the life cycle of PRCP in health and disease.

3   Endothelial Cell Reaction to sCD40L

High Level Problem Description. Assessment of classic cardiovascular risk factors has a central role in prognostic evaluation and prevention of cardiovascular disease, which is the leading cause of death worldwide. Epidemiological studies over the past 50 years have revealed numerous risk factors for atherosclerosis. The conclusions of the INTERHEART study are the definition of a number of risk factors, including abnormal lipids, smoking, hypertension, etc. Typical risk algorithms are based on the measurement of the these risk factors, and the most used are those derived from the US-American Framingham study and the German PROCAM study. However, these procedures fail in producing accurate predictions.

This has led to the search for novel biomarkers to better identify individuals at high risk. Inflammation is one of the main areas of investigation to identify such novel markers. The concept of the involvement of inflammation in atherosclerosis has started the discovery and adoption of inflammatory biomarkers for cardiovascular risk prediction [21]. Among these, CD40L plays an important role in the early stages of atherogenesis [21,22]. CD40L (also known as CD154) is a trimeric transmembrane protein of the tumor necrosis factor family expressed on several cell types, that together with its membrane receptor, CD40, mediates signals leading to responses which have a key role in immune activation, inflammation, atherosclerosis and thrombosis. All the main cell types involved in atherosclerosis, including endothelial cells, macrophages, T cells, smooth muscle cells, and platelets, expressing this proinflammatory cytokine as well as its receptor, CD40 [23].

When the endothelium is not injured, platelets and leukocytes move within blood vessels without any specific interaction with the endothelium. In case of injury or endothelium abnormal behaviour, it exposes specific proteins. Some of them, called *tissue factors*, are highly reactive with the platelets and bind to the specific receptors on their surface. Thus, interactions with the inflamed endothelium activate the surrounding platelets that release a wide range of mediators, such as the CD40L cytokine [23]. This mediator activates the endothelial cells by enabling their adhesive and chemotactic properties through the exposure of adhesion molecules on their cellular membrane [24]. Thus, CD40 ligation with CD40L triggers the endothelium activation, that is the expression of vascular adhesion molecules (VCAM-1) and the secretion of numerous cytokines and matrix metalloproteinases involved in extracellular matrix degradation [25]. This induces platelets and leukocytes to adhere to the endothelium even in absence of injuries or inflammation. Due to the diapedesis process, leukocytes migrate across the endothelium and in the long term can cause accumulation of thrombotic material. This dangerous phenomena, that is the atherosclerosis, can lead to the creation of thrombi, which may obstruct blood vessels.

In addition to CD40L expressed on activated platelets or T-cells, soluble fragments, sCD40L, could activate endothelial cells through ligation with endothelium CD40 receptors. Since it is known that more than 95% of the circulating sCD40L are due to platelets [26], the immediate objective of this experiment is to determine whether or not and to what extent an endothelial cell can be activated by sCD40L emitted by stimulated platelets in the absence of endothelium mechanical contact with cells exposing the CD40L ligand (see also [27]).

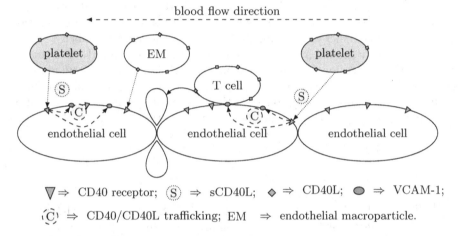

Fig. 4. Communication paths of sCD40L signaling in blood vessels in response to external stimuli and subsequent migration of T-cells in the subendothelium

Analytical and Simulation Modeling. A reliable model for communications among platelets, endothelial cells, and leukocytes is needed in order to improve focusing on targeted experiments and reduce the number of experimental animals needed. The effort to develop such models can open interactions among relevant research fields resulting in an improved understanding of the dynamics at the nanoscale in blood vessels. An example of this process is reported in [28], where the authors developed a specific experiment in order to validate the simulation model of nano particles propagation in blood vessels when the presence of large blood cells (specifically red blood cells) is simulated. In last few years, software tools specifically designed to simulate nanoscale communications have been developed, such as those presented in [29,30,31].

Laboratory Experiments. In this section we describe the in-vitro experiment carried out to analyze the interaction between sCD40L, produced by stimulated platelets, and CD40 on the human umbilical vein endothelial cells (HUVEC) surface. Platelets are stimulated with alpha thrombin for 10 minutes, then thrombin was neutralized with hirudin. Platelets are placed on the floor of the superior chamber, whereas HUVEC have been cultured on the bottom wells of a 96 well-plates. A section of a single transwell is reported in Figure 5a.

The transwell apparatus allows studying the effect of sCD40L released from stimulated platelets on cultured HUVECs, without direct platelet contact with endothelial cells, at different times starting from the thrombin neutralization (10, 30, 60, 120 and 240 minutes). At these times, a sample of 1500 HUVEC cells has been analyzed by flow cytometry [32]. This technique collects all events where the considered cell fluorescence is higher than basal fluorescence, leading to generation of a right-shift in flow cytometric pattern of cell fluorescence. This proves that fluorescent sCD40L interacted with HUVEC cells expressing CD40 receptors. In addition, after incubation, HUVEC have been analyzed with ELISA kit [33] to assess the VCAM-1 expression on HUVECs due to sCD40L diffusion from the upper chamber of the transwell plate into the lower chamber.

Flow cytometry showed a relevant presence of CD40L on the HUVEC surface after 10 minutes of co-incubation, indicating that sCD40L released from platelets binds HUVECs CD40 receptor within 10 minutes (Figure 5b, column 2). A significant VCAM-1 expression on HUVECs was visible starting 2 hours after co-incubation with platelets (Figure 5b, column 3), the experiment details are omitted here because it would be not only verbose but verbatim, however a thorough description of them can be found in [34].

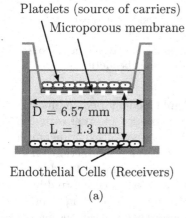

Platelets (source of carriers)
Microporous membrane
D = 6.57 mm
L = 1.3 mm
Endothelial Cells (Receivers)

(a)

Time (min)	CD40L/CD40 Bindings	VCAM-1 Expression
10	0.2607	0.009
30	0.3039	0.01
60	0.429	0.013
120	0.6836	0.085
240	0.7579	0.045

(b)

Fig. 5. Platelet experiment (a) Section of a well used for studying the interaction between stimulated platelets and HUVECs, and (b) results of experimental data analysis showing the fraction of endothelial cells exhibiting bindings between sCD40L carriers and CD40 receptors and the fraction of endothelial cells exposing VCAM-1 as a function of time from the stimulus neutralization time

4   Mapping Requirements to State of the Art

In this section, the state of the art in cellular communication modeling is examined in light of the objectives described in sections 2 and 3. To facilitate an orderly discussion the molecular communication architecture presented in [35] will be followed. In that reference, communications into 5 phases: encoding, sending, propagation, receiving, and decoding. In this section, each of these phases is discussed with a view towards providing modeling support for the experiments described previously. In each of the experimental cases, the interest is in understanding the cell's response to external stimuli. Therefore, the cell itself serves as a receiver and sender of information between the cell and the extracellular world, and there is a separate intracellular network to facilitate communications within the cell.

Encoding. In [35], encoding is defined as "the phase in which sender bionanomachine translates information into information molecules that the bionanomachine can detect." At the cell/extracellular interface, the specific information molecule to be detected by the cell is sCD40L in the case of the VCAM experiment and the corresponding receptors are CD40. The PRCP experiments have two parts. In the first part, Ang III is specific information molecule to be detected and the corresponding receptors are AT1 and AT2 receptors, which are at the cell plasma membrane. In the second part, lisinopril is the information molecule to be detected and the receiver is ACE. In each case, the result is a signal that contains information that goes directly to the nucleus.

Sending. In [35], sending is defined as "the phase by which a sender bionanomachine releases information molecules into the environment." In vivo, in addition to platelets, CD40L is expressed on the surface of many cell types, for example T cells, which are small lymphocytes, which in turn are a type of white blood cells. CD40L is expressed when platelets or other cells are activated to produce them. Ang III starts out life as Angiotensinogen, which is produced and released into circulation by the liver. Angiotensinogen is converted to Ang I by action of renin and then to Ang II by being acted on by ACE and then to Ang III by being acted on by aminopeptidases located in red blood cells and many other tissues. In the blood stream, Ang III has a half-life on the order of 15 seconds but is produced continuously. For modeling purposed, it can be assumed that both CD40L and Ang III can be available in the bloodstream when needed.

Propagation. Propagation is defined in [35] as the phase during which information molecules move from sender biomachines through the environment to the receiver bio-machines. From a review of the literature, it appears that propagation model are selected from an array of alternatives, mostly based on Brownian motion or random walks, rather than developing modes tailored to the problem at hand. Results are given in terms of the probability density function (PDF) for the latency between the transmitter and receiver for each piece of information for a given diffusion coefficient and parameterized by distance from the between the transmitter and receiver [35]. With regard to the state of the art in modeling the physical layer, [35] concludes

> These models are relatively simple and need to be extended to increase their applicability, for instance, by considering more complex geometry (e.g. intracellular environment, the human body), structure of molecules, interaction among molecules.

For the cases under discussion here, Ang III and CD40L must actually make contact with their respective receptors, which are on the cell's plasma membrane and vary in number depending on the activation level of the cell for the particular stimulant. Thus, the amount of time required for the stimulant to bind with the receptors to form complexes that activate the cell depends upon the number of receptors available on the cell which in turn depends on the cell's activation history as well as its initial conditions. In the case of the PRCP experiment, the target endothelial cells are stationary, the Ang III is suspended in solution above the endothelial cells, and the propagation channel is not an issue. But, in the case of the VCAM, one of the major steps requirements is to be able to account for reaction times of the endothelial cells, thus it is important to be able to factor out the information's propagation time. The propagation model proposed in [28] that accounts explicitly for collisions between nano particles and blood cells was adopted in [36].

Receiving. Receiving is defined in [35] as "the phase during which the receiver bio-machines captures information molecules propagating in the environment." In the experiments under discussion here, the cellular receivers are simply the receptors, and reception is modeled as binding between the stimulant-derived information molecule and the receptor. However, a fundamental issue in modeling the reception process in a communication system is to identify the signal strength needed to enable not only the reception of the signal, but also the decoding of the signal itself. In this regard, translating this requirements into a communication system that uses bursts of information molecules means evaluating the receiver sensitivity, that is the minimum number of nano particles to be bound with relevant receptors in order to trigger the decoding phase. In the case of the sCD40L signaling, the estimation of receiver sensitivity has been done in [36] using a theoretical model matched with the results of the experiment described in section 3.

Decoding. Decoding is defined in [35] as "the phase during which the receiver bio-machine, upon capturing information molecules, decodes the received molecules into a chemical reaction. Chemical reactions for decoding at the receiver bio-machine may include the production of new molecules, the performing of a simple task, or production of another signal (e.g., sending other information molecules)." In the case of the experiments described here, the result of receiving is a complex that is released in the cytoplasm directed towards the nucleus. However, the interesting part of the experiments is to determine what happens next; that is, what is the cell's reaction to the stimulus? Alternatively stated, the interesting question is "How does the cell work?".

5   Reaching the Next Level

Given the fact that the overriding objective of the research is to contribute to the understanding of how cells function in reaction to stimuli, consider the following excerpt from the 2001 article [37]:

> A bacterial cell, such as Escherichia coli (2 μm2 cross-sectional area) with a 4.6 million base-pair chromosome, has the equivalent of a 9.2 megabit memory. ... cell queries an extremely complex environment in a continuous and parallel manner and adapts its processing, sensing and actuating machinery to the needs at hand.

The author goes on to say that by 2014 it can be hoped that the silicon-based memory can reach about 490 bits.

Cells have a multitude of receivers and transmitters operating simultaneously on their membranes. In addition, there is a network of intracellular transmitters and receivers. It seems that a reasonable approach to characterizing cell behavior would be to severely limit the number of simultaneously operating receivers at the start so that the cell's reaction to a single stimulus can be understood in isolation before moving on to multiple simultaneous stimuli. This is, in fact, the approach that has been taken in biological research for a very long time, and significant progress has been made without question.

From the discussion of the previous sections, it can be concluded that there are at least three major obstacles to developing high fidelity models of cellular communications: lack of realistic extracellular propagation models, insufficient understanding of how cells react internally to external stimuli, and a system wide understanding of how cells interact in the presence of multiple stimuli. Thus, there are two questions: what are the shortcomings of the present approach, and what is the potential of communication systems modeling to improve the situation?

To illustrate one shortcoming of the present approach, the PRCP experiments involved incubating cells far a variety of periods of time including 12, 24, 48, and 72 hours. The reason for having multiple incubation periods is that there is no suitable way to predict the incubation period required to achieve their maximum PRCP expression in response to Ang III, or whether the cell would produce elevated PRCP for that matter and, if so, whether the cell would express PRCP externally. Given the model of PRCP-related flows presented in section 2, one possibility is to develop state machines, similar to those used to describe protocols in communications systems, to model intracellular behavior. From there, the state machine can be refined and additional hypotheses can be formulated for cell behavior iteratively until a suitable model results.

An alternative possibility is to develop a mathematical model that keeps track of the critical quantities that are involved in production of the end product, such as the Markov chain model of VCAM-1 production presented in [36]. In the case of PRCP-related experiments, the quantities of interest might include the number of PRCP molecules present in each to the following places: endoplasmic reticulum, Golgi, cytoplasm, lysosome, endosome, exosome, plasma membrane, and external to cell. It seems that a sensible approach would be to design both such a mathematical model in close coordination with a measurement program to ensure that the mathematical model and measurement programs are mutually compatible and supportive.

In the development of suitable state machines that resemble protocols, there are two basic issues: definition of the states and definition of the events that cause transitions among the states. With regard to the PRCP-related in vitro experiment, some potential candidates for states and events causing transitions are as follows:

Normality. There is no Ang III stimulant present at any receptor. In this basal state, the cell has a reserve of PRCP stored in the lysosomes, but there are no mRNA sequences being encoded to support additional PRCP transcription.

Alert. There is Ang III stimulant present and this information is being signaled to the nucleus, but the level of stimulant is insufficient to cause the nucleus to encode mRNA sequences for PRCP synthesis.

Response. Ang III stimulant has occurred for a sufficient period such that PRCP molecules are being released into the cytoplasm and being translocated to the plasma membrane to neutralize the stimulant. In addition some PRCP is being released from the cell.

Maintenance. Sufficient quantities of Ang III stimulant continue to be present at the receptors to cause the nucleus to encode mRNA to support synthesis and maintain the level of PRCP. In addition, the PRCP is still moving around within the cell. Simultaneously, receptor-stimulant complexes undergo endocytosis to curtail stimulation.

Normalization. Stimulant no longer continues to be be present and the cell is adjusting its PRCP level to basal either by degrading excess PRCP or synthesizing additional PRCP to replenish the shortage.

Compensation. If stimulation is chronic, basal level is adjusted to protect cell integrity.

It is pointed out that quality of the state definition of each state can be improved by augmenting the definition with a variable of interest, such as the number of molecules of PRCP present at a given time.

A state transition diagram based on these definitions is presented in Fig. 6. Some thought on the state definitions reveals that at least some level of mathematical modeling is needed to elucidate the cells activities while resident in each of the states. For example, during response, at what rate is the level of PRCP within the cell decreasing and what factors influence this decrease? What determines the period of time in the response state before the cell transitions to the maintenance state? Given that the PRCP may be in the lysosomes, vesicles, endosomes, etc., what is happening to the levels of each? In addition, at least some level of modeling is needed in order to determine when transitions occur and which events cause transitions. Clearly, many other questions can be posed to help formulate measurement plans.

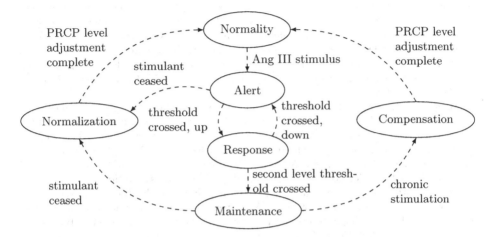

Fig. 6. State transition diagram for PRCP stimulation cycle

State machines and state transition diagrams are given for the VCAM-1 production and the platelet processes in [38], which is available to the interested reader but these are omitted here due to space limitations.

6   Conclusions

While in many cases, there is already a good understanding of the general reactions to stimuli, features such as reaction times, stimulant threshold levels, and molecule concentration levels required for expression are often poorly understood at best. Because a cell's reaction to stimuli is generally communication with other cells, an understanding of both reaction and reaction times is critical. The results presented here demonstrate that the joint efforts of communication engineers and biological researchers can lead to improving communication models of cells and the understanding of cellular systems, especially in terms of defining state machines and mathematical and simulation models of cell behavior that can be integrated into measurement programs.

References

1. Adams, G.N., LaRusch, G.A., Stavrou, E., Zhou, Y., Nieman, M.T., Jacobs, G.H., Cui, Y., Lu, Y., Jain, M.K., Mahdi, F., Shariat-Madar, Z., Okada, Y., D'Alecy, L.G., Schmaier, A.H.: Murine prolylcarboxypeptidase depletion induces vascular dysfunction with hypertension and faster arterial thrombosis. Blood 117(14), 3929–3937 (2011)

2. Shariat-Madar, B., Kolte, D., Verlangieri, A.: Prolylcarboxypeptidase (PRCP) as a new target for obesity treatment. Diabetes, Metabolic Syndrome and Obesity: Targets and Therapy 3(1), 67–78 (2010)
3. Diano, S.: New aspects of melanocortin signaling: a role for PRCP in alpha-msh degradation. Front Neuroendocrinol 32(1), 70–83 (2011)
4. Jeong, J.K., Szabo, G., Kelly, K., Diano, S.: Prolyl carboxypeptidase regulates energy expenditure and the thyroid axis. Endocrinology 153(2), 683–689 (2012)
5. Wallingford, N., Perroud, B., Gao, Q., Coppola, A., Gyengesi, E., Liu, Z.-W., Gao, X.-B., Diament, A., Haus, K.A., Shariat-Madar, Z., Mahdi, F., Wardlaw, S.L., Schmaier, A.H., Warden, C.H., Diano, S.: Prolylcarboxypeptidase regulates food intake by inactivating -MSH in rodents. J. of Clin. Invest. 119(8), 2291–2303 (2009)
6. Hagedorn, M.: Prcp: a key to blood vessel homeostasis. Blood 117, 3705–3706 (2011)
7. Tan, F., Morris, P.W., Skidgel, R.A., Erdos, E.G.: Sequencing and cloning of human prolylcarboxypeptidase (angiotensinase C). Similarity to both serine carboxypeptidase and prolylendopeptidase families. J. Biol. Chem. 268(22), 16631–16638 (1993)
8. Stinchcombe, J.C., Salio, M., Cerundolo, V., Pende, D., Arico, M., Griffiths, G.M.: Centriole polarisation to the immunological synapse directs secretion from cytolytic cells of both the innate and adaptive immune systems. BMC Biol. 9, 45 (2011)
9. Gordon, P.B., Kisen, G.O., Kovacs, A.L., Seglen, P.O.: Experimental characterization of the autophagic-lysosomal pathway in isolated rat hepatocytes. Biochem. Soc. Symp. 55, 129–143 (1989)
10. Swanson, J.A., Locke, A., Ansel, P., Hollenbeck, P.J.: Radial movement of lysosomes along microtubules in permeabilized macrophages. J. Cell. Sci. 103(pt 1), 201–209 (1992)
11. Isenman, L.D., Dice, J.F.: Selective release of peptides from lysosomes. J. Biol. Chem. 268(32), 23856–23859 (1993)
12. Daniele, T., Hackmann, Y., Ritter, A.T., Wenham, M., Booth, S., Bossi, G., Schintler, M., Auer-Grumbach, M., Griffiths, G.M.: A role for Rab7 in the movement of secretory granules in cytotoxic T lymphocytes. Traffic 12(7), 902–911 (2011)
13. Xu, S., Lind, L., Zhao, L., Lindahl, B., Venge, P.: Plasma prolylcarboxypeptidase (angiotensinase C) is increased in obesity and diabetes mellitus and related to cardiovascular dysfunction. Clin. Chem. 58(7), 1110–1115 (2012)
14. Mallela, J., Yang, J., Shariat-Madar, Z.: Prolylcarboxypeptidase: a cardioprotective enzyme. Int. J. Biochem. Cell. Biol. 41(3), 477–481 (2009)
15. Chajkowski, S.M., Mallela, J., Watson, D.E., Wang, J., McCurdy, C.R., Rimoldi, J.M., Shariat-Madar, Z.: Highly selective hydrolysis of kinins by recombinant prolylcarboxypeptidase. Biochem. Biophys. Res. Commun. 405(3), 338–343 (2011)
16. Zhu, L., Carretero, O.A., Xu, J., Wang, L., Harding, P., Rhaleb, N.-E., Yang, J.J., Sumners, C., Yang, X.-P.: Angiotensin II type 2 receptor-stimulated activation of plasma prekallikrein and bradykinin release: Role of SHP-1. Am. J. Physiol. Heart Circ. Physiol. (2012)
17. Velez, J.C.Q., Ierardi, J.L., Bland, A.M., Morinelli, T.A., Arthur, J.M., Raymond, J.R., Janech, M.G.: Enzymatic processing of angiotensin peptides by human glomerular endothelial cells. Am. J. Physiol. Renal. Physiol. 302(12), F1583–F1594 (2012)
18. Palmiter, R.D.: Reduced levels of neurotransmitter-degrading enzyme PRCP promote a lean phenotype [corrected]. J. Clin. Invest. 119(8), 2130–2133 (2009)
19. Bolsover, S.R., Shephard, E.A., White, H.A., Hyams, J.S.: Cell Biology: A Short Course, 3rd edn. Wiley-Blackwell (2011)

20. Zhu, L., Carretero, O.A., Liao, T.-D., Harding, P., Li, H., Sumners, C., Yang, X.-P.: Role of prolylcarboxypeptidase in angiotensin II type 2 receptoräimediated bradykinin release in mouse coronary artery endothelial cells. Hypertension 56(3), 384–390 (2010)
21. Szmitko, P.E., Wang, C.-H., Weisel, R.D., de Almeida, J.R., Anderson, T.J., Verma, S.: New markers of inflammation and endothelial cell activation. Circulation 108(16), 1917–1923 (2003)
22. Khot, U.N., Khot, M.B., Bajzer, C.T.: Prevalence of conventional risk factors in patients with coronary heart disease. ACC Current Journal Review 12(6), 23–23 (2003)
23. Schonbeck, U., Libby, P.: The CD40/CD154 receptor/ligand dyad. Cell. Mol. Life Sci. 58(1), 4–43 (2001)
24. Henn, V., Slupsky, J.R., Grafe, M., Anagnostopoulos, I., Forster, R., Muller-Berghaus, G., Kroczek, R.A.: CD40 ligand on activated platelets triggers an inflammatory reaction of endothelial cells. Nature 391(6667), 591–594 (1998)
25. Mach, F., Schonbeck, U., Libby, P.: CD40 signaling in vascular cells: A key role in atherosclerosis? Atherosclerosis 137(suppl. 1), S89 – S95 (1998)
26. André, P., Nannizzi-Alaimo, L., Prasad, S.K., Phillips, D.R.: Platelet-derived CD40L: the switch-hitting player of cardiovascular disease. Circulation 106(8), 896–899 (2002)
27. Chen, Y., Chen, J., Xiong, Y., Da, Q., Xu, Y., Jiang, X., Tang, H.: Internalization of CD40 regulates its signal transduction in vascular endothelial cells. Biochem. Biophys. Res. Commun. 345(1), 106–117 (2006)
28. Tan, J., Thomas, A., Liu, Y.: Influence of red blood cells on nanoparticle targeted delivery in microcirculation. Soft. Matter. 8, 1934–1946 (2012)
29. Felicetti, L., Femminella, M., Reali, G.: A simulation tool for nanoscale biological networks. Nano Communication Networks 3(1), 2–18 (2012)
30. Gul, E., Atakan, B., Akan, O.B.: Nanons: A nanoscale network simulator framework for molecular communications. Nano Communication Networks 1(2), 138–156 (2010)
31. Garralda, N., Llatser, I., Cabellos-Aparicio, A., Alarcón, E., Pierobon, M.: Diffusion-based physical channel identification in molecular nanonetworks. Nano Communication Networks 2(4), 196–204 (2011)
32. Ormerod, G., Novo, D.: Flow Cytometry: A Basic Introduction. M.G Ormerod (2008)
33. Lequin, R.M.: Enzyme immunoassay (EIA) / enzyme-linked immunosorbent assay (ELISA). Clinical Chemistry 51(12), 2415–2418 (2005)
34. Felicetti, L., Femminella, M., Reali, G., Gresele, P., Malvestiti, M.: Experimental campaign on the in-vitro platelet-endothelial cells interactions. Tech. Rep., http://conan.diei.unipg.it/pub/experiment.pdf
35. Nakano, T., Moore, M., Wei, F., Vasilakos, A., Shuai, J.: Molecular communication and networking: Opportunities and challenges. IEEE Trans. on NanoBioscience 11(2), 135–148 (2012)
36. Felicetti, L., Femminella, M., Reali, G., Gresele, P., Malvestiti, M., Daigle, J.N.: Modeling inter-cell communications in blood vessels. IEEE J. Sel. Areas in Com. (submitted)
37. Simpson, M.L., Sayler, G.S., Fleming, J.T., Applegate, B.: Whole-cell biocomputing. Trends Biotechnol. 19(8), 317–323 (2001)
38. Daigle, J.N., Femminella, M., Shariat-Madar, Z.: State transitions diagrams for vcam-1 production and platelet activity. Tech. Rep., http://conan.diei.unipg.it/pub/state_transition_diagrams.pdf

Substitution Networks Based on Software Defined Networking

(Invited Paper)

Daniel Philip Venmani[1,2], Yvon Gourhant[1], Laurent Reynaud[1],
Prosper Chemouil[1], and Djamal Zeghlache[2]

[1] Orange Labs, France Telecom R&D, Lannion, France
[2] TELECOM SudParis & CNRS, SAMOVAR / UMR 5157, Evry, France

Abstract. A Substitution Network (SN) is a rapidly deployable temporary wireless network that should be dynamically integrated within an existing base network. They back-up the base network inorder to meet temporary network overloaded conditions to keep providing services and to ensure the network connectivity, which could not be achieved by the base network alone. Within this context, in this paper, we propose a solution considering SNs as a means for provisioning backup path for Mobile Network Operators (MNOs) microwave backhaul to overcome network overload due to excessive wireless data traffic. Our approach considers Software Defined Networking (SDN) technology due to its flexibility to integrate diverse future generations of switches as well as its centralized approach for decoupling control-plane and data-plane. Our solution is based on exploring the OpenFlow protocol. Based on our experimental results, we demonstrate the feasibility of our proposal, which allows verifying the effectiveness of adopting SNs based on SDN. Here, our approach is considered in the context of emerging economies, since, from past research, studies have shown that OPEX/CAPEX may not have the same impact in emerging countries as they have in developed countries.

Keywords: OpenFlow, Software Defined Networking, Substitution Networks, Wireless Backhaul.

1   Introduction

Due to the continuous network and service evolution in wireless communications, future wireless ecosystem calls-for re-designing backhaul solutions to provide efficient and ubiquitous broadband wireless access to current and future Internet-based applications and to evolve seamlessly into the future "pure" packet network architecture. Data consumption has risen dramatically across the globe following the widespread availability of machine-to-machine communications, Wireless Sensor and Actuator Networks (WSAN), 3G and 4G-LTE which are being deployed worldwide [1]. Focusing towards the emerging markets such as the BRICS (Brazil, Russia, India, China, South Africa) economies and the Sub-Saharan African countries, in the light of the various challenges for the Mobile Network Operators (MNOs), traffic growth and

J. Zheng et al. (Eds.): Adhocnets 2012, LNICST 111, pp. 242–259, 2013.

the pressure to continuously deploy new services due to the gradual migration from 2G to 3G and further to 4G, raise one of the greatest challenges to support the backhaul capacity requirement. Furthermore, unlike in developed economies, there is generally no fixed line infrastructure to support this ever-rising traffic increase which creates a problem for backhauling.

Within this challenging context of addressing the problem of increased backhaul capacity, in a very competitive market in emerging economies, we propose in this paper a new architecture based on Substitution Networks (SNs). In simple words, a SN could be defined as any form of temporary wireless network that has rapid deployment capability to back-up a base network [2], [3]. SN is a new research area that is motivated by significant challenges among various disciplines such as wireless mesh networks, wireless sensor networks etc. However, its application towards fully demonstrating its behavior to practical technical systems such as the wireless mobile backhaul is very limited until today. Nevertheless, SN is foreseen to play a major role in future communication systems due to its simple but efficient design objective. While SNs are envisioned are to be highly autonomous, encompassing self-configuration, self-optimization and self-healing in a massively distributed environment, we claim that the non-centralized nature of SNs makes them sensitive to guarantee the required quality of service (QoS) to a wide variety of users, since in such networks, issues such as bandwidth management are expected to be transparent to the end-users. In addition, the requirement for bringing-in variety of vendor switches renders the networks increasingly complex, and therefore, more difficult to monitor, control, configure and manage.

Hence, this led to the necessity for a solution to deploy SNs through a centralized scheme, which is incidentally made possible by SDN, whose applicability and performance we study in this paper. That said, with this in mind, here in this article, we propose a new network design through which we appropriately suggest adopting SDN technology to SN. We incorporate SDN to tackle the problem of a centralized control of multiple diverse vendor equipments and thus we adopt OpenFlow to demonstrate the feasibility of our proposed network design. Moreover, through this solution, we demonstrate the possibility to adjust the bandwidth on a set of links and switches dynamically according to the traffic needs of individual end-users, which guarantees the required QoS. We believe that our proposal to incorporate SDN into SN will appeal to Internet Service Providers as well as the MNOs to solve the problem of network overload produced by varying user traffic demand at different periods of time.

2   Problem Characterization: Background and Existing Solutions

Problem 1: Network Overload. Network overload is a situation that generates an unexpected amount of traffic which exceeds the regular network capacity. This can be caused by a variety of factors, from too much traffic at one point in time to excessive traffic generated (i) under emergency situations like flood, earthquake, national emergency or other "chaotic" situations (ii) and in case of any other public social events. Thousands of cell sites installed throughout the country may determine the reach of the MNO, but it can not accommodate for the capacity increase in the backhaul to guarantee the required QoS to end-users. In order to prevent overload and the resulting network congestion, network traffic must be managed through a variety of methods. Bandwidth management [4], [5] and traffic shaping [6], [7] help stabilize network usage.

Problem 2: Cost of Resilience. Besides these technological advancements, setting up back-up paths is considered as another solution [8], [9] as shown in Fig. 1. Back-up paths are usually set up permanently across the locations where MNOs had predicted from previous statistical analysis that there could be network congestion or traffic spike under certain period of time. This typically involves over provisioning the core network and when the network gets overloaded, the exceeding traffic is re-routed through the back up networks; thereby avoiding congestion. Back-up paths are generally fixed paths and are not capable of being moved to another location whenever required. While setting up the back-up paths seem to be a feasible solution in developed countries, it may not have the same impact with regard to emerging countries due to the extremely high operational expenditures (OPEX) and capital expenditure (CAPEX).

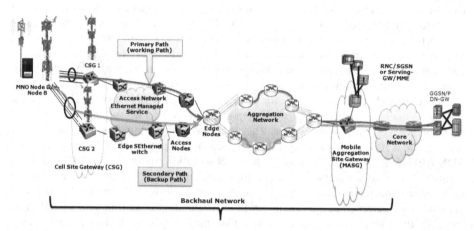

Fig. 1. Figure illustrating backup path protection in wireless microwave backhaul in 3G/4G

Problem 3: Reach of Service over Speed. Among others, one of the major focuses of the Telecom regulators all over the world is a system that enables people to get what they want and pay accordingly, i.e. the delivery of "unprecedented" broadband speeds should not be the guiding principle; rather what is important is to make sure that there is robust Internet connectivity in every nook-and-corner that gives atleast the minimum broadband coverage with minimum QoS as-and-when new Internet applications widely penetrate the related markets. This, in the first place, includes taking broadband coverage to rural and remote locations to prevent the tangible risk that some people and businesses may be left behind because of the inadequate access to the internet and all its benefits. Due to the cost involved in cell-site acquisition, Operation and Maintenance (O&M) etc. MNOs are reluctant to extend their broadband coverage to such rural and remote customers, unhesitatingly.

Problem 4: Heterogeneity. Today's communication network consists of heterogeneous networking vendor equipments and device models such as Cisco, Juniper, Ericsson, Nokia Siemens Networks, Alcatel Lucent etc. and hundreds of in-house developed applications not only based on different operating systems but also different versions of the same management protocol itself. These are deployed globally in hundreds of sites along the end-to-end wireless architecture (access/backhaul/core). They support tens of thousands of users, using a variety of network topologies and access mechanisms to provide connectivity. To complicate matters, with the proliferation of new technologies such as from 2G to 3G and now to 4G, networks are becoming more and more complex with different generations of technologies coexisting within the same network. This intensifies maintenance and network management, driving up OPEX.

3   Approaching the Problem through Substitution Networks (SNs)

Under these circumstances, solutions based on adaptive networks and low cost infrastructures are of major interest due to limited budget in emerging economies (also in developed economies for cost-sparring reasons), so that the services could be provisioned dynamically according to variable conditions. Therefore, the aforementioned factors lead to the consideration of an alternative approach called Substitution Networks.

3.1   Inspirations for Substitution Networks (SNs)

Our work here derives from a long line of related research [10]-[12] that inspired us towards the concept of SN to specify high-level policies at a logically centralized controller, which are then enforced across the network without the tedious concern of manually crafting switch-by-switch configurations. Distributed wireless sensor and actuator networks (WSANs) [13] that perform distributed sensing and acting tasks with the help of a controller that is responsible for monitoring and managing the overall network through communications with sensors and actuators is seen as another potential motivation towards our concept. There are three essential components in WSANs: sensors, actuators and a controller. Sensors observe information about the physical world, while actuators make decisions and perform appropriate actions upon the environments. The controller is responsible for monitoring and managing the overall network through communications with sensors and actuators. After sensors in the sensor/actuator field detect a phenomenon, they transmit their readings in one of the two following forms. They either transmit their readings to the resource-rich actuator nodes which can process all incoming data and initiate appropriate actions, or sensors route data hop by hop upto the sink which issues action commands to actuators. The former case is termed as Automated Architecture due to the nonexistence of central controller (human interaction) while the latter one is termed as Semi-Automated Architecture since the sink (central controller) collects data and coordinates the acting process.

The choice of centralized versus distributed approaches for WSANs has been in discussion [14], [15] and on a conclusive basis, we can infer that the pros of the semi-automated (centralized) architecture is to have a single view for taking the right decision versus the distributed architecture that takes decisions on partial knowledge and that may suffer from instability (in case of contradictory decisions taken by adjacent actuators). This may lead to an inefficient multi-actor global behavior. The cons are that centralized approach does not scale. Congestion is a consequence of scalability. Nevertheless, the problems of delay and potential congestion issues can be significantly mitigated, since the links close to the sink are those which are likely to exhibit the best quality (since they are close to the core network) with low latency and congestion, as opposed to those close to the actuators (since they will be close to the last mile in our target scenarios). Though it seems that the use of a centralized approach necessitates more hops, the extra hops alleviate the significant source of congestion and delay. With this motivation, we go forward to visualize our concept.

3.2   Substitution Networks (SNs) in Wireless Backhaul Networks

Within our context of wireless backhaul networks, a Substitution Network (SN) refers to network elements (NEs) (which could refer to elements of the access network, namely Node B or e-Node B or microwave backhaul equipped in a vehicle such as truck or car like Cell-on-Wheels (CoW)/Cell-on-Light Truck (CoLT) [16] as in Fig. 3) that are used for emergency services or temporary events) that can move or can be moved, and can be dynamically integrated into the base network. Accordingly, we propose SNs for different scenarios of network operation, e.g. during initial roll-out to carry-out radio planning or during early phases of operation where planned shutdown for maintenance is foreseen, or operation of a mature network with high load. In general, SN relies on Self Organizing Networks (SON) use cases which are related to self-configuration and coverage. These properties are the most important in the earlier phases, whereas quality and capacity-based use cases will be in the focus later. Hence, SNs do not apply only for overload traffic conditions but also to situations when a network is anticipated to be shutdown for maintenance reasons.

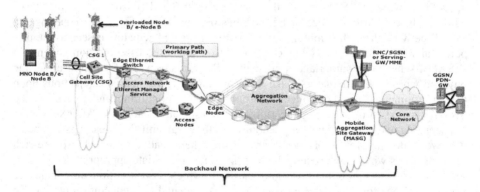

Fig. 2. Architectural design illustrating the elimination of back-up path

Now focusing towards emerging countries, the major concern is that the Mean-Time-To-Repair (MTTR) values are usually too high (in terms of days, sometimes weeks [17]) due to inadequate logistics facilities. With a rapid SN in-place, this could be considerably reduced to few hours. Adding to this, SN also allows reducing OPEX by optimized use of the existing NEs and physical resources, and prolonging equipment lifetime. Therefore the same coverage, capacity, and quality can be obtained with less investment in NEs, or those performance measures can be improved, thus allowing increased capacity, higher subscriber loyalty, and reduced failure events. This, therefore, can be of great interest for emerging countries where the cost of setting up a back-up network, only to handle additional traffic at peak hours or protect the last-mile link (which do not have double backup protection at all) is a real issue in terms of cost and technical complexity involved.

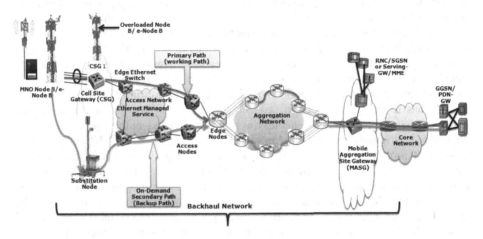

Fig. 3. Architectural design illustrating the integration of Substitution Node

3.3   Shortcomings of Substitution Networks (SNs) That Hinder a Wide Adoption into Wireless Backhaul Networks

Now, the question that arises is whether SNs can be generally exploited to a larger scale for solving some of the aforementioned pending problems for future networks. This question leads to a variety of open research challenges. Solutions to these challenges are pivotal in either leveraging the possible advantages of SNs, but could also turn out to be a heavy burden for both MNOs and end-users. The goal is clearly set: after purposefully introducing the SN either automatically or semi-automatically, the beneficial features often identified as the so-called self-properties should clearly out-weight the detrimental aspects, such as un-controllability, undesired instability or unpredictability. In this context, we do not consider mobility of the SN as a constraint; rather, we claim that the concept of controlled mobility may be based on operation research mechanisms that use empirical network monitoring statistics from the past for determining/predicting traffic load at a given period of time (e.g., every evening) and a given appropriate location. In any cases, this is the network traffic monitoring unit that accordingly decides the location of the SNs as well as the amount of time that the SN has to be present. Even if they are less reactive than traditional resilience mechanisms in case of unpredictable failures, they provide the same level of quality for scheduled management operations that take place largely more often than failures.

As previously mentioned, a SN is a spontaneous system made up of independent interacting entities often acting on simple rules. By independent, we imply that these systems do not necessarily have to comply with any standardized protocols and or any standardized vendor equipments. That does not make it easier to define the rules (protocols/algorithm) of the entities that are in-place in order to achieve a desired (emergent) behavior to back-up an existing network, so that a highly fault-tolerant and efficient network emerges with respect to pre-defined performance metrics. On the other hand, within the scope of microwave backhaul networks of MNOs, as mobile telecom market becomes more competitive, MNOs are increasingly at odds about the balance between choosing the NEs from "one" unique vendor alone and the cost associated with the equipment of that vendor. Adding to this, NE vendors, on the other hand, want to deliver standardized functionalities which are implemented in proprietary algorithms. This creates a dead-end to integrate SNs, specifically to mobile backhaul. In addition, but specific to SNs, if we want to integrate a SN into different networks at different periods of time, we need uniformity in management, or the SN has to evolve in order to produce the desired effect within the integrated network. Using open standards enables a variety of independent third-party tools to be applied to configuration, testing and troubleshooting. However, each NE has a limited amount of processing capacity and memory for storing and retrieving the data that travels over the network. When the amount of data on the network is excessive, the extra data can not be processed and has to be re-sent or dropped. This should be possible for the MNO, not as a burden of manual human intervention, but should be carried out autonomously. Thus, it is essential to design, optimize, and control complex backhaul architecture in a structured and centralized way together with the integration of an external node, i.e. the SN.

3.4   Towards a Centralized Approach for Substitution Networks (SNs)

This necessitates for an approach which is not inherently centralized to handle the additional burden of carrying out the data processing but also to co-operate with other NEs, since NEs are not necessarily based on a standardized implementation. A first critical issue is about integrating the SN into a base network automatically once it reaches the "spot". To do this, the SN has to discover the existing topology, configure resources, and integrate new resources at data, control and management levels, and release resources where they are not utilized anymore. There is no debate this can be best implemented in a distributed way within the SN and the base network. However, considering an environment such as the wireless mobile backhaul network, several independent SON functionalities coexist in the network and act on different algorithms. This may be conflicting sometimes. Indeed, these autonomic functionalities should ideally act in a coordinated manner to fulfill a common objective defined by the operator policy. Besides, in a distributed environment, the upper bound for communicating between any two nodes scales linearly with the longest loop free path. This could be sometimes higher than the time taken by a NE to reach a centralized controller. Furthermore, the fact that a real system might have only partial or error-prone knowledge of the existing neighbors and might not be able to detect all existing collisions adds whole new aspects to the problem. A specific centralized solution can locate a specific SON functionality in the NEs and can be further differentiated into the distributed case, where the SON functionality of multiple NEs need to collaborate and into the localized case, where the problem can be solved by a single NE without the need to communicate or coordinate. A centralized solution could address these needs by enabling a tight integration between an MNO's planning systems while maintaining the flexibility for MNO to adapt planning and visualizing diagnostics in a heterogeneous, multi-provider and multi-technology environment. This simplifies support of multi-vendor SON in a single geographic area. Since SNs within the scope of microwave backhaul are highly difficult to manage due to heterogeneity of networks, spontaneous set-up and negotiate the required QoS among the interconnected devices, we envision the centralized-based solution is cost-effective, suitable for different application scenarios, and simplifies O&M relatively.

4   Concept Visualization

4.1   The Application of the Approach to the Problem: OpenFlow

OpenFlow is a framework that is an implementation of SDN technology where policies are imposed by logically-centralized software, rather than by switch hardware or firmware. Thus, the OpenFlow protocol allows different vendor switches to be programmed without exposing the internal functionalities of the switches. A very brief description of the OpenFlow network functioning is elaborated below for the ease of understanding of our proposed solution. However, for further details, it is strongly recommended to refer to [18]-[20].

Understanding Flow Table: Since the control plane and the data plane are separated, the data path of an OpenFlow switch presents a clean flow table. Each flow table entry contains a set of packet fields to match (Fig. 4), and an *action* (such as send-out-port, modify-field, encapsulate and forward to the controller or drop). These *actions* associated with each flow table entry tell the OpenFlow switch how to process the flow. Ingress flows installed in an OpenFlow switch are stored in flow tables.

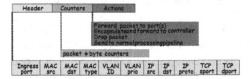

Fig. 4. Figure illustrating OpenFlow Fields that are used to match against flow table entries to match different actions to be performed by the switch upon receiving a packet. This header represents OpenFlow version 1.0.0.

Matching Flow Entries: When an OpenFlow switch receives a packet for the first time, for which it has no matching flow entries, it sends this packet to the controller. The controller then makes a decision on how to handle this packet. It can drop the packet, or it can add a flow entry directing the switch on how to forward similar packets in the future. OpenFlow switches use these flow entries that they have received from their controller to make forwarding decisions. In total the OpenFlow 1.0.0 specification includes 12 fields that can be matched upon as in the Fig. 4. A "microflow" rule (a microflow is equivalent to a specific end-to-end connection) matches on all fields of an incoming packet, whereas a "wildcard" rule can have "don't care" bits in some fields, meaning that a packet need not necessarily have to match all of the 12 fields in the OpenFlow table entry. Rules can be installed with a timeout that triggers the switch to delete the rule after a fixed time interval (a hard timeout) or a specified period of inactivity (a soft timeout). In addition, the switch counts the number of bytes and packets matching each rule, and the controller can poll these counter values.

Specifying Flows: A flow can be created for a specific stream of traffic by matching the fields in the flow table entry to that ingress flow. This means that the input port, source and destination MAC address, IP address, TCP/UDP port, etc. must all match with that flow. These flows are stored in a 'hash' table because the 12-tuple is hashed and then stored as an index in a table for fast lookups. If one or more of the fields are wild-carded, i.e. can match with any value, the flow is usually stored in a 'linear' table, to be looked at after the 'hash' table in a linear fashion. The hashes of the exact flows are typically stored in Static RAM (S RAM) on the switch. This memory allows for an indexed table of the hashes and a fast lookup procedure by the switch. This is done by matching against certain header fields while wildcarding others. Flows that do not match one of these "flow spec" categories are treated as best-effort.

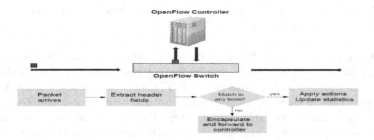

Fig. 5. Flow diagram of Open Flow packets

Thus, by specifying a standard interface (the OpenFlow Protocol) through which entries in the flow table can be defined externally, the OpenFlow Switch avoids the need to program the switch. While each vendor's flow-table is different, it will be interesting to identify a common set of functions that run in multiple switches and routers. OpenFlow exploits this common set of functions and thus provides an open protocol to program the flow table in different switches and routers. For high-performance and low-cost, the data-path must have a carefully prescribed degree of flexibility. This means forgoing the ability to specify arbitrary handling of each packet and seeking a more limited, but still useful, range of actions. Because OpenFlow connections are explicit, Network-as-a-Service is more secure and potentially provide improved QoS. This is because policies that set routes for packets can use application and even user priority to determine how traffic is allocated to resources, thus setting performance levels. Clearly, this property supports our approach.

4.2   Substitution Networks (SNs) Based on Software Defined Networking (SDN)

Taking Control of the Control-plane Traffic: As detailed previously, the split architecture in SDN technology assumes a logically centralized controller, which is physically separated from data plane forwarding switches. Thus, when the control plane is decoupled from the data plane, the traditional mechanisms that were commonly adopted to integrate a new node into an exiting network topology also changes. This means, since the control plane and the data plane of the OpenFlow are logically separated, any disruption in the control plane that incurs due to deployment of a temporary SN should not necessarily affect the existing communication sessions in the data plane. This is predominantly the desired effect when we introduce SN into a base network at times of network overload. With this we propose a solution based on the centralized SDN approach. Without emphasizing a separate centralized controller to integrate SON functionalities only for the SNs ignoring the base-network, our proposal include controlling the base network together with the SN in a joint fashion. This is done judiciously by incorporating OpenFlow protocol within the backhaul of the wireless networks. Fig. 5 illustrates the proposed network design.

Support for Flow-level Management for Backhaul Bandwidth: Flow-based switches, such as those enabled by the Open-Flow protocol, support fine-grained, flow-level control of Ethernet switching [20]. Such control is desirable because it enables (1) correct enforcement of flexible policies without having the need to craft switch-by-switch configurations, (2) visibility over all flows, allowing for near optimal management of network traffic, and (3) simple and future-proof switch design. This facilitates the deployment and the re-deployment of SNs, which is a critical part of the adaptation of the SNs to wireless mobile backhaul networks, because the protocols employed depend on the traffic patterns in the networks. A problem to tackle here is to provide an updated view of the traffic inside both the base and the substitution networks and to deliver this information to each NE (base or SN). OpenFlow will work best where traffic is made up of a modest number of predictable flows. That way, once the switches/routers learn the traffic rules from the controller, little additional interaction with the controller is needed. In the context of the control of base-to-substitution or substitution-to-base traffic within a wireless mobile backhaul, OpenFlow is particularly adapted to tackle this situation. This would apply to SN resources that would become under the control of the base network controller. With this approach the MNO does not need to have any prior reservation of network resources of the base network at any point in time and the integration of SN resources takes place dynamically. Our architecture does not include the flow concept inside the SN. In our architecture, the flow concept ends at the Bridge Router level, before entering into the SN. This is due to the computation time and memory constraints of the SN. Furthermore, even within SNs in a distributed case, OpenFlow could be expected to manage traffic within each distributed NE. In addition, OpenFlow can provide optimal admission control and flow-routing in support of QoS policies globally, in cases where a hop-by-hop QoS mechanism cannot always provide global optimality [21]. However, this does not mean that all flow setups should be mediated by a central controller. For instance, the controller can define flow categories that demand per-flow vetting which are required to guarantee particular QoS levels (e.g., "all flows to or from the specific e-Node B MAC or IP address"). Thus, only the flows that require guarantees actually need to be approved individually at setup time. Other flows can be categorically treated as best-effort traffic.

Energy-aware Routing: With SNs for emerging countries, it is worth pointing out that putting network components to sleep could save significant amounts of energy, which could result in significant cost savings for MNOs. This is because these networks typically have much aggregation and core switches that collect traffic from hundreds or thousands of servers. It is unlikely that ports can be transitioned from sleep state to wake state quickly enough to save significant amounts of energy on these switches [22]. It may be possible to perform energy-aware routing without full flow visibility. Here, the "microflows" should be aggregated along a set of least-energy paths using wildcard rules, while the "macroflows" should be detected and re-routed as necessary, to keep the congestion on powered-on links below some safety threshold. However, the performance evaluation on this proposal, is beyond the scope of this article.

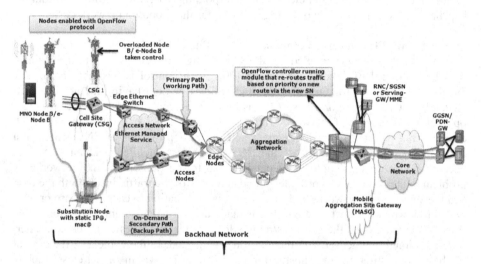

Fig. 6. Architectural design illustrating Substitution Networks based on SDN

In summary, we believe that the benefits of the centralized control in OpenFlow can be maintained by individually approving some flows, but categorically approving others. We conclude that some use of a centralized controller is necessary to build a power-proportional, energy and memory efficient, high-performance SNs.

5   Experimental Evaluations

In this section, we put forward our experimental results that were carried out on OpenFlow software-based implementation. Here, we have evaluated our approach that guarantees the required performance in terms of bandwidth management to satisfy QoS to every user within a network, irrespective of the "chaotic" situation, typically an overloaded network situation.

5.1   Design and Implementation

Our method outlines a bandwidth management framework based on OpenFlow. Briefly, when the centralized controller detects the OpenFlow enabled SN, it creates a new path via the SN and re-routes the traffic, thus guaranteeing the QoS to end-users. Thus, OpenFlow enabled SN uses the flow entries they have received from the controller to make forwarding decisions.

Topology Discovery and Traffic Re-route: For a SN to be integrated into an overloaded base network, the SN should be first detected by the controller. According to OpenFlow specification v1.0.0 [18], an OpenFlow switch must be able to establish the communication at a user-configurable (but otherwise fixed) IP address, using a user-specified port with a controller. Henceforth, we set the controller's IP address and port when starting the OpenFlow enabled SN. Then the controller and the SN will establish a TCP or TLS connection and *OFPT_HELLO* messages will be sent to each side of the connection. Now the controller knows that there is a new OpenFlow enabled node (SN) integrated into the network. Then the controller will let the SN itself to send out LLDP packets at a regular intervals to the controller, with each LLDP stamped with the sender's (here SN) datapath ID and outgoing port. If one outgoing port is linked to another switch, the LLDP packet will be sent to the controller by that switch and controller now knows the topology. The advantage of this sort of topology discovery scheme is that discovery packets sent by the SN can be appropriately prioritized so they get-through even on heavily loaded links.

Learning Switch: In order to setup paths, we use a simple learning switch application. This application associates MAC addresses to ports and installs respective flow entries on all OpenFlow-enabled nodes. The OpenFlow-enabled nodes will examine each packet and learn the source-port mapping. Thereafter, the source, i.e., MAC address, will be associated with the port. If the destination of the packet is already associated with some port, the packet will be sent to the given port, else it will be flooded on all ports of the switch. That is, once the SN is detected by controller, it results in the following:

a) The controller flushes all the exiting flow entries in all OpenFlow switches and now wildcards each flow entry based on source IP address and Ethernet address.

b) Accordingly, certain flows (based on source IP/MAC address) are now forwarded to the SN.

c) From this point, all of the data traffic from the base network starts to flow through the SN reducing the traffic load. However, at this point in time, the OpenFlow enabled SN is not aware of what to do with this first stream of packets that has just arrived from the base network. Hence it encapsulates and forwards the packet to the controller through a *packet_in* message (The message that a switch sends to the controller to inform it about an unknown flow is called a *packet_in* event message).

d) The controller now makes a decision on how to handle this traffic stream and forwards it to the SN by the *packet_out* message.

e) Accordingly, in this case specific to our situation, we choose to re-route the low-priority traffic through SN that can tolerate delay, while allowing the high priority traffic to continue to flow through the base network without any disruption. This is done by wildcarding the source IP address field of each low-priority user group traffic flow to be forwarded to the SN.

f) From then onwards, all the high priority traffic (delay-sensitive traffic, real-time traffic, premium customers, corporate customers) continues to flow through the base network, taking maximum advantage of the "now" available bandwidth and the low priority traffic (best effort traffic) is re-routed through the SN.

It is worth mentioning that that the bandwidth consumed for path setup is negligible. Thus, our evaluation results would still apply, even if we install all paths proactively. As mentioned earlier, in our approach mobility is not taken as a constraint, rather, it is assumed that the SN is brought in-place/ retained very close to the spots where there is usually traffic spikes (based on previous statistics). What we accomplish here distinctly due to the adaptation of OpenFlow is that, in general scenario, it is the network administrators who manually configure the SN when it is brought in-place as well as the traffic of the base network that has to re-routed every time when the SN integrated. But, with OpenFlow, the controller automatically takes care of re-routing the specific traffic flows by matching the fields of that flows, thereby retaining the required performance of the whole network. To maximize flexibility, the slice specifications can be applied to individual flows, aggregate traffic of certain flows, or even combination of them based on customer's requirements. The re-routing algorithm, implemented in the controller is the most important mechanism when considering the congestion control issue within our scenario. It decides (by prior configurations) which flows may be served through the base network and which should be re-routed through the SN. The pseudo-code below describes the view of the network resources from a base node perspective after a SN is integrated.

Algorithm to guarantee bandwidth management from an OpenFlow enabled base node perspective

```
 1 : for each flow entry ∉ Flow Table do
 2 : Send packet_out openflow message
 3 : If  packet_out message then
 4 :             //no Optimization needed
 5 :             Start Time Out to Increase
 6 :     else if  Reject  then
 7 :         if  maximum available bandwidth not reached then
 8 :             Change Bandwidth parameters
                     (increase data rate)
 9 :             go to 1:
10 :         end if
11 :     end if
13 : if Time Out to Increase  then
14 :     if  maximum available Bandwidth reached  then
15 :         Change Bandwidth parameters
                 (deccrease data rate)
16 :             go to 1:
17 :     end if
18 : end if
```

Most previous research works propose numerous queuing algorithms to guarantee QoS [23]-[25] by retaining certain flows and dropping the rest. These algorithms engage differently; however, the outcome of their functioning is almost identical. These algorithms implicitly give priority to the packets of flows whose peak rate is less than the current fair rate. The flows with rates less than the current fair rate are assigned high priority. This way, streaming flows with peak rates less than the current fair rate are subjects to the buffer-less multiplexing and, therefore, perceive low delays and losses [25]. However, our solution takes into account to route every flow within the network. Thus, it allows for fair access to the resources without any intervention form the user or the network administrator. To effectively manage the performance of a network, the controller needs to know about the current loads on most network elements. Maximizing some performance objectives may also require timely statistics on some flows in the network. (This assumes that we want to exploit statistical multiplexing gain, rather than strictly controlling flow admission to prevent oversubscription.) However, load-balancing does not require the controller to be aware of the initial setup of every flow.

5.2   Evaluation

Setup: In our experiments, we emulated an OpenFlow network using Mininet [30] hosted on a physical machine to generate the network topology, just as in Fig. 5. The controller that we utilized for our experiments is the standard NOX controller (destiny branch) [10].

Results: As a first step, we measure the latency by the controller to add a new flow entry directing the SN on how to forward the ingress flows. That is, when the SN establishes a connection with a controller, it sends to the controller, the first stream of packets which is receives and then the controller sends our *packet_out* messages. We measure this time to see how long it takes for the flows to be installed so that there is eventual forwarding without any disruption. To do so, we utilized a host machine with two Ethernet interfaces running OpenFlow v1.0.0, one connected to a switch port and one to the management port. The interface connected to the switch port starts to send unknown flows and listens on the control channel port for incoming *packet_in* messages. Based on the RFC2544, experiments with different frame sizes were conducted on latency test. The experiments were carried out five times for each packet size ranging from 60 bytes to 1024 bytes. The values are indicated in Table 1 and the variance of the latency is depicted in Fig.6.

Table 1. Average Latency values for 5 trails for measuring the time taken to install flow entries

Time (seconds)	15	30	45	60	75
Packet size (bytes)	64	128	256	512	1024
Latency (μs) Trail 1	4	6	8	8	15
Latency (μs) Trail 2	3	7	9	8	14
Latency (μs) Trail 3	4	5	8	11	13
Latency (μs) Trail 4	5	5	8	10	15
Latency (μs) Trail 5	4	7	10	9	13

From Fig. 6, it is very convincing to observe that latency time that is taken by an OpenFlow controller to install the first flow entries. As we described before, once the first flow entries are in-place in the flow table of an OpenFlow-enabled node, the node can forward similar packets in the future. Ignoring the time that is taken to move the SN to the spot (or if the SN has been already placed close to the spot because of the previous statistics), the time that is taken to configure flow entries in the flow table is totally negligible, which is only of the order of few microseconds. However, here we like to remark that the placement (location) of the controller has some significant role to play with this latency time that is measured. In [31], authors have measured the reaction-time requirements for the controller placement problem, by placing the controller in different locations in the country and presented the time to reach a controller.

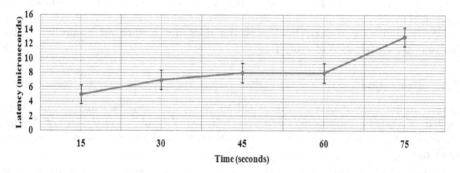

Fig. 7. Average latency to install flows on an OpenFlow switch

Next, through our experiments we aim to study average packet loss though a link, with and without the SN. To do this, we carried out experiments based on the steps described in section 5.1. Following this, we specified link bandwidth capacity on each link between the nodes that was created using the Mininet emulator. Each connected end-hosts runs UDP traffic. We overloaded the link more than our specified link capacity with and without the SN. Fig. 7 shows the packet loss on the link before and after the SN was introduced. It is interesting to see the influence of the new node on the packet loss parameter values. As expected, there is significant packet loss without the SN, which is avoided when the SN is introduced.

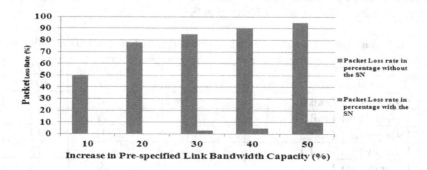

Fig. 8. Packet Loss Rate on a link before and after introducing SN

6   Discussions and Conclusion

Our approach here that embraces SDN and SN is completely a very new area of research. Instead of utilizing SNs that were classically considered to recover from failure, we propose to use them to increase efficiency with respect to desired performance metrics. This enables networks to evolve, e.g. to improve over time and to converge to a stable state that can be respected as a (local) optimum of the performance objective(s). It is unrealistic to simply reuse the homogeneous performance-related system design evaluation assumptions to illustrate a comparative evaluation or a quantification of the savings in terms of resource utilization or energy efficiency with any existing approach. Nevertheless, our past experience with OpenFlow [29] gives a good hold on this technology, atleast to some extent. Apart from the technical performance improvement, our approach depends very much on the economics, and cost models. Obviously it is hard to derive a final quantitative metric to capture all these aspects, in particular as the costs are confidential and highly dependent on the deployment scenario, region, strategy and work flows. Nevertheless some factors impacting the benefits can be quantified better, in particular the performance improvement (with respect to availability and Mean Time Between Failures (MTBF) and Mean Time To Repair) for a large base of end-users. We have discussed the performances as approximations to the real performance functions due to the fact that not all functions in a centralized scenario with possibly acting nodes can be optimized. We demonstrated the feasibility of the approach for wireless backhaul networks, where a topology is desired in which communication/routing cost is minimal.

Acknowledgement. This work was partially supported by the ANR-RESCUE project, grant ANR-10-VERS-003 of the French Agence Nationale de la Recherche.

References

1. Chen, A.C.: The evolution of wireless mobile data communication technologies and their market opportunities. In: 28th IEEE Annual Conference of the Industrial Electronics Society, vol. 4, pp. 3428–3433 (2002)
2. Razafindralambo, et al.: Promoting Quality of Service in Substitution Networks with Controlled Mobility. In: 10th International Conference on Ad Hoc Networks and Wireless (2011)
3. Miranda, K., Natalizio, E., Razafindralambo, T.: On the Impact of Router's Mobility on Substitution Networks. In: Twelfth ACM International Symposium on Mobile Ad Hoc Networking and Computing, Paris, France (2011)
4. Tong, S., Yang, O.W.W.: Bandwidth Management for Supporting Differentiated Service Aware Traffic Engineering. IEEE Transactions on Parallel and Distributed Systems 18, 1320–1331 (2007)
5. Shankaraiah, Venkataram, P.: Bandwidth management in a hybrid wireless network: For superstore applications. In: ICCS, pp. 517–521 (2010)
6. Georgiadis, L., Guerin, R., Peris, V., Sivarajan, K.N.: Efficient Network QoS Provisioning Based on Per Node Traffic Shaping. IEEE/ACM Transactions on Networking 4, 482–501 (1996)

7. Li, F.Y., Stol, N.: QoS Provisioning Using Traffic Shaping and Policing in 3rd-generation Wireless Networks. In: IEEE Wireless Communications and Networking Conference, WCNC 2002, vol. 1, pp. 139–143 (2002)

8. Chang, T., Pendarakis, D., Liu, Z.: Cost-Effective Configuration of Content Resiliency Services Under Correlated Failures. In: DSN 2006, pp. 536–548 (2006)

9. Venmani, D.P., Gourhant, Y., Zeghlache, D.: 3RIS for 4G: A New Approach for Increasing Availability and Reducing Costs for LTE Networks. In: ICACT, pp. 1025–1030 (2012)

10. Gude, N., Koponen, T., Pettit, J., Pfaf, B., Casado, M., McKeown, K., Shenker, S.: NOX: Towards an Operating System for Networks. In: SIGCOMM CCR (2008)

11. Tavakoli, A., Casado, M., Koponen, T., Shenker, S.: Applying NOX to the Datacenter. In: HotNets (2009)

12. Greenberg, A., et al.: A Clean Slate 4D Approach to Network Control and Management. SIGCOMM CCR 35, 41–54 (2005)

13. Amirijoo, M., Litjens, R., Spaey, K., Döttling, M., Jansen, T., Scully, N., Türke, U.: Use Cases, Requirements and Assessment Criteria for Future Self-Organising Radio Access Networks. In: Hummel, K.A., Sterbenz, J.P.G. (eds.) IWSOS 2008. LNCS, vol. 5343, pp. 275–280. Springer, Heidelberg (2008)

14. Ian, F.A., Ismail, H.K.: Wireless Sensor and Actor Networks: Research Challenges. Elsevier Journal of Ad hoc networks (2004)

15. Tommaso, M., Dario, P., Vehbi, C.G., Ian, F.A.: A Distributed Coordination Framework for Wireless Sensor and Actor Networks. In: 6th ACM International Symposium on Mobile Ad Hoc Networking and Computing, pp. 99–110 (2005)

16. Car-On-Wheels, http://en.wikipedia.org/wiki/Cell_on_wheels

17. Daniel Philip, V., Gourhant, Y., Zeghlache, D.: Preliminary Analysis of 4G-LTE Mobile Network Sharing for Improving Resiliency and Operator Differentiation. In: Yonazi, J.J., Sedoyeka, E., Ariwa, E., El-Qawasmeh, E. (eds.) ICeND 2011. Communications in Computer and Information Science, vol. 171, pp. 73–93. Springer, Heidelberg (2011)

18. OpenFlow Switch Specification v1.0. Brandon Heller (brandonh@stanford.edu), http://www.OpenFlowswitch.org/documents/OpenFlow-spec-v1.0.pdf

19. McKeown, N., et al.: OpenFlow Enabling Innovation in Campus Networks. ACM SIGCOMM Computer Communication Review 38(2), 69–74 (2008)

20. OpenFlow Switch Website, http://www.OpenFlowswitch.org

21. Kim, W., et al.: Automated and Scalable QoS Control for Network Convergence. In: INM/WREN (2010)

22. Heller, B., Seetharaman, S., Mahadevan, P., Yiakoumis, Y., Sharma, P., Banerjee, S., McKeown, N.: ElasticTree: Saving Energy in Data Center Networks. In: NSDI (2010)

23. Bonald, T., Oueslati, S., Roberts, J.: IP traffic and QoS control: Towards a Flow-Aware Architecture. In: World Telecom Conference, Paris (2002)

24. Roberts, J.: Internet Traffic, QoS and Pricing. IEEE Communication Letters 92(9) (September 2004)

25. Jajszczyk, A., Wojcik, R.: Emergency Calls in Flow-Aware Networks. IEEE Communications Letters 11, 753–755 (2007)

26. Cai, Z., Cox, A.L., Ng, T.S.E.: Maestro: A System for Scalable OpenFlow Control. Technical Report TR10-08, Rice University (2010)

27. Koponen, T., et al.: Onix: A Distributed Control Platform for Large-scale Production Networks. In: OSDI (2010)

28. Tam, A.S.-W., Xi, K., Chao, H.J.: Use of Devolved Controllers in Data Center Networks. In: INFOCOM Workshop on Cloud Computing (2011)

29. Venmani, D.P., Yvon, G., Djamal, Z.: OpenFlow as an Architecture for e-Node B Virtualization. In: Popescu-Zeletin, R., Jonas, K., Rai, I.A., Glitho, R., Villafiorita, A. (eds.) AFRICOMM 2011. LNICST, vol. 92, pp. 49–63. Springer, Heidelberg (2012)

30. Lantz, B., Heller, B., McKeown, N.: A Network in a Laptop: Rapid Prototyping for Software-Defined Networks. In: ACM SIGCOMM HotNets Workshop (2010)

31. Heller, B.: Sherwood. R., McKeown, N.: The Controller Placement Problem. In: ACM SigComm Workshop HotSDN (2012)

A Modular Architecture for Reconfigurable Heterogeneous Networks with Embedded Devices

José Cecílio, João Costa, Pedro Martins, and Pedro Furtado

University of Coimbra,
Coimbra, Portugal
{jcecilio,jpcosta,pmom,pnf}@dei.uc.pt

Abstract. Wireless SAN (WSAN) may include wired and/or wireless devices, PCs and control stations arranged in a heterogeneous distributed system. Instead of assuming that embedded device nodes (e.g. MicaZ or TelosB motes), gateways (e.g. PC running Linux) and control stations are disparate entities with their own programming and processing model, it should be viewed as a single heterogeneous distributed system, offering more uniformity, simplicity and flexibility. Enabling adaptivity in the higher layers of the network architecture such as the middleware and application layers, beside its consideration in the lower layers, becomes of high importance. In this paper we propose an approach to hide heterogeneity and offer a single common configuration and processing component for all nodes of that heterogeneous system. In particular, this proposal aims at providing an abstraction to facilitate development of adaptive Wireless Sensor and Actuator Network (WSAN) applications. The main contribution of this paper is how to design a middleware architecture with a single uniform component to work with such heterogeneous underlying parts as a WSAN. This advances the current state-of-the-art in middleware for WSANs, by providing a single component that abstracts the underlying differences in both devices such as PCs and motes and in communications such as TCP and proprietary stacks to create a global processor.

Keywords: Embedded Devices, SAN, Heterogeneous Network, Data Processing, (Re)Configuration.

1 Introduction

Motes are a small embedded device with computation, radio and extendible sensing and actuation capabilities and with an operating system that enables them to be programmed and to work in a network of devices. Motes have gained popularity due to the convenience of programming and deploying them quickly and easily in different contexts and for varied objectives.

In many industrial contexts the software infrastructure for enterprise networks needs data coming from nodes that can be PCs or pervasive devices, such as WSNs, and some contexts also need closed loop control over heterogeneous systems. The inclusion of pervasive devices (the mote) in industrial control and monitor applications provides flexibility and cost savings when compared to entirely cabled

J. Zheng et al. (Eds.): Adhocnets 2012, LNICST 111, pp. 260–274, 2013.

deployments. In a real industrial setup there will typically coexist wired sensors, wireless sensor and actuator networks (WSAN) and wired backbone nodes, forming a heterogeneous programmable distributed system.

Current solutions for deploying the heterogeneous systems that include WSAN nodes and the rest of the world involve programming every detail of processing and communication by hand, both within the WSAN and outside of it, or using middleware-based solutions that are limited to a single WSAN operating system and require the PCs to be coded separately and manually, in a different manner.

An important research issue in that context is how to provide interoperability between different nodes and provide a single configuration and data processing model in that kind of distributed system that handles different realizations, where the same operations can run without any custom programming over different SAN hardware or on different components of the system (sensors, sink nodes or controlling PCs), controlling different parts of the system. In this context we propose MidSN, a model to enable such vision.

Consider as an example that it is desired to configure a factory network for closed loop control. The factory network has multiple servers and multiple WSANs. With MidSN, as soon as the nodes MidSN components are installed in every computation-capable node, it is possible to issue configuration commands to program various parts of the closed loop (acquisition nodes, computing nodes and actuation conditions, actuation nodes) with exactly the same interface and syntax regardless of which nodes and node types will do which part. In spite of a completely heterogeneous WSN-wired-other WSN underlying environment, MidSN enables the view that nodes are just nodes with exactly the same abstraction and functionalities. Although this is a simple and very important vision, current state-of-the-art WSN middleware failed to realize it.

From the perspective of users, the approach offers a configuration API and a corresponding web services interface. Powerful (e.g. PCs) and embedded nodes (e.g. motes) are defined as nodes that can be configured, since they hold communication and data processing modules. There is always at least one powerful node in a system, a server PC node that contains the main configuration server.

The rest of the paper is organized as follows: section 2 discusses related work; section 3 describes the MidSN architecture's. Section 4 deals with node referencing, remote configuration and heterogeneity. Section 5 shows some results obtained from the experimental testbed and section 6 concludes the paper.

2   Related Work

The approach proposed in this paper provides configuration/reconfiguration capabilities for embedded devices such as WSN motes. With it, distributed sensor and actuator networks can be managed without any custom programming, using only simple configuration commands. Related work includes strategies to configure and program sensor network devices and to connect those to external applications / internet.

There are several aspects that should be kept in mind when (re)configuration mechanisms are studied. The first one involves the scatter of resources (memory aspects and processing power need to be into account). Nodes in a WSN don't have copious amounts of RAM such as a PC. The second one involves heterogeneity, or the ability of the network to have multiple node hardware.

Over-the-Air programming and dynamic software updating over WSNs was surveyed in [1, 2]. Such mechanisms allow reconfiguring the nodes without physically removing them from the deployment site, programming them and putting them back into the site. These approaches typically use a middleware to reprogram the network. Most consist of mobile agents which run over virtual machines. They receive agents over-the-air, and can put them to run over the middleware. Generically, over-the-air programming approaches offer code flexibility, but they have relevant differences when compared to our proposal:

Concerning performance and simplicity - in spite of all optimizations, there is a significant time overhead associated with dynamically loading the code or code fragments, and there are usually specific dynamic upload protocol requirements, while our approach is very fast. For instance, in our testbed it is able to (re)configure one or many nodes by sending simple commands through three 10 ms downstream slots (one per tree level) that were made available in the pre-planned schedule based tdma; the fact that our approach fits nicely into any runtime environment and requires no complex specific extra code updating protocols and related structures is a positive point for simplicity.

Concerning programming – typically the dynamic upload approaches are targeted a configuring a single WSN (e.g. TinyOS), while our approach configures heterogeneous mixed WSN-non-WSN environments; many dynamic uploading approaches also concentrate only on the technical uploading optimization issues, but the user needs to develop the code for the nodes. Therefore, this requires expertise in the programming languages of the platforms involved, plus developing the code by hand for the portion outside of the WSN and the interconnections. It is also a lengthy and buggy process (since the programmer will be coding multiple nodes in a distributed system that needs to interact correctly). In comparison, our approach only requires users to specify operation configuration commands with no further programming, and the API is available for external applications to use directly.

Approaches such as IrisNet[3] or GSN[4] are configuration-based solutions to connect sensor input to the internet, however those do not allow configuring functionality within sensor network WSNs, since they are only focused on wrapping data coming from sensor sources for sharing and processing over the internet. As an illustrative example, suppose we have a WSN organized as a tree of nodes, and that tree of nodes is connected to the internet through a sink node and a PC gateway. Approaches such as GSN will only allow you to configure a wrapper for the gateway to publish the data coming from the whole WSN into the internet, you would not be able to configure processing within the individual nodes of the WSN.

Finally, there are some middleware works that address reconfiguration of a WSN using software, but they are for a specific operating system, typically built on top of TinyOS, and are restricted to configuring processing within the WSN only.

TinyDB [5] is a query processing middleware system based on TinyOS. TinyDB approach treats the sensor network as a virtual database. Each sensor node contains a tiny database and this database is queried by using SQL like query language called

Tiny SQL. It has two different types of messages for query processing: Query Messages and Query Result Messages. It also has Command Messages for sending commands to sensor nodes. While TinyDB provides nice abstraction support and has a good aggregation model, it does not handle heterogeneous underlying contexts.

Agilla [6] is the "first mobile agent middleware for WSNs that is implemented entirely in TinyOS". It has a stack-based architecture which reduces code size. Up to four agents are supported on a single sensor node, running multiple applications on the network simultaneously. Agilla does not have any policy monitoring agent activities. Also, its assembly-like and stack-based programming model makes programs difficult to read and maintain.

TinyLime [7] is implemented based on TinyOS exploiting Crossbow's Mote platform. TinyLime follows an abstraction model based on shared tuple space. This tuple space contains sensed data. It supports data aggregation to find more information from collected data. Additionally, it does not provide good support for adaptability or scalability.

None of these works handles the issue of distributed configuration with heterogeneity that we are solving in this paper. Some of these approaches provide a programming infrastructure and assume that functionality and communication code are application-level issues would be hand-programmed for each node. Other approaches such as TinyDB are unable to run in heterogeneous sensor networks and do not provide homogeneous configuration capabilities, where every computation-capable node including server nodes should be viewed as a similar node for configuration and data processing.

3   MIDSN System

In this section we discuss the architecture of the middleware that enables the global processor, with uniform configuration and processing over heterogeneous underlying WSAN context. The heterogeneity concerns nodes, communication and operating systems.

The nodes can be heterogeneous, consisting of different classes of devices. They include resource-constrained sensor nodes, such as TelosB motes, and more powerful nodes, such as PCs or servers. In this model, any PCs are not just data sinks but fully participate in the global processor and offer exactly the same interface and modules of any node in the system.

3.1   MidSN Architecture

Instead of custom coding every node every time (e.g. when tuning a parameter) in the system, MidSN is developed once for each operating-system and included in any node in any practical deployment. A mote may be fitted with TinyOS plus the node engine for TinyOS, with Contiki plus the node operations for Contiki, or with Linux with the node engine for Linux.

Figure 1 shows the node engine architecture that ensures a similar configuration and processing interface for any node.

The Node Configuration architecture runs at application level and has a set of modules that provide: communication capabilities, whereby the node will be able to exchange messages with any other node in the system; data processor capabilities, whereby the node will be able to apply the configurations to determine alarms and actuations and to compute simple measures such as averages or maximum values for use in alarm or actuation functionalities or to send to other nodes; acquisition capabilities, whereby sensor nodes will be able to periodically acquire sensing values or issue actuation values (e.g. WSN motes, PC servers connected to wired analog sensor cables through DACs and ADCs); configuration management, whereby nodes will be able to configure themselves based on commands provided by other nodes or central server.

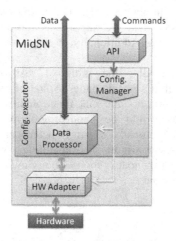

Fig. 1. MidSN Architecture

Node interactions are based on a small set of primitives: commands are used to configure nodes, and user configuration requests are routed to the appropriate node(s); messages (which specify a type) are used to send alarms, actuation values and notifications to nodes; streams are used to collect sensed data, compute and filter that data to exchange resulting data between nodes. The most important parts are defined next in more detail:

1)   Communication (API)
This module processes configuration commands, modifying processing, acquisition and communication according to issued configuration commands. The API is used by a web interface and any client applications to issue configuration commands.

The module has an important function in what concerns abstraction of proprietary network layer protocols. This module implements and abstracts network protocols needed to be able to communicate with all nodes in the network.

2)   Acquisition (HW Adapter)
This module must be present in nodes doing actual sensing and actuating. This module performs all sensor actions required to gather data from sensors.

Commands are used to configure the module that supports several configurations, such as activate or deactivate sensors and change sampling frequency. The data readings collected by sensors are stored in memory. The memory available for each data reading type is limited by a window size parameter specified during stream creation. The module uses a circular window which means that old readings, after the remaining window size has been filled, are overwritten by new readings.

3)   Config. Executor

The Config. Executor (CE), depicted in Figure 1, is a core component that provide configuration capabilities. It is composed by two sub-components: config. manager and data processor. The Config. Manager (CM) component allows dealing with events (e.g. time based events, network events, …) which are a core component of the nodes. CM manages those events, and is responsible for scheduling next events concerning sensor acquisition and computation. The CM component periodically checks all configurations and executes the corresponding action if conditions were matched.

When an event arrives at a node, CM analyzes its type (network event or timer event) through the Event Manager (EM), and executes the associated action. For instance, if a command arrives at a node (network event), the EM identifies it as a command and calls the parser to analyze the command type. The command types can be divided in two categories: node operation and stream types.

The node operation type is related with node's operation and supports commands such as start, stop, reboot and ping, while command stream type is related with data messages. If the command corresponds to a stream configuration, the Stream Manager (SM) is called to update an existing configuration or to create a new configuration. Table 1 shows the currently supported command stream types. If the event corresponds to a timer event, EM calls the Stream Executor (SE). The SE checks which event occurs (which configuration should be performed) and executes the configuration. This configuration can be meant to compute a message and send it to another node (specified in the stream creation command), or it can be meant to gather new samples from sensors.

Table 1. Command stream types

Command	Function
CTRL_ONE_TIME_QUERY	Used for a one-shot request to a node (e.g. read sensors) and send the sampled values back to the sink.
CTRL_NEW_STREAM	Creates a stream. Specify message parameters and format to send by mote to sink.
CTRL_RESTART_STREAM	Reset the counter associated to stream.
CTRL_SET_STREAM_SRATE	Changes the sending rate of stream.
CTRL_DROP_STREAM	Removes a stream from mote.
CTRL_SET_WINDOW_SIZE	When statistic information is required by users, this command allows defining how many samples are used to compose the statistical information.

The second component is a Data Processor (DP). The Data Processor (DP) module is responsible for managing all incoming data from sensors or other nodes.

It implements a simplified SQL engine over streams. It includes functionalities to apply in-network processing, which supports operations such as aggregation, merging or compression used to fit different application needs. It processes select and where clauses from configuration specifications, and composes stream messages with sensor data specified in the configuration. It also determines actuations based on where conditions. Through the analysis of the select measures, expressed during configuration, the DP also uses the sensor data readings to compose the stream messages to send elsewhere.

The DP module includes three common types of in-network processing (aggregation, merging and compression), besides the basic alternative of sense-and-send, where sensors periodically gather and send sensor data values without further processing. Each of these alternatives fits into different application needs – for instance, a sense-and-react system may require frequent detailed sensor data, while another application may tolerate a larger delay or accept statistically-summarized data. Figure 2 illustrates DP using streams with an example. In that Figure nodes were configured to collect, transform and deliver data into a control station to offer it to a visualization application.

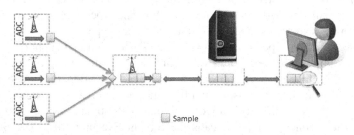

Fig. 2. Stream Processing Model

In the Figure a signal sample is collected periodically by each of three sensors, placed into a stream and routed into a relaying node. The relaying node computes some statistics (e.g. avg or max) over the three values and forwards the resulting value into the control station. The control station keeps a stream with the last values that were received, and offers it to a client application to visualize those values. It would be possible to configure differently any of the nodes in this illustrative example. For instance, sensor nodes could each compute some statistics over 10 samples and forward those to the control station directly, which would show the stream values or compute some other statistics.

4   Remote Configuration and Heterogeneity

Communication and remote access relies on a uniform distributed system. However, actual platforms with WSN and control stations are heterogeneous, with embedded devices featuring tiny OS and communication protocols.

Currently, implementation of the IP protocol stack on the sensor node is far from realistic due to the limitation of processing capability of the sensor nodes. It is not good because it is difficult to implement over different standards (802.15.4 and ZigBee) and it spends more memory, incurs high costs. Therefore, MidSN defines a gateway component to handle parts of the distributed system that do not support IP. This provides support for communication with non-IP embedded devices.

MidSN defines a scheme for saving the assignment information when assigning the IP addresses to ZigBee ID which is assigned to the sensor node in wireless sensor networks. The assigned IP address is IPv6 global unicast and gateway has to prepare it in advance (similar to DHCP server). The address assignment is managed and processed in gateway. Each IP address which is used in client requests is mapped to a corresponding ZigBee ID. The translation information can be found on the scheme, and it is used by gateway when sending the information of the client request to the sensor node.

The scheme of the IP address assignment consists of identifier (nodeID) of wireless sensor networks, the hostname, the group id (groupID) of the sensor node, and IPv6 address (ipADDR) which was allocated to sensor node.

MidSN maintains a catalog of nodes with scheme information and current node configuration data for each node, as well as a catalog of groups of nodes with group name and list of IPs. The global catalog identifies IPs that must be routed through the gateway, and the gateway is an IP node itself which implements proprietary protocols for non-IP sub-networks. The catalog is XML-based.

One important issue is how to join a new node to the network and how to assign the corresponding IP address. MidSN offers two mechanisms to join new nodes to the network. The first mechanism consists on connect a node to the gateway using serial interface. When a node is connected via serial interface, the gateway reads your ID and features, and a new entrance at the catalog is added. After that, node can be disconnected from serial interface and it will be available to be accessed by any remote client. The second mechanism consists on a remote addressing mechanism. When a node wants to connected to the network, a "wake up" message must be generated to signalize your intention to join to the network. This message will be received by the gateway and if the gateway doesn't have that ID on the catalog, a new IP assigned is done and stored at the catalog. When the process is concluded, the node receives an ACK message that signalizes that it is joined.

The MidSN communication protocol defines formats for control and data messages. There is a control message format for remote configuration of nodes which defines the configuration API method to call and parameters. A configuration application uses those control messages to send configuration commands to any nodes.

Remote configuration consists on sending configuration commands to nodes with combinations of measures, conditions and actuations. They are used to enable easy configuration or reconfiguration of system parts during the system lifetime. Conditions are used to compare threshold values with feature values. This comparison can either generate a specific message (that we call "alarm") or can originate the execution of an action. The functionality performed is specified by users or applications thought the WSI that is offered by the middleware interface with the external applications and users. To specify a configuration the user needs to create a stream message that includes multi-condition and actions. The multi-conditions are evaluated as "AND" conditions. To program an "OR" condition, a user should describe each set of configurations in separate commands.

The middleware supports configurations to select which sensors should be included into a stream. With the typical programming models used in WSN platforms, sensor nodes cannot be configured to apply mathematical functions to data readings, except by custom programming. MidSN middleware SQL model offers typical SQL functionalities to apply operations, and the result of theses computations can be requested and forwarded to any other node as if it were a sensor reading of that other node. Either conditions or action thresholds can be compared with the result of in-network processing to check if rules are matched for actuation or for alarms.

1)   Message formats

The communication adapter provides communication primitives for nodes interactions (exchange data messages or commands). These components use the lower-most components message (such as send and receive).

The MidSN implements two types of messages: downstream messages and upstream messages. These two types are identified by a flag "Msg Type" that is included into each message. Table 2 shows the currently implemented types with a small description of each one.

The message structure of MidSN is show in Figure 3. Each message includes a unique ID to identify the node source, one field to indicate the message type, a control type to introduce the information of a command (for MSG_CMD type), a sequence number, the length of payload and a set of parameters (payload).

Table 2. Supported types of messages

Types of messages	Description
MSG_WAKEUP	Used to send an intention to join to a network.
MSG_CMD	Used to send a command to the node.
MSG_ACK	Used to send a confirmation that a message was received by mote.
MSG_CMDDONE	Indicates that a command was performed.
MSG_DATA	Indicates that payload data contains the readings of sensors.

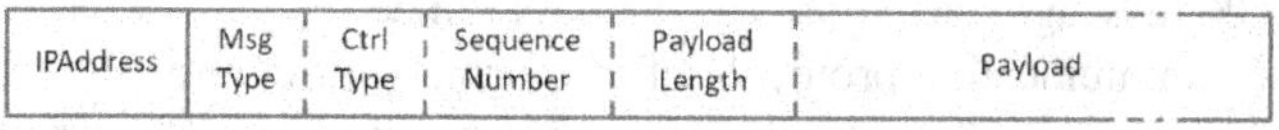

IPAddress	Msg Type	Ctrl Type	Sequence Number	Payload Length	Payload

Fig. 3. Format of downstream message

The control type field is used to specify the command that is sent in the message. Depending on the command, the payload field is filled with all parameters needed to configure a node correctly. Next we describe the payload specification for each command supported by the prototype that we developed for Ginseng according to the architecture.

2)   Payload specification

As we described before, the command types can be divided into two main categories: node operation and stream types.

The node operation type is related with node's operation and supports commands such as start, stop, reboot and ping. All of these commands have the same structure and we don't consider anything in the payload. For instance, if we want to send a start command to a node, we only need to fill the header of the message.

Concerning messages to create or change streams (Table 1), the payload must be filled with stream configuration parameters. Figure 4 shows how to fill the payload to configure an existing or a new stream.

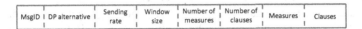

Fig. 4. Payload Specification for stream configuration

Where:

- MsgId is a unique identifier;
- DP alternative is a field that indicates the in-network processing technique. MidSN supports four techniques:

   "Sampled Sensor Data" (SD): sensors periodically collect and send sensed values to the sink without further processing.

   "Aggregated Delivery" (AD): this approach aggregates continuous data readings within the sensor node, and only sends the aggregated data to the control station. AD allows computing a summary of the sensed data, including statistic quantities that summarize and describe the data.

   "Merged Delivery" (MD): given a maximum packet size, it is beneficial to concatenate several data values to fit into a packet and send those in a single packet instead of sending one packet per reading. MD is used to keep all sensor data details and periodically, with a period that is a multiple of the sampling rate, send messages that contain several sampling readings at once to the sink node.

   "Compressed Delivery" (CD): this approach compresses the sensed data into an array to decrease the transmission rate. We used run-length encoding (RLE), which is simple and has a very low overhead. RLE is used to compress sequences containing repetitions of the same value. The idea behind it is to replace repeating values with just an instance of the value and a counter that counts the number of repetitions.

- Sending period can assume any value in ms that are converted to internal time units of motes (ticks).
- Window size specifies the number of samples that are considered in AD, MD and CD techniques.
- Number of measures and number of clauses indicates how many measures and clauses are included in message.

- Select measures specify the values that should be included in messages sent to other node(s) (PC or WSN node). This field assumes a single measure or a set of measures, depending on the number of measures indicated in the above field. Each measure is composed by two fields: sensor and metric. The sensor indicates which sensor should be included in the stream (e.g. temperature, humidity, light, ADC0, etc) and metrics indicate which in-network data processing technique must be applied over sensor readings.
- Clauses (where Clauses) represent the condition that should be checked before sending a message to the control station. This field is composed by one or more expressions connected by AND or OR where each expression has five fields (sensor, metric, operator, sensor, metric). The operator can assume one of the following values: >, <, =, >=, <=.

This format allows users to define expressions such as (avg (temperature) > 25). The fields are exactly the same used in the Select field and can take any of the values described before.

5   Experimental Evaluation

In this experimental section we use a prototype to show that we are able to configure any node in the whole SAN (WSN nodes, intermediate PCs and a control station) using the same remote interface. We also show that the configuration resulted in corresponding behavior modification.

We have deployed MidSN in an industrial environment in context of European FP7 research project - Ginseng on performance-controlled WSNs, in which applicability in actual industrial scenarios is an important aspect. In that setting, MidSN allows users to configure and change what any part of the system is expected to do easily and remotely, concerning data collection, alarms and actuation.

We have used both industrial and lab testbed to test our approach. The testbed is a totally planned network (Ginseng focuses on totally planned networks with performance guarantees) with two sub-networks where each one include PC nodes and TelosB nodes. The first (sub-network 1) includes 16 TelosB nodes organized hierarchically in a 3-2-1 tree and one sink node (PC). The second one (sub-network 2) includes 6 TelosB nodes organized hierarchically in a 1-2-1 tree. The setup also includes a control station that receives the sensor samples and alarm messages. All PC nodes (sink 1, sink 2 and control station) are connected with Ethernet cable and GigaBit network adapter.

In our setup the WSN nodes of the first tree run the Contiki operating system (sub-network 1) with a TDMA network protocol (GinMac [8]) to provide precise schedule-based communication. The TDMA schedule had an epoch time of 640 ms. The nodes of the second tree run TinyOS (sub-network 2) with an S-MAC protocol implementation [9]. All WSN nodes are time-synchronized and awake for their predefined slot time. The other nodes (PC nodes) are also time-synchronized using NTP protocol.

MidSN was implemented in three programming languages, C-Contiki to be supported by ContikiOS in the first tree, nesC to be deployed in TinyOS and java to run in PC nodes with linuxOS.

Each sink is connected to the WSN through a bridge, which allows configuring both WSN nodes and sink with any of the pre-defined operations (e.g. getting data from other nodes, firing alarms based on conditions, closed-loop control logic from input signals that come from other nodes).

The evaluation of MidSN will be done in two parts. The first part consists on evaluating the resources needed to run MidSN, since that component will have to be able to run in memory and computation resource constrained motes. The second part will evaluate performance. Furthermore, we describe how MidSN can be used in real-world applications.

Memory Footprint

The Typically, WSN devices have limited memory and computation capabilities, so the occupied memory is an important issue. MidSN can be deployed on WSN devices or more powerful nodes, such as PCs.

In this sub-section we will evaluate the amount of memory needed when MidSN is deployed in a WSN node, such as TelosB node. Table 3 shows the amount of memory needed by each component of MidSN when it is ported to ContikiOS.

The main part of MidSN is the Config. Executor (CE). This module includes Config. Manager (CM) and Data Processor (DP) components. The size of CM depends of the flexibility required by the application context, because its size depends on the number of commands that are to be sent and interpreted by the node.

The values presented are the size of the runtime code; they exclude the operating system, the network stack, and other services included by Contiki. The Contiki implementations consume just 36,4 KB of program memory (operating system is included). Our implementation is based on proto-threads [10]. Since proto-threads cannot use local variables, some functions use pointers to store their state in variables passed as parameters. For other nodes that are not motes, implementation size limitations are less stringent because they are less constrained devices. Even there, MidSN also needs just a few KB.

Table 3. Memory Consumption

Component	Memory [Bytes]
I/O Adapter	1262
Config. Manager	880
Data Processor	834
HW Adapter	514

Performance of the Runtime System

To test the MidSN we have written a simple web service client to submit commands at specific time instants and we collected data logs in the control station to analyze timings and modifications to sampled data coming from the SAN. With this data we have built timeline charts to show the results.

The time taken to deliver a command is an important measure of reliability in performance controlled WSNs, partly enforced by a TDMA protocol. Figure 5 shows the measured maximum, minimum and average delay to deliver a command for TelosB nodes of each sub-network. These networks are identified with a prefix number before each node id (e.g 1.2 – node two of sub-network 1).

The sub-network 1 has 16 nodes and runs ContikiOS while the sub-network 2 has 5 nodes that run TinyOS. There is also a network composed by 2 PCs that run Linux and are connected by Ethernet and to the WSN sub-networks.

The results in the Figure 5 concern sending commands to WSN nodes. They show that all commands sent to TelosB nodes were delivered in less than 500ms on average, and always below 1200 ms. These times reflect the TDMA schedules: every node transmits in its slot every complete cycle. The delays were smaller in network 2, which is mostly due to its smaller size. We also measured the delay to deliver a command to each PC node, but that one was less than 1ms.

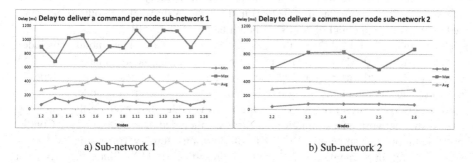

a) Sub-network 1   b) Sub-network 2

Fig. 5. Time taken to deliver a command

Figure 6a) shows the average time and standard deviation of actuation latency. We analyze the time from the abnormal event to delivery at the control station, process an actuation command and deliver it to an actuator. The following time intervals were considered:

- time to detect and send a message to the control station – time to detect;
- time for the control station to evaluate and determine the actuation condition – time to process;
- time for the control station to send the actuation command and for the actuation node to receive it and act – time to act.

In our experiment, the detection time was about 370 ms in average, processing time was about 1 ms and actuation time was about 362 ms. Figure 6b) shows the average total time (sum of the components) along the experiment time.

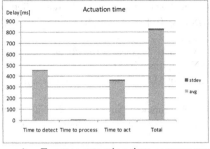
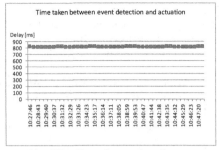

a)   Event to actuation time components   b)   Timeline of actuation time

Fig. 6. Actuation time

6   Conclusion

In this paper we proposed a middleware model for uniform configuration and operation over heterogeneous networks comprising WSNs and nodes outside the WSNs (PCs or control stations). The model advances the state-of-the-art since it views the whole system as a distributed system and any computing device as a node (inside or outside of the WSN, regardless of hardware or operating system) with the same configuration, remote configuration capabilities and operation interface. We have described the modules and details of the component. Then we used an industrial experimental testbed and defined a set of tests that show the system is able to configure both sensor nodes and control stations very easily and using exactly the same calls. From our test runs we extracted logs and displayed a timeline that proves correct configuration of both sensor nodes and control station using the approach. We also show results on delay statistics for the data, data consistence and reliability for our SAN.

References

1. Han, C.-C., Kumar, R., Shea, R., Srivastava, M.: Sensor network software update management: a survey. Int. J. Network Mgmt. 15, 283–294 (2005)
2. Suriyachai, P., Brown, J., Roedig, U.: Poster Abstract: A MAC Protocol for Industrial Process Automation and Control. In: IEEE EWSN (February 2010)
3. Wyckoff, P., McLaughry, S.W., Lehman, T.J., Ford, D.A.: T Spaces. IBM Systems Journal, 454–474 (1998)
4. Welsh, M., Mainland, G.: Programming Sensor Networks Using Abstract Regions. In: Proc. of the 1st Symp. on Networked Systems Design and Implementation (2004)
5. Gupta, V., Junsung, K., Pandya, A., Lakshmanan, K., Rajkumar, R., Tovar, E.: Nano-CF: A coordination framework for macro-programming in Wireless Sensor Networks. In: IEEE SECON (2011)
6. Fok, C.-L., Roman, G.-C., Lu, C.: Agilla: A mobile agent middleware for self-adaptive wireless sensor networks. ACM Transactions on Autonomous and Adaptive Systems 4 (2009)

7. Suriyachai, P., Brown, J., Roedig, U.: Time-Critical Data Delivery in Wireless Sensor Networks. In: Rajaraman, R., et al. (eds.) DCOSS 2010. LNCS, vol. 6131, pp. 216–229. Springer, Heidelberg (2010)

8. Suriyachai, P., Brown, J., Roedig, U.: Poster Abstract: A MAC Protocol for Industrial Process Automation and Control. In: IEEE EWSN (February 2010)

9. Ye, W., Heidemann, J., Estrin, D.: An Energy-Efficient MAC Protocol for Wireless Sensor Networks. In: IEEE INFOCOM (June 2002)

10. Dunkels, A., Schmidt, O., Voigt, T., Ali, M.: Protothreads: Simplifying Event-Driven Programming of Memory-Constrained Embedded Systems. In: Proc. of the 4th Int. Conf. on Emb. Netw. Sensor Syst. (2006)

CiNetStrain - Wireless Strain Gauge Network - Calibration and Reliability Measurements

Timo Hongell, Jukka Ihalainen, and Ismo Hakala

University of Jyväskylä / Kokkola University Consortium Chydenius
P.O. Box 567, FI-67701, Kokkola, Finland
{timo.hongell,jukka.ihalainen,ismo.hakala}@chydenius.fi

Abstract. Wireless sensor networks can be extended to include numerous different sensing devices. Strain gauges are the most common non-destructive sensing elements for measuring surface strain. This paper discusses the design, for the wireless CiNet network, of a strain gauge measurement system, which would make strain measurements more flexible while opening new targets of application in addition to those that traditional wired strain measuring systems can offer. The calibration and validation of the wireless strain measurements as well as energy consumption issues are also brought under observation.

Keywords: calibration, reliability of the system, strain gauges, wireless sensor network.

1 Introduction

In recent years, study of wireless sensor networks (WSN) has become a rapidly developing research area. WSN is a set of wireless sensor nodes where each node measures a physical value using selected sensor probes and sends the value to a database through specific sink nodes. Nowadays, WSNs are widely used in civil and industrial applications such as smart home or environment monitoring [1,2,3]. Compared to traditional sensing methods, wireless sensor networks technology offers some additional benefits: wide areas can be covered with inexpensive, energy-efficient battery-powered devices, which make long-term monitoring of and real time access to measuring data possible. Often the nodes of WSN also are able to self-configure themselves, which enables quick and easy system deployment.

When compared to traditional wired strain gauge systems, wireless solution provide more adaptiveness to the measurements. Wired systems require that the installation cables be mounted from the measurement location to the end device. The extra cables may cause interference to the measurements, and they also make the installation process more complicated and increase the costs. Depending on the measurement environment and the radio solution used, the wireless systems have transmission ranges from few meters up to few hundred meters. The advantage of a wireless system compared to wired one is that it can operate

J. Zheng et al. (Eds.): Adhocnets 2012, LNICST 111, pp. 275–288, 2013.

in different difficult-to-reach surroundings such as rural areas and rotating objects, which are impossible to be measured effectively using wired systems. The networks are flexible and scalable and can be easily widened if an additional measurement point is required. Wireless solutions are ideal for temporary network setups, where the measurement data gathering is done only for a known period of time and where the measurement system is to be removed afterwards.

This paper discusses the design of a strain gauge measurement system for a wireless IEEE802.15.4 standard CiNet network and the reliability of the experiment results. The network can configure and send data automatically after the node deployment. The main focus of the paper is on the describing, designing and evaluating the strain gauge sensor platform.

The paper is organized as follows: First we provide a brief description of some related research and describe the technologies used. Section 3 presents the CiNetStrain system created for this research and the CiNetStrain node calibration. Sections 4 and 5 describe the strain gauge measurements done for validating the CiNetStrain nodes operation and discuss the analysis of the results. Finally, some ideas about real wireless applications and future development are discussed and acknowledgements are made.

2   Related Work

Strain gauge measurements are widely used in different systems and deployments, but the study of those measurements in a wireless environment is quite marginal. The general features of wireless strain gauge system requirements and system design are discussed in [4]. Bielen et al. have developed a WMS 80 based wireless measurement system for rotating structures that can support strain gauges [5]. Their study mainly focuses on building the complete system; the basic data gathering procedures or the initial calibration with any reference device of the nodes are not explained. In [6] Jian et al. describe the development of an IEEE802.15.4 based wireless strain mapping system, where they use commercial WSN RF modules and mainly focus on strain mapping.

Some new commercial solutions have been developed, but they are relatively costly and limited. It can be stated that our CiNetStrain node solution costs roughly only one fifth of the commercial strain measurement nodes. One wireless solution is the Microstrain SG-Link® -mXRS^{TM} Wireless Strain Node developed by MicroStrain Inc [7].

Although, the basics of strain gauge measurements are explained in detail in the related papers, some interesting features and constrains of wireless strain gauge systems are discussed only briefly or not at all taken into consideration. These features include e.g. the sensor platform design, the used measurement protocols, the accuracy and the reliability of the strain results and also the systems true energy consumption that is very important for wireless systems.

It is known that wireless strain gauge systems are able to produce strain values, but the reliability and accuracy those systems is not a widely studied topic. The basic information concerning how the strain measurement values are produced and collected in wireless systems is typically not explained in great many details in most of the strain measurement related articles.

In this paper, we also explain in detail our solution on how to procedure wireless strain measurements. The CiNetStrain system differs from the referenced systems by its scalability and capability to support multiple different sensor solutions at the same time. Additional nodes can easily be introduced to the network, and the data produced by them can be analyzed together with other nodes. This paper also describes the data gathering procedure, calibration and the energy consumption of the CiNetStrain nodes.

3   CiNetStrain System

The wireless CiNetStrain system was built for the CiNet network nodes [2][8] (see Figures 1 and 2). CiNet is a research and development platform for the WSN implemented in Kokkola University Consortium Chydenius, University of Jyväskylä. The hardware in the CiNet node is specially designed for WSNs and consists of inexpensive, standard off-the-shelf components. The CiNet node includes all the basic components necessary for WSNs.

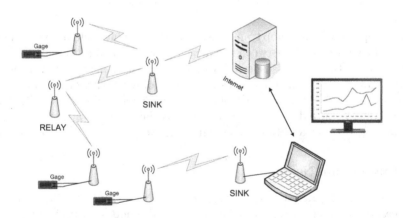

Fig. 1. The system structure of CiNetStrain network

The CiNet WSN includes the measurement nodes, relay nodes and sink nodes that can communicate and transmit data between each other using wireless radio transmitters. The CiNet network uses typically multi-source single-sink (MSSS) topology. The CiNet nodes are able to automatically configure the network structure and, therefore, it is very simple to add more nodes to the measurement network. Typically the sink node gathers and transmits the measurements to a specified database, which usually is defined to be a web server. This can be done using i.e. GPRS transmission or direct USB, Ethernet or serial cable connection from a sink to the computer. The data transmission between the nodes can be multi-hop

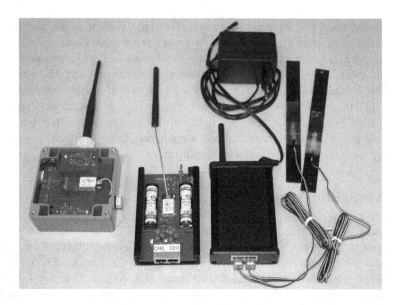

Fig. 2. Wireless strain measurement devices (SINK and nodes) and attached strain gauges

or single-hop based. Multi-hop transmission allows relaying nodes to be used when there are longer distances between the measurement node and the sink node.

The network that was used basically operates in the same way as is presented and illustrated in [9], which discusses the design of networking and communication parts for a noise measurement network in a CiNet environment. The CiNet network is synchronized and uses the CiNet cross-layer protocol stack that allows data sharing, without additional messaging, between different protocol layers.

3.1   CiNetStrain Nodes

The nodes are using 2.4 GHz Jennic IEEE802.15.4 radio modules [10], and all the nodes can work seamlessly in the CiNet network. The nodes are typically powered with two industrial 3.6 volt AA-batteries, but they can also be connected straight to an electric power network. The strain gauges, which are the main sensors of this system, are attached to the nodes using the gauges' lead wires. The nodes can be configured to measure strain values at user-defined time intervals. For example, strain values can be measured continuously, or the nodes can be defined to go to sleep mode and wake up to measure strain values on defined intervals.

Measurement Sensors. One of the CiNet nodes benefits is that the nodes can also be equipped with various kinds of sensors to measure, e.g., temperature, humidity, noise, vibration and strain. For example, the nodes typically have built-in temperature and humidity sensors, whose data can be used together with the strain measurement data. Another way to collect additional data is to introduce to the network new nodes that have been equipped with specific measurement sensors.

Strain Gauges. The CiNetStrain nodes (see Figure 2) are modified from the basic CiNet nodes by equipping them with two Wheatstone bridge resistor setups by using precision resistors and applying required electronics and connectors for the strain gauges.

The Wheatstone bridge is an electric circuit suitable for detection of very small resistance changes. It is typically used to measure resistance changes of a strain gauge. The two bridges allow the nodes to have two independent measurement channels that both can measure strain values. Basically this means that one two-channel node can replace two one-channel nodes.

In this study we are using strain gauge sensors. A strain gauge is a sensor whose resistance varies with applied force. It converts force, pressure, tension, weight, etc., into a change in electrical resistance which can then be measured. When external forces are applied to a stationary object, stress and strain are the result. Stress is defined as the object's internal resisting forces, and strain is defined as the displacement and deformation that occurs in the object.

3.2   Strain Data Sampling

In this study case, the CiNetStrain nodes measures 20 raw-data ADC samples to produce one strain measurement. The raw-data samples are taken at 2 ms intervals. The samples are sorted from the smallest to the largest, and the largest and the smallest values are ignored to reduce false sampling. The average of the remaining 18 values is calculated and stored to a sliding average buffer. The buffer size and the length of the sliding average can be defined by the user. In this paper's measurements, the nodes' final output is the sliding average of the five most recent averaged measurements. Figure 3 illustrates the strain sampling procedure. This double averaging is done to minimize the noise and errors in the ADC raw data measurements.

The CiNetStrain node has two different strain measurement channels, and they both can be used virtually at the same time, as one node can support two strain gauges. The node does first the measurements sampling for channel 0 and then for channel 1. By doing this, the measurement bridges are not on at the same time, which reduces the power consumption. The time difference between the two sampled channels is 15 ms.

Depending on the measurement case and application, the requirements for the time intervals between two measurements change. For the measurements of this study, the data sampling cycle is defined as shown in Figure 4.

3.3   CiNetStrain Interface

The CiNetStrain application (see Figure 5) is designed to be used with the CiNetStrain nodes. In the CiNetStrain system, this application is the controlling software that is used to visualize and control the collected data. It is basically

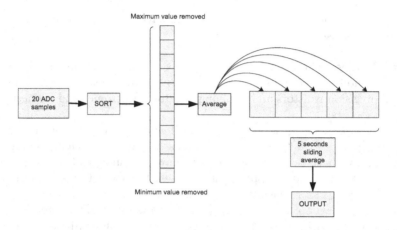

Fig. 3. CiNet nodes ADC sampling of the strain gauges

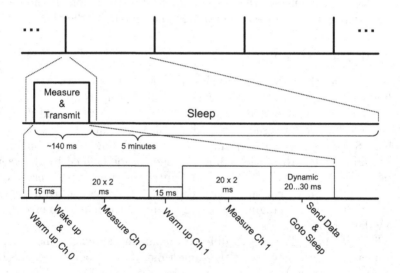

Fig. 4. CiNetStrain data sampling cycle

one executable program that can be used with a PC or laptop computer. The application reads and displays the measured strain values with a graphical user interface window. The application can be used to zero the initial strain values, and user-defined offset values can be set if needed. Strain data for each channel of every strain node is automatically shown in the graphical display with different line colors. With the software, it is possible to define the different channels whose strain and other data is wanted to be recorded to a data file. In longer experiments, the application automatically saves separated data files for different dates in order to avoid data loss in error situations.

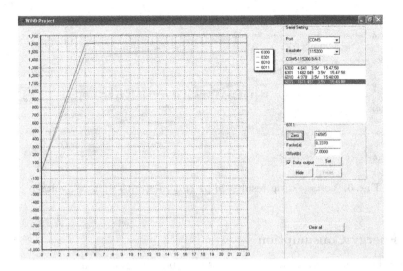

Fig. 5. CiNetStrain application

3.4   Node Calibration

The calibration of the CiNetStrain nodes were done using the Model D4 Data Acquisition Conditioner (D4) [11]. The strain gauge was attached to a composite material, and different weighted objects were used to produce constant stress values on the material. The ADC value of the node and the strain value of the D4 were recorded with the different weights. Based on these results, the linear conversion equation can be defined as

$$y = 0.337x + 7.0, \tag{1}$$

where x is the input in ADC values and y is the output as micro strain value. Using Equation 1, the wireless nodes are linearly calibrated to produce micro strain values, equal to the D4 reference devices' strain value. The equation is given for the CiNetStrain application, and it automatically converts the ADC values to micro strain values. This conversion is done to make the measured strain values more easily comparable with the strain values given by the D4 reference device.

The battery duration measurements showed that the strain values will decrease once the battery's voltage level has fallen below a critical threshold. The battery voltage will then be too low to produce reliable strain values. The voltage drop test showed (see Figure 6) that, with the current measurement-node system design, the critical threshold is around 3.0 volts. On the other hand, the nodes' transmitter radio becomes unstable when operated below 3.0 volts. Therefore, the node's practical operation voltage threshold should be set to 3.0 volts.

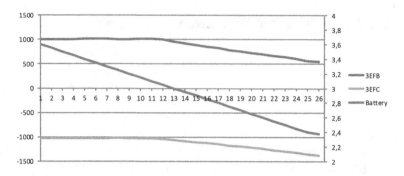

Fig. 6. Voltage drop results, in $\mu\varepsilon$ (micro strain) units vs. voltage

3.5 Energy Consumption

The wireless CiNetStrain nodes are tested in both a long term measurement test and a shorter laboratory measured test to find out the energy consumption and the practical battery life for the nodes. The idea of the long term measurements is to simulate typical and practical strain gauge deployment scenarios, where the strain values are taken with relatively long time intervals over longer period of time. This kind of application can be i.e. structural monitoring of a bridge or a building. In the long term measurement, the nodes are equipped with AA-batteries and programmed to measure strain data and transmit the data packets once in every five minutes. The packets are received by the sink node at real time. The long term battery duration measurements are done simultaneously with the reliability tests discussed later in this paper.

In the shorter laboratory test, the node is measuring data once in every five minutes with both of it's channels. The power supply is constant 3.6 V. The measuring and transmitting takes less than 140 ms, and for the rest of the time the node will be in sleep mode (see Figure 4). This goal of the this test is to be able to get controlled data about the nodes energy consumption in relatively short time to minimize the measurement device related interference to the results. Based on the laboratory measurements, the current consumption of one node during a strain measurement, with 5 minute-long sleeping cycles, is on average 595 μA. The continuous energy consumption of the device is in sleep mode 490 μA. The maximum current consumption caused by the data transmission is 23.396 mA.

Our nodes can support two AA-batteries. When the nodes are equipped with two 3.6 volt 2600 mAh industrial AA-batteries, the computational operation time of the nodes is one full year. The measurement cycle for this setup is defined in Figure 4.

4 Strain Gauge Measurements

We used Micro-Measurements' Model D4 Data Acquisition Conditioner [11] as a commercial measurement and reference device. We also employed 350 Ω

strain gauges, which are Micro-Measurements & SR-4 General Purpose C2A-06-125LW-350 strain gauges [12] that are suitable for composite materials. The tested material we used is 205 mm x 19 mm x 2 mm carbon-fiber composite, provided by Exel Composites Plc.

4.1 Experimental Setup

Samples, where two strain gauges were attached side by side was kept in a closed room - see Figure 7. The gauges were connected to the wireless CiNetStrain and wired D4 systems. The test materials were attached with clamp tools to a table side and stressed with a constant force, using hanging weights. The initial strain values of both of the gages were similar. Additionally, each of the CiNetStrain nodes and the reference D4 device were equipped with strain gauges that were not connected to materials and are therefore sensitive to temperature variations.

Fig. 7. Experimental measurement setup

The wireless nodes sent their measurement data to a sink node connected to a tabletop computer with a USB-cable, and the measurement data was stored in the computer's hard drive using the CiNetStrain application. The D4 measurement unit was connected to a laptop computer with a USB-cable, and its control software stored the measurement data to the computer's hard drive. Additionally the room temperature was constantly measured with another wireless CiNet node that stores the temperature information to a web server.

4.2 Measurement Procedure

The different measurements are independent and do not affect each other. The measurement values of each of the measurement cases were stored to different data files and analyzed separately. The basic measurement procedure consisted of different phases. First, the measurement systems were connected to the strain gauges and the initial strain values were zeroed. The second phase was to produce tension to the materials, and that was done by adding hanging weights to the materials' free ends.

4.3   Reliability Test

In the beginning of the test, all the strain gauges were set to zero value in the measurement devices, without any stress load. Each of the bending setups was set to produce initial strain values to the composite materials. The strain was increased until all the specimen reached the strain value readings of around 1450 to 1600 $\mu\varepsilon$ (micro strain) units according to the measurement systems. This initial bending was done to simulate large material displacements in different strain related applications.

Measurements were taken continuously once every five-minute period, and the data was collected. The goal was to detect that does the measurement systems produce constant reliable and constant results during the whole test measurement. The wired D4 device is electrically operated, and it updates its real time display constantly, but stores the values once every five minutes. The nodes use 3.6 volt batteries, and they were set to take measurements and transmit them once every five minutes and go to the sleep mode between the measurements. The battery voltage levels were also monitored during these tests, but they did not drop significantly enough to affect the results.

5   Data Analysis

Using the data files, each of the strain gauges were separately analyzed, and also mutually compared. The data comparison was based on the synchronized data sets from the data files. The data set synchronization was done with the help of the time stamps of the measurements samples. The Microsoft Excel and Matlab calculation programs were used in the data analysis.

5.1   Reliability Test

The goal of the reliability test is to ensure that the wireless device can produce reliable and valid results in short and long term measurements when compared to the wired one. When the reliability test results are analyzed in a large scale, it can be stated that both of the systems can produce relatively constant strain values with a constant bending force, see Figure 8.

According to [13], when identical "high" accurate strain gauges are compared with each other that may produce typically about 1 to 3 % difference in values, but the gauge error will be constant. Measurement units typically have an accuracy of 0.1 %. Also some external factors, such as temperature and humidity, can affect the results. The total accuracy of the measurement can be calculated using

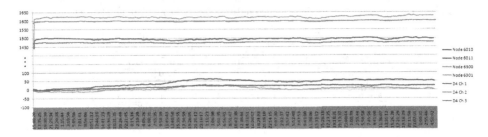

Fig. 8. Reliability test results in $\mu\varepsilon$ (micro strain) units

$$e_{total} = \sqrt{e_{gauge}^2 + e_{device}^2 + e_{other}^2},\qquad(2)$$

where e_{total} is the total accuracy of the measurement and e_{gauge} is the strain gauge accuracy, e_{device} is the measurement device's accuracy, and e_{other} is the error caused by the external factors. Based on the formula, the total accuracy of the strain measurements can be stated to be about 2 %. With micro strain value 1600 ± 2 %, this means an acceptable range from 1568 to 1632 $\mu\varepsilon$ units.

When the measurement scale is zoomed in, both of the systems seem to produce variation to the results. The variation seems to follow the same pattern for both the wired and the wireless system, only the magnitude is slightly larger in the wireless solution. See Figure 9. The numerical analysis of the results is shown in Table 1. The analysis show that the wireless results have more variation than the wired ones.

The reason why the wireless and wired D4 results are not exactly the same is due to the strain gauge placements. Even though the strain gauge pairs are

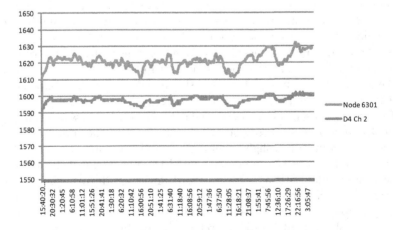

Fig. 9. Wireless node 6301 vs. D4 Ch 2 in $\mu\varepsilon$ (micro strain) units

Table 1. Numerical analysis of the reliability tests in $\mu\varepsilon$ (micro strain) units

stats	Wireless CiNetStrain node				D4 device		
	6010	6011	6300	6301	Ch 1	Ch 2	Ch 3
standard deviation	15.9	3.9	10.2	4.1	9.1	1.9	2.0
variance	254.3	15.0	104.3	16.9	82.0	3.7	4.1
maximum value	63.4	1501.7	30.2	1632.3	27.0	1602	1478
average value	44.0	1494.2	5.4	1621.1	17.1	1598	1475
minimum value	-1.2	1411.7	-12.5	1530.4	-3.0	1587	1464

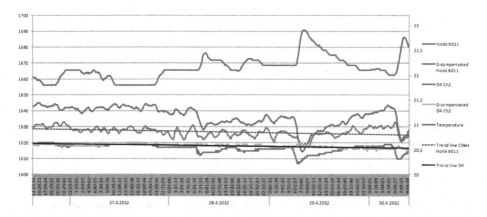

Fig. 10. Temperatures [C°] (right scale) affect strain values (left scale) and "zero-" gauge compensation results in $\mu\varepsilon$ (micro strain) units

in the same material sample, the strain caused by bending the material is not equal all over. Even a slight change in the strain gauges' placement will lead to a different strain value.

The commercial D4 device have built-in filters and signal processing [11] that can diminish the deviation in the measured strain values. Our nodes seem to react with larger intensity than the D4 to strain changes, presumably because our nodes do not process or filter the raw data as much as the D4 device.

When the temperature values are analyzed together with strain values, our measurements indicate that the room temperature changes affect the strain results. We used temperature compensated strain gauges, but the compensation is only for the gauges. Temperature variation affect the test materials behavior and this affect can be seen from our measurements. Figure 10 shows the correlation between the room temperature and strain values, when the room temperature decreases, the strain values slightly increase and vice versa.

The electrically operated commercial wired D4 measurement device can produce constant results with a small standard deviation during whole measurement time. Temperature changes caused by automatic ventilation in the room are clearly visible from the data curves in Figure 10. Wireless battery operated CiNetStrain nodes can also produce relatively constant results with adequate standard deviation. The temperature changes can be observed more precisely in the wireless result graphs. This shows that the wireless devices are more sensitive to temperature changes. The commercial device has built-in filters that can somewhat manage the temperature changes. More effective filtering of wireless results is one of the potential future developments and study issues.

Zero-gauge compensation is typically done to neglect the temperature effect to the strain measurements. Strain gauges which are connected to a material similar to the materials measured but which are not put under tension are called Zero-gauges. This way only the temperature affects the material, and its effect can then be taken into consideration. Figure 10 also shows the zero-gauge compensated strain values for both of the measurement systems.

The test shows that when comparing trend lines of the zero-gauge compensated results, the lines seem to act similarly for both of the systems. Temperature compensation improves the measurement accuracy and reliability.

6   Conclusions

In this paper, we have presented a working strain-based wireless CiNetStrain monitoring system that can be used to diagnose structures and easily extended to large deployments at low cost. The measurements presented and analyzed show that the CiNetStrain system can produce reliable strain values with a low standard deviation. The CiNetStrain nodes have relatively low power consumption, and with a typical setup the nodes can be operational for one year without a battery change. Thus the presented system shows that the strain measurements can be performed with wireless sensor network, where the resources, such as; energy, memory, computing capacity and even the price, are constrained.

The easily installable CiNetStrain network is automatically scalable and additional nodes can easily be introduced to the network, and the data produced by them can be analyzed together with other nodes. The additional nodes can produce information that can be used to support the strain measurements, e.g. temperature and humidity.

The system can be applied to a wide range of target types, and it is equipped with a multi-hop wireless communication capability. The strain sensor board using a Jennic radio that we have designed was proven as a reliable source of strain data. GUI-based monitoring software was developed to analyze and visualize the strain data. Thus, in order to monitor structural conditions, we have developed a wireless system for measuring strain, wherefore the measured data can be directly used to trigger maintenance events and report alerts in real time scenarios.

For future work, the idea is to improve the adaptiveness of the wireless CiNetStrain nodes to be able to use different strain gauges, without large modifications on the hardware. The raw-data calculation has been programmed to include more effective filtering and averaging to reduce noise from the results. For example, filtering that is based on confidence intervals is been studied. The energy consumption is always an issue with WSNs and that is also one topic that we need to improve in our system.

In summary, we have discussed the main topics in the design of a wireless strain gauge measurement system and the reliability comparison of wired and wireless strain gauge measurements. We have also shown the calibration and energy consumption of the CiNetStrain nodes.

Acknowledgments. The work presented in this paper was supported by the Tekes' Boat program's WiND (Wireless sensor technology and NDT-methods in plastic composites quality assurance) project.

References

1. Chen, Y., Chiang, J., Chu, H., Huang, P., Tsui, A.: Sensor-Assisted WI-FI Indoor Location System for Adapting to Environmental Dynamics. In: Proceedings of the 8th ACM Symposium on Modeling, Analysis and Simulation of Wireless and Mobile Systems, Montreal, Quebec, Canada, pp. 10–13 (October 2005)
2. Hakala, I., Ihalainen, J., Kivelä, I., Tikkakoski, M.: Evaluation of Environmental Wireless Sensor Network - Case Foxhouse. International Journal on Advances in Networks and Services 3(1-2), 22–32 (2010)
3. Hu, Y., Li, D., He, X., Sun, T., Han, Y.: The Implementation of Wireless Sensor Network Visualization Platform based on Wetland Monitoring. In: Second International Conference on Intelligent Networks and Intelligent Systems (2009)
4. Arms, S., Townsend, C.P.: Wireless Strain Measurement Systems – Applications & Solutions. In: NSF-ESF Joint Conference on Structural Health Monitoring, Strasbourg, France, pp. 3–5 (October 2003)
5. Bielen, P., Lossie, M., Vandepitte, D.: A Low Cost Wireless Multi-channel Measurement System for Strain Gauges. In: Proceedings of ISMA 2002, vol. 2, pp. 663–670 (2002)
6. Jian, L., Lishchynska, M., Delaney, K.: Distributed Adaptive Networked System for Strain Mapping. In: Third International Conference on Mobile Ubiquitous Computing, Systems, Services and Technologies, UBICOMM 2009, pp. 71–76 (2009)
7. MicroStrain Inc.: User Manual Version 4.0.2 SG-Link® Wireless Strain Node. MicroStrain Inc., 459 Hurricane Lane, Suite 102, Williston, VT 05495 (July 2011)
8. Hakala, I., Tikkakoski, M.: From vertical to horizontal architecture: a cross-layer implementation in a sensor network node. In: Proceedings of the First International Conference on Integrated Internet Ad Hoc and Sensor Networks, vol. 138(6) (2006)
9. Kivelä, I., Gao, C., Luomala, J., Hakala, I.: Design of Noise Measurement Sensor Network: Networking and Communication Part. In: The Fifth International Conference on Sensor Technologies and Applications, SENSORCOMM 2011, pp. 280–287 (August 2011)
10. NXP Laboratories: Data Sheet: JN5148-001-Myy JenNet, ZigBee PRO and IEEE802.15.4 Module, CHIPCON, http://www.jennic.com/files/support_files/JN-DS-JN5148M0-1v4.pdf
11. Vishay Precision Group: Model D4 Data Acquisition Conditioner Instruction Manual Version 1.10. Micro-Measurements, P.O. Box 27777 Raleigh, NC 27611 USA (April 2011)
12. Vishay Precision Group: STRAIN GAGES - C2A Series. Vishay Micro-Measurements (July 2004)
13. Vishay Precision Group: Tech Note TN-505-4 Strain Gage Selection: Criteria, Procedures, Recommendations. Vishay Micro-Measurements, http://www.intertechnology.com/Vishay/pdfs/TechNotes_TechTips/TN-505.pdf

Design Challenges and Solutions for Multi-channel Communications in Vehicular Ad Hoc NETworks

Claudia Campolo and Antonella Molinaro

Università Mediterranea di Reggio Calabria,
Loc. Feo di Vito, 89060, Reggio Calabria, Italy
{name.surname}@unirc.it

Abstract. Vehicular Ad-Hoc Networks rely on a multi-channel architecture to support vehicle-to-vehicle and vehicle-to-infrastructure communications. Multiple service channels are assigned in the 5GHz spectrum for non-safety data transfer, while a unique control channel is used for broadcasting safety messages and service advertisements. Single-radio vehicular devices stay tuned on one radio channel at a time and alternately switch between channels to monitor safety messages and to access information and entertainment services; while dual-radio devices can simultaneously stay tuned on both types of channels. Multi-channel coordination, synchronization, and access are big challenges in VANETs; many design choices are still open issues in ETSI and IEEE standardization bodies. In this paper, counter-measures and recent trends in standardization bodies are discussed to cope with inefficiencies related to multi-channel operation for single-radio devices (*e.g.,* inefficient spectrum utilization, synchronized frame collisions, bandwidth waste), and dual-radio devices (*e.g.,* cross-channel interference, coexistence with single-radio devices).

Keywords: VANET, 802.11p, WAVE, ETSI, IEEE, multi-channel.

1   Introduction

Research activities in governmental, industrial and academy bodies have been underway to accelerate the deployment of Vehicular Ad Hoc Networks (VANETs) that provide wireless communications among moving vehicles (Vehicle-to-Vehicle, V2V) and between vehicles and roadside infrastructure (Vehicle-to-Infrastructure, V2I).

Potential applications for VANETs are categorized based on their targets as: *safety* applications, geared primarily toward avoiding the risk of car accidents; *transport efficiency* applications, focusing on optimizing flows of vehicles; and *commercial* applications, aimed at providing the road traveller with information support and entertainment to make the journey more pleasant. The last two categories are also known with the generic term of *non-safety* applications.

The history leading to the development of VANETs goes back in the early 1990s when the U.S. Department of Transportation (DOT) and the Intelligent Transportation Society of America (ISTA) developed a plan for Intelligent Transportation Systems (ITSs) to make road traffic safe, efficient, and environmentally friendly.

J. Zheng et al. (Eds.): Adhocnets 2012, LNICST 111, pp. 289–301, 2013.
© Institute for Computer Sciences, Social Informatics and Telecommunications Engineering 2013

Since the beginning IEEE 802.11 was identified as the key enabling technology for the delivery of ITS services. In 2004, the task group *p* started developing an amendment to IEEE 802.11 to provide Wireless Access in Vehicular Environments (WAVE) [1]; the standard 802.11p was released in July 2010. The IEEE 1609 working group undertook the task of developing specifications covering additional layers in the WAVE protocol suite.

The milestone for the development of vehicular communications was the allocation by the Federal Communications Commission (FCC) of 75 MHz of bandwidth in the 5.85-5.925 GHz spectrum for Dedicated Short Range Communications (DSRC)-based ITS radio services. The U.S spectrum includes seven 10MHz-wide channels (Figure 1(a)): Channel 178 is the common control channel (CCH) for the exchange of safety and control messages, the other ones are service channels (SCHs) for the exchange of non-safety related data. A similar frequency allocation has been fixed in Europe by the European Telecommunications Standards Institute (ETSI). A 50 MHz-wide spectrum has been allocated (Figure 1(b)), with 30 MHz reserved in the ITS-G5A bandwidth for road safety purposes, and 20 MHz in the ITS-G5B for non-safety traffic [2].

On the one hand, the availability of multiple channels is beneficial in terms of throughput performance [3]; on the other hand, the multi-channel organization in the dynamic vehicular environment raises several issues. Indeed, VANET features, like the heterogeneous nature and requirements of vehicular applications, the absence of central coordination, the unstable, distributed, and quickly changing nature of wireless links, uniquely challenge the coordination of multi-channel activities.

To the purpose of concurrently supporting safety and non-safety applications, single-radio devices may periodically and synchronously switch between CCH and SCHs, according to rules defined by the IEEE 1609.4 standard [4], whereas dual-radio devices, mainly considered by ETSI [2], could have one radio tuned to the CCH and the second radio tunable to one of the available service channels. Dual-radio devices promise better spectrum usage at the expenses of a higher level of implementation complexity. Nonetheless, due to cross-channel interference issues, the multi-channel operation is still an issue.

Although a plethora of works have been published in the recent years on vehicular networks, most of them ignore the multi-channel operation envisioned in the frequency spectrum reserved for ITS, with the exception of a few excellent surveys, recently published and covering the topic of vehicular networking standardization efforts [5-7]. This work differs from the previous ones since it focuses on multi-channel operations and clearly identifies potential concerns left unspecified in the standards, describes strengths and weaknesses of single-radio and dual-radio devices, reviews preliminary solutions proposed in the related literature and discusses open issues which require further investigations.

The paper is organized as follows. Section 2 summarizes the basics of the IEEE 802.11p and the IEEE 1609 multi-channel specifications; Section 3 discusses the main open issues of the multi-channel operation and describes related counter-measures; conclusive remarks are reported in Section 4.

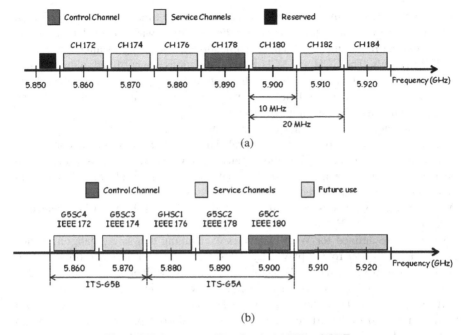

Fig. 1. ITS frequency allocation in (a) US and (b) Europe

2   The IEEE 802.11p/WAVE Multichannel Framework

The IEEE 802.11p task group [1] has recently ratified specifications of the physical (PHY) and medium access control (MAC) layers to support communications in the rapidly changing vehicular environment. It inherits the main principles of 802.11a at the PHY layer with some modifications introduced to cope with the hostile mobile radio propagation environment. At the MAC layer, 802.11p relies on the main rules of the baseline standard with prioritized channel access, but it simplifies the authentication and association operations, which are considered time-consuming for short-lived vehicular communications.

Higher layers in the WAVE protocol suite are covered by the IEEE 1609 standard family [5] that consists of five set of specifications: 1609.0 defines the overall 1609 framework; 1609.1 defines services, interfaces and data flows; 1609.2 covers security and privacy issues; 1609.3 defines the addressing and routing functions associated with the Link Layer Control, the network and the transport layers; 1609.4 specifies extensions to the MAC layer for multi-channel operations; it supports channel coordination, routing and data transfer from the upper layers to the designated channel at the MAC layer. The overall WAVE stack is illustrated in Figure 2.

The 1609.4 specifications [4] define four modalities for channel switching in case of single-radio devices, as shown in Figure 3. According to the *continuous* mode, a node stays always tuned to the CCH to exchange safety-related data; this mode requires no channel coordination. A single-radio device working in the *alternating* mode switches between the CCH and a SCH at scheduled time intervals. Specifically, the channel time is divided into *synchronization intervals* with a fixed length of 100 ms (to meet the requirements of safety applications), consisting of alternating CCH and SCH intervals. The CCH and SCH interval durations are not fixed, although they are typically 50 ms-long intervals. At the beginning of each channel interval, no transmission is allowed for a 4 ms-long guard time to account for radio switching delay and timing inaccuracies in the devices.

The *immediate* access mode allows immediate data transfer over the SCH without waiting for the beginning of the SCH interval. The *extended* access allows continuous communications over the SCH without pauses for CCH access; it is useful for a service which requires a huge amount of data to be transferred and takes several channel intervals to be delivered.

Multi-channel operations are still under discussion in ETSI, who created a specialist task force, STF 420, devoted to this purpose.

Two roles are defined for WAVE devices exchanging non-safety data on service channels. The *provider* role is played by a device offering services and broadcasting WAVE Service Advertisements (WSAs)[1] to indicate its availability for data exchange on one or more SCHs. The *user* role is played by a device wishing to access the advertised services and monitoring the CCH waiting for WSAs. WSAs contain information related to the offered services and the network parameters necessary to join the provider (selected SCH, channel access parameters, etc.).

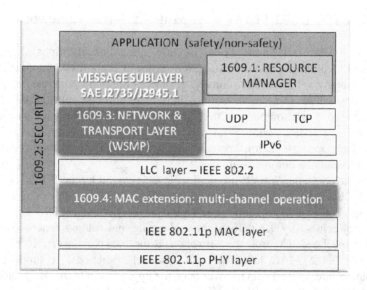

Fig. 2. WAVE protocol stack

---

[1] Similarly to WSAs, Service Announcement Messages (SAMs) are specified by ETSI to notify neighbors about the availability of non-safety services. In the current draft standard SAMs are sent over the CCH and the announced services on the service channels.

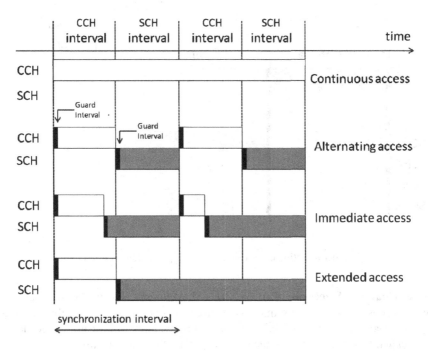

Fig. 3. WAVE channel switching modes

3 Multi-channel Operations: Issues and Countermeasures

The WAVE multichannel organization and related channel switching schemes unavoidably lead to some shortcomings which are exacerbated by the challenges of the vehicular environment and applications. The main identified issues are summarized in the following with related countermeasures proposed in the literature.

Spectrum Utilization. Single-radio devices are obliged to temporarily freeze all running activities on a given channel when switching on another channel. This implies inefficient spectrum utilization. By referring to the alternating switching mode, the theoretical channel capacity would be more than halved when also considering the guard time between channel intervals (Figure 4).

The negative consequences are a significant throughput reduction for non-safety services on the SCHs and an increase in the delay of safety and control messages on the CCH, with the risk of conveying outdated information, which are useless or even detrimental for cooperative road applications [7], [16].

Dual-radio devices can achieve higher spectrum utilization since they can simultaneously exploit two channels. Notwithstanding, full spectrum usage cannot be achieved, unless devices with a number of radios equal to the number of available channels are considered.

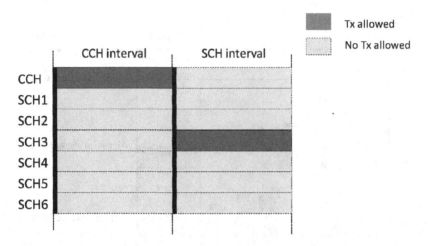

Fig. 4. Spectrum utilization for the alternating channel access scheme

Service Channel Selection. The WAVE Management Entity (WME) in each provider keeps track of SCHs that are in use by nearby devices, so that the *least congested* channel can be selected. Criteria and procedures to measure congestion on a channel and to select the target one are not specified in the standard.

If WAVE providers in radio proximity are able to select *non-overlapping* SCHs, then data exchange would occur without reciprocal interference and with positive effects on network throughput and channel utilization. Nevertheless, the choice of non-frequency overlapping channels in a dynamic environment is challenged by the unstable and quickly changing nature of vehicular links, the limited assigned spectrum, the distributed control, the mobility of nodes and the hidden terminals phenomenon, etc.

The limited number of SCHs has obviously a big impact; the lower the number of SCHs the higher the interference and the probability of choosing overlapping channels. The risk of overlapping SCH selection is exacerbated by the fact that VANETs are infrastructureless, so there is no central authority that assigns channels or coordinates the choice among providers in non-line of sight. The mobility of providers also plays a role; it could neutralize the effectiveness of any procedure for SCH selection. For example, two providers reciprocally hidden could select the same SCH, but users in the common overlapping area would suffer from interference. Even if there are no common users, when the providers move and fall in reciprocal radio coverage they would reciprocally interfere.

Another issue adversely affecting the SCH selection is the loss of WSA packets. This event can be due to several reasons: *(i)* collisions among WSAs simultaneously transmitted by different providers; *(ii)* collisions among WSAs and other types of messages broadcasted over the CCH (e.g., event-triggered safety messages, or periodic short status *heartbeat* messages like *beacons*); *(iii)* channel errors and interference. Whichever the reason of the WSA loss, a provider that misses the WSA from a nearby provider could blindly reserve the same SCH and then generate interference.

The SCH selection is also an issue for dual radio devices; they also have to choose the service channel where the second radio will be tuned into with the aim of reducing interference with nearby nodes.

Just a few works in the literature addressed the SCH selection issue. In [8] the authors propose splitting the control channel into two sub-channels: one used for Request to Send (RTS)/Clear to Send (CTS) exchange to reserve a given SCH, and the other one for ACK transmission to confirm the SCH selection. Pairs of nodes asynchronously switch on the selected SCH and transmit in a collision-free manner after the RTS/CTS handshaking and ACK confirmation. RTS and CTS packets convey channel status information that can be collected by any node when overhearing these packets; this information is used to drive the SCH selection. The main drawback of this proposal is the signalling overhead due to the RTS/CTS and the ACK exchange on the CCH, which could penalize the delivery of safety critical messages transmitted on the same channel. A similar approach with RTS/CTS exchange on the CCH is proposed in [9] to allow sender-destination nodes agreeing on the SCH to use. By listening RTSs/CTSs all nodes record the time the reserved channel will be freed. Although these proposals can achieve significant improvements in data delivery, they are not recommended for single-radio devices. In fact, since these devices asynchronously switch from CCH to SCH after the SCH negotiation, they would miss emergency messages transmitted on the CCH when they are tuned on the SCH. Moreover, the asynchronous approach could have negative consequences on the transmissions of beacons, which are requested to be sent *periodically* on the CCH.

Standard-compliant solutions are proposed in [10] and [11], which follow the 1609.4 channel switching rules and exploit *legacy* service advertisements without adding overhead on the CCH. In [10] each node maintains a *channel utilization table* to record the busy/idle channel status and the related number of active providers, identified on the basis of received WSAs. The solution in [11] leverages cooperation among vehicular nodes to allow providers to offer their services on different SCHs. WAVE providers use *enhanced* WSA frames to advertise information about their own SCH and the SCHs reserved by nearby providers whose WSAs have been heard. By doing so, unreliability of WSAs transmission and hidden providers can be kept under control.

Cross-Channel Interference. The parallel usage of adjacent channels may generate interference that adversely affects the communication quality. 802.11p limits the out-of-band energy of a transmitter by associating a spectral mask to each class of devices, characterized by a given maximum transmission power. The mask specifies a frequency-dependent upper bound on the permitted power spectral density (PSD) of the transmitted signal. At a frequency offset of ± 10 MHz from the signal center frequency, corresponding to the adjacent channel center frequencies in the considered spectrum, the PSD values are not negligible (*e.g.,* for a class A device, the loss is equal to 28 dB). This creates problem of cross-channel interference, also known as adjacent channel interference (ACI).

Some preliminary test results [12], showed that ACI creates significant packet errors if the interferer is an order of magnitude or more closer than the desired transmitter to the receiver, thus strongly penalizing performance.

The cross-channel interference problem could be exacerbated in dual-radio devices with co-located antennas simultaneously working on different channels if they are adjacent, *i.e.*, CCH and SCH 176 or 180. Therefore, the positioning of antennas on the car surface and also the channels for tuning the available transceivers should be carefully planned.

In [13] a preliminary solution to reduce cross-channel interference is proposed, which follows the most conservative approach: a potential transmission on the SCH is delayed until the transmission on the adjacent CCH is completed. Further efforts are required to design more efficient techniques to face ACI.

WAVE Service Advertisement Procedures. Non-safety data exchange on SCHs is conditioned on the reception of WSAs by vehicles under the provider's coverage. Channel impairments or collisions on CCH could hinder the WSA reception and prevent potential users to know about the services advertised by the provider and access them, with consequent inefficient exploitation of the SCH capacity. This could be particularly detrimental for short-lived vehicular connections (*e.g.*, between a vehicle and a roadside unit (RSU) due to the high vehicle speed, or between vehicles moving in opposite directions). WSA losses could also adversely affect the effectiveness of the SCH reservation procedure.

To the purpose of increasing the reliability of service advertisement, the standard suggests to send multiple WSAs, but without specifying neither the number nor the scheduling of WSA replicas. Intuitively, the higher the number of WSAs, the higher the probability to detect the provider. Nevertheless, a higher number of WSAs increases the traffic load and, consequently, the collision probability with adverse effect on *heartbeat* and safety messages. It is of crucial importance to tune the number of WSA repeats for the best trade-off between the successful delivery of safety/heartbeat messages and the capability of vehicles to detect nearby providers.

In [14] a set of solutions are proposed and evaluated aimed at improving the spreading of WSA information in the network, with little-to-none overhead. The main idea is that vehicles detecting a provider piggyback the main WSA information in their heartbeat messages, thus counteracting WSA losses.

Multi-hop Communications. The effective use of multiple channels becomes even more challenging in case of multi-hop communications. Nearby nodes need to tune into the same SCH in order to communicate, but coordinating switching decision between neighboring nodes over multiple-hops is a tough task, especially for single-radio devices.

In [10] two multi-hop forwarding schemes are designed for scenarios where vehicles need to transmit information to a RSU, which is outside their radio coverage. The first scheme relies on sender-initiated broadcasting; the source and every intermediate node broadcast data only after becoming a provider and having advertised the service. In the second scheme each forwarding node broadcast a *'forward-req'* WSA frame during the CCH interval to seek for a nearby node available to forward the unicast received data. Although this work is one of the pioneers in dealing with multi-hop forwarding in WAVE, it has some drawbacks. The first scheme suffers from high redundancy related to the naive flooding technique. The second scheme generates additional overhead on the CCH due to the 'forward-req' frames, which compete with safety messages.

The work proposed in [15] shares a similar objective, but proposes a counter-based scheme coupled with overhearing techniques to reduce the overhead and cancel duplicated transmissions. To deal with the fact that a WAVE node cannot simultaneously act as a provider and as a user and, hence, it can only take part in data exchange in a given Basic Service Set (BSS) at a time, the solution in [15] leverages a feature introduced in 802.11p [1], which allows data transmission *outside the context of a BSS* (OCB). OCB relies on the use of a wildcard BSS identifier (BSSID). By removing the BSSID filtering, packet forwarding towards the RSU is facilitated.

Tuning the Channel Interval Duration. The standard does not specify mandatory CCH and SCH interval durations. Therefore, the research community has devoted some attention to the the trade-off for optimal CCH/SCH duty cycle. On the one hand, giving more time to the CCH will help the timely delivery of safety messages; on the other hand, longer SCH intervals could be beneficial to handle the high traffic volume of some non-safety applications, which have the great potential to accelerate the market penetration of VANETs. Results in [16] show that even under light traffic conditions, the alternating switching every 50 ms suggested by the standard is not able to meet the safety reliability requirements; poorer performance are experienced in dense network scenarios [17].

Similarly, in [18] the authors suggest low usage of the spectrum from non-safety traffic in highly dense road segments and during peak hours to ensure reliability of safety applications. According to [16] also bandwidth-intensive video applications cannot be supported by the alternating channel access scheme.

Starvation of Non-safety Applications. Because of the alternating WAVE access scheme, bandwidth demanding applications could starve while waiting for being transmitted over the SCH. To this purpose the standard has recently introduced the *immediate* and *extended* channel access schemes in Figure 3. The quite obvious benefits of the extended access have been investigated in [19]. However, the paper does not study to which extent this approach may cause either losses of emergency messages or their expired reception. The latter issues are addressed in [20]; a multi-radio RSU broadcasts traffic view reports to all neighboring vehicles in all channels, so that vehicles under its coverage can be tuned into a SCH as long as they require. In the proposed solution, a vehicle tuned on SCH also during the CCH interval may fail to receive/transmit heartbeat status information from/to those nearby vehicles, which are different from the neighbors of the RSU. The consequent lack of timely and accurate neighborhood-awareness may be detrimental for several applications (e.g., cooperative cruise control).

We consider critical the specification of use cases to properly exploit the newly defined switching schemes. In [21] we identify in vehicles stopped at a gas station or at intersections the best candidates for the extended access scheme without being a threat to road safety. In fact, vehicles that do not move during a given time period need neither to transmit nor to receive updated position/kinematics information from/to nearby vehicles. The proposed solution, DREAM, has been designed to allow vehicles to self-control their switching mode according to the their mobility patterns in drive-thru scenarios.

Synchronized Frame Collisions. Other events unique to the WAVE channel switching are the *synchronized* frame collisions at the beginning of each channel interval [7]. At beginning of the CCH interval several devices may have one packet (e.g., heartbeat message, WSA) ready to be transmitted. At the beginning of the SCH interval, some vehicles may have bulk of data to transfer (e.g., file sharing).

If the application layer is not *aware* of channel switching, packets intended to be transmitted on CCH might be generated during the SCH interval and buffered in the MAC queue, and vice versa. The probability of collisions increases with the number of contending devices and the number of packets per device.

Collisions are particularly detrimental for broadcasted messages, like WSAs and safety/heartbeat messages, due to lacking of acknowledgements and contention window adaptation mechanisms.

To counteract synchronized collisions, the 1609.4 standard suggests that backlogged nodes undergo a random back-off before accessing the channel. This helps to avoid, but not to prevent, collisions. Collisions can be reduced if *(i)* the application is *aware* of channel switching and passes packets to the MAC layer only during the proper interval [17] (Figure 5); *(ii)* transmission attempts, instead of being concentrated at the beginning of the channel interval, are distributed in random instants during the channel interval, in order to improve time diversity [22].

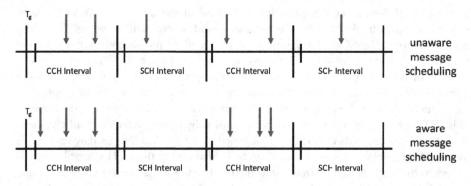

Fig. 5. Unaware and aware message transmission scheduling

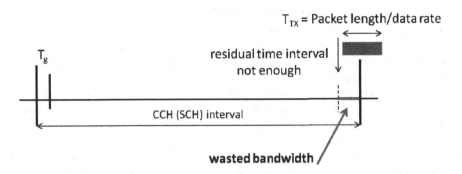

Fig. 6. Bandwidth wastage at the end of a channel interval

Bandwidth Wastage. The WAVE channel switching has another unique negative issue: the bandwidth wastage at the end of a channel interval. If the residual channel interval is not long enough to accommodate an incumbent packet transmission, the standard recommends to postpone its transmission to the next synchronization interval (Figure 6). This wastes channel bandwidth and causes higher packet delay.

In [23] this issue is mitigated through fragmentation schemes that adapt the packet size in order to make the best use of the residual channel interval. However, packets whose lifetime is bounded to a channel interval (e.g., heartbeat, safety and WSA messages) can be neither fragmented nor queued. They can only be dropped to avoid the conveying of outdated information. A possible solution to reduce bandwidth wastage is to use shorter packets whenever possible, by renouncing to some extra information. For example, the security overhead can be shortened by omitting signatures and certificates in situations where they are not strictly necessary [24]. In such a case, the security-efficiency tradeoff needs to be carefully considered.

Time Synchronization. Despite the asynchronous 802.11p channel access rules, switching between CCH and SCH requires an accurate and absolute synchronization among devices. The standard suggests relying on the Coordinated Universal Time (UTC) signals for maintaining devices synchronized, but this approach suffers from being centralized. In fact, because of the limitations of satellite positioning systems, *e.g.*, in tunnels, urban canyons, densely treed streets, the UTC signal could be lost. Therefore, it is likely that WAVE networks will adopt a combination of the global time reference signal and some other distributed approaches that rely on timing signals received from other devices [6]. The *Timing Advertisement* frame has been introduced in IEEE 802.11p just to this purpose [1].

Co-existence between Dual-Radio and Single-Radio Devices. While advantages of dual-radio devices are quite obvious when all nodes are equipped with dual transceivers, they are unclear when single-radio and dual-radio devices co-exist. Since the co-existence of single-radio and dual-radio devices is expected in the mid-term deployment of VANETs, designing coexistence solutions becomes an issue.

Three approaches have been proposed in [25] to improve the delivery performance of safety messages in case of coexistence of single-radio and dual-radio devices.

The simplest solution foresees that single-radio devices always stay tuned into the CCH, where also dual radio devices tune one of their radios. In this case, single-radio devices cannot participate in non-safety data exchange.

According to the second approach, single-radio devices alternately tune into the CCH while dual-radio devices have one radio tuned into a dedicated safety channel (Channel 172, according to the latest trend in standardization groups) and the other radio following the alternating channel access. In this case, dual-radio devices which detect the presence of a single-radio neighbor, send safety messages on both the CCH and the dedicated safety channel. The non-safety data exchange occurs on the SCH interval for both single-radio and dual-radio devices.

The third solution exploits the same idea, but single-radio devices that are not interested in non-safety data exchange notify their neighbors about their intention to remain permanently tuned to the CCH. The two last approaches call for one extra bit to provide information about the channel switching capability/intention of the single-radio device.

4   Conclusions

In this paper an analysis is presented of the main open issues related to the use of multiple channels in vehicular networks. The analysis suggests that several issues unique to the vehicular environment need to be addressed in order to take decisions on the adoption, adaptation, and improvement of IEEE 802.11p/1609 multi-channel networks. Existing literature has been surveyed which provide some countermeasures for both single-radio and dual-radio devices; some hints for possible future research direction are also given. Especially if single-radio devices will be considered in the near future, capabilities and constraints of the standard, requirements and nature of vehicular applications shall be understood carefully.

References

1. IEEE 802.11p, Amendment 6: Wireless Access in Vehicular Environments (July 2010)
2. Strom, E.G.: On Medium Access and Physical Layer Standards for Cooperative Intelligent Transport Systems in Europe. Proceedings of IEEE 99(7), 1183–1188 (2011)
3. So, J., Vaidya, N.: Multi-channel MAC for ad hoc networks: handling multi-channel hidden terminals using a single transceiver. In: ACM International Symposium on Mobile Ad Hoc Networking and Computing (MOBIHOC), pp. 222–233 (2004)
4. IEEE 1609.4. IEEE Standard for Wireless Access in Vehicular Environments (WAVE) - Multi-channel Operation (February 2011)
5. Morgan, J.L.: Notes on DSRC WAVE Standards Suite: Its Architecture, Design and Characteristics. IEEE Communications Surveys and Tutorials 12(4), 1–15 (2010)
6. Uzcategui, R.A., Acosta-Marum, G.: WAVE: a Tutorial. IEEE Communications Magazine 47(5), 126–133 (2009)

7. Kenney, J.B.: Dedicated Short-Range Communications (DSRC) Standards in the United States. Proceedings of IEEE 99(7), 1162–1182 (2011)

8. Ni, M., Zhong, Z., Zhao, D.: A Novel Multichannel Multiple Access Protocol for Vehicular Ad Hoc Networks. In: IEEE International Conference on Communications, ICC (2012)

9. Han, C., Dianati, M., Tafazolli, R., Kernchen, R.: Asynchronous Multi-Channel MAC for Vehicular Ad Hoc Networks. In: IEEE Vehicular Networking Conference, VNC (2012)

10. Wang, S.Y., Lin, C.C., Hong, W.J., Liu, K.C.: On the performances of forwarding multihop unicast traffic in WBSS-based 802.11(p)/1609 networks. Computer Networks 55, 2592–2607 (2011)

11. Campolo, C., Cortese, A., Molinaro, A.: CRaSCH: A Cooperative Scheme for Service Channel Reservation in 802.11p/WAVE Vehicular Ad Hoc Networks. In: Net4Cars (2009)

12. Rai, V., Bai, F., Kenney, J., Laberteaux, K.: IEEE 802.11 11-07-2133-00-000p. Cross-Channel Interference Test Results: A report from VSC-A project (2007)

13. Lasowski, R., Gschwandtner, F., Scheuermann, C., Duchon, M.: A Multi Channel Synchronization Approach in Dual Radio Vehicular Ad-Hoc Networks. In: IEEE Vehicular Technology Conference, VTC-Spring (2011)

14. Campolo, C., Cozzetti, H.A., Molinaro, A., Scopigno, R.: Augmenting Vehicle-to-Roadside Connectivity in Multi Channel Vehicular Ad Hoc Networks. Journal of Network and Computer Applications (2012)

15. Campolo, C., Molinaro, A.: Vehicle-to-Roadside Multihop Data Delivery in 802.11p/WAVE Vehicular Ad Hoc Networks. In: IEEE GLOBECOM (2010)

16. Misic, J., Badawy, G., Rashwand, S., Misic, V.: Trade Off Issues for CCH/SCH Duty Cycle for IEEE 802.11p Single Channel Devices. In: IEEE GLOBECOM (2010)

17. Qi, C., Jiang, D., Delgrossi, L.: IEEE 1609.4 DSRC multi-channel operations and its implications on vehicle safety communications. In: IEEE Vehicular Networking Conference, VNC (2009)

18. Wang, Z., Hassan, M.: How much of DSRC is available for non-safety use? In: 5th ACM International Workshop of VehiculAr Inter-NETworking, VANET (2008)

19. Wang, S.Y., Chou, C.L., Liu, K.C., Ho, T.W., Hung, W.J., Huang, C.F., Hsu, M.S., Chen, H.Y., Lin, C.C.: Improving the Channel Utilization of IEEE 802.11p/1609 Networks. In: IEEE WCNC (2009)

20. Liu, K., Guo, J., Lu, N., Lu, F.: RAMC: A RSU-Assisted Multi-channel Coordination MAC protocol for VANET. In: NiVi Workshop, Co-Located with IEEE GLOBECOM (2009)

21. Campolo, C., Molinaro, A.: DREAM: IEEE 802.11p/WAVE Extended Access Mode in Drive-Thru Vehicular Scenarios. In: IEEE International Conference on Communications, ICC (2012)

22. Campolo, C., Molinaro, A., Vinel, A.: Understanding the Performance of Short-Lived Control Broadcast Packets in IEEE 802.11p/WAVE Vehicular Networks. In: IEEE Vehicular Networking Conference, VNC (2011)

23. Wang, S.Y., Chao, H.L., Liu, K.C., He, T.W., Lin, C.C., Chou, C.L.: Evaluating and Improving the TCP/UDP Performances of IEEE 802.11(p)/1609 Networks. In: IEEE ISCC (2008)

24. Schoch, E., Kargl, F.: On the Efficiency of Secure Beaconing in VANETs. In: IEEE WiSec (2010)

25. Hong, K., Kenney, J., Rai, V., Labertaux, K.: Evaluation of Multi-Channel Schemes for Vehicular Safety Communications. In: IEEE WiVEC (2010)

Prefix Delegation Based Route Optimisation in Cooperative Ad Hoc Interconnected Mobile Networks

Rehan Qureshi[1] and Arek Dadej[2]

[1] Faculty of Engineering, Sciences and Technology, Iqra University, Karachi, Pakistan
riqureshi@gmail.com
[2] School of Electrical and Information Engineering, University of South Australia,
Mawson Lakes, SA 5095, Australia
arek.dadej@unisa.edu.au

Abstract. We consider a scenario where a number of mobile networks, e.g. vehicles equipped with Mobile Routers, travel together interconnected in a dynamic mesh structure, here called Ad Hoc Interconnected Mobile Network or AIMNET. The mesh topology interconnecting the mobile networks not only facilitates inter-mobile-network communications, but more importantly allows sharing of Internet access available to individual Mobile Routers. We first discuss the route optimisation problem in AIMNET and the prefix delegation based solutions. We then propose a two-level addressing scheme that minimises the overhead and improves route optimisation. Then, we discuss routing in the AIMNET and provide experimental results to verify our proposals.

Keywords: Ad Hoc Networks, NEMO, MIPv6, Route Optimisation.

1 Introduction

The advances in mobile technology have enabled the devices to connect to the Internet while they move. With mobile devices it became possible to have mobile networks as well. Networks deployed on a ship, in a vehicle or on a person are all mobile networks due to the mobility of the ship, vehicle and the person respectively. These mobile networks help the nodes they carry in communicating with each other and with nodes in external networks or the Internet.

Different nodes may require help in Internet access for different reasons. Some nodes may want to save power by connecting to the local network instead of transmitting data to a far away base station. Others may not be capable of utilising a wireless access technology that is available at their location. While some nodes may not be capable of handling IP layer mobility, thus require assistance from another entity to do it on their behalf. In all cases, the nodes rely on their *mobile networks* to provide Internet access.

A mobile network has at least one *mobile router* (MR) and one or more mobile network nodes (MNN). The mobile router is like a gateway to the mobile

J. Zheng et al. (Eds.): Adhocnets 2012, LNICST 111, pp. 302–315, 2013.

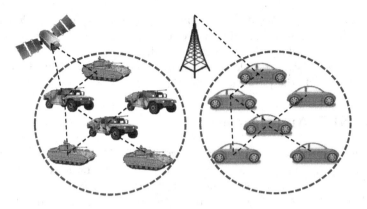

Fig. 1. Ad Hoc Interconnected Mobile Networks

network; MNNs access external networks through it. A mobile router can be any device from a general purpose mobile phone to a dedicated router. Since it can be like any other node, it has its own set of limitations. In a heterogeneous wireless access environment, it is reasonable to assume that not all access technologies are available everywhere and that a mobile router is compatible with only selected access technologies. Therefore a mobile router is unlikely to maintain ubiquitous Internet connectivity on its own.

Interesting scenarios occur when a group of mobile networks are operating together. These mobile networks can interconnect to exploit their diversity in capabilities and conditions in order to achieve ubiquity in communication. Application of such collaborative mobile networks can be seen in many areas, e.g. in disaster recovery where emergency vehicles and personnel with a variety of devices/sensors communicate amongst themselves and with the emergency response control centre, in a battlefield where military vehicles moving together communicate with each other as well as with other components of the Command and Control hierarchy, or on roads where multiple vehicles and their passengers interconnect to take advantage of the heterogeneous wireless Internet access.

In all of these scenarios, the mobile networks that are operating in the vicinity of other mobile networks can collaborate with each other to increase their chances of ubiquitous communication. The collaboration is assisted by forming an ad hoc network between the mobile networks, forming an architecture that we call 'Ad Hoc Interconnected Mobile Networks' (AIMNET). In the examples given above, AIMNET in emergency services allows a mobile network to be reachable by a base station when it can not be reached directly due to obstacles; in militarily communications scenario, the AIMNET allows redundancy in connections so that the mobile networks can find alternative routes to the command centre if their nearest gateway becomes unavailable; and in the case of a group of cars on the road, the AIMNET allows them to be accessible by the Internet while individually they might not be able to do so.

We give further details of the AIMNET architecture in section 2. We then discuss the issue of route optimisation for AIMNET in section 3. We follow in section 4 with an evaluation of candidate AIMNET addressing schemes that support prefix delegation based route optimisation, and propose a new two-level addressing topology. In section 5, we discuss routing in AIMNET with our proposed addressing topology and provide simulation results in section 6. Finally, we conclude the paper in section 7.

2   AIMNET Architecture

The Ad Hoc Interconnected Mobile Networks (AIMNET) has different types of communicating nodes present at different levels. The basic component of an AIMNET is a mobile network. A mobile network is a network segment that is able to change its point of attachment to the Internet. A mobile network can only be accessed via one or more 'mobile routers' (MRs) that act as gateway for the mobile network. The devices that belong to the mobile network or obtain connectivity through the MR are called mobile network nodes (MNNs).

A mobile router can have three types of interfaces: an ingress or internal interface that is attached to a link inside the mobile network, an external interface that attaches to an access network and a MANET interface that participates in the inter-MR ad hoc network of AIMNET. A MNN sends packets, destined to a correspondent node (CN) outside its mobile network, to the ingress interface of the mobile router. The mobile router then routes the packets, according to its

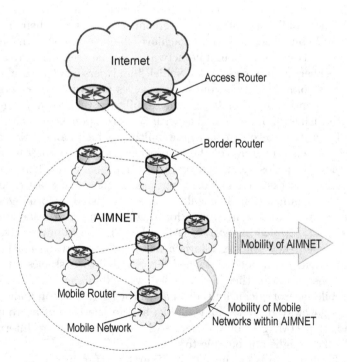

Fig. 2. AIMNET architecture

routing policy, using the external interface or the MANET interface. A mobile router that has no external interface, or does not have an active connection on any external interfaces, can only send its packets via the MANET interface.

In AIMNET, any mobile router that establishes a direct connection with an Internet access network becomes a border router and announces this status in the AIMNET. When a border router loses its external connection, it ceases to be a border router and becomes a simple mobile router. The mobile routers that do not have direct Internet connectivity at their external interfaces send their packets to the border routers that can forward them into the Internet. Similarly, the mobile routers with no direct Internet access can be reached via border routers of AIMNET.

The mobile routers in AIMNET face two kinds of mobility, mobility of all mobile routers as a group and mobility of mobile routers within the AIMNET. The first type of mobility causes changes in location of the entire AIMNET with respect to available access networks and results in changes of the global IP address of the AIMNET. The second type of mobility results in changes in the AIMNET's internal topology. Thus the internal topology of AIMNET is volatile, however the internal topology of a mobile network remains relatively stable.

3 Route Optimisation

3.1 Problem

When a mobile node is moving independently and reaches a visiting (foreign) network, it is no longer reachable at its home address (HoA), hence it requires a Care-of Address (CoA) from the visiting network to be reachable. This IP mobility support for individual mobile nodes is provided by Mobile IPv6. To provide IP mobility support to mobile networks, IETF-NEMO Working Group has proposed Network Mobility Basic Support Protocol (NEMO BSP) [1]. In NEMO BSP only the MR gets CoA, other nodes in the mobile network continue to use their home address; thus NEMO BSP hides network mobility from the nodes inside the mobile network and relieves them from mobility management. However, the NEMO BSP protocol dictates that all packets from a node inside a mobile network must travel to their destination via the home agent of the mobile network, leading to sub-optimal routes and related overheads [2]. This gets worse with nested mobile networks because packets from nodes in mobile networks have to follow a path that involves home agents of all MRs along the way to the Top Level MR that is directly connected to the visiting access network.

In AIMNET, only a border router is directly connected to the visiting network. If NEMO BSP is applied to AIMNET, the border router will become the Top Level MR of AIMNET and only the border router will receive a CoA from the visiting network. This will result in all traffic from a node in AIMNET to not only go through the home agent of its serving mobile router, but also through the border router's home agent as well. This routing path is obviously not an optimal path and thus it will incur higher overheads.

3.2 Solutions

In order to solve the problem of route optimisation of NEMO BSP, several solutions have been proposed in the literature. An overview of the available solutions can be found in [3,4]. Generally, the subject literature mentions three major approaches. These are Recursive approach, Hierarchical approach and Aggregate & Surrogate approach [5].

The *recursive approach* aims at reducing tunnelling overheads in NEMO BSP. The number of tunnels and home agents (HAs) along the path can be decreased by providing information about the nesting of networks hosting the mobile node to its HA and to the correspondent node (CN). Recursive approach then uses source routing due to HA and CN know the path from the Access Router (AR) to the mobile node. This approach can adversely affect the network performance in high mobility environments because every time a mobile node changes its nesting position, it has to send path information update to its HA and CN. Recursive approach also causes higher delay and memory costs [5]. Scalability is another concern as this approach requires extensions/changes to functionality of network components and protocols.

In the *hierarchical approach*, the TLMR (top level MR connected to access router) is used as a virtual home agent or a mobility anchor point. A mobile node's tunnel to its HA is encapsulated by MR-to-TLMR tunnels of all the MRs between the mobile node and the TLMR. The TLMR removes all tunnels and encapsulates the original MN-to-HA tunnel in another tunnel from TLMR to MN's HA. This approach does not require source routing and avoids routing via HAs of nested MRs, but uses tunnels to provide route optimisation. In scenarios where MRs are highly mobile inside AIMNET, this approach reduces the number of binding updates (BUs) sent to HA and CN, as all BUs generated as a result of local mobility are processed locally by the TLMR. Another benefit of this approach is that it requires no change in the functionality of CNs. Overall performance of schemes following this approach is better than that of recursive approach but, due to additional tunnels, delays are comparatively higher than those in the aggregate & surrogate approach [5].

The *aggregate & surrogate approach* supports route optimisation by relaying network prefix of the AR to the nodes inside the mobile network. This enables them to configure a topologically correct care-of-address (CoA) and be directly accessible to CNs without involving HAs of any intermediary MRs. This approach does not require unnecessary tunnels or changes in the functionality of CN, HA etc. As a result, packet delays and memory costs are relatively low [5], and scalability is good [6]. A side effect of providing AR's prefix to the mobile nodes is that when the mobile network changes its point of attachment to the Internet (i.e. changes the AR), CoAs of all nodes also change, resulting in a binding update storm.

In short, as MRs can move frequently inside the AIMNET, the binding update costs due to this local mobility is lesser with hierarchical approach as opposed to recursive approach. This advantage of hierarchical approach comes with extra tunnelling costs. When ad hoc routing protocols are used to facilitate routing among MRs, they remove the need to nest MRs in other MRs. Also, registrations with TLMR for local reachability are not required. Due to the mobile nature of AIMNET, top level MRs may change dynamically resulting in a change of the entire hierarchical structure of AIMNET hence the need to detect and register with the new TLMR if hierarchical approach is used. The aggregate & surrogate approach is better suited for AIMNET as it can support random local mobility without additional tunnelling costs. It is also better than recursive approach because the source routing mechanisms in the recursive approach do not perform well for highly dynamic AIMNETs.

4   Topologies Based on Prefix Delegation

In the previous section we have discussed that the aggregate & surrogate or the prefix delegation based approach to support route optimisation is better suited for AIMNET than other approaches. The network prefix of the access network can be delegated to AIMNET in a number of ways, resulting in different addressing topologies in AIMNET. In this section, we discuss the options for AIMNET addressing topology i.e. a flat topology and a hierarchical topology of addressing. In the end we propose our own two-level topology that is better than the other two topologies.

4.1   Flat Topology

A flat topology can be formed within the AIMNET by enabling all mobile nodes to directly configure their CoA with the subnet prefix delegated by the AR. This can be achieved by using MRs as neighbour discovery proxies (ND-Proxy) [7]. In this scenario, an MR directly connected with the AR forms its CoA with the prefix advertised by the AR, and then relays this prefix to other MRs and to nodes within its network. This way the prefix delegated by the AR reaches all nodes, enabling them to configure a globally routable CoA. This results in a flat single domain network layer overlay on the multi-network physical topology of AIMNET.

In flat topology, CoA of a node has no relation with the node's position inside AIMNET, hence it avoids reconfiguration of CoA every time its MR changes position inside AIMNET. However, the disadvantage is that since all mobile networks in the AIMNET share the same prefix, the duplicate address detection (DAD) upon configuration of a CoA has to involve the entire AIMNET. As the neighbour solicitation (NS) message for Duplicate Address Detection (DAD) is not meant for multi-hop distribution, it needs to be extended [7] so that ND-Proxies (MRs) can assist mobile nodes in performing AIMNET-wide DAD.

In traditional MANETs, the number of routes increases with the number of network nodes [8]. In AIMNET, only MRs participate in ad hoc routing, hence the number of routes is not greatly affected by the number of end user nodes. However, MRs have to maintain next hop routes to all mobile nodes in the AIM-NET, and whenever a route is unknown the MR has to multicast NS messages in the AIMNET for address resolution. The associated overheads increase rapidly with the number of mobile nodes, limiting the AIMNETs scalability.

4.2 Hierarchical Topology

If, instead of relaying the unchanged AR prefix, each intermediate MR relays a subnetted prefix, a hierarchical topology is formed. This can be achieved by using IPv6 prefix options for DHCPv6. The top-level MR obtains a network prefix from the AR and delegates subnetted prefixes to MRs directly connected to it. These MRs further subnet the prefixes and delegate to other MRs. Consequently, all nodes configure CoAs with subnetted versions of the prefix originally delegated by the AR, forming a hierarchical network overlay. The CoAs are globally routable IP addresses that allow route aggregation inside the AIMNET.

In a hierarchical topology the subnetted prefixes can be aggregated to simplify routing. A subnet prefix higher in the hierarchy can, for the purpose of routing, represent all lower nodes. Thus, for successful routing, an MR has to know only about subnets directly attached to it. This reduces the routing overheads. However, since the CoA of a node now represents its position in the hierarchy,

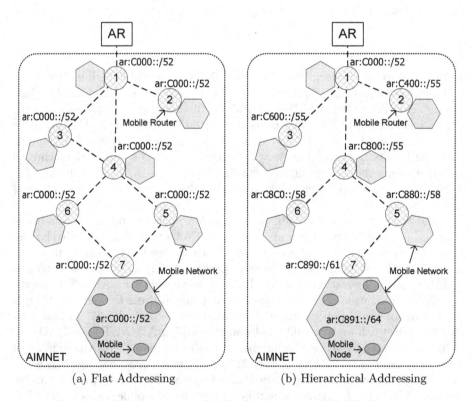

(a) Flat Addressing   (b) Hierarchical Addressing

Fig. 3. Prefix delegation in Ad Hoc Interconnected Mobile Networks

whenever the node changes its position, it may have to change its subnet prefix, configure a new CoA and perform a binding update. Also, if an MR (mobile network) changes its position in the AIMNET hierarchy, the resulting change in the AIMNET hierarchical topology may require a large scale reconfiguration of subnet prefixes and CoAs.

Route aggregation in hierarchical topology reduces routing overheads and improves scalability. On the other hand, hierarchical addressing may prevent optimal routing between two nodes within AIMNET. For example, in Fig. 3 MR7 and MR6 may be connected by a direct short route if flat addressing is used (Fig. 3a), but with hierarchical addressing this route may be eliminated (Fig. 3b). Consequently, communications between MR6 and MR7 have to be routed via MR4 and MR5.

4.3   The Proposed Two-Level Topology

For the same degree of mobility, nodes in a flat topology need to change their CoA less frequently than in a strictly hierarchical topology. However, this comes at a higher cost of routing and AIMNET-wide DAD. The hierarchical topology reduces these costs by creating a hierarchy of subnets. The hierarchical subnetting, however, results in nodes changing CoA more often than in flat topology. It is therefore desirable that the addressing topology for AIMNET balances these costs and benefits.

We propose to logically divide the AIMNET into two levels. The inter-MR ad hoc network forms the first level, and the mobile networks attached to the MRs form the second level. The first level can be seen as a semi-meshed backbone network of the AIMNET. The second level features networks of nodes attached to individual MRs, mobile with respect to external world but of relatively stable internal topologies.

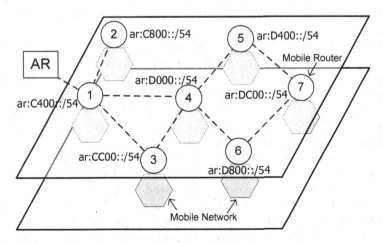

Fig. 4. Prefix delegation in AIMNET with two-level addressing topology

Since mobile networks at the lower level are separate entities, it is reasonable to assign them separate subnet addresses. This partitions the network into subnets formed around individual MRs and avoids AIMNET-wide duplicate address detection for each newly formed CoA. All nodes in a mobile network can be, for the purpose of routing, represented by their subnet address. Thanks to the flat structure of the ad hoc network of MRs (first level), the movement of MRs within AIMNET does not imply change of addresses and requires only update of routing information for a small number of MRs.

The implementation of prefix assignment to MRs will require multihop propagation of subnetted prefixes from AR to MRs along the ad hoc backbone of the AIMNET. The MRs assign prefix to their MNNs via router advertisement.

5   Routing in AIMNET

The prefix delegation mechanism and the proposed two-level addressing architecture allows the AIMNET and the mobile networks within it to look like an extension of the access network. This simplifies the routing and global access to the hosts inside mobile networks. Since the care-of-address (CoA) of a host in the mobile network is formed with the network prefix delegated by the access router, it reflects the actual location of the host in the Internet. As a result, any node in the Internet that knows the CoA of the host can directly send packets to it. These packets, bearing CoA of the host as the destination address, reach the access network via standard IP routing. The access network recognises the network prefix and subnet information and sends the packets to the appropriate border MR in the AIMNET. The border MR uses local routing mechanisms to forward these packets to their destination. Similarly, since a node in a mobile network has topologically correct CoA, it no longer needs to evade ingress filtering at access router by sending its packets through the tunnel between its MR and HA. The packets bearing CoA of the node as the source address are forwarded to the MR, then to BR, AR and eventually to the destination in the Internet.

One of the benefits of the proposed two-level topology is that a MR does not have to advertise individual routes to all nodes in its mobile network. It can use route aggregation and advertise a route to its mobile network using the allocated care-of prefix. In this scenario, when a node in a mobile network wishes to communicate with a node in another mobile network in AIMNET using destination node's CoA, the source node's MR only needs to find the MR that has advertised a route to the destination prefix.

In some cases the source node may not know the care-of address (CoA) of the destination node or may not know that the destination node is located within the AIMNET. If so, the source node will send packets to the Home Address (HoA) of the destination. When the source node's MR receives the packet, it knows that the destination address is not within the AIMNET and sends the packet outwards via a border router. The packet will eventually reach the home network of the destination where the HA will intercept the packet and send it to

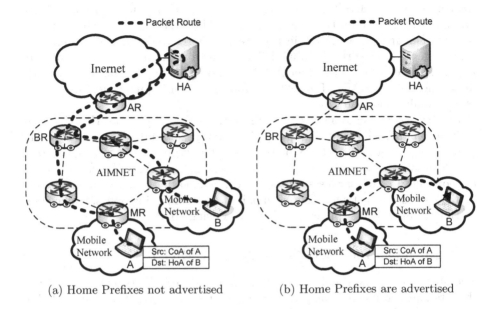

(a) Home Prefixes not advertised   (b) Home Prefixes are advertised

Fig. 5. Packet route between two nodes in AIMNET

the current CoA of the destination in the AIMNET. Thus a packet originating from AIMNET takes a long path through the destination's HA back to the AIMNET (fig 5a). This sub-optimal path will last until the destination node informs the source node about its current CoA as part of route optimisation procedure. However, when there is no Internet connection available to AIMNET, two nodes in the neighbouring mobile networks may not be able to communicate with each other.

To address the above (and related) problems, we propose that the MRs should advertise their home prefixes as well as their care-of prefixes. With this, packets using home addresses of the nodes within AIMNET as destination address can be routed directly without including home networks in the route. This will also help in the scenario when there is no Internet access available, and hence no valid care-of addresses can be formed in AIMNET. If this occurs, two nodes in different mobile networks of an AIMNET can communicate with each other using their home addresses.

6   Performance

We used OPNET simulation software to judge communication performance of AIMNET nodes. First we observed communication between different nodes in AIMNET, then we observed communication between nodes in AIMNET and nodes in the Internet. For both tasks we considered two scenarios. First we considered AIMNET moving in open areas where there are little geographic/geometric limitations on the shape of AIMNET e.g. in open field, desert, sea etc. The area of AIMNET in this scenario is set to 500m x 500m implying that all mobile networks remain within this area while moving as a group. In the second scenario, we consider AIMNET moving along a road. This scenario limits the area of AIMNET to 500m x 15m, representing movement of vehicles along a multi-lane road.

In both scenarios mobile networks move randomly within the AIMNET area while also moving forward as a group. The average speed of all mobile networks (AIMNET) is set to $\approx$ 60 km/h. However at any given time, the speed of a mobile network can be above or below this average. The AIMNET moves across the coverage area of an access router. All communicating nodes in AIMNET are in different mobile networks. For each pair of communicating nodes, traffic is set to 1KByte per second application layer data using UDP.

6.1   Communication between Nodes in AIMNET

The objectives of the simulation results presented here are twofold: i) to verify that standard ad hoc routing protocols can perform reasonably well in AIMNET and ii) to verify that two nodes in AIMNET can communicate with each other directly without involving their home agents and with reasonable quality. Since experimenting with a large number of protocols for a wide range of possible AIMNET scenarios is a task beyond the scope of this project, we only considered the most general classes of ad hoc routing protocols. Traditionally these protocols are classified into proactive (table-driven) and reactive (demand-driven) protocols. Proactive protocols require each node to maintain tables to store routing information, and use route updates (periodic and triggered by topological change) to maintain a consistent view of the network. The reactive protocols maintain only information for active routes i.e. they determine and maintain routes only when nodes need them to send data packets. For these simulations we selected AODV [9] and OSPFv3-MANET [10] as representative protocols of reactive and proactive routing respectively. We assume that if these protocols can perform adequately, future experiments can be conducted to see how the performance can be further improved by changing the inter-MR routing protocols.

Figures 6 and 7 show the simulation results for the open field and road scenarios respectively. The error bars represent the standard error of means. We can observe that with the increasing number of communicating nodes, the routing overheads of AODV increase whereas the overheads of OSPFv3 do not change much. This can be expected as AODV finds routes for each pair of communicating nodes while OSPFv3 maintains routing information irrespective of how many nodes are communicating. Therefore, for smaller AIMNETs where numbers of communicating nodes are expected to be low, AODV appears to be effective. Otherwise, for larger numbers of communicating nodes, OSPFv3 will be more suitable. It can also be observed that in the open field scenario the overall routing

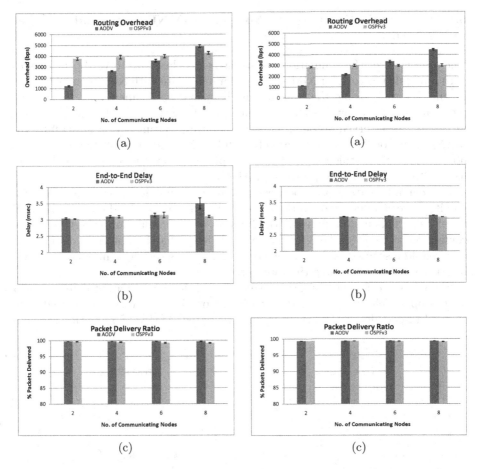

Fig. 6. Communication between nodes in AIMNET, area = 500m×500m

Fig. 7. Communication between nodes in AIMNET, area = 500m×15m

overheads are higher than in the road scenario. This is because the road scenario has a smaller area, which corresponds to higher node density; thus more mobile networks can find direct routes to other mobile networks. With these provisions in mind, we can easily conclude that routing overheads in AIMNET architecture are acceptable.

The end-to-end delay of packets in the simulated AIMNET scenarios generally remains around 3 msec. The packet delivery ratio remains high under all conditions. This demonstrates that data packets from a node in a mobile network can be routed to nodes in other mobile networks of the AIMNET. It also shows that under the simulated conditions, nodes in different mobile networks can communicate with each other with reasonable quality.

6.2   Communication between Nodes in AIMNET and Nodes in the Internet

The objectives of the simulation results presented here are to verify that nodes within mobile networks of AIMNET can communicate with correspondent nodes in the Internet using the routing mechanisms we defined and to observe performance of communication between nodes in AIMNET and nodes in the Internet. It was observed in the previous section that routing overhead of OSPFv3-MANET protocol remains relatively stable when number of communicating nodes increase. For this reason the results presented in this section are obtained using OSPFv3 as routing protocol in AIMNET.

The communication path between a node in a mobile network of AIMNET and its correspondent node in the Internet includes an IP cloud node in OPNET simulation. This node represents the Internet in the simulation. The IP cloud is configured to route packets with a random delay that is uniformly distributed between 40 msec and 60 msec. This delay represents the random delay incurred by packets when traversing the Internet.

Figures 8 and 9 show the average end-to-end delay and packet delivery ratio for the open field and the road scenarios respectively. It can be observed that the end-to-end delay of packets in the simulated AIMNET scenarios remains

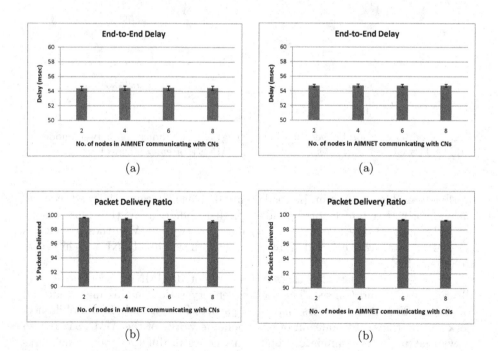

Fig. 8. Communication between nodes in AIMNET and Internet, AIMNET area = 500m×500m

Fig. 9. Communication between nodes in AIMNET and Internet, AIMNET area = 500m×15m

under 55 msec. The packet delivery ratio remains high under all conditions. This demonstrates that data packets from a node in a mobile network of AIMNET can be routed to nodes in the Internet and vice versa. It also shows that under the simulated conditions, the nodes in AIMNET can communicate with nodes in the Internet with reasonable quality.

7 Conclusion

In this paper we analysed different route optimisation methods and suggested the use of prefix delegation to support route optimisation in Ad Hoc Interconnected Mobile Network (AIMNET). We have also proposed a two-level addressing topology for AIMNET that supports prefix delegation based route optimisation. Finally, via simple simulation experiments, we have obtained results in support of our expectation that the proposed architecture is feasible and the nodes within it can communicate easily. These results encourage us to investigate the proposed scheme further. A more comprehensive performance assessment of the proposed scheme can be made when costs such as overheads due to routing and binding updates can be combined with address configuration overheads.

References

1. Devarapalli, V., Wakikawa, R., Petrescu, A., Thubert, P.: Network mobility (NEMO) basic support protocol. Rfc 3963. IETF (2005)
2. Ng, C., Thubert, P., Watari, M., Zhao, F.: Network mobility route optimization problem statement. Rfc 4888. IETF (2007)
3. Ng, C., Zhao, F., Watari, M., Thubert, P.: Network mobility route optimization solution space analysis. Rfc 4889. IETF (2007)
4. Khan, M.Q., Andresen, S.H., Khan, K.N.: Pros and cons of route optimization schemes for network mobility (NEMO) and their effects on handovers. In: Proceedings of the 8th International Conference on Frontiers of Information Technology, vol. 24, pp. 24:1–24:6 (2010)
5. Lim, H.J., Lee, D.Y., Kim, T.K., Chung, T.M.: A model and evaluation of route optimization in nested NEMO environment. IEICE Transactions on Communications E88-B (7), 2765–2776 (2005)
6. Hossain, M., Shahriar, A., Atiquzzaman, M., Ivancic, W.: Scalability analysis of NEMO prefix delegation-based schemes. In: International Conference on High Performance Switching and Routing (HPSR), pp. 107–112 (2010)
7. Jeong, J., Lee, K., Park, J., Kim, H.: Route optimization based on ND-proxy for mobile nodes in IPv6 mobile networks. In: IEEE 59th Vehicular Technology Conference, vol. 5, pp. 2461–2465 (2004)
8. López, J., Barceló, J.M., García-Vidal, J.: Analysing the overhead in mobile ad-hoc network with a hierarchical routing structure. In: International Working Conference Performance Modelling and Evaluation of Heterogeneous Networks (2005)
9. Perkins, C., Belding-Royer, E., Das, S.: Ad hoc On-Demand Distance Vector (AODV) Routing. Rfc 3561. IETF (2003)
10. Ogier, R., Spagnolo, P.: Mobile Ad Hoc Network (MANET) Extension of OSPF Using Connected Dominating Set (CDS) Flooding. Rfc 5614. IETF (2009)

Movement Speed Based Inter-probe Times for Neighbour Discovery in Mobile Ad-Hoc Networks

Matthew Orlinski and Nick Filer

School of Computer Science, University of Manchester, Manchester, M13 9PL, UK
{orlinskm,nick}@cs.manchester.ac.uk

Abstract. It is widely known that topology, wireless range, and the movement patterns of devices often impose severe limitations on the ability of devices to communicate in Mobile Wireless Ad-hoc Networks (MANETs). However, there has been less research into the effect of devices' movement speeds on network connectivity. In this paper we will look at two commonly used MANET movement patterns, Working Day Movement (WDM) and Random Walk Movement (RWM). This report will demonstrate using both of these movement patterns, that the time between neighbour discovery scans called the inter-probe time, can have a drastic effect on network connectivity. We will suggest a mechanism to choose inter-probe times based on the movement speeds of devices which can efficiently detect more than 99% of encounters between mobile devices carried by pedestrians. We will then propose a dynamic approach (PISTONS) which allows devices to alter inter-probe times based on context whilst preserving much of the network connectivity.

Keywords: mobile ad-hoc networks, pocket switched networks, neighbour discovery, inter-probe times.

1 Introduction

Network topology, wireless range and the movement of devices often impose severe limitations on the ability of devices to communicate in Mobile Wireless Ad-hoc Networks (MANETs). In two specific types of MANETs, Pocket Switched Networks (PSNs), and Vehicular ad-hoc networks (VANETs), data is often exchanged in a "store-wait-forward" [1,2] model which is constrained by the movement speed of devices [3]. Slower movement can mean longer inter-contact times, and messages are stored for longer periods.

Movement speed can also impact device discoverability. When one electronic device searches for another it can either do this continuously, consuming valuable power and channel capacity [2,4,5], or it can probe periodically using inquiry intervals as shown in Fig. 1. During an inquiry interval, Neighbour Discovery Requests (NDREQs) [6] are broadcast, listened for and replied to resulting in encounters between devices and perhaps data connections forming between devices a short time after they come into range of one another.

J. Zheng et al. (Eds.): Adhocnets 2012, LNICST 111, pp. 316–331, 2013.
© Institute for Computer Sciences, Social Informatics and Telecommunications Engineering 2013

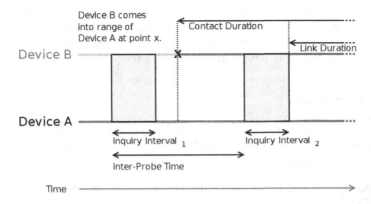

Fig. 1. Link and Contact Duration. Once a Neighbour Discovery Response (NDRES) has been received, a link can be established.

Choi et al. [3] reported that as the movement speed of devices increases in bounded simulations, devices encounter each other more frequently and energy consumption of devices can increase. The goal of this work is to provide a mechanism with which to choose inter-probe times (time between entering inquiry states, see Fig. 1) without detailed movement pattern information, whilst still giving predictable results. The aim is to suggest reasonable inter-probe times for changing network topologies where limited knowledge makes it difficult or impossible to base decision on past behaviours, or it is undesirable to have separate interfaces monitoring a devices' environment. To achieve this, we explore the use of movement speed, not only as a hindrance or help to network performance as Choi pointed out, but also as a means for choosing sensible inter-probe times and prolonging battery life.

Qin et al. [2] observed that smaller inter-probe times lead to smaller differences between link and contact durations, yet little work has been done on adequate inter-probe times for MANETs with movement patterns such as those found in PSNs [7]. In Section 3, we will look at the effect inter-probe times have in PSNs on the numbers and lengths of contacts detected.

Inter-probe times are of critical importance to some delay tolerant routing schemes for PSNs, as they often consider devices to be disconnected if they are not seen for one or more NDREQs [6]. Neighbouring devices may also be incorrectly considered connected for inordinate amounts of time when there is a lengthy wait between NDREQs. Data routing schemes such as [8,9,10] base routing decisions on the current environment in which mobile devices exist by using parameters such as movement direction, or the inter-connection time between two successive encounters. We will show in Section 3 that the accurate evaluation of inter-connection times is affected by the inter-probe times used. Furthermore, we will show that the Working Day Movement (WDM) [11] and Random Walk Movement (RWM) models upon which many simulated conclusions are reached, can affect conclusions reached about suitable inter-probe times. For example, in [12] it is stated that devices which move in the WDM pattern rather than RWM exhibit more continuous co-location and as a result, networks created using this model are more resilient to longer inter-probe times. Yet, as we will show in Section 3, the WDM is not resilient to long inter-probe times.

1.1 Related Work

It is important to understand the distinction between inter-probe times and inquiry intervals [5]. The difference between the two is shown in Fig. 1 and can be summarised as follows:

1. An inquiry interval is the period in which devices broadcast and listen for NDREQs.
2. Inter-probe time is the time between inquiry intervals.

The length of inquiry intervals is important to both broadcasting and listening devices because if the interval is too short to completely understand a NDREQ, a loss of an NDREQ happens [5]. In the MobiClique experiments [13], 50% of participant devices are successfully detected during the day whereas at night, success rates go up to nearly 100%. This difference has been attributed to static devices in hotel rooms at night and could be caused by inquiry interval length, inter-probe times, or both.

To find moving devices, inquiry intervals must happen frequently enough to ensure that changes in network topology are detected. The inter-probe times can be constant, or dynamically derived from network or other environmental and contextual sensors. Some schemes already exist for inter-probe time choices based on a wide range of different variables such as energy levels and inter-contact distributions [1,5]. However, the existing methods used to determine inter-probe times have a number of drawbacks, including but not limited to: Reliance on high level information such as commuter traffic levels, complex calculations to estimate encounter probabilities, and the need to store large amounts of information on past encounters.

Work from Qin et al. [2] considered the impact of inter-probe times on link durations. The outcome was a method to calculate optimum inter-probe times to maximise device throughput with limited energy using the Random Waypoint (RWP) and RWM movement patterns which we now know have different inter-contact and duration distributions to those found in PSNs. To exploit the self-similar behavioural patterns of human movement [7,14], Wu et al. [4] calculated inter-probe times from periods of rush hour traffic using a method which requires a high level knowledge of the devices' empirical environment.

Wang et al. [15] proposed an optimisation framework to compute optimal inter-probe times as a function of arrival rate called STAR. Extensive work on STAR introduced the concept of the "Missing Probability", the probability that a contact will not be detected in different contact distributions assuming the inter-probe time is the same between devices. After observing that inter-contact distribution differs over time, they also stated that optimal inter-probe times will vary with time, and that inter-probe times should be shorter in time slots with "high arrival rates" so the missing probability can be minimised. However, STAR misses a relatively large fraction of short term contacts [15], which has implications for network connectivity as we will show later in Section 3.4.

All the methods seen so far require in-depth knowledge of either energy usage or contact statistics. DWARF [1] requires no prior knowledge of contact patterns but performs best with continuous monitoring of environmental conditions in order to initiate inquiry intervals.

2   Experimental Environment

Our experiments will be conducted using the synthetic movement models Working Day Movement (WDM) [11] and Random Walk Movement (RWM) [16]. Unlike research topics such as the opportunistic delivery of data, empirical data-sets found in the CRAWDAD repository [1] can not be used to validate methods for choosing inter-probe times. At the core of each empirical experiment is the inter-probe time giving GPS or encounter information for participants. In many cases inter-probe times are measured in minutes, and can not easily be lowered retrospectively. Accurate studies into the effects of inter-probe times require a higher degree of fidelity.

RWM's inter-contact times are distinct from that of WDM in that they are light-tailed [17], and the devices it models move independently and are identically distributed in a bounded region. WDM is being used for realistic pedestrian movement as devices are not evenly distributed and inter-contact times follow a power-law distribution [11]. In [12] it is stated that devices which move in the WDM pattern rather than RWM exhibit more continuous co-location and as a result, networks created using this model are more resilient to longer inter-probe times. Yet, Section 3 will show that WDM is not actually as resilient to long inter-probe times as we once thought.

Synthetic movement models also allow us to experiment with a higher level of participation than is usually possible in real life experiments. Acquiring enough devices and participants for an empirical study is extremely difficult and we often limit ourselves in our predictions and applications based on this difficulty. To give our research some lasting impact [13], we should instead be striving to achieve what is possible within realistic limits.

For realism, the movement models used in this paper restrict participants to paths found in real life city layouts. The scenarios used are shown in Table 1. The Manhattan and Helsinki scenarios are bundled with The One Simulator [12]. The University scenario ensures that device movement is restricted to a map of the Kilburn and IT building in the University of Manchester shown in Fig. 2. University was created especially for this work to replicate the densely populated campus and conference environments found in many empirical data-sets [2].

---

[1] CRAWDAD Repository http://crawdad.cs.dartmouth.edu/
[2] The scenario files used with The One Simulator can be downloaded at http://bit.ly/JNOeQU

Table 1. Simulation Environment Sizes

	University	Manhattan	Helsinki
Number of devices	235	200	200
Wireless Range (m)	10		
Area Size (m)	380 x 265	6000 x 5600	7200 x 6800
Days	3		

When paired with the WDM movement model, the scenario maps give a similar contact distributions as those found in Reality Mining data-sets. Empirical studies [6,14] have found that inter-contact times of humans follow a power-law distribution (over the range of 10 minutes to 1 day) in office and conference settings. In the University model, the same heavy-tailed inter-contact and contact durations are present as shown in Fig. 2 with a power of 2.1 between the same range.

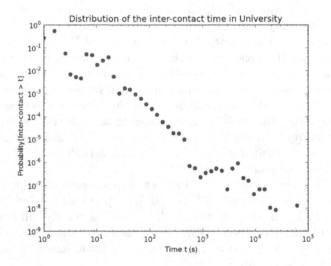

Fig. 2. Power-law distribution of inter-connection times between 1 second and 1 day for the University using WDM

The range of movement speeds used in these experiments were 0.8-1.4 and 7-30 m/s. For convenience the different speed ranges are referred to as "slow" and "fast" respectively. Slow movement closely resembles human walking speeds, and has been restricted to a maximum of 1.4 m/s. Fast movement mimics fast traffic speeds up to 30 m/s.

3   Choosing Inter-probe Times

When a continuous inquiry interval is not possible, what should the inter-probe time which separates inquiry intervals be so devices do not miss crucial encounters? In this section inter-probe times are calculated based on the movement speeds of the wireless device carriers in a manner which guarantees over 99% of encounters are detected in different movement patterns. Furthermore, our equations allow for acceptable levels of network connectivity loss to be specified using the variable α. A smaller α will result in longer inter-probe times, fewer detected encounters, and produce a less connected network.

Our method for choosing inter-probe times depends on knowing the maximum speed at which devices can travel B measured in metres per second, as well as the range of the wireless interface in metres R. As human interactions can be measured using inter-connection or mixing times (time needed to "mix" with all other devices) which could suggest frequencies of interactions, we have adopted an approach similar to that of the Nyquist–Shannon sampling theorem but using the speed of devices, not the bandwidth. The method is called the Inter-Probe time Calculation (IPC). Given an approximate acceptable ratio of missed encounters via the variable α, the inter-probe time can then be calculated using the IPC Equations 1 and 2:

$$f_s \geq \frac{2B}{R} \tag{1}$$

$$\tau = \frac{\frac{1}{f_s}}{\alpha} \tag{2}$$

To give an example, an inter-probe time τ is calculated using a uniform sampling rate f_s which should be more than twice the maximum relative movement speed of target devices in m/s. In other words, $f_s \geq \frac{2B}{R}$. This form is taken from the work by Nyquist and Shannon with baseband bandwidth, B replaced with speed in m/s. The final inter-probe time τ is then calculated by dividing the fraction $\frac{1}{f_s}$ by the ratio α.

The ratio α, can be within the range $0 < \alpha \leq 1$. It represents the proportion of encounters that we wish to detect. For example, take someone walking at a leisurely 1.4 m/s with a Bluetooth device with communication range 10 m. Then the uniform sampling rate f_s should be at least 3.57 s (Equation 1). If detecting every device in range is not a priority then the ratio α can be lowered. For example, an α of 0.01 will produce a very long inter-probe time of 357.14 s in our walking example because $\tau = \frac{\frac{1}{f_s}}{\alpha} = \frac{\frac{1}{0.28}}{(0.01)} = 357.14$ s.

What value α finally takes will be application specific. An α of 1 should be used for applications where maximum connectivity is crucial and a continuous inquiry interval is impossible. In energy constrained environments, or applications where the probability of missing an encounter can be quite high, a longer inter-probe time is desirable and α should be lowered. Examples of inter-probe times calculated by IPC for cases where the maximum speed of devices are set at 1.4 m/s and 30 m/s are provided in Fig. 3.

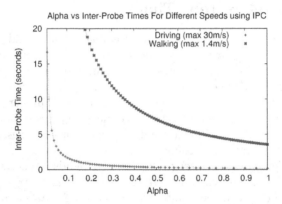

Fig. 3. Inter-probe times produced by the IPC algorithm for slow and fast moving devices and α values between 0.01-1

3.1 Encounters Captured

The results of different α ratios on various network measurements for different movement patterns are presented in the following subsections.

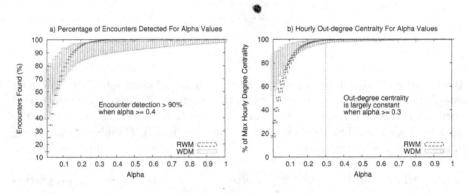

Fig. 4. Encounters captured and hourly out-degree centrality percentage using α values 0.01-1 in IPC in different movement models

Fig. 4a shows the effect α has on the number of encounters captured for different movement patterns. Encounter percentage is measured against continuous, never ending inquiry intervals in the same experiments. The results in Fig. 4a show that that IPC produces a higher range of values for captured encounters in the WDM model scenarios. This variation is partly caused by the different movement patterns present in the WDM model, and also the different mixing times between the scenario densities. When using the WDM pattern in sparse scenarios, there is less of an effect when longer inter-probe times are used as brief encounters are so rare.

3.2 The Effect of Inter-Probe Times on Hourly Out-Degree Centrality

To show how inter-probe times affects the network connectivity, we have plotted hourly out-degree centrality rather than link duration [2] against different α values in Fig. 4b. Hourly out-degree centrality is used to measure the number of devices encountered in hourly time frames and therefore has implications for data dissemination. As connections in PSNs are asymmetrical, hourly out-degree centrality measures the number of connections that a device directs to others — it is a measure of gregariousness of devices. In contrast, in-degree centrality would be a separate measure to gauge the popularity of a device.

Using the IPC equations 1 and 2 from Section 3, hourly out-degree centrality follows the same curved shape as the total number of events captured in the previous Section 3.1. When α is greater than 0.3, 99% of the devices which come within range are detected using IPC.

3.3 Total Encounter Time

The total cumulative connection time of all devices in the network is critically dependent on inter-probe times. Figs 5a and 5b show that average encounter time increases with decreases to α, whilst total encounter time in the network goes down.

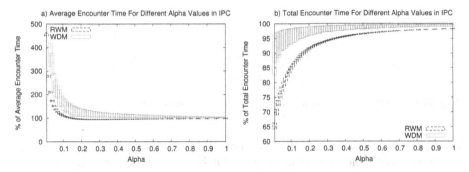

Fig. 5. Average encounter times and total encounter times per experiment for IPC using different α values compared with continuously scanning

Fig. 6a and Fig. 6b show that fewer shorter encounters are detected when inter-probe times are longer. The number of shorter encounters recorded drops dramatically with longer inter-probe times in both the RWM and WDM models. What affect missing these shorter encounters has on network connectivity is covered in more detail in the next section.

3.4 Short Encounters Matter

Encounter duration in the WDM model and in PSNs has a heavy tailed distribution [6,14], with the vast majority of encounters being brief. Fig. 7 shows

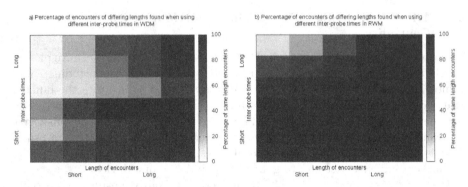

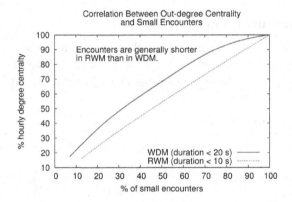

Fig. 6. A reduction of short duration encounters using inter-probe times compared to continuously scanning is more prominent when using RWM

Fig. 7. Correlation between number of short term encounters and degree centrality

the relationship between two of the measurements introduced so far, hourly out-degree centrality and shorter encounters for both the WDM and RWM movement models. Fig. 7 shows a very high correlation between the number of shorter encounters discovered and out-degree centrality in both the RWM and WDM models. This near linear relationship suggests that network connectedness in PSNs comes from the devices which move around a lot, rather than the static devices. Detecting the shorter encounters will be essential for preserving network connectivity, as the devices which connect to the most others, do so for short periods of time.

4   Dynamic Inter-probe Times

The previous section highlighted the importance of short encounters to network connectivity. However, because of the need to preserve battery life, the short inter-probe times needed to detect shorter encounters should only be applied during times with high arrival rates [15]. There are a number of different challenges when considering this problem:

1. Firstly, How is a "correct" inter-probe time chosen? Is this choice based on efficiency like in [2], or is the desire to encounter a single device or every device possible? This challenge has been addressed somewhat using the IPC system in the previous sections.
2. Secondly, how is a device to determine whether the inter-probe interval should be changed? A single interface cannot see the world around it at a higher frequency than it is probing.
3. Lastly, how can devices choose their own inter-probe times, thus making the devices truly independent and asynchronous?

The answer to the first challenge is simple, it is down to the devices being used and the application. For pertinence to a variety of different scenarios, this topic shall be left open. As for the second and third challenges, there are many different ways with which to shorten inter-probe times, including but not limited to:

1. Periodically lowering inter-probe times to see if more events are captured; And if so, choose a more suitable inter-probe time.
2. Lowering inter-probe times when an encounter takes place to see if more events around it can be captured.

An inter-probe time of 3.57s for PSNs made entirely of pedestrians would be sufficient to discover over 99% of encounters due to the limited maximum speed and movement patterns of the participants (see Section 3). However, such a fast time between inquiry intervals is not needed throughout as no new devices are seen for long periods of time [3]. Discovering what inter-probe times to use and when, and achieving this using asynchronous, distributed methods are discussed in the following sections.

4.1   Distributed Dynamic Inter-probe Time Selection

In this section we will present an inter-probe time selection process called PIS-TONS which alters inter-probe times based on movement speed and the results of inquiry intervals. We will compare PISTONS to 2 recent methods from the literature, STAR [15] and DWARF [1] by testing each algorithm using the scenarios and movements speeds presented in Section 2.

PISTONS increases inter-probe time when an inquiry interval results in no neighbouring devices being discovered as presented in Algorithm 1. When an encounter between two devices has been detected in PISTONS, α is reset to $\alpha = 1$ and inter-probe times are recalculated on both devices. This is because a single encounter is treated as an indication that more may follow due to the bursty nature of PSNs [14]. Ideally, PISTONS would give longer average inter-probe times than IPC whilst giving encounter discovery rates, and an out-degree centrality close to that of a continuous inquiry interval.

PISTONS does not partition time into arbitrary time frames, or attempt to base inter-probe times on previous encounters because of the possibility of not

---

Algorithm 1. PISTONS algorithm

 1: **if** CurrentTime > (LastChecked + InterProbeTime) **then**
 2: *EnterInquiryInterval*
 3: **if** Neighbour Detected **then**
 4:   $\alpha = 1$
 5:   SetInterProbeTime(α)
 6: **else**
 7:   **if** $\alpha > 0.3$ **then**
 8:    $\alpha = \alpha - 0.01$
 9:   **end if**
10:   SetInterProbeTime(α)
11: **end if**
12: LastChecked = CurrentTime
13: **end if**

14: **procedure** SETINTERPROBETIME(α)
15: $f_s = \frac{2B}{R}$
16: InterProbeTime $= \tau = \frac{\frac{1}{f_s}}{\alpha}$
17: **end procedure**

---

matching individual scenarios. Furthermore, framing requires complicated strat-ification as human contact behaviour is self-similar [14] (See all the variations of STAR in [15]). Stratification of time frames may improve the performance of PISTONS in some real world networks, but is costly in terms of implementation and not easy to translate to other movement patterns or device densities.

In PISTONS, inter-probe times are increased by decrementing the α used in the IPC algorithm from Section 3 after each unsuccessful neighbour discovery attempt until α reaches 0.3. At $\alpha = 0.3$, the curve of hourly out-degree centrality seen in Section 3.2 decreases rapidly and PISTONS must guard against the loss of short encounters in order to preserve network connectivity (see Section 3.4). For example, when α has no minimum value in fast moving, dense scenarios using RWM, average hourly out-degree centrality is 0.581. However, if the minimum allowed α is set to 0.3, average hourly out-degree centrality is much higher at 0.629.

By decreasing α after each unsuccessful neighbour discovery, the rate at which inter-probe times increase in PISTONS varies depending on the movement speed of devices. The rate of inter-probe time increase can affect network connectivity differently depending on the movement model being used. Increasing inter-probe times more quickly affects network out-degree centrality negatively in RWM Models as shown in Table 2. As a result, the decrement by 0.01 method for α is used. However, it is worth noting here that when using WDM patterns, the effect on out-degree centrality of increasing inter-probe times more quickly is much less noticeable, and decreasing α quickly can lower the number of inquiry intervals necessary to detect a high proportion of network out-degree centrality.

Table 2. Network Out-Degree Centrality (ODC) and percentage of Inquiry Interval Saved (IIS) compared to continuously scanning at the rate $\alpha = 1$ for different α decrease methods in PISTONS

Scenario	α decrease method and results							
	No Decrease		$\alpha - 0.01$		$e^{-(\alpha-0.01)}$		$e^{-(1.5*(\alpha-0.01))}$	
	ODC	IIS	ODC	IIS	ODC	IIS	ODC	IIS
RWM, Sparse, Slow	0.060339	-	0.060187	45.77%	0.059252	62.79%	0.059120	63.61%
RWM, Sparse, Fast	0.352501	-	0.262916	88.15%	0.224611	89.59%	0.220828	89.95%
RWM, Dense, Slow	0.102024	-	0.101966	33.85%	0.101641	55.42%	0.101552	56.85%
RWM, Dense, Fast	0.731342	-	0.628351	86.15%	0.488322	90.31%	0.470920	91.09%
WDM, Sparse, Slow	0.001315	-	0.001314	20.13%	0.001314	20.27%	0.001314	20.34%
WDM, Sparse, Fast	0.001262	-	0.001234	26.58%	0.001233	27.04%	0.001233	27.44%
WDM, Dense, Slow	0.008506	-	0.008487	56.66%	0.008368	60.51%	0.008379	60.68%
WDM, Dense, Fast	0.005284	-	0.004348	82.43%	0.004274	82.70%	0.004268	82.94%

4.2 Results

The resulting inter-probe times of PISTONS, STAR, and DWARF for WDM experiments are presented in Fig. 8. The figures show that PISTONS tends to lower the mean inter-probe times more than the other algorithms as movement speed increases. The inter-probe time of DWARF does not change with speed. This is partly due to the algorithm provided in [1] which does not alter inter-probe times when a remote device is discovered. Furthermore, as the device density in slow and fast experiments is the same, the mechanism for choosing inter-probe times in DWARF is not effected by the movement speed.

PISTONS performs as well if not better than DWARF and STAR in terms of preserving cumulative encounter time in just about every random movement scenario as shown in Fig. 9. When movement speeds are increased, PISTONS provides the longest cumulative connection time in both sparse and dense environments because of the lower inter-probe times. When using the WDM pattern, movement speed has little affect on cumulative connection times as devices are stationary for long periods, therefore those results are not presented here.

Fig. 10 and Fig. 11 show the resulting out-degree centrality loss associated with the different algorithms. Generally, because of low inter-probe times, DWARF performs well in slower environments with PISTONS being better at preserving network connectivity as speeds increase.

Fig. 10 shows the out-degree centrality loss associated with random movement patterns. The results show that as speed increases, the algorithms start to lose the ability to detect shorter encounters and out-degree centrality suffers. PISTONS handles faster scenarios better than either DWARF or STAR because it detects the shorter encounters. For all of the fast moving random scenarios, the outcome of this is that PISTONS looses on average 20% of out-degree centrality, whereas STAR loses 73%.

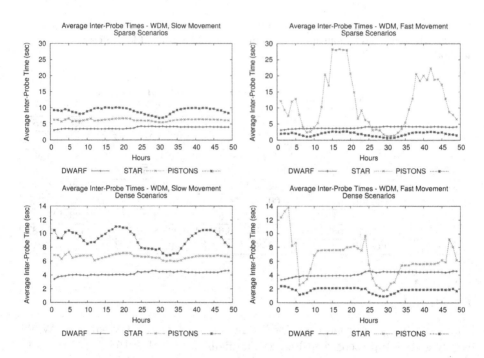

Fig. 8. Average hourly inter-probe times for different movement speeds

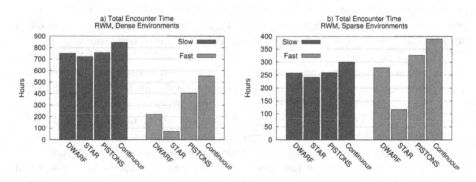

Fig. 9. Total connection times in fast moving scenarios

Fig. 11 shows out-degree centrality for the WDM experiments. In the slow moving WDM experiments, DWARF detects slightly more (but less than 1%) short term connections than STAR due to its ability to detect changes in signal strength, and thus DWARF produces a slightly higher average hourly out-degree centrality then STAR. PISTONS outperforms both STAR and DWARF in terms of out-degree centrality in fast moving environments at the expense of more inquiry intervals. In dense WDM senarios, PISTONS only loses 18% of the mean

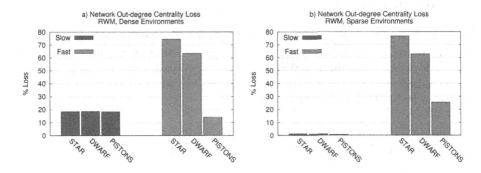

Fig. 10. Out-degree centrality loss for PISTONS, STAR, and DWARF modes compared to continuous inquiry intervals in random movement patterns

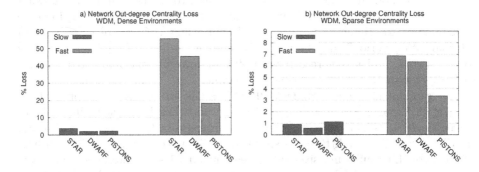

Fig. 11. Out-degree centrality loss for PISTONS, STAR, and DWARF modes compared to continuous inquiry intervals using the WDM model

hourly out-degree centrality when speed is increased, where as DWARF loses 45% and STAR 55%. However, DWARF will actually use a quarter of the inquiry intervals produced by PISTONS in this case. Further improvements in the out-degree centrality/number of inquiry intervals ratio for PISTONS may be gained in WDM experiments by decreasing α faster after unsuccessful inquiry intervals as shown in Table 2, or in future work by:

1. Including information on past behaviours as in STAR-PTS [15].
2. Changing base speed, B to be dependent on actual movement speed at the time, detected for example by accelerometers on mobile phones.
3. Contextual adaptation of α, for example, if large numbers of devices are detected without subsequent data being exchanged, then it may be desirable to decrease α to preserve battery life.

5   Conclusions

We investigated the design of an inter-probe times calculation algorithm which uses the movement speeds of devices as a method of ensuring encounters between mobile devices are not missed. We used the hourly out-degree centrality measure as an indication of temporal network connectivity due to the ever changing nature of PSNs. Our key contributions were:

1. The IPC calculation for inter-probe times in PSNs.
2. Design and validation of PISTONS which can vary inter-probe times in order to save energy.
3. Discovery that the detection of shorter encounters is crucial to preserving hourly out-degree centrality and thus network connectivity in dynamic networks.

Our IPC method from Section 3 can also be used to calculate inter-probe times in the first instance for other dynamic methods, not just PISTONS. In some preliminary experiments we have found that using IPC where $\alpha = 1$ in an "initialisation period" may be useful for finding the rate of topological change of a network, and therefore can be useful for lowering the number of inquiry intervals for the remainder of some time frame.

For random movement models, PISTONS has an average inter-probe time that is 78% longer when movement is slow than when it is fast (using the two speed ranges in this paper). In contrast, the inter-probe times of both STAR and DWARF change very little with speed in random scenarios, and thus both of these algorithms suffer massive out-degree centrality losses when speeds increase.

When using the WDM pattern, contact durations are Pareto distributed and new contact arrivals are self-similar [14]. Despite exploiting this self-similar behaviour, STAR was shown in Fig. 10 to be less reliable than PISTONS in preserving hourly out-degree centrality in dense scenarios and when movement speed is fast. PISTONS gave encouraging overall results in the fast WDM experiments, suffering an overall 11% loss of hourly out-degree centrality, compared to 26% using DWARF and 31% using STAR.

Compared with IPC using $\alpha = 1$, PISTONS loses 2.7% of the hourly out-degree centrality but reduces the number of inquiry intervals needed by 65%. Whether this 2.7% loss in out-degree centrality is critical for data dissemination applications remains to be seen, it may depend on a number of other questions not yet explored:

1. How are mixing and inter-connection times affected by IPC and PISTONS?
2. Should inquiry interval lengths be adapted in a similar way to that of inter-probe times?
3. What are the effects of inter-probe times on end-to-end data link times?

References

1. Izumikawa, H., Pitkanen, M., Ott, J., Timm-Giel, A., Bormann, C.: Energy-efficient adaptive interface activation for Delay/Disruption tolerant networks. In: ICACT, vol. 1, pp. 645–650 (February 2010)
2. Qin, S., Feng, G., Zhang, Y.: How contact probing affects the transmission capacity and energy consumption in DTNs. In: ICC (June 2011)
3. Choi, B.J., Shen, X.: Adaptive asynchronous sleep scheduling protocols for delay tolerant networks. Mobile Computing 10(9), 1283–1296 (2011)
4. Wu, X., Brown, K., Sreenan, C.: Exploiting rush hours for Energy-Efficient contact probing in opportunistic data collection. In: ICDCSW, pp. 240–247 (June 2011)
5. Yang, D., Shin, J., Kim, J., Kim, C.: Asynchronous probing scheme for the optimal energy-efficient neighbor discovery in opportunistic networking. In: PERCOM 2009, Washington, DC (2009)
6. Hui, P.: People are the network: experimental design and evaluation of social-based forwarding algorithms. Tech. Rep. (2008)
7. Gonzalez, M., Hidalgo, C., Barabasi, A.: Understanding individual human mobility patterns. Nature 453(7196), 779–782 (2008)
8. Sandulescu, G., Nadjm-Tehrani, S.: Adding redundancy to replication in window-aware delay-tolerant routing. JCM 5(2), 117–129 (2010)
9. Small, T., Haas, Z.: Resource and performance tradeoffs in delay-tolerant wireless networks. In: SIGCOMM, pp. 260–267 (2005)
10. Zhang, X., Neglia, G., Kurose, J., Towsley, D.: Performance Modeling of Epidemic Routing. In: Boavida, F., Plagemann, T., Stiller, B., Westphal, C., Monteiro, E. (eds.) NETWORKING 2006. LNCS, vol. 3976, pp. 827–839. Springer, Heidelberg (2006)
11. Ekman, F., Keranen, A., Karvo, J., Ott, J.: Working day movement model. In: SIGMOBILE, pp. 33–40 (2008)
12. Keranen, A., Ott, J., Karkkainen, T.: The ONE simulator for DTN protocol evaluation. In: SIMUTools, p. 55 (2009)
13. Pietilainen, A.K., Oliver, E., Lebrun, J., Varghese, G., Crowcroft, J., Diot, C.: Experiments in mobile social networking. Tech. Rep. (2008)
14. Wang, Y., Krishnamachari, B., Valente, T.: Findings from an empirical study of fine-grained human social contacts. In: WONS, pp. 153–160 (February 2009)
15. Wang, W., Motani, M., Srinivasan, V.: Opportunistic energy-efficient contact probing in delay-tolerant applications. Trans. Netw. 17(5), 1592–1605 (2009)
16. Keranen, A., Karkkainen, T., Ott, J.: Simulating mobility and DTNs with the ONE (Invited paper). Journal of Communications 5(2) (2010)
17. Sharma, G., Mazumdar, R., Shroff, B.: Delay and capacity Trade-Offs in mobile ad hoc networks: A global perspective. Trans. Netw. 15(5), 981–992 (2007)

Online Algorithms for Adaptive Optimization in Heterogeneous Delay Tolerant Networks

Wissam Chahin[1], Francesco De Pellegrni[2],
Rachid El-Azouzi[1], and Amar Pazad Azad[3]

[1] CERI/LIA, University of Avignon, 339, chemin des Meinajaries, Avignon, France
[2] CREATE-NET Via alla Cascata 56/D, Povo, Trento, Italy
[3] SOE, UCSC, USA

Abstract. We study in this paper heterogeneous delay tolerant networks formed by different classes of nodes. We assume that two hop is the forwarding strategy to deliver messages from a source node to destination node and the goal is to optimize the probability of delivering a message in the presence of different classes of mobiles, while satisfying a given energy budget. Using our model, in particular, we transform the joint energy constraint into separate constraints, one per class. This allows us to characterize the optimal strategies and provides us with a suitable framework for the design of multi-dimensional stochastic control algorithms that achieve optimal performance at runtime in spite of the lack of full information on the network state and in presence of different classes of mobiles. A thorough analysis of the convergence properties and stability of our algorithms is presented.

Keywords: Delay tolerant networks, multi dimensional optimal control, stochastic approximation, projected ODE.

1 Introduction

Delay Tolerant Networks (DTNs) gained the interest of the research community in recent past [1] since they have been identified as a promising mean to transport data in intermittently connected networks. DTNs in particular, are able to sustain communications in a networked system where continuous connectivity cannot be assumed [2,3,1]. In DTNs, messages are carried from source to destination via relay nodes adopting the so-called "store and carry" forwarding, which basically leverages on the underlying node mobility pattern. The key problem in DTNs is thus to efficiently route messages towards the intended destination. It is worth observing that due to frequent disruptions, traditional techniques for routing perform very poorly in this context. Furthermore, mobile nodes rarely possess information on the upcoming encounters they are going to experience [4].

An intuitive and robust solution is to disseminate multiple copies of the message in the network. This is meant to ensure that at least some of them will reach the destination node within some deadline [5,6] with high probability. The above scheme is referred as epidemic forwarding [7], in analogy to spread of infectious

J. Zheng et al. (Eds.): Adhocnets 2012, LNICST 111, pp. 332–350, 2013.
© Institute for Computer Sciences, Social Informatics and Telecommunications Engineering 2013

diseases. In literature, several variants of epidemic forwarding exist, including *spray and wait* [5] and *two hop routing protocol* [8], implementing different trade-offs between delay and number of released copies.

We consider a heterogeneous DTN, that is, a DTN with heterogeneous relay nodes and with different physical characteristics, e.g. transmission range, mobility, etc, [9,10,11].

To this respect, our starting assumption, as in [9], [10], and [12] is that according to their physical characteristics, nodes group into classes homogeneous with respect to routing. More precisely, two nodes belong to the same class if they have *same intermeeting intensities with source and destination nodes*. Each node is different in terms of mobility and other characteristics. Heterogeneous DTNs are the subject of early on papers, mainly adopting algorithmic approach [9] or oriented towards implementation issues [13].

In this context, the fundamental question that arises naturally when one models the trade off of network resources for delivery probability, is how to exploit diversity of contact patterns in order to improve the message delivery performance in DTNs.

In [12], we derived the closed-form structure of the optimal forwarding policy for heterogeneous DTNs using tools from optimal control. Then we were able to identify the existence of a peculiar order among classes that exists with respect to optimal forwarding; such order is fully determined by the network parameters, i.e., the intermeeting intensities of each class of mobiles with the source and the destination. Leveraging on the properties of the so determined optimal forwarding policy, we could design online algorithms exploiting this order and able converge to the optimal control policy over time.

In this paper, we provide major enhancements of these algorithms and make a step forward by introducing the two-time scale stochastic approximation and presenting thorough analysis of their convergence. More precisely, we deeply investigate these algorithms' performance and rigourously prove their convergence to some limit set of Ordinary Differential Equations (ODEs), then we use Lyaponuv functions to confirm their stability. Furthermore, we show that the online implementation of such algorithms does not require explicit estimation of the system parameters.

In literature, some attempts to address optimal control for heterogeneous DTNs have been performed in [11] and [10]. The algorithmic formulation that we provide here introduces not only a characterization of the optimal strategy, but also an algorithmic distributed implementation suitable for disconnected operations.

Related Studies: With the aim of optimizing network performance, several previous works addressed the control of forwarding schemes in DTNs [4,14,8,6]. The work [8] proposed to control two-hop forwarding and optimized the system performance by choosing the average duration of timers for message discarding. Authors of [6] considered a homogeneous network and described a general framework for the optimal control of monotone relay strategies. The optimal control was proved there to be of dynamic type; the first work claiming the optimality of dynamic policies was [14], limited to epidemic routing. In line with [11], our formulation builds also on multidimensional control. Also, we extend the approach in [15] leveraging stochastic approximation algorithms because they overcome the explicit estimation of network parameters. In fact, such an estimation is per se a difficult task in disconnected systems [16]. Furthermore, we observe that this operation becomes critical in the case of multiple classes of mobiles since a number of such estimates would be required.

The heterogeneity in mobile ad hoc DTNs is well documented in literature, [17,18]. However, very few papers addressed this aspect from the modeling perspective. One such work is [10]; the authors assume that nodes may migrate from one class to another. In our framework nodes are fixed within one class. Also, in [13], the authors showed that the presence of heterogeneity has controversial effect on the delivery probability. I.e., it cannot be related in a straightforward manner to the performance of the system. In [11] a general setting for the optimality of controls of a DTN was presented.

Overall, the main contributions of this work are the following. First, we introduce a new perspective of the optimal forwarding problem in DTNs and characterize its structure in section 3. Second, based on this structure, we develop in section 4 our stochastic approximation algorithms and rigourously prove their stability.

2   System Model

Consider a network composed of $N + 2$ mobile nodes: a source node, denoted by s which generates messages, a destination node, denoted by d which acts as sink of the data packets, and N potential relay nodes. We consider a sparse network

Table 1. Glossary of Notations

Symbol	Meaning
N_i	number of nodes of class i
λ_{si}	intermeeting intensity for nodes of class i with the source
λ_{id}	intermeeting intensity for nodes of class i with the destination
τ	timeout value
h	time threshold
Δ	time slot
K	$\frac{\tau}{\Delta}$
X_i^k	number of infected nodes of class i at slot k
$\widehat{X}(\theta_i^k)$	estimate of the average number of infected nodes of class i that could potentially be attained at slot k
Ψ	energy constraint
$F_D(t)$	delivery probability at (t)
u_i	forwarding probability to class i
θ_i	$= \sum_{k=0}^{K-1} u_i(k), i = 1, 2$
ψ_i	the maximum number of nodes of class i that can be infected

where the average euclidean distance of nodes is much larger than the communication range. Hence, a network where any two nodes are not in contact at any time instant, i.e., no two nodes are in communication range of each other with high probability. We assume that two nodes are able to communicate when they are within reciprocal radio range, and communications are bidirectional. Thus, as customary in DTNs literature, we consider nodes *meeting times* only, i.e., time instants at which a pair of not-connected nodes fall within reciprocal radio range. However, we also assume that contact intervals are sufficient to exchange an entire message and every message sent by a node is received successfully by its neighbor.

Heterogeneous DTNs considered in this paper are composed of M classes of relay nodes: class i, $1 \leq i \leq M$, contains N_i nodes, and $N = \sum_i N_i$. We will often refer to the case $M = 2$ for the sake of clarity; results shown later easily extend to hold in general unless otherwise stated. We refer to the M class system as the M-dimensional (mD) system for the sake of brevity.

We denote intermeeting times, briefly intermeetings, the successive contact times between a node with another node. Intermeetings are considered to follow an exponential law with given intensity; this model was shown to fit well random synthetic mobility, e.g., Random Walk, Random Direction, Random Waypoint [19]. The validity of models based on contact times have been well studied in several previous papers [6,15]. However, in heterogeneous networks, intermeetings of s and d with relay nodes have intensity that *depends on the class relays belong to*. We let λ_{si} and λ_{id} be the intermeeting intensity for nodes of class i with the source and the destination, respectively.

The source node s generates a message at a time $t = 0$. Such a message is intended for destination d and it is useful till time τ. No acknowledgment is sent to notify whether the message was delivered to the destination within τ.[1]

We confine our analysis to the *two hop routing protocol* because of two major technical advantages: first, compared to plain epidemic routing it performs natively a better trade-off between the number of released copies and the delivery probability [6]. Second, and most relevant with respect to the algorithmic design that we propose in this paper, forwarding control can be fully implemented on board of the source node. Under two hop routing, the source transmits a message copy to mobiles it encounters. A relay forwards the message copy it has to the destination only.

We adopt a discrete time model where the time axis is divided into slots of duration Δ. Time slot n is the interval $[n\Delta, (n+1)\Delta]$ and the number of slots is equal to $K = \lceil \tau/\Delta \rceil$. Moreover, the control during $[n\Delta, (n+1)\Delta]$ is a constant, denoted by $u(n)$. This model provides a useful framework for the subsequent algorithmic development that we detail for the 2D case.

---

[1] There could exist multiple source–destination pairs in general; we consider only one source node and one destination for the sake of simplicity. We also neglect the effect of beaconing and related issues including the possibility that messages are not detected due to missed beacons.

Forwarding Control: The source node has the possibility to control dynamically the forwarding process to relay nodes: it will forward to nodes in class i with probability u_i. This will slow down the generation of message copies within class i.

The problem we address in this paper is to maximize the delivery probability of the packet by the K-th time slot, under a constraint on the expected number of infected nodes.

Message Delivery Distribution: The source node aims at maximizing the fluid approximation for the cumulative distribution function (CDF) of the delay[2] $F_D(t) := P(T_d \leq t)$. It is based on a generalization of [6]:

$$F_D(t) = 1 - \exp\left(-\sum_j \lambda_{jd} \int_{s=0}^t X_j(s)ds\right). \tag{1}$$

Energy Consumption: The number of infected nodes is related to the total energy consumption. They are proportional if we assume that most of the energy is consumed for transmission and a constant per-contact energy expenditure in order to forward a message.

In the following section we characterize optimal strategies. Then in section 4 we show how the source can learn online the optimal policy. In Table 1 the notation used throughout the report is described.

3   Optimal Control Characterization

In the 2-D case, the source aims to optimize over the 2-dimensional control vector $\mathbf{u} = (u_1, u_2)$, where $u_i : \{0, \ldots, K-1\} \to [u_{\min}, u_{\max}]^2, i = 1, 2$. Denote the delivery rate by J, then the optimal control problem reads

$$\max_{u_1, u_2} \int_0^\tau \lambda_{1d} X_1(t) + \lambda_{2d} X_2(t)dt, \qquad \text{s.t. } X_1(\tau) + X_2(\tau) \leq \psi$$

where the number of message copies $X(n)$ (which is a Markov chain) can be characterized as follows:

$$X_i^{n+1} = X_i^n + (N_i - X_i^n)(1 - e^{-\lambda_{si}\Delta u_i(n)}), \tag{2}$$

where i=1,2. Therefore, we can easily put the objective functional:

$$J = \sum_{i=1,2} \tau N_i \lambda_{id} - \frac{\lambda_{id}}{\lambda_{si}} \sum_{n=0}^{K-1} (N_i - X_i^n) \frac{1 - e^{-\lambda_{si}\Delta u_i(n)}}{u_i(n)} \tag{3}$$

---

[2] The controlled version reported in (1) derives from the separable differential equation in the form $\frac{d}{dt}F_D(t) = \lim_{h\to 0} \frac{\mathbb{P}[T_d > t+h] - \mathbb{P}[T_d > t]}{h} = [1 - F_D(t)] \sum_j \lambda_{jd} X_j(s)$.

Definition 1. *A policy $u = \{u_1, u_2\}$ is a static policy if u is a constant function, i.e. $u(n) = u \in [0, 1]$, for $n = 0, 1, 2, \ldots, K$. A policy u is a threshold policy with parameter h, if there exist $h \in \{0, 1, 2, \ldots, K - 1\}$ (the threshold) such that*

$$u(n) = \begin{cases} u_{max}, & \text{if } n < h \\ u_{min}, & \text{if } n > h \end{cases} \tag{4}$$

Theorem 1. *(**Static case**): Consider the problem of maximizing $\bar{F}_D(K)$, in a static policy, the following holds :*

i. *If $X(\tau) > \psi$ at $\{u_1 = u_{min}, u_2 = u_{min}\}$ there is no feasible solution.*
ii. *If $X(\tau) < \psi$ at $\{u_1 = u_{min}, u_2 = u_{min}\}$ and $X(\tau) > \psi$ at $\{u_1 = u_{max}, u_2 = u_{min}\}$, then the optimal policy is $\{u_1^* = u_1(u_{min}), u_2^* = u_{min}\}$ where*

$$u_1(u_{min}) = \frac{-1}{\lambda_{s1}\tau} \log\left(\frac{N - \psi}{N_1 - X_1^0} - \frac{N_2 - X_2^0}{N_1 - X_1^0} e^{-\lambda_{s2}\tau u_{min}}\right).$$

iii. *If $X(\tau) \leq \psi$ at $\{u_1 = u_{max}, u_2 = u_{min}\}$, then the optimal policy is $\{u_1^* = u_{max}, u_2^* = u_1^{-1}(u_{max})\}$ where*

$$u_1^{-1}(u_{max}) = \frac{-1}{\lambda_{s2}\tau} \log\left(\frac{N - \psi}{N_2 - X_2^0} - \frac{N_1 - X_1^0}{N_2 - X_2^0} e^{-\lambda_{s1}\tau u_{max}}\right).$$

Proof: The proof of this theorem is proved in [12].   ◇

Theorem 2. *(**Dynamic case**) There exists an optimal threshold policy. A non threshold policy is not optimal.*

Proof: The existence of an optimal policy follows from elementary properties of Markov decision processes. We need to prove that a non threshold policy cannot be optimal. Let us consider a non threshold policy $\mathbf{u} = (u_1, u_2)$ that satisfies the constraint $(X_1(\tau) + X_2(\tau) \leq \psi)$: there must exist some time $k < K$ and some $\epsilon > 0$ such that $u_i(k) < u_{max} - \epsilon$ and $u_i(k + 1) > u_{min} + \epsilon$ $(i = 1, 2)$.

Let $\mathbf{u}^\epsilon = (u_1^\epsilon, u_2^\epsilon)$ be the policy obtained from $\mathbf{u}$ by setting $u_1^\epsilon(k) = u_1(k) + \epsilon$ and $u_1^\epsilon(k + 1) = u_1(k + 1) - \epsilon$ and without loss of generality, we leave $u_2(n)$ unchanged (the other components are the same as those of $\mathbf{u}$). Let $X_1^{n\epsilon}, J^\epsilon$ the corresponding variables under $\mathbf{u}^\epsilon$. From (2) it follows that $X_1^{n\epsilon} = X_1^n$ for $n \neq k$ and $X_1^{k\epsilon} > X_1^k$ then substituting $X_1^{k\epsilon}$ in (3) we can find that $J^\epsilon \geq J$

$$J^\epsilon = J + \frac{\lambda_{1d}}{\lambda_{s1}}(N_1 - X_1)\Big(\frac{1 - e^{\lambda_1 \Delta(u_1(k)+\epsilon)}}{u_1(k) + \epsilon} - \frac{e^{-\lambda_1 \Delta(u_1(k)+\epsilon)}}{u_1(k+1) - \epsilon}$$
$$+ \frac{e^{-\lambda_1 \Delta(u_1(k)+u_1(k+1))}}{u_1(k+1) - \epsilon} - \frac{1 - e^{\lambda_1 \Delta u_1(k)}}{u_1(k)} + \frac{e^{-\lambda_1 \Delta u_1(k)}}{u_1(k+1)} - \frac{e^{-\lambda_1 \Delta(u_1(k)+u_1(k+1))}}{u_1(k+1)}\Big).$$

It is easy to show the following relations

$$\frac{1 - e^{\lambda_1 \Delta u_1(k)}}{u_1(k)} < \frac{1 - e^{\lambda_1 \Delta(u_1(k)+\epsilon)}}{u_1(k) + \epsilon},$$

$$\frac{e^{-\lambda_1 \Delta(u_1(k)+\epsilon)}}{u_1(k+1) - \epsilon} < \frac{e^{-\lambda_1 \Delta u_1(k)}}{u_1(k+1)},$$

$$\frac{e^{-\lambda_1 \Delta(u_1(k)+u_1(k+1))}}{u_1(k+1)} < \frac{e^{-\lambda_1 \Delta(u_1(k)+u_1(k+1))}}{u_1(k+1) - \epsilon},$$

from which $J^\epsilon > J$. Also, since $X_1(\tau) + X_2(\tau) = X_1^\epsilon(\tau) + X_2^\epsilon(\tau) \le \psi$, the new policy satisfies the constraint and improves the delivery probability. Hence a non threshold policy can't be optimal, which concludes the proof.   ◇

A consequence of the last theorem is the following: either the optimal threshold strategy is the static policy with $u_i^*(k) = u_{max}$, for all k, $i = 1, 2$, or it saturates the constraint $(X_1(\tau) + X_2(\tau) \le \psi)$. In what follows we focus only on the optimal threshold strategy in which the constraint is saturated.

Under the optimal strategy (u_1^*, u_2^*), let ψ_1 denote the number of infected nodes of class 1. This implies that $\psi - \psi_1$ is the number of infected nodes of class 2. Then the optimal threshold policy (u_1^*, u_2^*) satisfies the following relation

$$U_i(\psi_i) \overset{def}{=} \sum_{k=0}^{K-1} u_i^*(k, \psi_i) = -\frac{1}{\lambda_{si}\Delta} \log(\frac{N_i - \psi_i}{N_i - X_i^0}),$$

Let $h_i(\psi_i)$ the threshold for the optimal policy u_i^*. Then we have

$$U_i(\psi_i) = h_i(\psi_i) \cdot u_{max} + (K - 1 - h_i(\psi_i)) \cdot u_{min} + g(\psi_i) \tag{5}$$

where

$$g(\psi_i) = -\frac{1}{\lambda_{si}\Delta} \log(\frac{N_i - \psi_i}{N_i - X_i^0}) - (h_i(\psi_i) \cdot u_{max} + (K - 1 - h_i(\psi_i)) \cdot u_{min})$$

Notice that (5) defines a bijection, so that $(u_1^*, u_2^*) \sim (\psi_1^*, \psi - \psi_1^*)$: we can now consider the problem from slightly different perspective of the one defined in (2). The equivalent problem is defined as follows: the source goal is to find the optimal ψ_1^* that maximizes the delivery probability. The advantage of the new formulation is that the joint constraint is replaced by two separate constraints, one per class. In turn we can express our initial optimization as

$$\max_{\psi_1} \bar{J}(\psi_1) = \max_{\psi_1}(\bar{J}_1(\psi_1) + \bar{J}_2(\psi - \psi_1)) \quad \text{s.t. } X_1(\tau) \le \psi_1, X_2(\tau) \le \psi - \psi_1 \tag{6}$$

where $\bar{J}_i(.)$ is given by

$$\bar{J}_i(\psi_i) = \tau N_i \lambda_{id} - \frac{\lambda_{id}}{\lambda_{si}} \sum_{k=0}^{K-1} (N_i - X_i(k, \psi_i)) \frac{1 - e^{-\lambda_{si} \Delta u_i(k, \psi_i)}}{u_i(k, \psi_i)}, i = 1, 2.$$

It is clear that the solution of this new problem solves directly the original optimization problem (2).

Theorem 3. *There exists an unique optimal value* (ψ_1^*) *that maximizes the delivery probability in (6).*

Proof. In order to prove the uniqueness, it is sufficient to prove that J is concave in ψ_1. We start by proving that $\bar{J}_1(\psi_1)$ is concave. From equation (5), it follows that $\frac{dg(\psi_1)}{d\psi_1} = \frac{1}{\lambda_{s1}\Delta}$, then the derivative of function $\bar{J}_1$ can be expressed as follows:

$$
\frac{d\bar{J}_1(\psi_1)}{d\psi_1} = -\frac{\lambda_{1d}}{\lambda_{s1}}(N - X_1^h(\psi_1)).\frac{\lambda_{s1}\Delta.g(\psi_1)e^{-\lambda_{s1}\Delta.g(\psi_1)} - 1 + e^{-\lambda_{s1}\Delta.g(\psi_1)}}{U_1^h(\psi_1)^2}
$$

$$
+\frac{\lambda_{1d}}{\lambda_{s1}}\frac{1 - e^{-\lambda_{si}\Delta.u_{min}}}{u_{min}}.\sum_{k=h+1}^{K-1}\frac{dX_1^k(\psi_1)}{d\psi_1} \tag{7}
$$

The first term is clearly decreasing in ψ_1, since $g(\psi_1)$ is an increasing function in ψ_1. Let us now determine the derivative of second term as follows:

– For $k = h + 1$, we have

$$
X_1^{h+1}(\psi_1) = X_1^h + (N_1 - X_1^h)(1 - e^{-\lambda_{s1}\Delta.g(\psi_1)}),
$$

then

$$
\frac{dX_1^{h+1}(\psi_1)}{d\psi_1} = (N_1 - X_1^h)e^{-\lambda_{s1}\Delta.g(\psi_1)}. \tag{8}
$$

– For $k = h + 2$, we have

$$
X_1^{h+2}(\psi_1) = X_1^{h+1}(\psi_1) + (N_1 - X_1^{h+1}(\psi_1))(1 - e^{-\lambda_{s1}\Delta.u_{min}}), \tag{9}
$$

then

$$
\frac{dX_1^{h+2}(\psi_1)}{d\psi_1} = \frac{dX_1^{h+1}(\psi_1)}{d\psi_1}e^{-\lambda_{s1}\Delta.u_{min}}. \tag{10}
$$

– Making all the steps up to $k = K - 1$ we can derive the useful formula of the derivative of the second term in (7):

$$
\sum_{k=h+1}^{K-1}\frac{dX_1^k(\psi_1)}{d\psi_1} = \frac{dX_1^{h+1}(\psi_1)}{d\psi_1}e^{-\lambda_{s1}\Delta.\sum_{k=h+2}^{K-1}u_{min}}, \tag{11}
$$

Since $g(\psi_1)$ is increasing function in ψ_1, it is easy to check that the derivative of function $X_1^{h+1}(\psi_1)$ is a decreasing function, It follows from (11) that the second term is decreasing function in ψ_1. Hence the function $\bar{J}_1$ is a concave function. Using the same steps we can show that $\bar{J}_2(\psi - \psi_1)$ is a concave function in ψ_1, and since the sum of two concave functions is a concave function, $\bar{J}(\psi_1)$ is a concave function, hence the proof.   ◇

4   Blind Online Algorithms for Adaptive Optimization

In this section we first present out static algorithm proposed in [12] and provide a rigorous investigation of its convergence and stability. Then we propose an improved and advanced version of the online algorithm to attain optimal dynamic control of forwarding by developing a two-time scale concept, here too, a thorough analysis of convergence is provided. Both algorithms are designed based on stochastic approximation theory.

Algorithm (1) is used by the source to achieve the optimal policy for the static control, it is the same algorithm introduced in [12] but Algorithm (2) applies to the dynamic threshold control. Both algorithms are *blind*: they do not require a-priori knowledge of network parameters (intermeeting intensities and number of mobiles). Observe that in the heterogeneous case, each class of nodes has its own (unknown) parameters: intermeeting intensities (λ_{si} and λ_{id}) and the number of nodes (N_i) for each class i. These algorithms will only depend on the source ability to distinguish between classes, e.g., according to node's type (whether it is a throwbox, a smartphone, etc): leveraging on the structure of the optimal solution, this will be enough to find the optimal forwarding control that the source should adopt without explicit estimation of such parameters.

Our approach is based on stochastic approximation theory [20] that allows us to facilitate online estimation of network parameters. This framework generalizes Newtons method to determine the root of a real-valued function when only noisy observations of such function are available.

We can approach online estimation of static and dynamic control in the same way. Let us denote $\theta_i = \sum_{k=0}^{K-1} u_i(k), i = 1, 2$, then θ_i identifies both the static and dynamic policies: the static policy is $u_i = \theta_i/K$, while for the dynamic policy threshold writes $h_i = \max\{h \in \mathbb{N} : v(h) = h \cdot u_{max} + (K - h) \cdot u_{min} \leq \theta_i\}$, and $u_i(h) = \theta_i - v(h)$. Define $\epsilon > 0$ a tolerance and given interval $I = [\theta_{min}, \theta_{max}]$, Π_I is the projection over I defined as follows:

$$\Pi_I(\theta_i) = \begin{cases} \theta_{max} & \text{if} & \theta_i \geq \theta_{max} \\ \theta_i & \text{if} & \theta_{min} \leq \theta_i \leq \theta_{max} \\ \theta_{max} & \text{if} & \theta_i \leq \theta_{min} \end{cases}$$

4.1   Blind Online Algorithm for Static Control

Our static algorithm is an extension of [15] to the multi-dimensional case. Each step of the algorithm corresponds to a round of duration τ. For sake of notation, we let $\widehat{X}(\theta_i^k, t), i = 1, 2$ the number of nodes of the ith class that are potentially infected by the source in the current round up to time t.

The algorithm works as follows:

1: By averaging over several consecutive rounds, using interpolation, the source node is able to obtain an estimate of the average number of copies ($\widehat{X}(\theta_i^k)$) that could potentially be attained using the current set of K policies.

2: Using $\widehat{X}(\theta_i^k)$, the source updates the value of θ_i according to the formula showed in Algorithm 1.

3: Repeat steps 2 and 3 until the algorithm converges.

This stochastic approximation algorithm will implicitly discover the fastest class, this permits to adjust the values of (θ_1, θ_2) for the next round in order to, eventually, estimate the optimal (θ_1, θ_2) in I, which uniquely determine the optimal static policy $\mathbf{u} = (u_1^*, u_2^*)$. In the following theorem we discuss the convergence of our algorithm.

Theorem 4. *If the sequence $\{a_k\}$ verifies that $a_k > 0$, for all k, $\sum_{k=0}^{+\infty} = +\infty$ and $\sum_{k=0}^{+\infty} a_k^2 < +\infty$, then the sequence (θ_1^k, θ_2^k) converges to the optimal solution (θ_1^*, θ_2^*).*

Proof: First we show that the sequence (θ_1^k, θ_2^k) converges to some limit set of the following Ordinary Differential Equation (ODE)

$$\dot{\theta}^1 = G_1(\theta^1) + z_1 = \Psi - E[X_1 + X_2 | (\theta^1, \theta_{min})] + z_1 \tag{12}$$
$$\dot{\theta}^2 = G_2(\theta^1, \theta^2) + z_2 = \Psi - E[X_1 + X_2 | (\theta^1, \theta^2)] + z_2, \tag{13}$$

where $z = (z_1, z_2) \in -C((\theta^1, \theta^2))$ and z_i, $i = 1, 2$, is the minimum force needed to keep the solution θ_i in $[\theta_{min}, \theta_{max}]$ and the set $C(\boldsymbol{\theta})$ is defined as follows. For $\boldsymbol{\theta} = (\theta_1, \theta_2) \in (\theta_{min}, \theta_{max})^2$, $C(\boldsymbol{\theta}) = \{(0, 0)\}$; for (θ_1, θ_2) in the boundary of $[\theta_{min}, \theta_{max}]^2$, let $C(\boldsymbol{\theta})$ be the infinite convex cone generated by the outer normals at $\boldsymbol{\theta}$ of the faces on which $\boldsymbol{\theta}$ lies. For example, if $\theta_1 = \theta_{max}$ and $G_1(\theta_1)$ point out of $[\theta_{min}, \theta_{max}]$ then $z_1(t) = G_1(\theta_1)$. Hence the function $z(.)$ is determined by $[\theta_{min}, \theta_{max}]^2$ and the functions $G_i(.)$, $i = 1, 2$.

Algorithm 1. Stochastic approximation of the optimal policy using online estimation (2D static case)

1: **input:** $I = [0, K - 1]$, $\theta_1^0 = \theta_2^0 = K/2$, $k = 0$
2: **while** $max(|\theta_1^{k+1} - \theta_1^k|, |\theta_2^{k+1} - \theta_2^k|) > \epsilon$ **do**
3:     $\widehat{X}_1(\theta_1^k) = \text{interp}(\widehat{X}_1(\theta_1^k), \theta_1^k)$
4:     $\widehat{X}_2(\theta_2^k) = \text{interp}(\widehat{X}_2(\theta_2^k), \theta_2^k)$
5:     **if** $\widehat{X}_1(\theta_1^k) >= \widehat{X}_2(\theta_2^k)$ **then**
6:         $\theta_1^{k+1} = \Pi_I(\theta_1^k + a_k(\Psi - \widehat{X}_1(\theta_1^k)))$
7:         $\theta_2^{k+1} = \Pi_I(\theta_2^k + a_k(\Psi - \widehat{X}_1(\theta_1^k)) - \widehat{X}_2(\theta_2^k)))$
8:     **else**
9:         $\theta_1^{k+1} = \Pi_I(\theta_1^k + a_k(\Psi - \widehat{X}_1(\theta_1^k)) - \widehat{X}_2(\theta_2^k)))$
10:        $\theta_2^{k+1} = \Pi_I(\theta_2^k + a_k(\Psi - \widehat{X}_2(\theta_2^k)))$
11:    **end if**
12:    $k \leftarrow k + 1$
13: **end while**

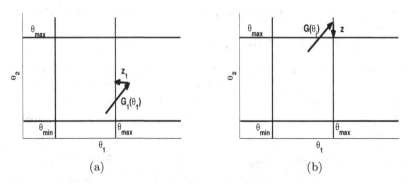

Fig. 1. Projection of the value θ_i over I

Since $G_1(\theta_1)$ (resp. $G_2(\theta_1, \theta_2)$) is decreasing function in θ_1 (resp. θ_1 and θ_2), then the equilibrium is unique. Moreover, it is easy to check that the optimal solution (θ_1^*, θ_2^*) (see theorem 1) is the unique equilibrium of (12)-(13). As discussed in [20], the convergence of such stochastic algorithm is guaranteed when the sequence (a_k) verifies, $a_k > 0$, for all k, $\sum_{k=0}^{+\infty} a_k = +\infty$ and $\sum_{k=0}^{+\infty} a_k^2 < +\infty$. We now need to show that (θ_1^*, θ_2^*) is globally asymptotically stable for system (12)-(13). We use the Lyapunov function $V(\theta_1, \theta_2) = (\theta_1 - \theta_1^*)^2 + (\theta_2 - \theta_2^*)^2$. Then we have

$$\dot{V}(\boldsymbol{\theta}) = 2\dot{\theta}_1(\theta_1 - \theta_1^*) + 2\dot{\theta}_1(\theta_2 - \theta_2^*) \tag{14}$$
$$= 2(G_1(\theta_1) + z_1)(\theta_1 - \theta_1^*) + 2(G_2(\theta_1, \theta_2) + z_2)(\theta_2 - \theta_2^*)$$

Since there is almost one active constraints, we have two cases (see Fig. 1):

- If $\theta_{min} < \theta_i < \theta^{max}$ for $i = 1, 2$, then $z_1 = 0$ and $z_2 = 0$
- If $\theta_i = \theta_{max}$ (resp. θ_{min}) and $G_i(\theta_{max}) > 0$ (resp. $G_i(\theta_{min}) < 0$) for only one class i, then $z_i = -G_i(\theta_{max})$ (resp. $z_i = -G_i(\theta_{min})$) and $z_{-i} = 0$ for other class

Since G_1 and G_2 are strictly decreasing function, it is easy to check that $\dot{V}(\boldsymbol{\theta})$ for all θ_1 and θ_2. Hence the optimal solution is asymptotically stable.

4.2   Blind Online Algorithm for Dynamic Control

We apply the *two-time-scale stochastic approximation algorithm*, which is a stochastic recursive algorithm. Compared to standard stochastic approximation techniques in literature [20], here some of the components are updated using a step-size much smaller than those of the remaining components. For further insight into the convergence properties of this class of algorithms, i.e., almost sure convergence of sample paths to the ODE, the reader is referred to [21].

Let ψ_1 be the maximum number of nodes of class 1 that can be infected: then the source can infect ($\psi_2 = \psi - \psi_1$) nodes of class 2. The algorithm tries to find the optimal (ψ_1) that maximizes the probability of success $F_D(\tau, \psi_1) = 1 - \exp\left(-\sum_j \lambda_{jd} \int_{s=0}^t X_j(\psi_1, s)ds\right)$. Since the system parameters (such as N_i and λ_i, $i = 1, 2$) are unknown, the value of $F_D(\tau, \psi_1)$ is also unknown, but a noisy estimate of it is known, namely $f(\psi_1)$ such that $\mathbb{E}[f|\psi_1] = F_D(\tau, \psi_1)$.

The two-time-scale stochastic approximation algorithm is then formulated as follows:

$$\theta_i^{k+1} = \Pi_I\left(\theta_i^k + a_k(\psi_i^k - X_i(\theta_i^k))\right), \tag{15}$$

$$\psi_1^{k+1} = \Pi_H\left(\psi_1^k + b_k\frac{f(\psi_1^k + c_k) - f(\psi_1^k - c_k)}{c_k}\right) \tag{16}$$

where $i = 1, 2, \psi_2^k = \psi - \psi_1^k$, $I = [0, K-1]$, $H = [0, \psi]$ and $\{a_k\}, \{b_k\}$ are sequences of non-increasing positive constants satisfying $\sum_{k=0}^{+\infty} a_k = +\infty, \sum_{k=0}^{+\infty} a_k^2 < +\infty, \sum_{k=0}^{+\infty} b_k = +\infty, \sum_{k=0}^{+\infty} b_k^2 < +\infty$, and $\lim_{k\to+\infty} \frac{b_k}{a_k} = 0$. The last condition implies that $b_k \to 0$ at a faster rate than a_k, implying that (16) moves on a slower timescale than (15). An example of such stepsizes are $a_k = \frac{1}{k}, b_k = \frac{1}{1+k\log k}$ and so on. Further requirements are imposed on sequence (c_k), which we defer to Thm. 6 for the sake of clearness.

More in detail, at each round k the following steps are executed:

1: Fix (ψ_1) at the value (ψ_1^k) and learn the optimal values of θ_1^k, θ_2^k for $(\psi_1^k + c_k), (\psi_1^k - c_k)$ using the following algorithm:

$$\theta_1^{k+1} = \Pi_I\left(\theta_1^k + a_k(\psi_1^k - X_1(\theta_1^k))\right),$$
$$\theta_2^{k+1} = \Pi_I\left(\theta_2^k + a_k(\psi_2^k - X_2(\theta_2^k))\right).$$

2: Measure the noisy estimate of the success probability, $f(\psi_1)$, at $(\psi_1^k + c_k), (\psi_1^k - c_k)$ when θ_1^k, θ_2^k, obtained at the first step, are applied.
3: Use $f(\psi_i^k + c_k), f(\psi_i^k - c_k)$ to update the value of (ψ_1^k) according to Kiefer-Wolfowitz algorithm as shown at step (11) of algorithm 2.

In the following theorem we proof the convergence of the Kiefer-Wolfowitz part of the algorithm that appears in (16); this serves as an introduction to theorem 6.

Theorem 5. *If the sequence (b_k) verifies: $b_k > 0$, for all k, and $\sum_{k=0}^{+\infty} b_k = +\infty, \sum_{k=0}^{+\infty} b_k^2 < +\infty$ and $c_k \to 0$, then (ψ_1^k) converges to the optimal solution (ψ_1^*).*

Proof: Consider two sequences $\{b_k, c_k, k \geq 1\}$ satisfying $c_k \to 0, \sum_k b_k = \infty, \sum_k b_k c_k < \infty, \sum_k (b_k/c_k)^2 < \infty$, and the recursive updates of ψ_1:

$$\psi_1^{k+1} = \psi_1^k + b_k\frac{f(\psi_1^k + c_k) - f(\psi_1^k - c_k)}{c_k} \tag{17}$$

This recursive schema converges stochastically to the optimal value (ψ_1^*) that maximizes $F_D(\tau, \psi_1)$ provided that $F_D(\tau, \psi_1)$ satisfies the following conditions:

1) $F_D(\tau, \psi_1)$ is a strictly quasi-concave function.
2) There exists β and B such that $|\psi_1^a - \psi_1^*| + |\psi_1^b - \psi_1^*| < \beta$ implies $|F_D(\tau, \psi_1^a) - F_D(\tau, \psi_1^b)| < B|\psi_1^a - \psi_1^b|$.
3) There exists ρ and R such that $|\psi_1^a - \psi_1^b| < \rho$ implies $|F_D(\tau, \psi_1^a) - F_D(\tau, \psi_1^b)| < R$.
4) For every $\delta > 0$ there exists a positive $\pi(\delta)$ such that $|\psi_1 - \psi_1^*| > \delta$ implies

$$\inf_{0 < \epsilon < \frac{\delta}{2}} \frac{|F_D(\tau, \psi_1 + \epsilon) - F_D(\tau, \psi_1 - \epsilon)|}{\epsilon} > \pi(\delta).$$

In order to prove that $F_D(\tau, \psi_1)$ satisfies these conditions, we only need to prove that $F_D(\tau, \psi_1)$ is concave and has a unique maximum solution ψ_1^* ([22]-lemma 2, theorem 1) which is already proved in theorem 3, hence the proof.

Theorem 6. *The sequence (θ_i^k, ψ_1^k) defined in the iteration (15) and (16) converges a.s. to $(\theta_i(\psi_1^*), \psi_1^*)$.*

Proof. This can be proved directly by the results of ([23], Chapter 6) together with the sure convergence of the two related single-time-scale stochastic approximation algorithms – those defined in (15) and (16), respectively – and that each algorithm has a globally asymptotically stable equilibrium, appearing in the following.

The first algorithm is the aforementioned algorithm (Alg. 1) taking as entries the fixed values of $\widehat{X}_1(\theta_1^k), \widehat{X}_2(\theta_2^k)$ (which are ψ_1^k, ψ_2^k for the current round k). In fact, (15) sees ψ_1 as quasi-static (i.e., 'almost a constant') and it is easy to prove that the sequence (θ_1^k, θ_2^k) converges to some limit set of the following Ordinary Differential Equation (ODE)

$$\dot{\theta}_1 = G_1(\theta_1) + z_1 = \psi_1 - E[X_1 | \theta_1] + z_1, \quad z_1 \in -C_1(\theta_1) \tag{18}$$

$$\dot{\theta}_2 = G_2(\theta_2) + z_2 = (\psi - \psi_1) - E[X_2 | \theta_2] + z_2, \quad z_2 \in -C_2(\theta_2) \tag{19}$$

where $z_1 \in -C_1(\theta_1), z_2 \in -C_2(\theta_2)$ and $z_i, i = 1, 2$, is the minimum force needed to keep the solution θ_i in $I = [\theta_{min}, \theta_{max}]$.

Following the same reasoning in the proof of theorem 4, it is easy to verify that each of the ODEs (18) and (19) has a globally asymptotically stable equilibrium $\theta_i^*(\psi_1)$.

The second algorithm is the Kiefer-Wolfowitz whose convergence is proved in theorem 5 and its asymptotic behavior is characterized [20] by the ODE

$$\dot{\psi}_1 = G(\theta_1(\psi_1), \theta_2(\psi_1), \psi_1) + z_3 = \frac{\partial F_D(\tau, \psi_1)}{\partial \psi_1} + z_3, z_3 \in -C_3(\psi_1) \tag{20}$$

where z_3, is the minimum force needed to keep the solution ψ_1 in $H = [0, \psi]$. We now need to show that (ψ_1^*) is globally asymptotically stable of the ODE (20). We use the Lyapunov function $V(\psi_1) = (\psi_1 - \psi_1^*)^2$. Then we have

---

Algorithm 2. Stochastic approximation of the optimal policy using online estimation (2D Dynamic case)

1: **input:** $I = [0, K-1], H = [0, \psi], \theta_1^0 = \theta_2^0 = K/2, \psi_1^0 = \psi, c_k = \frac{1}{k^{0.001}}$

2: **while** $|\psi_1^{k+1} - \psi_1^k| > \epsilon$ **do**

3:     set $\psi_1^+ = \min(\psi_1^k + c_k, \psi)$, $\psi_2^+ = \psi - \psi_1^+$

4:     $\theta_1^k = \Pi_I\left(\theta_1^k + a_k(\psi_1^+ - \widehat{X}_1(\theta_1^k))\right)$

5:     $\theta_2^k = \Pi_I\left(\theta_2^k + a_k(\psi_2^+ - \widehat{X}_2(\theta_2^k))\right)$

6:     Measure $f(\psi_1^+) = func(\theta_1^k, \theta_2^k)$

7:     set $\psi_1^- = \max(\psi_1^k - c_k, 0)$, $\psi_2^- = \psi - \psi_1^-$

8:     $\theta_1^k = \Pi_I\left(\theta_1^k + a_k(\psi_1^- - \widehat{X}_1(\theta_1^k))\right)$

9:     $\theta_2^k = \Pi_I\left(\theta_2^k + a_k(\psi_2^- - \widehat{X}_2(\theta_2^k))\right)$

10:    Measure $f(\psi_1^-) = func(\theta_1^k, \theta_2^k)$

11:    $\psi_1^{k+1} = \Pi_H\left(\psi_1^k + b_k(\frac{f(\psi_1^+) - f(\psi_1^-)}{c_k})\right)$

12:    $k \leftarrow k + 1$

13: **end while**

$$\dot{V}(\psi_1) = 2\dot{\psi}_1(\psi_1 - \psi_1^*) \tag{21}$$
$$= 2\frac{\partial F_D(\tau, \psi_1)}{\partial \psi_1}(\psi_1 - \psi_1^*) < 0$$

Asymptotic global stability follows from Lyapunov's theorem.

5   Numerical Investigation

In this section we illustrate numerical experiments that validate our results. Using Matlab® scripts, we have studied the impact of the energy constraint (ψ) and the number of nodes of a class (N_i) on the 2-D system optimal dynamic policy. We are interested in the performance of the stochastic approximation algorithms described earlier; we will investigate their ability to drive the two hop forwarding both in the static as well as dynamic scenario to the optimal operating point.

An important aspect is the impact of the energy constraint on the dynamic policies adopted by the source (see Fig. 2). We notice that the larger the energy constraint is, the higher the switch times are (Fig. 2(a) and 2(c)). This is because increasing ψ allows the source to infect more nodes by augmenting the optimal switch times while satisfying the constraint (Fig. 2(b) and 2(d)). An interesting observation is captured in Fig. 2(b) 2(d)): when ψ has a small value ($\psi = 10$), the source forwards the message only to class 1 (class 2) nodes, respectively. This indicates that under a tight energy constraint, the source should rely on one class only (the one with higher λ_s) to have its message delivered. For the case where $\psi = 40$, the source will forward the message all the time to both classes in order to saturate the constraint.

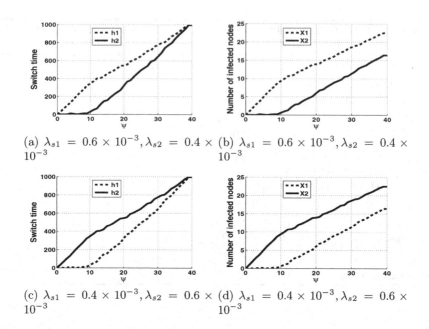

(a) $\lambda_{s1} = 0.6 \times 10^{-3}, \lambda_{s2} = 0.4 \times 10^{-3}$

(b) $\lambda_{s1} = 0.6 \times 10^{-3}, \lambda_{s2} = 0.4 \times 10^{-3}$

(c) $\lambda_{s1} = 0.4 \times 10^{-3}, \lambda_{s2} = 0.6 \times 10^{-3}$

(d) $\lambda_{s1} = 0.4 \times 10^{-3}, \lambda_{s2} = 0.6 \times 10^{-3}$

Fig. 2. The impact of the energy constraint (ψ) on switching times and number of infected nodes in the 2-D case, where $N_1 = N_2 = 50$

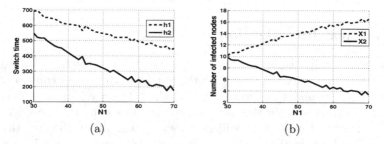

Fig. 3. The impact of the number of class1 nodes (N_1) on switching times and number of infected nodes in the 2-D case, where $\psi = 20$, $N_2 = 50$, $\lambda_{s1} = \lambda_{1d} = 0.0006$, $\lambda_{s2} = \lambda_{2d} = 0.0004$, $\tau = 1000$

In Fig. 3 we observe the impact of number of nodes of a class on the switch times. We observe that the source infects both classes for shorter time with the increase of the number of nodes of class 1 (Fig. 3(a)), which corresponds to the intuition: a larger number of relays per class increases the number of infected nodes (Fig. 3(b)) and increases the message delivery probability.

Fig. 4 shows sample paths of our learning algorithm for the problem of static control. In Fig. 4(a) the algorithm is showed to converge to $(u_1^*, u_2^*) = (u_1^*, u_{\min})$

with $0 < u_1^* < 1$. Indeed, since the source may affect at most 30 nodes, from theorem 1, the optimal solution is $(u_1(u_{\min}), u_{\min})$ with $u_1(u_{\min}) = \frac{-1}{\lambda_{s1}\tau}\log\left(\frac{N-\psi}{N_1-X_1^0} - \frac{N_2-X_2^0}{N_1-X_1^0}e^{-\lambda_{s2}\tau u_{\min}}\right)$, we can see that u_1 converges to $u_1(u_{\min})$ and u_2 to $u_{\min}$.

In Fig. 4(b) we plot case ii) of theorem 1 where the energy constraint is 60 and the algorithm converges to $(u_1^*, u_2^*) = (u_{\max}, u_2^*)$ with $u_2^* = u_1^{-1}(u_{\max}) = \frac{-1}{\lambda_{s2}\tau}\log\left(\frac{N-\psi}{N_2-X_2^0} - \frac{N_1-X_1^0}{N_2-X_2^0}e^{-\lambda_{s1}\tau u_{\max}}\right)$. In this case the source will infect nodes of both classes in order to saturate the constraint by giving the message with probability 1 to the class with larger intermeeting intensities $\lambda_{si}, \lambda_{id}$ (class 1) and with some probability u_2^* to the other class.

Fig. 4(c) shows the case where the constraint has a large value ($\psi = 90$) and the source can not reach the constraint even when forwarding to both classes with probability 1.

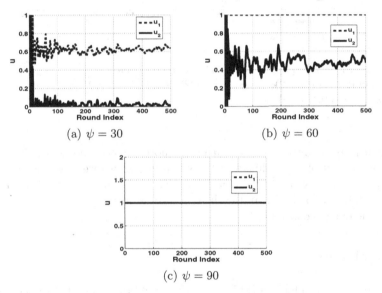

(a) $\psi = 30$

(b) $\psi = 60$

(c) $\psi = 90$

Fig. 4. The stochastic approximation using online estimation ($\lambda_{s1} > \lambda_{s2}$) in the 2-D case (static algorithm 1), where $\tau = 1000, N_1 = N_2 = 1000, \lambda_{s1} = \lambda_{1d} = 0.34 \times 10^{-4}, \lambda_{s2} = \lambda_{2d} = 0.14 \times 10^{-4}$.

The performance of our learning algorithm in the dynamic case is shown in Fig. 5. In Figs. 5(a) and 5(b) we depict the convergence of ψ_1 (the maximum number of nodes of class 1 that can be infected) to the optimal value that maximizes the delivery probability under two different values of the energy constraint, and in Figs. 5(c) and 5(d) we show the corresponding switch times for both cases.

To better understand Fig. 5, let us observe Figs. 5(a) and 5(c) where the energy constraint has a small value ($\Psi = 20$), we notice that since class 1 has bigger intermeeting intensities ($\lambda_{s1}, \lambda_{1d}$), the algorithm forward the message to

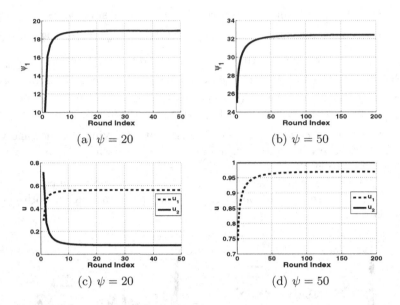

Fig. 5. The stochastic approximation using online estimation ($\lambda_{s1} > \lambda_{s2}$) in the 2-D case (Dynamic algorithm 2), where $\tau = 1000, N_1 = N_2 = 1000, \lambda_{s1} = \lambda_{1d} = 0.34 \times 10^{-4}, \lambda_{s2} = \lambda_{2d} = 0.14 \times 10^{-4}$

class 1 with larger probability resulting in more infected nodes in class 1 (19 infected nodes out of 20). While in Figs. 5(b) and 5(d) where ψ is large ($\psi = 50$), the algorithm converges to $(u_1^*, u_2^*) = (u_{max}, u_2^*)$ which means giving the message with probability 1 to class 1 and with some probability u_2^* to class 2 in order to saturate the energy constraint.

6   Conclusion

In this paper we considered a DTN network formed by different classes of nodes. We used two hop as the forwarding strategy to deliver messages from a source node to destination node: the goal is to optimize the probability of delivering a message in the presence of different classes of mobiles, while satisfying a given energy budget. Using our model we characterized the optimal strategy in the family of the multi-dimensional dynamic policies. Moreover, we are able to design stochastic approximation algorithms that attain optimality when multiple classes of relays exist. Furthermore, this can be done with a novel online implementation that does not require explicit estimation of the system parameters. A rigorous analysis of the convergence properties and stability of our algorithms is provided.

References

1. Pelusi, L., Passarella, A., Conti, M.: Opportunistic networking: data forwarding in disconnected mobile ad hoc networks. IEEE Communications Magazine 44(11), 134–141 (2006)
2. Chaintreau, A., Hui, P., Crowcroft, J., Diot, C., Gass, R., Scott, J.: Impact of human mobility on opportunistic forwarding algorithms. IEEE Transactions on Mobile Computing 6, 606–620 (2007)
3. Burleigh, S., Torgerson, L., Fall, K., Cerf, V., Durst, B., Scott, K., Weiss, H.: Delay-tolerant networking: an approach to interplanetary Internet. IEEE Comm. Magazine 41, 128–136 (2003)
4. Zhao, W., Ammar, M., Zegura, E.: Controlling the mobility of multiple data transport ferries in a delay-tolerant network. In: Proc. of IEEE INFOCOM, Miami USA, March 13–17 (2005)
5. Spyropoulos, T., Psounis, K., Raghavendra, C.: Efficient routing in intermittently connected mobile networks: the multi-copy case. ACM/IEEE Transactions on Networking 16, 77–90 (2008)
6. Altman, E., Basar, T., De Pellegrini, F.: Optimal monotone forwarding policies in delay tolerant mobile ad-hoc networks. In: Proc. of ACM/ICST Inter-Perf. ACM, Athens (2008)
7. Vahdat, A., Becker, D.: Epidemic routing for partially connected ad hoc networks. Duke University, Tech. Rep. CS-2000-06 (2000)
8. Hanbali, A.A., Nain, P., Altman, E.: Performance of ad hoc networks with two-hop relay routing and limited packet lifetime. In: Proc. of Valuetools, p. 49. ACM, New York (2006)
9. Spyropoulos, T., Turletti, T., Obraczka, K.: Routing in delay-tolerant networks comprising heterogeneous node populations. IEEE Transactions on Mobile Computing 8(8), 1132–1147 (2009)
10. Chaintreau, A., Boudec, J.-Y.L., Ristanovic, N.: The age of gossip: Spatial mean-field regime. In: Proc. of ACM SIGMETRICS, Seattle, Washington, USA (June 2009)
11. De Pellegrini, F., Altman, E., Basar, T.: Optimal monotone forwarding policies in delay tolerant mobile ad hoc networks with multiple classes of nodes. In: Proc. of WiOpt WDM Workshop, Avignon, France (June 4, 2010)
12. Chahin, W., El-Azouzi, R., De Pellegrini, F., Azad, A.: Blind online optimal forwarding in heterogeneous delay tolerant networks. In: Wireless Days (WD), October 10-12. IFIP (2011)
13. Lee, C.-H., Eunt, D.Y.: Heterogeneity in contact dynamics: helpful or harmful to forwarding algorithms in DTNs? In: Proc. of WiOPT, Seoul, Korea, pp. 72–81 (2009)
14. Neglia, G., Zhang, X.: Optimal delay-power tradeoff in sparse delay tolerant networks: a preliminary study. In: Proc. of ACM SIGCOMM CHANTS 2006, pp. 237–244 (2006)
15. Altman, E., Neglia, G., De Pellegrini, F., Miorandi, D.: Decentralized stochastic control of delay tolerant networks. In: Proc. of INFOCOM, Rio de Janeiro, Brazil, April 19-25 (2009)
16. Guerrieri, A., Carreras, I., De Pellegrini, F., Miorandi, D., Montresor, A.: Distributed estimation of global parameters in delay-tolerant networks. Elsevier Comput. Commun. 33(13), 1472–1482 (2010)

17. Hui, P., Crowcroft, J., Yoneki, E.: Bubble rap: social-based forwarding in delay tolerant networks. In: Proc of ACM MobiHoc, pp. 241–250. ACM, New York (2008)
18. Conan, V., Leguay, J., Friedman, T.: Characterizing pairwise inter-contact patterns in delay tolerant networks. In: Proc. of ACM Autonomics, pp. 1–9 (2007)
19. Groenevelt, R., Nain, P.: Message delay in MANETs. In: Proc. of Sigmetrics, pp. 412–413. ACM, Banff (2005); see also Groenevelt, R.: Stochastic Models for Mobile Ad Hoc Networks. PhD thesis, University of Nice-Sophia Antipolis (April 2005)
20. Kushner, H.J., Yin, G.G.: Stochastic Approximation and Recursive Algorithms and Applications, 2nd edn. Springer (2003)
21. Borkar, V.S.: Stochastic approximation with two time scales. Elsevier (February 1997)
22. Gong, C., Girard, A., Wang, W.: Stochastic approximation to optimize the performance of human operators, June 30-July 2, pp. 5644–5649 (2010)
23. Borkar, V.S.: Stochastic Approximation: A Dynamical Systems Viewpoint. Cambridge University Press (September 2008)

Implementation and Analysis of FMIPv6, an Enhancement of MIPv6

Johan Pieterse[1], Riaan Wolhuter[2], and Nathalie Mitton[3]

[1] Department of Electronic Engineering, University of Stellenbosch,
South Africa 7600
15041077@sun.ac.za
[2] Department of Electronic Engineering, University of Stellenbosch,
South Africa 7600
wolhuter@sun.ac.za
[3] Inria Lille - Nord Europe, France
nathalie.mitton@inria.fr

Abstract. The initial IP Mobility protocol was first presented in 1993 for IPv4. The Mobile IP protocol solves the TCP/IP Layer 3 mobility, by assigning a permanent IP address to the mobile node. Mobile IP consists of both MIPv4 and MIPv6, but IPv4 has a couple of drawbacks, the main one being IP address exhaustion, making MIPv6 the future option for mobility protocol in IP Networks.The main goal of the mobility protocol is to enable network applications to operate continuously at the required quality of service for both wired and wireless networks. MIPv6 uses the existing IPv6 protocol to enable seamless roaming between different access points. MIPv6 on its own needs optimization techniques to improve the handover latency of the protocol and to minimize the latency. This paper proposes FMIPv6 protocol to minimize handover latency. Both MIPv6 and FMIPv6 protocols introduce some new terminologies as proposed by the Internet Engineering Task Force (IETF), which require prior familiarisation to understand the working of MIPv6 and FMIPv6.

Keywords: MIPv6, FMIPv6, handover latency, Fast binding update, AR, NAR, PAR.

1 Background

The Mobile IP protocol solves the TCP/IP Layer 3 mobility, by assigning a permanent IP address to the mobile node. Mobile IP consists of both MIPv4 and MIPv6, but IPv4 has a couple of drawbacks, the main one being IP address exhaustion, making MIPv6 the future option for mobility protocol in IP Networks [1].The main goal of the mobility protocol is to enable network applications to operate continuously at the required quality of service for both wired and wireless networks [2]. MIPv6 uses the existing IPv6 protocol to enable seamless roaming between different access points [2, 3]. MIPv6 on its own needs optimization techniques to improve the handover latency of the protocol and to minimize the latency. FMIPv6 proposes some enhancements to minimize

J. Zheng et al. (Eds.): Adhocnets 2012, LNICST 111, pp. 351–364, 2013.

the handover latency of a MIPv6 network. The MIPv6 and FMIPv6 protocol also introduces some new terminologies as proposed by the Internet Engineering Task Force (IETF), which require prior familiarisation to understand the workings of MIPv6 and FMIPv6 [4].

1.1   Internet Protocol Version 6

With the rappid growth of the internet the current IP version 4 is becoming exhausted and will make way for the "next generation" IP version 6 that is designed to enable ongoing expansion of the Internet. The continuous growth of the Internet requires an evolution of the overall IP architecture to accommodate new technologies that support increasing numbers of users, applications and services. In terms of IP services integrated into the architecture, IPv6 most notably offers integrated auto-configuration, expanded IP addresses, enhanced mobility, end-to-end security and quality-of-service (QoS). The design of IPv6 is intentionally targeted for minimal impact on upper and lower layer protocols by avoiding the random addition of new features [5].

- Large address space: IPv6 increases the IP address size from 32 bits to 128 bits, to support more levels of addressing hierarchy, a much greater number of addressable nodes, and simpler auto-configuration of addresses. A 'scope' field was added to the multicast addresses to improve the scalability of multicast routing. A new type of address called the 'anycast address' was also defined. This packet is used for sending a packet to any one of a group of nodes.
- Extensibility: IPv6 can easily be extended for new features by adding extension headers after the IPv6 header. Unlike options in the IPv4 header, which can only support 40 bytes of options, the size of IPv6 extension headers is only constrained by the size of the IPv6 packet.
- Better support for prioritized delivery: A new capability is added to enable the labelling of packets belonging to particular traffic 'flows' for which the sender requests special handling, such as non-default quality of service or 'real-time' service. And the IPv6 also has built-in support prioritized delivery, IPSec, and mobility [5].

1.2   Mobile Internet Protocol Version 6

Mobile Node (MN): The MN is a node that moves between different networks, namely the home network and foreign networks.

Home Network (HN): The MN is permanently connected to this network. The subnet of this network corresponds to the home address of the MN and home agent.

Home Agent (HA): The home agent is a router in the HN responsible to forward packets destined for the MN when the MN has moved to a foreign network.

Foreign Network (FN): This is the network to which the MN moves and attaches when not in the HN.

Foreign Agent (FA): The foreign agent is a router in the FN to which a MN attaches when not in the HN. The FA assigns a care-of-address to the MN and is used to forward and receive packets destined for the MN.

Correspondent Node (CN): The CN is a node located somewhere in any network and communicates with the MN.

Care-of-Address (CoA): This address is a IPv6 address assigned to the MN via the foreign agent and can be a agent care-of-address, or a collocated care-of-address. The MN uses this address to communicate when not in it's home network.

- *Foreign Agent Care-of-Address (FA CoA)*: The MN gets the the IP of the foreign agent by use of Agent Advertisements.
- *Co-located Care-of-Address (CCoA)*: The MN receives this IP when the foreign network temporarily assigns an IP to the MN using Router Advertisements, or Dynamic Host Configuration Protocol.

MIPv6 makes use of triangular routing and route optimization to forward packets to and from the MN [6]. The route optimization protocol enables the MN and the CN to send packets directly to each other via direct routing despite the changes in IP connectivity, by using tunneling. The main problem with MIPv6, is the handover delay when moving between nodes and it consists of the following delay components [7]:

$$T_{THO} = T_{HRD} + T_{CRD} + T_{L2D} + T_{RDD} + T_{RRD} + T_{DAD}$$

Where:

$T_{THO} = Total\ Handover\ Delay$
$T_{HRD} = Home\ Registration\ Delay$
$T_{CRD} = Correspondent\ Registration\ Delay$
$T_{L2D} = Layer\ 2\ Handover\ Delay$
$T_{RDD} = Router\ Discovery\ Delay$
$T_{RRD} = Return\ Routability\ Delay$
$T_{DADD} = Duplicate\ Address\ Detection\ Delay$

1.3 Fast Mobile Internet Protocol Version 6

Access Router (AR): This router refers to the MN's default router.

Access Point (AP): The AP refers to the device that enable wireless connection to the MN and is a Layer 2 device connected to a IP subnet.

Previous Access Router (PAR): This router refers to the MN's default router prior to its handover.

New Access Router (NAR): This router refers to the MN's new router subsequent to its handover.

Previous Care-of-Address (PCoA): The valid IP address on the PAR's subnet.

New Care-of-Address (NCoA): The valid IP address on the NAR 's subnet.

FMIPv6 attempts to enhancement the handover strategy in a MIPv6 network. The main goal of FMIPv6 is to configure a new Care-Of-Address (NCoA) or Previous CoA (PCoA) for the mobile node before the mobile node moves to the new access router. The FMIPv6 protocol enables a MN to request information about neighbouring AP's and the subnets information of AR's. There are two types of handovers that have been identified in the FMIPv6 protocol, namely Predictive and Reactive handover.

The MN sends a Router Solicitation for Proxy Advertisement (RtSolPr) to the current AR requesting information for a potential handover. The AR replies with a Proxy Router Advertisement (PrRtAdv) containing information about neighbouring links. This message also acts as a trigger for network-initiated handover. After the PrRtAdv was received, the MN formulates a prospective NCoA and sends a Fast Binding Update (FBU) to the PAR. The purpose of the FBU is to bind the PCoA to the NCoA so that the arriving packets can be tunnelled to the new location of the MN. The PAR sends a FBack to the MN and this means that the packet tunneling is already in progress by the time the MN attaches to the NAR. This scenario is called the "predictive" mode of operation. The MN will then send a Fast Neighbour Advertisement (FNA) as soon as the MN is connected to the NAR. This message is used to announce attachment between the MN and the NAR and to confirm the use of the NCoA. [5]

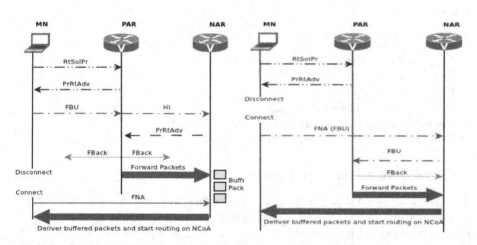

Fig. 1. FMIPv6 Handover Predictive   **Fig. 2.** FMIPv6 Handover Reactive

The reactive handover mechanism represents the case where the MN could not anticipate the handover. The reactive mode can be seen in Figure 2. In this case the MN was only able to react once the handover was already in progress. In the reactive case the FBU is send from the NAR's link and is encapsulated in the FNA message after the Layer 2 handover has completed. The NAR forwards the FBU to the PAR, this is followed by a HI/HACK exchange and the PAR then starts to tunnel packets to the NAR.

2 Objectives

The objectives of this investigation was to develop a test bed, in order to evaluate different handover strategies in a Mobile IPv6 network. This would also evaluate the capability of the IPv6 network protocol in a mobile network environment. Efficient handover strategies are important for MIPv6, as this is the main cause of packet loss thus reducing service quality in mobile networks. To reduce the handover latency FMIPv6 was implemented on the network to evaluate the improvements on the handover latency of MIPv6. After implementation of FMIPv6 the results of the FMIPv6 network was compared with those of the MIPv6 network to evaluate improvements of FMIPv6 on the network performance.

3 Methodology

Initially, the handover latency between access points in a WLAN IPv6 network was determined by simulating the network using Omnett++ Network Simulator. Next, the simulated network was built and MIPv6 implemented on the test bed for evaluation of the actual network. We consider a single MN moving between two AR's in two different subnets between the home network and a visited network in MIPv6. See Figure 3. After the MIPv6 network was functioning,we implemented FMIPv6 on the same network to evaluate the handover latency of the network with FMIPv6. Simulations and hardware performance of handover latencies could than be compared.

These complementary results were used to investigate different handover techniques and possible optimization of the current handover technique. After investigation of different handover techniques, FMIPv6 was implemented on the test bed to improve the handover latency of the MIPv6 network. The FMIPv6 protocol was tested by moving MN visiting new subnets link between PAR and NAR as seen in Figure 4. The performance measurement of the FMIPv6 network includes TCP/UDP throughput, packet loss and handover latency measurement with the Jperf network application.

4 Implementation

4.1 MIPv6 Network

The implementation of the protocol was done on a IPv6 test bed, consisting of various Linux based PC's set up as routers. Figure 3 depicts the network topology of the test bed. Table 1 shows the hardware and software setup of

Table 1. MIPv6/FMIPv6 Test Bed Setup

Device name	Network Configuration	Software setup
HA	Consists of multiple nic's and IPv6 forwarding is enabled to act as router.	Linux MIPv6 2.6.38 compiled kernel, radvd 1.7 and MIPv6 UMIP 0.4 home agent setup.
FA	Consists of multiple nic's and IPv6 forwarding is enabled to act as router.	Linux 2.6.38-generic kernel and radvd 1.7.
MN	IPv6 802.11n access point	Linux MIPv6 2.6.38 compiled kernel and MIPv6 UMIP 0.4 mobile node setup.
CN	IPv6 ready IP Camera	Linux MIPv6 2.6.38 compiled kernel and MIPv6 UMIP 0.4 CN setup.
CN Router	Consists of multiple nic's and IPv6 forwarding is enabled to act as router.	Linux 2.6.38-generic kernel and radvd 1.7.
AP	IPv6 802.11n access point	OpenWrt Firmware and Linux 3.2.5 compiled kernel with IPv6 enabled.
AR	Consists of multiple nic's and IPv6 forwarding is enabled to act as router.	Linux MIPv6 2.6.38 compiled kernel, radvd 1.7 and FMIPv6 daemon running.

the various nodes. The MIPv6 stack used in the implementation, is the (UMIP) Mobile IPv6 stack for Linux [8]. The corresponding node consists of a IPv6-ready IP camera transmitting live video streaming to the MN. The live streaming is used to measure packet loss and the handover latency produced by the MIPv6 protocol, when the MN moves from one access point to another.

The network consists of three subnets as shown in Figure 3. IPv6 addresses are assigned by the routers using Router Advertisements broadcast messages. The Linux kernels for the MN,CN and HA was recompiled to include the MIPv6 extensions for the kernels. The access points are based on Omnima Embedded Linux Wifi boards, running Openwrt Linux distributions for embedded wireless devices.

4.2   FMIPv6 Network

The implementation of the protocol was done on the MIPv6 test bed as already setup. The setup for the various hardware components can be seen in Table 1. The MN will first move from the home network to AR1. From this point on, the FMIPv6 protocol will handle the handover between the PAR and the NAR, as seen in Figure 4.

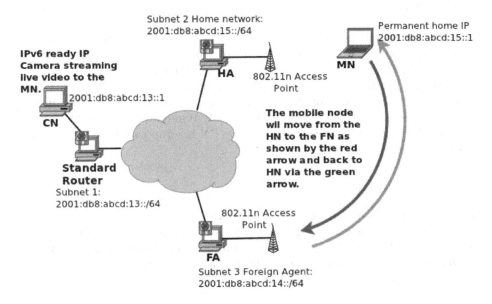

Fig. 3. MIPv6 network setup

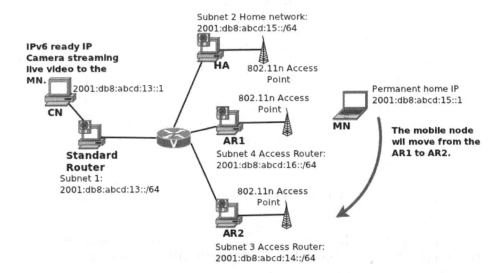

Fig. 4. FMIPv6 network setup

5   Results

The following results were captured using the Jperf application. Jperf is an application used to measure the jitter, throughput and bandwith for network protocols. [9] During the experiment, we transmit UDP traffic at the rate of 10 Mbps and we use the Jperfs default values of packet size and buffer size for both UDP and TCP environment. For the TCP measurement we use the Jperfs default values for the TCP buffer length, TCP Windows Size, and TCP Max Segment Size. The the jeperf apllication the CN is setup as the server and the MN as the client.

5.1   MIPv6 Test Bed

The MIPv6 Test Bed was used to test the MIPv6 protocol on a physical level, the protocol was implemented and successful results were obtained from the test bed. The sought for results are in terms of protocol performance when live video is streamed to the mobile node and to investigate the affect of handover latency on real-time applications between the MN and CN.

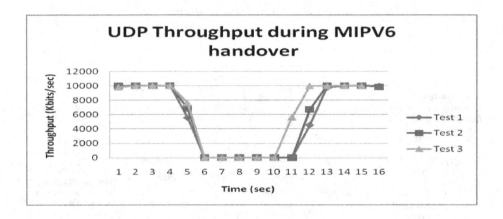

Fig. 5. MIPv6 UDP throughput

Figure 5 shows the UDP throughput of the test bed during a handover. This indicates that the latency for MIPv6 network with UDP transmission is around 5 seconds.

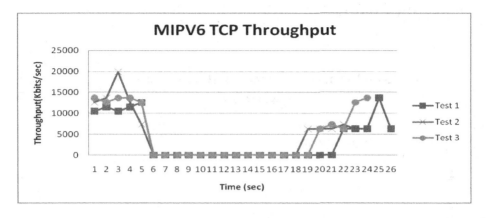

Fig. 6. MIPv6 TCP throughput

Figure 6 shows the TCP throughput of the test bed during a handover, giving a latency for MIPv6 network with TCP transmission around 13 seconds.

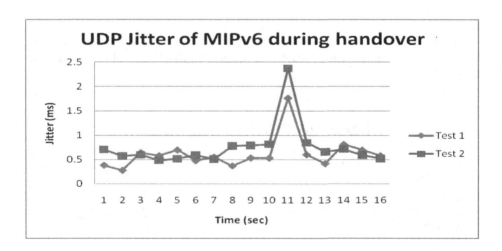

Fig. 7. MIPv6 UDP jitter during handover

Figure 7 shows the UDP jitter of the MIPv6 network. The average UDP jitter for the 10 Mbps is 0.588 ms.

It is clear from the results that MIPv6 handover needs to be optimise to enable effective live video streaming and VOIP during the handover process.

5.2   FMIPv6 Test Bed

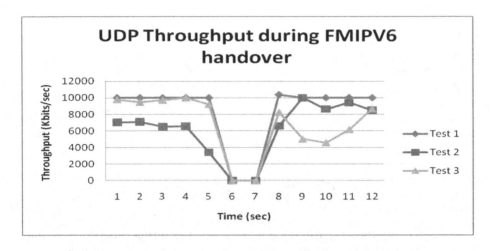

Fig. 8. FMIPv6 UDP throughput

Figure 8 shows the UDP throughput of the test bed during a handover. This indicates that the latency for FMIPv6 network with UDP transmission is around 3 seconds.

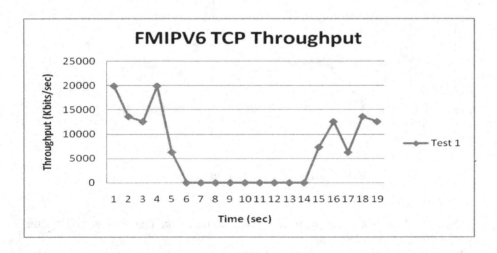

Fig. 9. FMIPv6 TCP throughput

Figure 9 shows the TCP throughput of the test bed during a handover, giving a latency for FMIPv6 network with TCP transmission around 8 seconds.

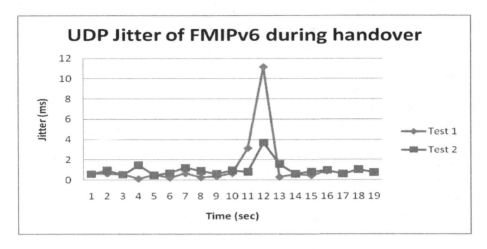

Fig. 10. FMIPv6 UDP jitter during handover

Figure 10 shows the UDP jitter of the FMIPv6 network. The average UDP jitter for the 10 Mbps is 1.01 ms.

5.3   MIPv6 and FMIPv6 Comparison

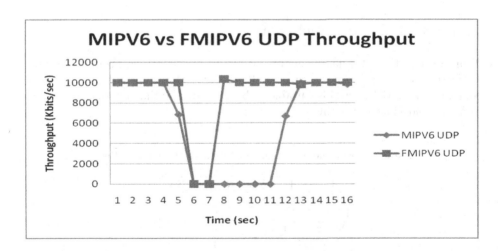

Fig. 11. MIPv6 vs FMIPv6 UDP throughput

We find that the FMIPv6 in predictive mode supports a faster handover, and thus reduces the handover latency of the network. The total handover time of MIPv6 is 5 seconds and FMIPv6 in predictive handover is minimum 3 seconds, resulting in a significantly lower latency time in the network.

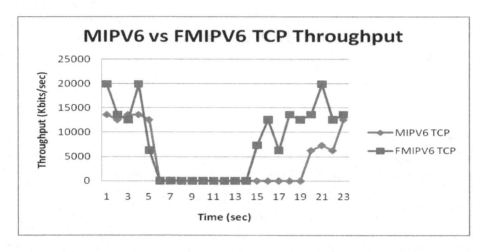

Fig. 12. MIPv6 vs FMIPv6 TCP throughput

We find that the FMIPv6 in predictive mode supports a faster handover, and thus reduces the handover latency of the network. The total handover time of MIPv6 is 13 seconds and FMIPv6 in predictive handover is minimum 8 seconds. The FMIPv6 reported a better performance due to a lower latency during handover process.

6   Summary and Conclusion

Table 2 shows the total handover time of MIPv6 and FMIPv6. From the results in Section 5 and Table 2 we can conclude that FMIPv6 performs well when compared with MIPv6 and is suitable to be used for real time applications, such as VOIP and video streaming.

Table 2. Total handover time of MIPv6/FMIPv6 Test Bed

Protocol	Handover time (Sec)
MIPv6 TCP	13
FMIPv6 TCP	8
MIPv6 UDP	7
FMIPv6 UDP	3

For UDP throughput and jitter comparison, the UDP throughput as per Figure 11 shows that FMIPv6 in predictive mode also performs better than MIPv6. For comparison of UDP jitter, Figure 7 and Figure 10 show the comparison of average UDP jitter of the two protocols. In Table 3, we see the average UDP jitter calculated in Jperf for the two protocols. The UDP jitter for MIPv6 is

0.588 and 1.01 for FMIPv6. This indicates that MIPv6 has the minimal jitter of
the two protocols. The reason for this result is the way that FMIPv6 is deployed.
When running FMIPv6 the MIPv6 daemon also needs to run and this means
that the number of processes on the FMIPv6 nodes will be more than on the
MIPv6 nodes.

Table 3. Average UDP Jitter (ms) of MIPv6/FMIPv6 Test Bed

Protocol	Average UDP Jitter (ms)
MIPv6 UDP	0.588
FMIPv6 UDP	1.01

Further tests on the MIPv6 and FMIPv6 protocols will include various router
advertisement time intervals and file transfer using a FTP application. The
sought for results would be the packet loss during handover with different file
sizes and the average transmission time of FTP applications. The router advertisements will be changed to see the effect on the handover latency of the
protocols. To measure the video quality performance of the protocols, the network will also be tested using Jinzora Media Server with Mean Opinion Score
(MOS) used to evaluate transmission quality [10].

In summary, the FMIPv6 protocol outperforms the MIPv6 in all aspects.
However the implementation of the FMIPv6 protocol still has several limitations
and still requires refinement, but this does not affect the test results. For example,
after a while of running FMIPv6, the MN will disconnect and the performance
of the network will slow down. We also find a lot of packets being dropped when
the MN needs to scan for neighbouring AP's, but adding an additional wireless
card to the MN resolves this problem. We look forward to further improvements
of FMIPv6.

References

1. Prasad, R., Dixit, S. (eds.): Wireless IP and Building the Internet. The Artech
   House Universal Personal Communications Series. Artech House (2003)
2. Xie, G., Chen, J., Zheng, H., Yang, J., Zhang, Y.: Handover latency of mipv6
   implementation in linux,
   http://ieeexplore.ieee.org/stamp/stamp.jsp?tp=&arnumber=4411253
3. Chandrasekaran, J.: Mobile ip: Issues, challenges and solutions. Master's thesis,
   Department of Electrical and Computer Engineering Rutgers University (2009)
4. Mobility support in ipv6 (June 2004), http://www.ietf.org/rfc/rfc3775.txt
5. Ngamtura, P.: Performance comparison of mipv6 and fmipv6 over wlans. Master's
   thesis, Faculty of Graduate Studies Mahidol University (2010),
   http://www.li.mahidol.ac.th/thesis/2553/cd439/4737231.pdf
6. Enhanced route optimization for mobile ipv6 (May 2007),
   http://www.ietf.org/rfc/rfc4866.txt

7. Yousaf, F.Z., Bauer, C., Wietfeld, C.: An accurate and extensible mobile ipv6 (xmipv6) simulation model for omnet++. In: 1st International Conference on Simulation Tools (March 2008)
8. Umip: Usagi-patched mobile ipv6 for linux,
   `http://umip.linux-ipv6.org/index.php?n=Main.HomePage`
9. JPerf, `http://sourceforge.net/projects/jperf/`
10. Mean opinion score, `http://en.wikipedia.org/wiki/Mean_opinion_score`

Author Index

Abreu, Thiago   1
Amato, Giuseppe   72
Amraoui, Asma   119
Antoniadis, Panayotis   29
Aristomenopoulos, Georgios   43
Aung, Zeyar   103
Azad, Amar Pazad   332
Azim, Mohammad Abdul   103

Baynat, Bruno   1
Begin, Thomas   1
Bellalta, Boris   149
Bendimerad, Fethi Tarik   119
Benmammar, Badr   119
Botta, Miroslav   17

Cairns, David   87
Campolo, Claudia   289
Cao Minh, Trang   149
Casilari, E.   196
Cecílio, José   260
Chahin, Wissam   332
Chemouil, Prosper   242
Chessa, Stefano   72
Costa, João   260

Dadej, Arek   302
Daigle, John N.   226
Denkovski, Daniel   135
De Pellegrni, Francesco   332
Dutta, Ratna   164

El-Azouzi, Rachid   332

Fan, Xinxin   180
Fayed, Marwan M.   87
Fdida, Serge   29
Femminella, Mauro   226
Filer, Nick   316
Furtado, Pedro   260

Gavrilovska, Liljana   135
Gennaro, Claudio   72
Gong, Guang   180

González-Cañete, F.J.   196
Gourhant, Yvon   242
Griffin, Christopher   29
Guérin-Lassous, Isabelle   1

Hakala, Ismo   275
Hongell, Timo   275

Ihalainen, Jukka   275

Jin, Youngmi   29

Kenny, Warren   212
Kesidis, George   29
Khadkikar, Vinod   103
Krief, Francine   119

Magklara, Kalypso   59
Martins, Pedro   260
Mitra, Sarbari   164
Mitton, Nathalie   351
Molinaro, Antonella   289
Mouftah, Hussein T.   87
Mraz, Lubomir   17
Mukhopadhyay, Sourav   164

Nguyen, Nghi   1

Oliver, Miquel   149
Orlinski, Matthew   316

Papavassiliou, Symeon   43
Pavlovska, Valentina   135
Pieterse, Johan   351
Pokorny, Jiri   17

Qureshi, Rehan   302

Razafindralambo, Tahiry   59
Reynaud, Laurent   242
Romaszko, Sylwia   135

Shariat-Madar, Zia   226
Simek, Milan   17
Stathopoulos, Christos   43

Triviño-Cabrera, A.   196

Vairo, Claudio   72
Venmani, Daniel Philip   242

Weber, Stefan   212
Wolhuter, Riaan   351

Xiao, Weidong   103

Zeghlache, Djamal   242
Zorbas, Dimitrios   59